MW01056716

HERNANDO DE SOTO AND THE INDIANS OF FLORIDA

The Ripley P. Bullen Series
Florida Museum of Natural History

Jerald T. Milanich
and
Charles Hudson

HERNANDO DE SOTO

AND THE

INDIANS OF FLORIDA

University Press of Florida
Florida Museum of Natural History
Gainesville Tallahassee Tampa Boca Raton Pensacola
Orlando Miami Jacksonville

Excerpts from an English translation of the early sixteenth-century Spanish document the *Requerimiento* from Robert S. Chamberlain, *The Conquest and Colonization of Yucatan, 1517–1550* (Washington, D.C.: Carnegie Institution of Washington, 1948), Publication 582, pp. 24–25.

The University Press of Florida is the scholarly publishing agency for the State University System of Florida, comprised of Florida A&M University, Florida Atlantic University, Florida International University, Florida State University, University of Central Florida, University of Florida, University of North Florida, University of South Florida, University of West Florida.

Library of Congress Cataloging in Publication data
appear on the last printed page of the book.

University Press of Florida
15 Northwest 15th Street
Gainesville, FL 32611

COLUMBUS QUINCENTENARY SERIES
FLORIDA MUSEUM OF NATURAL HISTORY

Publication of this book was
made possible in part by grants from The Program for
Cultural Cooperation between Spain's Ministry of Culture and
United States Universities and the Florida Department of
Natural Resources.

FLORIDA MUSEUM OF NATURAL HISTORY
RIPLEY P. BULLEN SERIES
JERALD T. MILANICH, GENERAL EDITOR

Tacachale: Essays on the Indians of Florida and Southeastern Georgia during the Historic Period, edited by Jerald T. Milanich and Samuel Proctor (1978).

Aboriginal Subsistence Technology on the Southeastern Coastal Plain during the Late Prehistoric Period, by Lewis H. Larson (1980).

Cemochechobee: Archaeology of a Mississippian Ceremonial Center on the Chattahoochee River, by Frank T. Schnell, Vernon J. Knight, Jr., and Gail S. Schnell (1981).

Fort Center: An Archaeological Site in the Lake Okeechobee Basin, by William H. Sears, with contributions by Elsie O'R. Sears and Karl T. Steinen (1982).

Perspectives on Gulf Coast Prehistory, edited by Dave D. Davis (1984).

Archaeology of Aboriginal Culture Change in the Interior Southeast: Depopulation during the Early Historic Period, by Marvin T. Smith (1987).

Apalachee: The Land Between the Rivers, by John H. Hann (1988).

Key Marco's Buried Treasure: Archaeology and Adventure in the Nineteenth Century, by Marion Spjut Gilliland (1989).

First Encounters: Spanish Explorations in the Caribbean and the United States, 1492–1570, edited by Jerald T. Milanich and Susan Milbrath (1989).

Missions to the Calusa, edited by John H. Hann, with Introduction by William H. Marquardt (1991).

Excavations on the Franciscan Frontier: Archaeology at the Fig Springs Mission, by Brent Richards Weisman (1992).

The People Who Discovered Columbus: The Prehistory of the Bahamas, by William F. Keegan (1992).

Hernando de Soto and the Indians of Florida, by Jerald T. Milanich and Charles Hudson (1993).

CONTENTS

LIST OF FIGURES *ix*

PREFACE *xi*

ACKNOWLEDGMENTS *xiii*

I THE SEARCH 3

Reconstructing the Route 7

II PRELUDE TO THE EXPEDITION 19

Hernando de Soto, Conquistador 26
De Soto's Charter 28

III THE LANDING 39

The Harbor 39
The Landing and the Camp 48
Archaeological Evidence 61

IV NORTH TO OCALE 71

The Location of Urriparacoxi 73
The River of Mocoso 76
From the River of Mocoso to Ocale 81
The Crossing of the Swamp and River of Ocale 87
Ocale 91
Acuera 96
Archaeology in the Cove of the Withlacoochee and Ocale 98

V NATIVE PEOPLES OF SOUTHERN AND CENTRAL FLORIDA 111

The Tequesta of Southeast Florida 114
The Calusa of Southwest Florida 117
Indians of the Tampa Bay Region 121
Inland Native Groups 127
Archaeological Correlations 129

VI OCALE TO AGILE 133

To the River of Discords 134
Trails and Sites in North Florida 148
Aguacaleyquen 154
To the River of the Deer 158
Agile 166

VII NATIVE PEOPLES OF NORTHERN FLORIDA 169

Potano 170
Northern Utina: Aguacaleyquen, Uriutina, Napituca 177
Uzachile/Yustaga 183
Eastern Utina and the St. Johns River 186
Saturiwa and Other Northeast Florida Indians 205

VIII TO APALACHEE 211

The March to Iniahica 212
Winter Camp 216
The Governor Martin Archaeological Site 222
The Apalachee 226
North from Apalachee 230

IX AFTER DE SOTO: SPAIN IN SIXTEENTH- AND SEVENTEENTH-CENTURY LA FLORIDA 237

More Failed Settlements: Luna and Villafañe 237
Menéndez, St. Augustine, and Santa Elena 241
The Mission System 243
Timucuan Missions 245
Apalachee Missions 248
Demise of the Missions 250

AFTERWORD 255

NOTES 259

BIBLIOGRAPHY 263

INDEX 281

LIST OF FIGURES

1. The Alonzo de Chaves map, ca. 1544 10
2. Section of John Lee Williams's 1837 map of Florida 12
3. Civil War period map of Florida 14
4. The Caribbean and the southeastern U.S. 20
5. Map from Pineda's voyage 23
6. Diego Ribero's world map of 1529 24
7. Route of the Pánfilo de Narváez expedition 25
8. The Florida Gulf coast 40
9. Tampa Bay 44
10. The route of de Soto into Tampa Bay 51
11. Unloading men and horses in Tampa Bay 52
12. Moving to Uzita's village 54
13. Archaeological sites just east of Tampa Bay 65
14. The Thomas site 67
15. Archaeological sites and Urriparacoxi's territory southwest of Orlando 75
16. Route from the camp on Tampa Bay to Ocale 77
17. Archaeological sites north and northeast of Tampa Bay 79
18. The Mill Point site 80
19. Section of a Civil War map showing sandhills 85
20. Archaeological sites in the Cove of the Withlacoochee 89
21. The Cove of the Withlacoochee, typical terrain 91
22. "Eloquale" (Ocale) and "Aquouena" (Acuera) 95
23. Central Florida 97
24. Glass beads from Tatham Mound 105
25. Glass beads from Tatham Mound 106
26. Armor from Tatham Mound 107
27. Iron chisel from Tatham Mound 108
28. Glass beads from Weeki Wachee Mound 109

29. Native groups in south Florida and the Tampa Bay region 113
30. Pottery of the Safety Harbor culture 130
31. Route from Ocale to Aguacaleyquen 135
32. Trails and archaeological sites south of the Santa Fe River 137
33. Pottery of the Alachua tradition 139
34. Potano 141
35. Stuart-Purcell map 142–43
36. Trails and archaeological sites in north Florida 149
37. Pottery of the Suwannee Valley assemblage 151
38. 1829 map of the Ichetucknee River 155
39. Route from Aguacaleyquen to Agile 159
40. Native groups in northern Florida 171
41. The battle between chiefs Utina and Potano 175
42. "Apalatci" 181
43. East Florida 188
44. The Mission Trail and the "Itoniah scrub" 191
45. The St. Johns River drainage 195
46. Saturiwa preparing for war 206
47. Saturiwa and Timo-ga 208
48. Archaeological sites and the Mission Trail in northwest Florida 213
49. Route from Agile to Georgia 217
50. Clarksdale bells 220
51. Fort Walton culture pottery 223
52. Crossbow dart tip from Martin site 225
53. Chain mail from Martin site 226
54. Route of the expedition through the southern United States 234–35
55. Sixteenth-century locations 238
56. Route of the Tristán de Luna expedition 240
57. Route of the expeditions of Juan Pardo 243

PREFACE

We beseech and demand ... that you accept the Church and the Superior Organization of the whole world and recognize the Supreme Pontiff, called the Pope, and that in his name you acknowledge the King and Queen, ... his representatives, as the lords and superior authorities of these islands and mainlands. ... If you do not do this, or resort maliciously to delay, we warn you that, with the aid of God, we will enter your land against you with force and will make war in every place and by every means we can and are able, and we will then subject you to the yoke and authority of the Church and of Their Highnesses. We will take you and your wives and children and make them slaves. ... And we will take your property and will do you all the harm and evil we can. ...

From the Requerimiento *read by Spanish conquistadors to the people of the New World (Chamberlain 1948:25)*

To contemporary Americans, Hernando de Soto is perhaps the most famous Spanish conquistador. We have counties, towns, hotels, bridges, automobiles, caverns, geological formations, shopping malls, and even pecan stores named for him. But the average American knows little about the de Soto expedition and its historical importance to our own past. We hope that this volume will help to remedy that shortcoming and bring to the public some understanding of de Soto's odyssey in Florida as well as an appreciation of the native peoples he encountered.

That encounter with Europeans was a prelude to a demographic disaster for the aboriginal peoples of Florida. Old World diseases, perhaps introduced by the de Soto expedition and certainly by Europeans in the later sixteenth and seventeenth centuries, killed hundreds of thousands of Florida Indians. By the eighteenth century, the indigenous populations of Florida had been severely decimated; by midcentury, only a few remained alive. Today, the only way we can learn about these peoples as they were at the time of European contact is through documents, such as those written by the members of the de Soto expedition, and through archaeological research. The story of the Hernando de Soto expedition, then, is also the story of the Florida Indians.

Further, a study of the de Soto expedition through Florida enhances our understanding of Spain's role in the European colonization of our nation. More than a hundred years before the Pilgrims landed at Plymouth Rock in 1621, the Spaniard Juan Ponce de León made his own landing on the Atlantic coast of Florida. Understandably perhaps, colonial American history has emphasized the English attempts to establish colonies at Roanoke, Jamestown, and Plymouth. But we hope that this book about de Soto's exploration of Florida will show that the English were latecomers to the eastern United States.

And, as noted, studies of European activities in sixteenth-century North America are also helping to bring to light the story of the native peoples who inhabited the region for thousands of years before either the Spanish or the English arrived on these shores. The accounts of the de Soto expedition and other sixteenth-century European intrusions and excursions into Florida contain valuable information on the native societies. Once we are able to locate the activities of these explorers in specific geographical locations—and particularly the route of the de Soto expedition—we can use this information to help reconstruct and interpret these native societies. We can begin to flesh out archaeological information on groups such as the Uzita, Aguacaleyquen, and Apalachee, and in so doing we can write a new social geography of the indigenous peoples of the Southeast (e.g., Swanton 1932).

The Hernando de Soto expedition provides us with a privileged moment when we can peer through the mists of several centuries into the past, to a time when hundreds of thousands of native peoples lived in Florida. Perhaps this is the expedition's most important legacy.

ACKNOWLEDGMENTS

This project had its genesis in 1983 at the first meeting of the Florida De Soto Trail Committee. The committee was organized under the sponsorship of Ney C. Landrum, then director of the Florida Division of Recreation and Parks, an agency of the Florida Department of Natural Resources (DNR). It was chaired by Michael V. Gannon, director of the University of Florida's Center for Early Contact Period Studies. We are grateful to Ney and Mike for helping to arrange funding from DNR for much of the research reported here. DNR also provided a portion of the publication costs of this book, as did the Program for Cultural Cooperation between Spain's Ministry of Culture and United States Universities. Lanette H. Radel, John A. Scafidi, and James A. Stevenson, DNR staff members, facilitated research on the Hernando de Soto expedition in Florida and the marking of the De Soto Trail.

Members of the De Soto Trail Committee are also due our thanks for their contributions. They are Elizabeth Alexander, Jeffrey Brain, Amy Bushnell, David Colburn, Kathleen Deagan, Charles Fairbanks, José Fernández, William Goza, Guy Lacine, Lyle McAllister, Samuel Proctor, Rolfe Schell, Marvin Smith, Louis Tesar, and Leitch Wright. Gannon, Hudson, Landrum, and Milanich also served on the committee.

Milanich's initial thoughts on de Soto in Florida were stimulated by students in a graduate seminar taught at the University of Florida in 1984. Participants were Doran Cart, William Fisher, Kenneth Johnson, Jonathan Leader, Jeffrey Mitchem, Donna Ruhl, Marvin Smith, and Robert Wilson. William Goza, a lifelong student of history and archaeology, also participated in the class. Ken, Jeff, and Marvin went on to write dissertations on topics related to native peoples in La Florida and the early contact period. The dissertation research carried out by Ken and Jeff at the University of Florida was especially pertinent to this study, and their work is cited extensively. They were students of Milanich, and he is very proud of their contributions. Dale Hutchinson's dissertation at the University of Illinois, which used collections from Florida, was also important to our study.

Other archaeologists and field workers who were a part of the de Soto project in Florida and whose work is utilized here include William Burger and his associates, friends, and students in the Tampa Bay region and at New College; Frank Keel; Cliff Nelson; Claudine Payne; and Keith Terry. Calvin Jones and John Hann, Florida Bureau of Archaeological Research, graciously shared their thoughts and extensive knowledge with us or our field teams. And Calvin, along with Charles Ewen, excavated the Governor Martin site in Tallahassee. Their work was funded in part by the National Endowment for the Humanities (NEH). John went well beyond the call of duty in reviewing two drafts of this manuscript. John Worth also critiqued a draft, and Jeffrey Mitchem and Dale Hutchinson were kind enough to comment on our interpretations of their own research.

In addition to funds from DNR and NEH, funds from SantaFe HealthCare, Inc., the Florida Division of Historical Resources, the University of Florida's Division of Sponsored Research, and Piers Anthony and his family allowed the various research projects whose results we have utilized to be completed. Piers's novel *Tatham Mound*, published in 1991 by William Morrow and Company, is a marvelous chronicle of the native peoples associated with the archaeological site called Tatham Mound, the data from which are cited in chapter 4.

Hudson expresses his thanks to the University of Georgia Research Foundation, which awarded him a Senior Faculty Research Grant providing time for research and writing in the summer and fall of 1988.

The maps used in this report were prepared by Janis Callahan and Melanie Knapp. Larry Leshan provided the expertise for final production of all the art work.

Special thanks are due three individuals who were critical to this project. First is Senator Bob Graham, who, while governor of Florida, set in motion the events that led to the Florida De Soto Trail and all that has transpired since that first Trail Committee meeting in May 1983. The others are Ney Landrum and Michael Gannon, mentioned above, who were the movers and shakers—

the *sine qua nons*—whose personal support and interest, not to mention administrative skills, kept us on what we hope was the right path.

Last, we thank all those landowners and informants, ranging from large corporations in Tallahassee to owners of small farms in Manatee County, who allowed access to their properties and provided archaeologists with information on site locations. We hope that in return we have provided them with a clearer picture of Hernando de Soto and the Indians of Florida.

HERNANDO DE SOTO AND THE INDIANS OF FLORIDA

CHAPTER I

THE SEARCH

On May 18, 1983, we were invited along with seventeen other scholars to attend the premier meeting of the "Committee to Establish the Route of Hernando de Soto through Florida, 1539–1540" at the University of Florida in Gainesville. Chaired by historian Michael V. Gannon, the committee was formed at the behest of Ney C. Landrum, then director of the Florida Division of Recreation and Parks. Landrum had in turn been asked by Governor Bob Graham to mark the general route of de Soto in Florida so that Floridians and visitors to the state could drive along the route and learn about the history of the largest Spanish overland expedition in the United States.

Using the information arrived at by consensus at that first de Soto committee meeting, as well as at a second meeting held March 21, 1984, the Division of Recreation and Parks set about designating and marking the De Soto Trail along appropriate Florida highways. A distinctive logo was created, and roadside signs and exhibit kiosks were installed. The northern portion of the trail, from Inverness to Tallahassee and from there to the Florida-Georgia border, was dedicated by Governor Graham in a ceremony held May 3, 1985 in Inverness. The southern portion of the trail, from Inverness to Tampa Bay, was marked later.

The process of designating de Soto's route in Florida, however, has been fraught with more difficulty than is evident from this brief history of the committee. At the initial meeting, held almost 444 years to the day after de Soto first sighted the Gulf coast of Florida, the participants quickly reached agreement on the northern portion of the route, from Ocala to Georgia. But we could not agree on the actual landing site, whether Tampa Bay, Charlotte Harbor, or the area of San Carlos Bay and the mouth of the Caloosahatchee River. Consequently, the De Soto Trail was left up in the air while we all scurried to our books and maps to see whether enough evidence existed to favor one route over another.

Hudson, aided by his associates at the University of Georgia, especially Chester DePratter and Marvin T. Smith, had been working on interpretations of the route within the southeastern United States north of Florida since the early 1980s. Using both documentary and archaeological information not available at the time of the 400th anniversary of the de Soto entrada, when John R. Swanton had edited the *Final Report of the United States de Soto Expedition Commission* (Swanton 1939), Hudson, DePratter, and Smith had worked out new reconstructions of portions of de Soto's route. The experience and knowledge they gained from their research was directly applicable to unraveling the Florida portion of the trail, which had not been conclusively reconstructed by the Hudson team at the time of the initial meeting of the Florida committee.

Stimulated by that first De Soto Trail Committee meeting, Hudson and Milanich both returned to their respective offices and began examining the Florida route in detail. Initially they worked independently, but not for long. Soon they were exchanging ideas and interpretations via telephone calls and letters. Putting knowledge gained from his previous de Soto research to work, Hudson wrote a draft of a paper arguing that the landing site was Tampa Bay (Hudson 1984). Milanich, aided by graduate students participating in a de Soto seminar at the University of Florida, built a case for Charlotte Harbor. But as more information surfaced and Hudson pressed his arguments, Milanich was forced to concede the point. The available evidence all pointed toward Tampa Bay as the landing site. And now, like a reformed smoker, Milanich (1989) strongly advocates Tampa Bay as the landing site.

Hudson and Milanich began writing two separate papers interpreting the de Soto expedition route in Florida, often using different data to reach the same conclusions. At that point the research had become so entwined that the only reasonable thing to do was to combine efforts.

What began as an interpretation of a bare-bones de Soto expedition route has expanded to include an examination of the social geography of the native peoples whom the Spaniards encountered along the way. To learn more about those people the authors consulted other sixteenth-century French and Spanish sources. It became clear that these sources, when treated together and with seventeenth-century sources, provided a great deal of information on the social geography of the Florida natives, both those encountered by the Hernando de Soto expedition and others. The result is this book.

The initial collaboration provided information for the De Soto Trail Committee. By the time of the committee's second meeting in 1984, it was evident the first collective reconstruction of the route north of Alachua County (through Columbia and Suwannee counties) was in error. This meant that the Division of Recreation and Parks, which had labored to gain access to roadside sites needed for the exhibit kiosks, was forced to scrap much of the work it had done. The authors also were able to convince the committee members that the Marion County portion of the route was in error; it was far more probable that the route was farther west. It is doubtful if the entrada actually passed through the vicinity of present-day Ocala. Based on the deliberations of the second meeting, the route was subsequently marked southward to Inverness.

Although they hope that the reading of the data will persuade readers that the landing site of Hernando de Soto was indeed Tampa Bay, the authors have no illusions that some people will easily be divested of differing interpretations and opinions. Like religion and politics, Hernando de Soto engenders passion. Many people have responded in print to Swanton's 1939 report, disagreeing with all or portions of his reconstruction of the route in Florida, especially the landing site (see Bullen 1952a; Wilkinson 1954; Schell 1966; Williams 1986, 1989). And for every author's published ideas about de Soto's route in Florida, there are perhaps a hundred people who expound on their own theories in letters. The authors of this book have accumulated large files of such correspondence. Moreover, because people love to heap blame on politicians for decreeing where the De Soto Trail lies in Florida and for marking the trail to Tampa Bay, the authors are periodically showered with confirmation copies of letters, ranging from polite to downright irate, that people have sent to their public servants with dozens of copies to "interested parties." We can wish that de Soto and his army landed at every port in Florida and visited all points of interest in the state, but they did not.

The principal reason for so many theories about the route is that people tend to focus only on that portion of the route that is geographically important to them: a landing location, an aboriginal village the expedition visited, or a river crossing. In focusing on only one part of the total trail, they are breaking what the authors have come to see as a cardinal rule of de Soto route reconstruction: the route must be considered and interpreted in its totality. Many rivers may satisfy documentary accounts of a particular river crossing. For instance, any of several Florida rivers flow relatively swiftly, fulfilling a description of a swift river in the de Soto narratives. But, if the narratives describe a swamp, then a swift river, then an Indian village, and then a region of broad roads and good agriculture, this constellation of conditions may only fit one Florida locality. When many such localities can be strung together in a sequence, this favors a single correct fit between the geographical and cultural features mentioned in the documents of the expedition and observable physiographical features and archaeological sites.

Another common mistake of de Soto researchers is to use Garcilaso de la Vega's account of the de Soto expedition as the principal source of information for reconstructing the route. Many researchers use John and Jeanette Varner's translation of Garcilaso's *La Florida*, published as *The Florida of the Inca* (Varner and Varner 1951). It is the most readily available of the four de Soto narratives. But there are serious problems in using Garcilaso, especially on matters relating to the sequence of geographical features and villages encountered in Florida. Garcilaso frequently scrambles the sequence of village names, and the locations where events took place are also confused.

Garcilaso began researching his account several decades after the de Soto expedition was over. He had finished about one-quarter of the manuscript by 1587, he did not complete it until 1599, and it was first published in 1605 (Varner and Varner 1951). *La Florida* is not a firsthand account. Rather, it is primarily based on interviews with survivors of the expedition whom Garcilaso met in Peru and Spain. Garcilaso also used two or more primary documents, now lost. Some historians regard Garcilaso's *La Florida* to be more a work of literature than a work of history (see Henige 1986, for example). And recently John Hann has pointed out problems with the Varners' translation of *La Florida* (Hann 1989a).

RECONSTRUCTING THE ROUTE

How, then, can we be confident of our reconstruction of the route of the Hernando de Soto expedition through Florida? How do we know, for instance, that the expedition landed at Tampa Bay and not at the Caloosahatchee River or Charlotte Harbor, as some scholars have claimed (Wilkinson 1954; Schell 1966; Williams 1986, 1989)? We have proceeded by using data-gathering techniques from several disciplines, cross-checking and cross-referencing the collected data, and then continuing to test and refine the reconstruction. In this interdisciplinary approach, which draws on documentary/historical research, cartographic /geographical interpretations, and archaeological investigations, we have been detectives seeking to solve a very large puzzle. Like good detectives, our *modus operandi* has been to gather facts, fit them together in a pattern, and then test the pattern against more facts. A single piece of evidence decides nothing. But when many such pieces of evidence are put together, a scenario of the expedition takes shape.

Our research has made use of both previously known sources of information and new sources. Previously known documentary sources consist first and foremost of the three firsthand narratives of the expedition written by participants. All three are available in English, although in some details the older translations are lacking (see Hann 1989a). The first account is by an unknown Portuguese knight from the town of Elvas who participated in the expedition (Elvas 1922). It was originally published in 1557 in Portugal (Swanton 1939:4). What appears to be an official account of the expedition was written by Luys Hernández de Biedma, who was the crown's representative (Biedma 1922).[1] The original manuscript, first filed in the Simancas archive in Spain as early as 1544, still exists. It is the shortest of the accounts. Both the Elvas and Biedma accounts were translated into English by Buckingham Smith and published in 1866 (Smith 1866)

De Soto's personal secretary on the expedition was Rodrigo Ranjel. The original manuscript of his relation or diary (Ranjel 1922), which has almost daily entries for the Florida portion of the route, has been lost, but what is generally taken to be an account based on the original was included in a work by the Spanish historian Gonzalo Fernández de Oviedo y Valdés. Fernández de Oviedo's five-volume *Historia General y Natural de las Indias* was written in the sixteenth century (1851). Volume I, which contains the Ranjel account (as Book 17, chaps. 21–28), was first published in 1851. It was translated into English by Edward G. Bourne and published in 1904 along with the Buckingham Smith translations of Elvas and Biedma. All three were reprinted in 1922 in the two-volume Allerton Book Co. edition edited by Bourne. We have used the 1922 editions of Elvas, Biedma, and Ranjel in our study, occasionally consulting the printed Spanish texts. For convenience, we have cited them by author, rather than by translator or editor (e.g., Biedma 1922).

Other translations also exist and we have used them where appropriate. One of the better of these is the translation of the narrative of the Gentleman of Elvas done by James A. Robertson and published by the Florida State Historical Society in 1933.[2]

In 1988, stimulated by the need for more accurate translations of the three firsthand de Soto accounts, John H. Hann of the Florida Bureau of Archaeological Research undertook new translations of portions of those accounts. He retranslated the sections that dealt with the expedition's route in Florida from Ocale (near the Withlacoochee River in the west-central part of the state) north into Apalachee. Hann also translated anew those sections of the Garcilaso de la Vega account that covered the same geographical region, as well as what are interpreted to be two separate versions of the account written by Alvar Núñez de Cabeza de Vaca who was in Florida and Apalachee in 1528 as part of the Pánfilo de Narváez expedition (see chapter 2). In 1989 Hann wrote an introduction to these six translations, including a critique of the translations of the de Soto–related accounts previously done by Buckingham Smith, James A. Robertson, and John and Jeanette Varner. That critique makes it clear that de Soto researchers using the de Soto documents to interpret, for instance, the native societies encountered by the expedition, must be aware "that all of them [the translators] (with the exception of James Alexander Robertson's translation of the Fidalgo [Elvas] account) are relatively free translations in which the translators took considerable liberty with the Spanish and Portuguese text, and, what is worse, often without adequately warning the reader about the degree of his or her tampering with the original paragraph and sentence structure, syntax, choice of words, and so forth in rendering these accounts into readable English" (Hann 1989a).

Hann graciously made his unpublished translations available to us in 1989, along with his introduction, and we cite them as "Hann 1989a." Where these new translations add to or correct the older translations we have cited Hann; otherwise we have cited the various editions as noted above.

Several pages from a fourth firsthand account, also written by a survivor of the expedition, have been found by Eugene Lyon in the Archivo General de Indias in Seville, Spain (Lyon 1982). This brief document, by Father Sabastián de Cañete, contains a description of native life in the chiefdom of Cofitachequi (in South Carolina), but is of no use in interpreting the Florida portion of the route.

In addition to the above, there are also documents and letters relating to the entrada, its preparation, and its aftermath. Some of these were published as appendixes to Buckingham Smith's translations of the Biedma and Elvas narratives. They include a letter dated May 18, 1539 from Havana to the Spanish crown, written by Juan Gaytan, Juan de Añasco, and Luys Hernández de Biedma; a letter from de Soto to the king of Spain, written at Tampa Bay (Espiritu Santo) on July 9, 1539; the Memorial of Alonso Vázquez, which contains the testimony of several individuals who participated in the entrada, including Ana Méndez, a woman; and the *asiento* or contract between the crown and de Soto, dated April 20, 1537. Other documents are as yet unpublished. Some of these (this list was provided by Eugene Lyon, a historian with the Historic St. Augustine Research Foundation) are: a 3720-page *Justicia* covering the period 1540–1545 and containing a lengthy lawsuit filed by Isabela de Bobadilla (de Soto's widow) against Hernán Ponce de León, former partner of de Soto in Peru and Nicaragua; voluminous documents recounting the controversies among de Soto's heirs and Francisco Vásquez de Coronado, Hernán Cortéz, and the viceroy of Mexico; and de Soto's *Residencia*, the posthumous investigation carried out in 1554 to determine whether he had fulfilled his responsibilities as outlined in his *asiento*. These materials, however, do not contain new information relative to the route in Florida.[3]

Still other pre– and post–de Soto entrada documents are available and provide evidence on the landing. Alonso de

Figure 1

This pen-and-ink hand-drawn map from the Archivo General de Indias in Seville, Spain was first used as an illustration by Henry Harrisse in 1892. It is believed to have been drawn about 1544 by Alonso de Santa Cruz, the royal Spanish cosmographer. The interior names are native villages mentioned in the de Soto accounts and could only have come from information provided by survivors of the de Soto expedition (see Robertson 1933:2:426–427 and Harrisse 1961).

Chaves's guide to navigators (ca. 1537) describes Bahía Honda, where de Soto's fleet went ashore on the Gulf coast, leaving little doubt that it is Tampa Bay (Castañeda, Cuesta, and Hernández 1983). And bits and pieces about the expedition, especially the survivors, are found in Ignacio Avellaneda's *Los Sobrevivientos de la Florida: The Survivors of the de Soto Expedition* (1990). Another important post–de Soto document, a 1612 Spanish account of a military expedition to Tampa Bay, mentions by name one of the same Indian groups mentioned in Ranjel's narrative and says that the bay was the same one in which de Soto had landed, providing two pieces of evidence that de Soto landed there (Quinn 1976:137).

Documents recounting explorations by the French and the Spanish in northern Florida in the 1560s and documents from the period of the Spanish missions also provide excellent clues to locations of Indian villages mentioned in the de Soto narratives. Unlike Georgia, the Carolinas, and other more northerly parts of de Soto's route, in Florida we have an almost continuous documentary record from 1539 into the eighteenth century, due in part to the Spanish presence at St. Augustine and the Spanish-Indian missions.

These historical materials, especially the narratives of the Gentleman of Elvas, Biedma, and Ranjel, provide descriptions of natural and cultural features along the route that we attempt to locate on modern maps. For instance, if the accounts say the expedition stopped at an Indian village by a lake, then crossed a very large swamp, bridged a swift river and came to another Indian village, we must attempt to locate the lake, swamp, and river. Florida has many lakes and swamps, but not so many rivers. Consequently, there may be several locations that satisfy the combination of geographical features (lake, swamp, river). However, as noted above, when the entire de Soto route is considered, not just one segment, the alternatives often drop to one best-fitting answer. In this fashion a solution to the entire puzzle can be achieved.

Some locations named in the de Soto narratives can be correlated with modern place-names, e.g., the native town of Agile and the modern Aucilla River. Since place-names can easily be moved from one location to another, these correlations are much stronger when we can also tie the modern names to seventeenth-century names, such as the seventeenth-century mission of San Miguel de Asile, located near the Aucilla River in westernmost Madison County. Other names in the narratives can also be tied to seventeenth-century mission locations, e.g., the Apalachee town of Ivitachuco and the mission of San Lorenzo de Ivitachuco. Although place-names must be used with all due caution, some of them are quite secure (e.g., Asile) and can be used because of Florida's unique history to help locate other relative sites along the route. In contrast, the use of place-names to establish the route north of Florida has often been positively misleading.

Another line of evidence that can be used in tracing the expedition is the use of old maps that show trails and paths which existed prior to modern roads. From the narratives themselves it is clear that de Soto and his army usually traveled along Indian

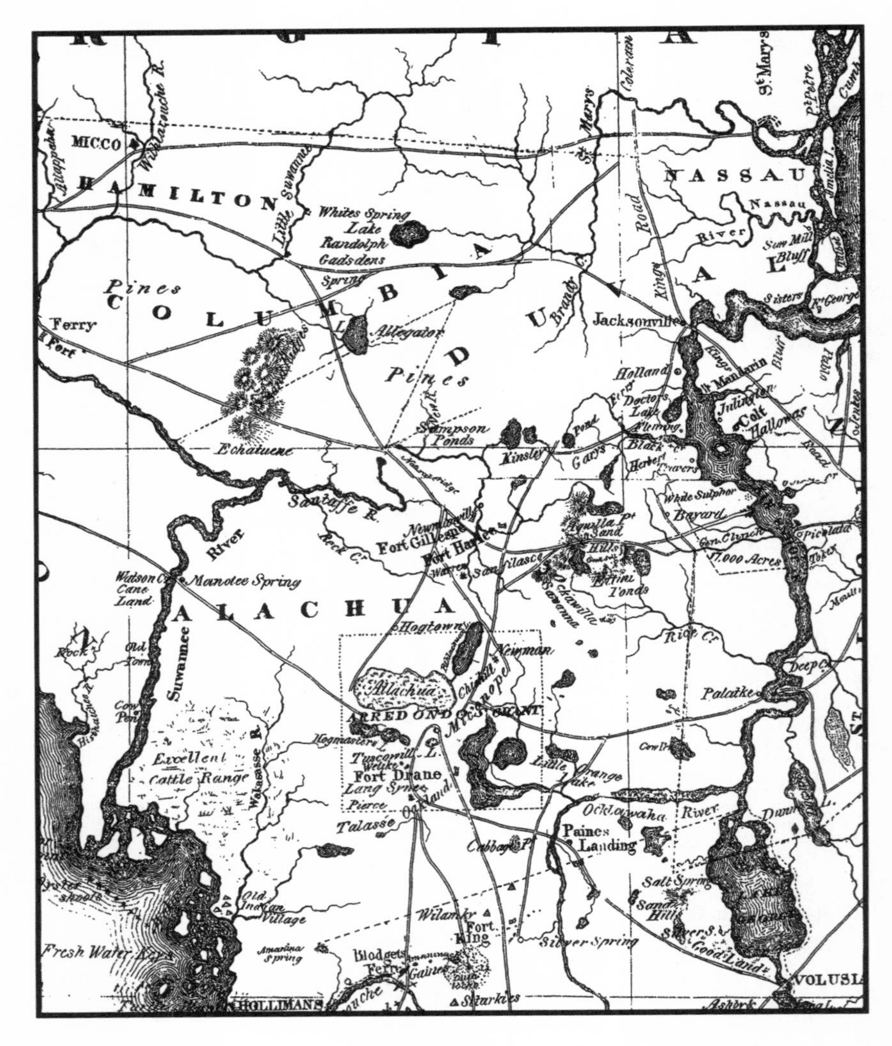

Figure 2

The 1837 John Lee Williams map of Florida shows many early trails. As can be seen in this section of the map, however, the depiction of the trails is more schematic than exact (see Williams 1837).

trails, moving from one native town to another. Many of those same trails continued to be used into the 1830s and during the Second Seminole War, when the first accurate maps of much of interior Florida were compiled (and many of these same trails have become our modern highways and railroad beds). By using early maps in conjunction with modern maps and aerial photographs on which old trails sometimes can be seen, we can locate those trails along which de Soto's army might have traveled. Field surveys, such as those by Kenneth Johnson (1991) in northern Florida, have been used to locate some of these trails on the ground.

Still another clue is the river crossings mentioned in the narratives. Because Florida has relatively few rivers that the Spanish needed to bridge, the sequence of river crossings is reasonably easy to work out. The Withlacoochee, Santa Fe, Suwannee, and Aucilla rivers all can be distinguished, and others, such as the Alafia, Ichetucknee–Rose Creek, and St. Marks, can be located in between.

Using these documentary and cartographic sources of information we worked out a hypothesized reconstruction of the route, then we set about seeking evidence to test whether our reconstruction was correct. The best proof would seem to be physical evidence that could be gathered through archaeological investigations. If our interpretation of a particular lake, swamp, river, and trail was correct, then we should be able to find the archaeological sites corresponding to the Indian villages mentioned in the narratives. The correct sites would have been occupied into the early sixteenth century and they should contain at least some artifacts that could have been left by the de Soto expedition (e.g., Fairbanks 1968; Brain 1975; Smith and Good 1982; Deagan 1987; Smith 1987; Mitchem 1989a,b).

Fortunately, the Florida Bureau of Archaeological Research maintains a file of all known archaeological sites in the state. Archaeological research in Florida has been ongoing since the nineteenth century, and much information has been gathered and is available in published sources, museum collections, and archives. The use of the site files and the reports from earlier archaeological investigations were used to help locate known sites that fit both the descriptions and locations given in the narratives and the reconstructed route. For example, the site files provided us with information on a site located on Lake Tsala-Apopka in Citrus County. Indian pottery recovered from the site is of a type that was still being made in the sixteenth century. Also, a Spanish iron ax was found there. The site's location is quite near our predicted location of the Indian town of Tocaste, visited by the de Soto expedition on July 24, 1539, and said to have been on a large lake.

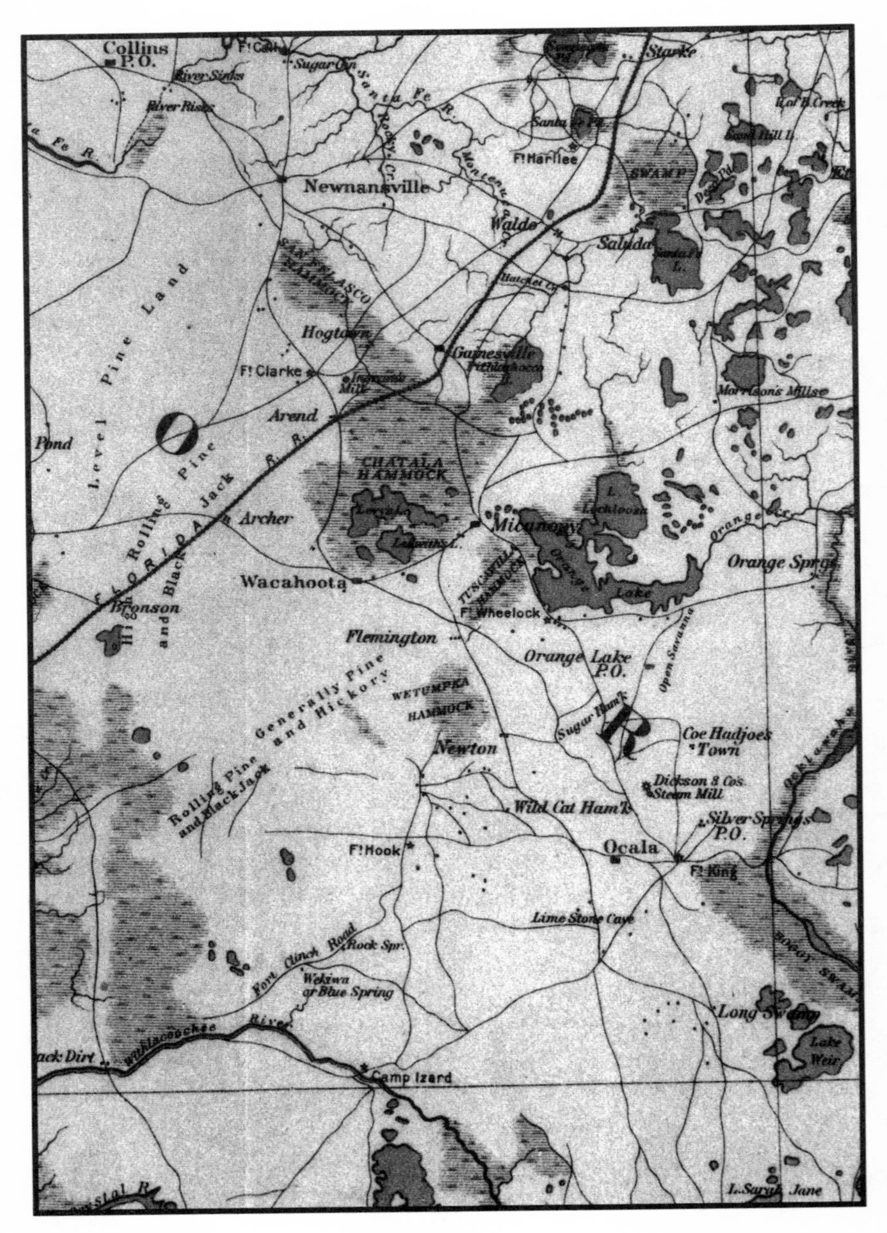

Figure 3

This Civil War period map (Bien n.d.) of Florida is more exact than the 1837 Williams map. It shows a number of the early trails mentioned in chapters 4 and 6, which also are indicated on other maps from the Second Seminole War (1837–1842) and later periods.

Our predicted location for de Soto's Tampa Bay camp is near the mouth of the Little Manatee River near Ruskin. The narratives tell us that the camp was established at an Indian village with a large mound. At the turn of the century an archaeologist investigated a site, Thomas Mound, on the Little Manatee River. The report of those excavations describe a mound as well as Spanish artifacts. More recent surveys and archival work have revealed that extensive village midden deposits, as well as other mounds, were distributed nearby along the Little Manatee (Moore 1900:358–359; Bullen 1952b). Their presence lends support to our selection of that location as de Soto's campsite.

The archaeological site files were also extremely useful for the Apalachee region (Jefferson and Leon counties). Frank J. Keel, an archaeologist employed by the Florida Museum of Natural History to work on the de Soto project, used data on eighty sites to plot potential locations for the Apalachee towns de Soto traveled through in that native province (Keel 1989), and Kenneth Johnson, another museum archaeologist, did the same for northern Florida (Johnson 1986, 1987, 1991; Johnson, Nelson, and Terry 1988).

A third way to find predicted sites is to look for them. Florida archaeologists have expended a great deal of effort over seven years looking for the Indian villages that are predicted by our reconstruction of the route. For example, more than 800 sites have been surveyed by Johnson and his archaeological crews. Only a few of these sites are related to de Soto. Another archaeologist on the de Soto project, William B. Burger, surveyed and tested sites in the greater Tampa Bay region. One example of a site search is the towns of Uqueten and Ocale, visited by de Soto in late July 1539 after crossing a large swamp and then the River of Ocale. Johnson's archaeological surveys have located a group of sites east of the Cove of the Withlacoochee wetlands area that lay close to the Withlacoochee River, possibly Uqueten, and a group of sites farther to the northeast, possibly the village of Ocale. Their relative locations fit the locational conditions present in the narratives (see chapter 4). While Spanish artifacts have yet to be found at either site, such artifacts have come from sites on the opposite side of the river.

Because Florida has a long history of Spanish exploration and settlement—from 1513 into the nineteenth century—just finding Spanish artifacts is not strong evidence of de Soto's presence. We must be able to show that the artifacts date from the 1530s or earlier and are not items salvaged from Spanish ships or given out by seventeenth-century Spanish missionaries. Using information gathered from elsewhere in the Southeast, the Caribbean, Central and South America, and from Spanish museums and other sources, we now have a list of early sixteenth-century Spanish artifacts that are arguably items brought by de Soto. It is when these artifacts are found in archaeological sites that are on or near our predicted village locations that we have the best evidence for de Soto's route. In Florida, many such artifacts have been found around Tampa Bay and at several sites along the route. Some of these artifacts—beads and other materials—are exactly the same as those found at de Soto contact sites elsewhere in the Southeast.

Recent archaeological investigation of an aboriginal mound in Citrus County has unearthed quantities of such artifacts, more in fact than have been found anywhere else along de Soto's route north of Florida (Mitchem 1989b). In addition to Spanish artifacts of the right time period, a mass burial of more than seventy people was found in this mound: possibly they were victims of an epidemic introduced by the Spanish. Moreover, some of the bones exhibit injuries which may indicate sword wounds (Hutchinson 1991).

Quantities of Spanish artifacts similar to those of the Citrus County site have come from a second site in Citrus County, located directly on the route, and from a third site that lies west of the route in Hernando County (Mitchem and Weisman 1984; Mitchem, Weisman, et al. 1985). Additional research has turned up additional sites, and additional Spanish artifacts are being found (Mitchem 1989a).

Not all of these discoveries are a result of recent research. For example, probable de Soto artifacts excavated from Urriparacoxi's territory in central Florida were located using clues published in 1897. Many artifacts are no doubt stored in museums, waiting to be discovered.

A spectacular archaeological discovery was made in early 1987 when B. Calvin Jones of the Florida Division of Historical Resources located the Indian village of Iniahica where the de Soto expedition spent the winter of 1539–1540. Iniahica, the major town of the Apalachee Indians, is in downtown Tallahassee, quite near the trail we have argued that de Soto's men followed. Excavation of the site by Jones and Charles Ewen has revealed beads, broken pottery, coins, and hundreds of pieces of chain mail, all lost or discarded by the expedition members (Ewen 1989). Excavators even found the tooth of a pig, probably one of the pigs that the expedition drove across La Florida.

The research in Citrus County and at the Governor Martin site in Tallahassee, as well as other work being done elsewhere in the Southeast, demonstrate that it is indeed possible to use archaeology to help reconstruct the route of the Hernando de Soto expedition 450 years after those Spanish explorers traveled through Florida.

Archaeological research also has provided a great deal of information about the settlement patterns of Florida native societies in the sixteenth century. These data tell us where the native populations lived and where they did not and they make it clear that the native populations were not scattered randomly across the landscape. Understanding the locations of people in the sixteenth century at the time of de Soto is important in reconstructing the route of his army.

Extensive archaeological data—both from surveys and excavations—were not available to John Swanton when he reconstructed the Florida segment of the de Soto route in the 1930s. The physical evidence provided by archaeological sites and artifacts is important to our investigations because such evidence provides refinement and verification of the route as reconstructed from other sources of information. This process of refining the reconstruction of the route will no doubt continue for a long time as new information continues to come in from archaeological sources.

Our methodology, then, was to use the information contained in the de Soto narratives to draw a line or lines on a map approximating the route of the expedition. In this initial reconstruction, available cartographic and archaeological sources were also used. Then we set out to collect other pertinent information, especially evidence from archaeological research. What is presented here is the "best fit" based on all of these sources.

Although we continue to write about the "route" as though the expedition traveled as a single unit along a single path, in reality the de Soto expedition cut a much wider swath through Florida. The expedition was organized as an army composed of several units, both cavalry and infantry, and all existed in a chain of command.

From the narratives it is apparent that mounted scouting parties, sometimes with infantry, were sent out from the main body of the army to explore and to search for Indian villages where the Spaniards could secure food and lodging. Occasionally, foot soldiers were also sent on these excursions. At times scouting parties ranged ahead several days or more, and parties were sent out on the flanks to search for food and to explore. Thus, although the main army, including the supply train, may have followed a single route several hundred yards across, the actual width of the de Soto expedition's activities through Florida and the southern United States could have been considerably greater, perhaps twenty-five to thirty miles in some places. In our reconstruction we trace the path of the main army and some of the side excursions, such as the ones to Urriparacoxi and to Acuera.

The de Soto expedition, the first major European overland expedition into what is now the eastern United States, is certainly important. It was a major historical event. But it also is important in two additional respects. It was a part of Spain's effort to explore and colonize the eastern United States, and the expedition's firsthand observers provide invaluable information on aboriginal Florida—the region and its native peoples before the European invasion. Let us turn first to the events in La Florida and the New World that set the stage for de Soto's expedition.

CHAPTER II

PRELUDE TO THE EXPEDITION

The Spanish empire's effort to explore and colonize the Southeast emanated from the nascent settlements on Hispaniola and nearby Caribbean Islands, which were founded in the late fifteenth and early sixteenth centuries. On his initial voyage in 1492, Christopher Columbus had attempted to found a settlement, La Navidad, on the north coast of Hispaniola (now Haiti). Returning to La Navidad on his second voyage, Columbus found that the settlement had been destroyed by the native peoples.

From the site of La Navidad Columbus then sailed further west along Hispaniola's north coast and established a second town, La Isabela. More settlements quickly followed as Spanish sailors and explorers sailed throughout the Caribbean and then to the mainlands of Central and South America, claiming lands and wealth for Spain.

The Spanish empire also looked toward the north. Perhaps word of lands in that direction first came from Spanish slavers who illegally—without royal sanction—raided native groups living along the Florida coasts. Or perhaps Indians captured or encountered in the Bahamas or the Caribbean knew of the northerly land. If the 1502 Juan de la Cosa map depicts the Florida peninsula, as some historians and geographers have suggested, it is evidence that European sailors had reached the southeastern United States coast by that time, a decade earlier than the first official Spanish expedition (see Cumming, Skelton,

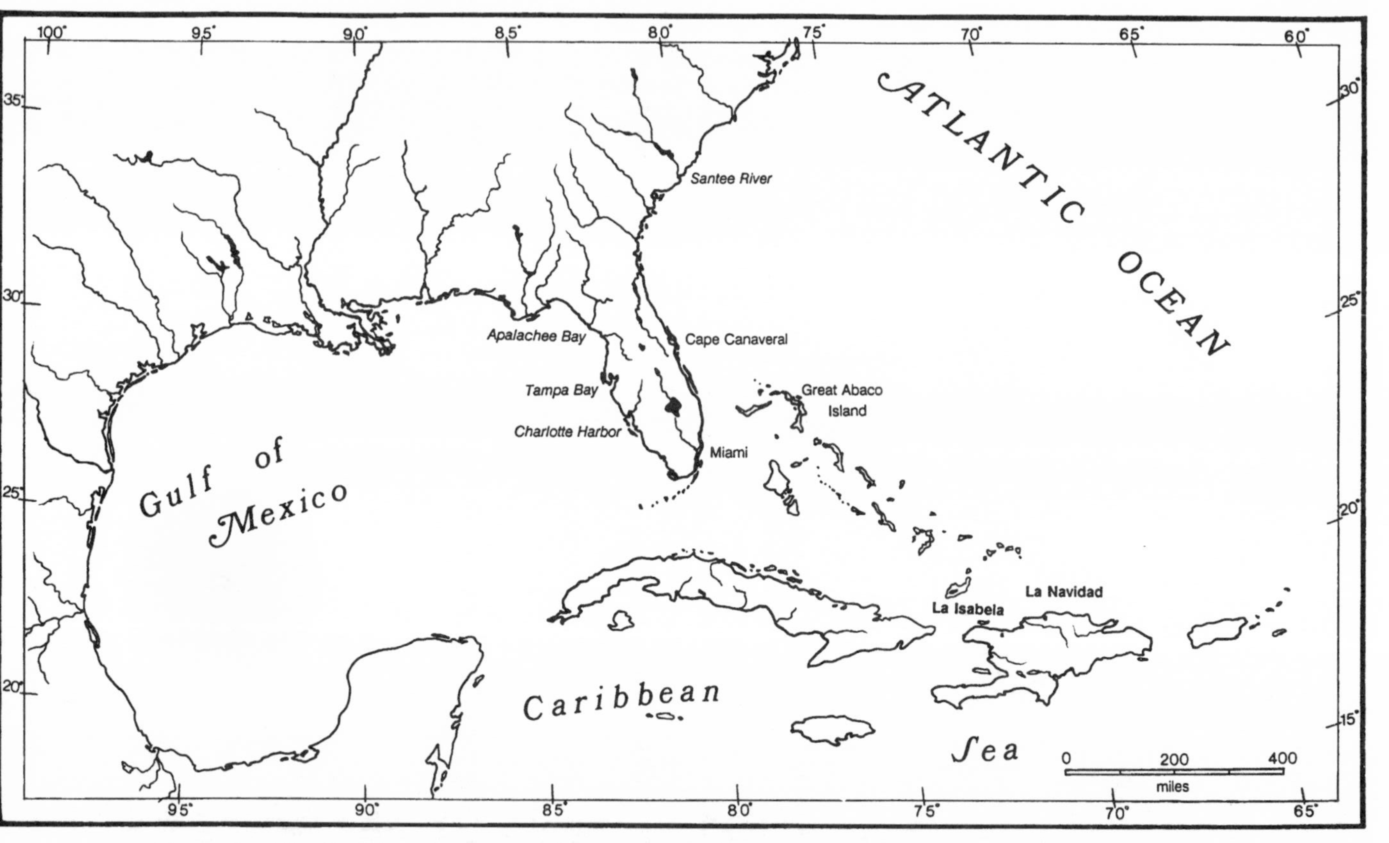

Figure 4. *The Caribbean and the southeastern United States, showing locations mentioned in the text.*

and Quinn 1972:56–57). Other scholars, however, suggest that the mainland shown north of Cuba is that portion of the North American Atlantic coast to which John Cabot sailed on his expeditions of 1497 and 1498 (Harrisse 1968:135–141).

That first official Spanish exploratory voyage was led by Juan Ponce de León, the former governor of the island colony of San Juan (today Puerto Rico) (see Davis 1935; Weddle 1985:38–53). The Spanish crown had given Ponce a three-year *asiento,* or charter, to explore and settle Bimini, an island thought to lay to the north of the Lucayos (Bahama Islands). Such charters typically spelled out the responsibilities and rights of the conquistadors vis-à-vis their respective sovereign, as well as stating what benefits each would receive if the search for new lands was successful (e.g., shares of booty from the colony). Future Spanish conquistadors to La Florida would have similar royal charters.

Ponce set sail on March 3, 1513 on a northerly heading out of Puerto Rico that took him along the Atlantic side of the Bahama Islands. He rounded Great Abaco Island and then turned more northwesterly, a course that brought him to the east coast of north Florida. His arrival coincided with the Feast of Flowers, Easter Holy Week, leading him to name the new land La Florida.

Ponce then turned southward, sailing down the Atlantic coast of peninsular Florida past Cape Canaveral and what is now Miami before rounding the Florida Keys and traveling up the Gulf coast to Charlotte Harbor, which was at first named for him. The Bahía de Juan Ponce appears on sixteenth-century maps (Harrisse 1961) as well as in the ca. 1537 Chaves *derrotero,* a navigation rutter compiled at the behest of the Spanish crown (Castañeda, Cuesta, and Hernández 1983:366).

Antonio de Herrera's history of Juan Ponce's expedition records the first documented Spanish encounter with the Florida natives (Davis 1935). Ponce and his men met native peoples along Florida's Atlantic coast as they sailed southward. On the lower Gulf coast the Spaniards entered the territory of the Calusa Indians, who were led by their chief, Carlos. The Calusa were a nonagricultural people who lived in the Charlotte Harbor–Fort Myers coastal region (Goggin and Sturtevant 1964; Marquardt 1987, 1988; Widmer 1988). On his return to San Juan, Ponce visited the Chequescha (Tequesta) who lived in the vicinity of modern Biscayne Bay and Miami (Goggin 1940).

In 1521 Juan Ponce returned to La Florida, probably again to the Calusa in the greater Charlotte Harbor area, to attempt a settlement. The effort failed when the Spaniards were driven off by the native inhabitants of the region (Davis 1935).

Following Juan Ponce's first voyage, other Spaniards sought to take advantage of his discoveries, leading to additional voyages of exploration along the coasts of La Florida. Diego de Miruelo possibly reached Apalachee Bay (at the northern end of the Florida peninsula on the Gulf side) in 1516; Francisco Hernández de Córdova reached the southwest coast in 1517; and Alonzo Alvarez de Pineda sailed the entire Gulf coast in 1519, drawing the first map of the lands surrounding the Gulf of Mexico (Weddle 1985:55–65, 95–108). No information about Florida natives is provided by these early exploratory voyages, although the sketch map from Alvarez de Pineda's voyage does show Charlotte Harbor and Tampa Bay. All of these early contacts with the Florida aborigines were fleeting and of a limited nature, although slaving probably took place and European diseases were possibly introduced among the native peoples.

Other Spaniards explored the Atlantic coast of La Florida. In 1521 Pedro de Quexo and Francisco Gordillo, on a slaving expedition, sailed into the Santee River and encountered a native group or town called Chicora. That voyage would give rise to Peter Martyr's description of a fabled land "abounding in timber, vines, native olive trees, Indians, pearls, and, . . . , perhaps gold and silver" that quickly spread through Europe in the first half of the sixteenth century (Hoffman 1984:419). The Chicora legend would lure Spaniards and Frenchmen to the southeastern Atlantic coast in search of nonexistent wealth (Hoffman 1990).

The first colonizing expedition to the Atlantic coast was in 1526. It was led by Lucas Vásquez de Ayllón, who had been the backer of Francisco Gordillo (Morison 1971:332–334; Hoffman 1984:423, n. 13, 1990:60–83). Ayllón's royal charter required him to colonize Chicora and establish forts and settlements. But the attempt to establish San Miguel de Gualdape, a colony of 600 persons on the Georgia coast, was a failure, lasting only a few months. The site of Ayllón's short-lived colony has never been found, but is thought to be on or near Sapelo Sound, Georgia (Hoffman 1990:328).

Spain's earliest efforts to explore and colonize La Florida were centered on the coasts, with no significant penetration of the

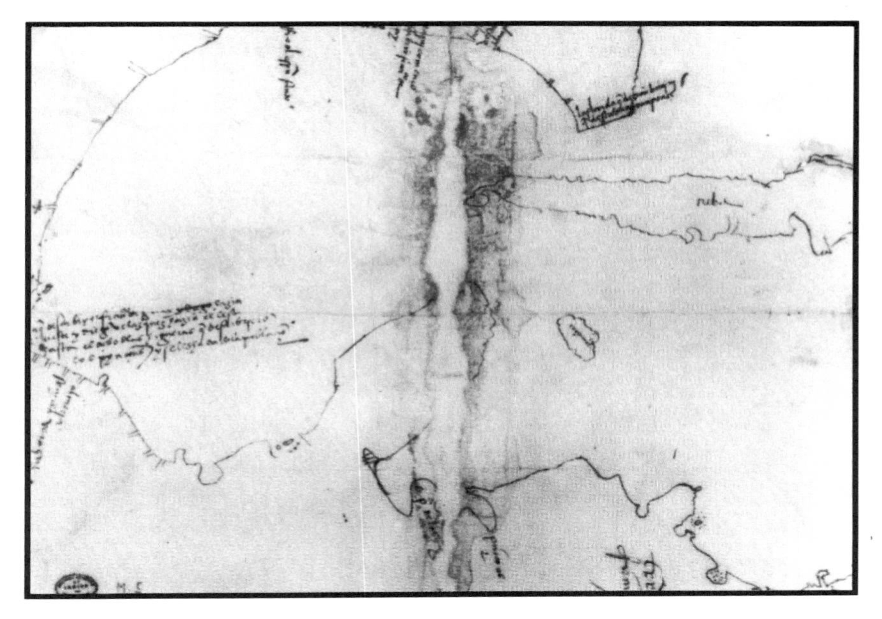

Figure 5

The map from Pineda's voyage along the Gulf of Mexico coast shows both Charlotte Harbor and Tampa Bay. The original is in the Archivo General de Indias.

interior. The first overland expedition was in 1528. Led by Pánfilo de Narváez, an army of 400 men and forty horses landed on the Gulf coast near Tampa (Weddle 1985:185–207). Narváez was to explore La Florida from the Florida peninsula around the Gulf of Mexico to northern Mexico, to the "Rio de las Palmas," probably the Rio Soto la Marina (see Weddle 1985:104–105). The relation of Alvar Núñez Cabeza de Vaca, a survivor of this ill-fated expedition, provides a surprisingly detailed firsthand account of his experiences, although he wrote it nearly a decade after the fact (Bandelier 1905).

Apparently the expedition landed south of the entrance of Tampa Bay and then moved inland and north, locating the harbor. After reconnoitering the eastern portion of the bay and encountering various native groups, the expedition proceeded northward, probably paralleling the coast as it made its way toward the territory of the Apalachee Indians in northwest Florida.

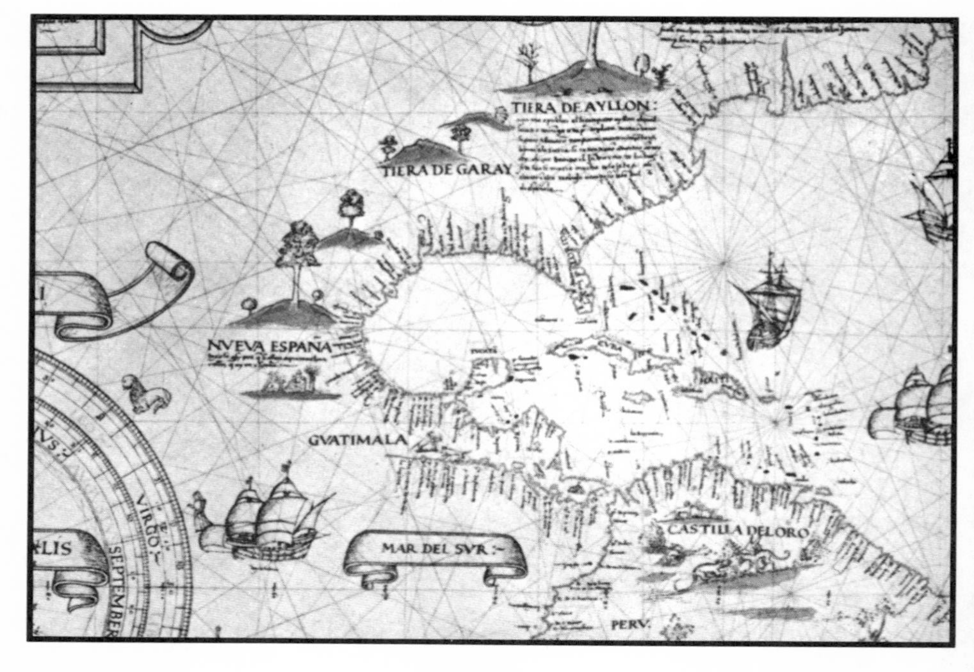

Figure 6

This section of Diego Ribero's world map of 1529, the original of which is in the Vatican, shows the growth of European geographical knowledge about the Western Hemisphere. "Tiera de Ayllón," written on the southeastern United States, refers to Ayllón's colony on the southeast Atlantic coast.

The expedition encountered few native people until it reached Apalachee, where it stayed for twenty-five days before departing and traveling nine days to reach the native village of Aute on the Gulf coast, probably near the mouth of the St. Marks River (Mitchem 1989a). Illness struck the army in Aute. Attempts to travel farther westward through the marshy coastal region also thwarted the Spaniards, who instead chose to build several boats and make their way to New Spain (Mexico) by water.

They failed miserably in the attempt, and most of the men were either swept out into the Gulf never to be seen again or washed ashore where they were taken captive by native peoples. Four of the survivors, including Cabeza de Vaca, who was held captive in Texas for nearly eight years, escaped and made their way westward into the southwestern United States and northern Mexico, where they were found by Spanish slavers. Their tales of wealthy native towns on the northern Rio Grande River later led

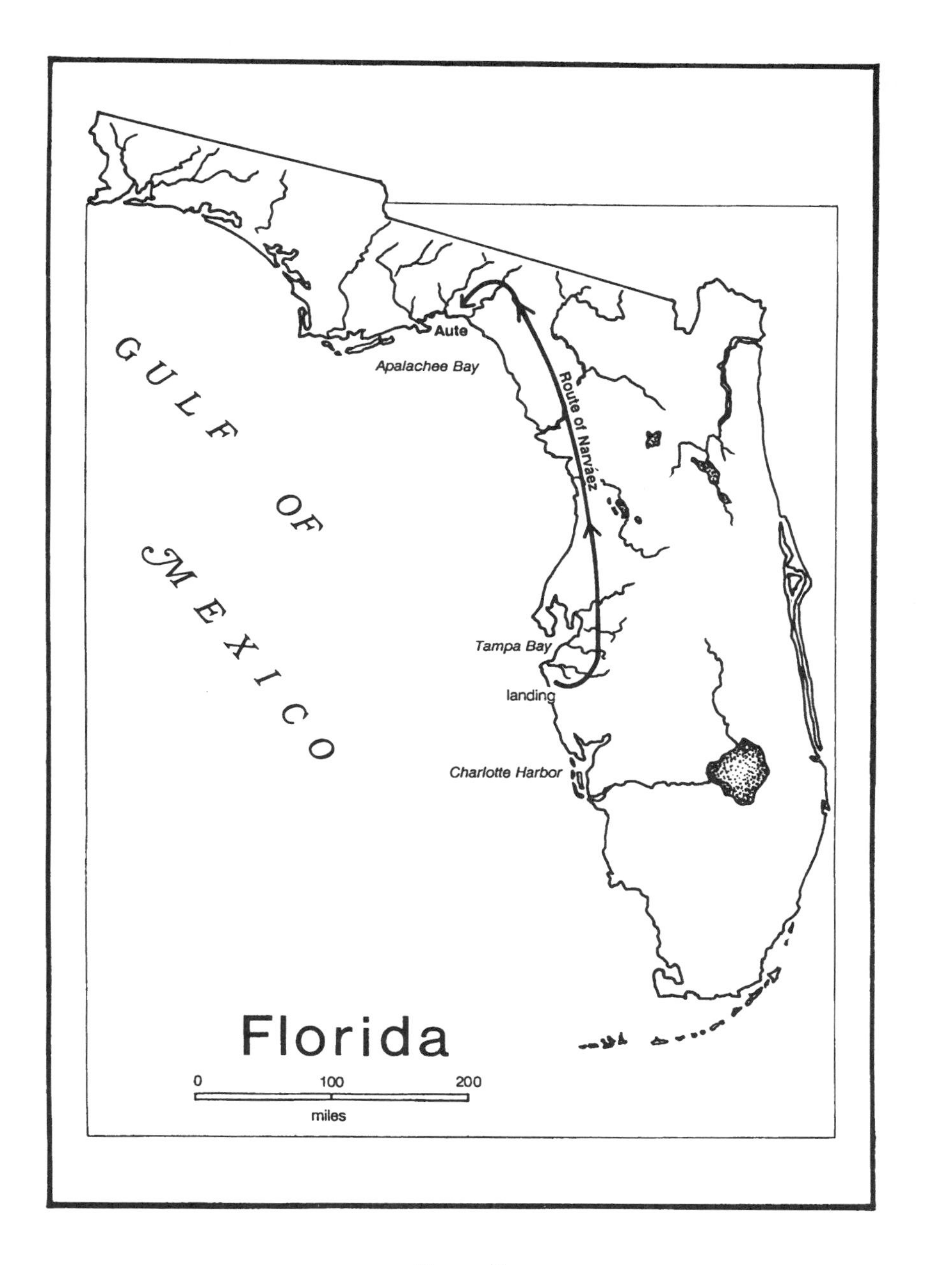

Figure 7

Route of the Pánfilo de Narváez expedition in Florida.

to the 1539 Fray Marcos de Niza and the 1540–1542 Francisco Vásquez de Coronado expeditions into that region (Cordell 1989:25).

Following his ordeal, Cabeza de Vaca arrived at the Spanish court in Seville in 1538. There he led people "to understand that it [La Florida] was the richest country in the world" (Elvas 1922:6). De Soto, in Seville, tried to enlist Cabeza de Vaca in his planned expedition to La Florida but failed. The stories Cabeza de Vaca told the crown apparently did convince others to join de Soto, however. Some of them, including relatives of Cabeza de Vaca, even sold their properties in Spain to finance their participation (Elvas 1922:6–9).

HERNANDO DE SOTO, CONQUISTADOR

De Soto's expedition would be the most ambitious of the Spanish attempts to explore the interior of La Florida. He was born about 1500 in Jeréz de los Caballeros in Extremadura, a Spanish province that produced many of the Spanish New World conquistadors, including Vasco Núñez de Balboa, Hernán Cortéz, and Francisco Pizarro. Tourist brochures today refer to Extremadura as "Land of the Conquistadors." Like many of the Spanish aristocracy, de Soto's ancestors had distinguished themselves in fighting the Moors during the *reconquista.* Military successes had embellished the family's coat-of-arms and resulted in many family members being knighted.[1]

Little is known about de Soto's early years in Spain, and it is uncertain exactly when he came to the New World. The best evidence suggests that he sailed in 1514 in the entourage of the newly named governor of the Castilla del Oro (modern Panama), Pedrárias Dávila (Elvas 1922:3–4). Also accompanying the governor was Francisco Vásquez de Coronado, who later would explore the southwestern United States.

By 1520, at the age of about twenty, de Soto was a captain who had already participated in military actions against the Panamanian Indians. As a portion of his share of booty, he received the right to use a number of Indians as laborers, providing him a source of revenue. His partner in many ventures was Hernán Ponce de León; another associate was Francisco Pizarro.

Throughout the 1520s, de Soto participated in military exploits in Panama and Nicaragua, some against rival Spaniards. By late 1531 when he left Panama, de Soto had amassed great wealth from slave trading and from gold taken from the Indians. With his wealth he was able to build ships and to expand his activities, including maintaining a cadre of military aides, infantry, and cavalry. By the standards of the day, he was already a notable conquistador.

But de Soto was to garner even greater wealth. From 1531 through 1535 he accompanied Pizarro and other Spaniards in the conquest and looting of the Inca civilization in Peru. De Soto played an important part in the military engagements, experience that would later serve him well in La Florida. After the Spanish executed the captive Inca leader Atahualpa and occupied Cuzco, de Soto helped distribute the stolen wealth to the conquistadors. He left Peru in late 1535, sailing on to Spain in early 1536. With him were men who would later accompany him on the Florida expedition.

Back in Spain, de Soto used his wealth to hire a number of servants and secure other trappings befitting someone of his station. He was presented at court and, along with his entourage of military aides who had accompanied him to Spain, must have created quite a stir. While in Spain he married Isabela de Bobadilla, the daughter of Pedrárias Dávila with whom de Soto had first traveled to the New World.

De Soto next attempted to persuade the crown to grant him the right to New World lands that he could govern and exploit. He asked for either lands in Ecuador and Colombia, north of Pizarro's holdings, or, failing that, Guatemala. Though these requests were denied, he was able to successfully negotiate an agreement to conquer and govern La Florida. The *asiento* given to de Soto by Carlos V is dated April 20, 1537 (Swanton 1939: 75–76).

The language of de Soto's charter was much the same as that in the contracts awarded by the crown to other New World adventurers.[2] The charter required de Soto to conquer, pacify, and settle 200 leagues of La Florida's coast, taking with him 500 men and supplies for eighteen months, and he was to build three stone forts, using his own funds. In return he was to receive titles, lands, and a share of the colony's profits.

DE SOTO'S CHARTER

A translation of de Soto's royal charter follows.[3] It is a relatively simple but comprehensive document that spells out de Soto's rights and duties and, in considerable detail, the sovereign rights of the crown, especially the division of booty that might be found in La Florida.

CONCESSION MADE BY THE KING OF SPAIN TO HERNANDO DE SOTO OF THE GOVERNMENT OF CUBA AND CONQUEST OF FLORIDA, WITH THE TITLE OF ADELANTADO

The King

Inasmuch as you, Captain Hernando de Soto, set forth that you have served us in the conquest, pacification, and settlement of the Provinces of Nicaragua and Peru, and of other parts of our Indias [Spain's New World lands]; and that now, to serve us further, and to continue to enlarge our patrimony and the royal crown, you desire to return to those our Indias, to conquer and settle the Province of Río de las Palmas to Florida, the government whereof was bestowed on Pánfilo de Narváez, and the Provinces of Tierra-Nueva, the discovery and government of which was conferred on Lucas Vázquez de Ayllón; and that for the purpose you will take from these, our kingdoms and our said Indias, five hundred men with the necessary arms, horses, munitions, and military stores; and that you will go hence, from these our kingdoms, to make the said conquest and settlement within a year first following, to be reckoned from the day of the date of these article of authorization; and that when you shall leave the Island of Cuba to go upon that enterprise, you will take the necessary subsistence for all that people during eighteen months—rather over than under that time—entirely at your own cost and charges, without our being obliged, or the kings who shall come after us, to pay you, nor satisfy the expenses incurred therefore, other than such as you in these articles may be authorized to make; and you pray that I bestow on you the conquest of these lands and provinces, and with it the government of the said Island of Cuba, that you may from there the better control and provide all the principal and important material for the conquest and settlement, whereupon I have ordered to be made with you the terms and contract following:

First, I give you, the said Captain Hernando de Soto, power and authority, for us and in our name, and in that of the royal crown of Castilla, to conquer, pacify, and populate the lands that there are from the Province of the Rio de las Palmas to Florida, the government of which was bestowed on Pánfilo de Narváez; and further, the Provinces of the said Tierra-Nueva, the government thereof was in like manner conferred on the said Licentiate Ayllón.

Also, purposing to comply in this with the service of God our Lord, and to do you honour, we engage to confer on you the dignity of Governor and Captain-General of two hundred leagues of coast, such as you shall designate, of what you discover, so that within four years, to be reckoned from the time you arrive in any part of the lands and provinces before mentioned, you shall choose and declare whence you would have the two hundred leagues begin; that from where you designate they shall be measured along the coast, for all the days of your life, with the annual salary of fifteen thousand ducats, and five hundred ducats gratuity, in all two thousand, when you shall receive from the day you set sail in the Port of San Lucar, to go upon your voyage, to be paid to you from the duties and profits appertaining in those said lands and provinces which you so offer to conquer and colonize; and in that time should there be neither duties nor profits, we shall not be obliged to order that you be paid anything.

Also, we will confer on you the title of Adelantado over the said two hundred leagues which you shall thus select and make known for your government in the said lands and provinces you so discover and colonize, and will likewise bestow on you the office of High-Constable (Alguazile mayor) over those territories in perpetuity.

Also, we give permission, the judgment of our officers of said province being in accord, that you build there as many as three stone fortresses in the harbours and places most proper for them, they appearing to you and to our said officers to be necessary for the protection and pacification of that country; and we confer on you the Lieutenancy of them, and on one heir for life, or successor whom you shall name, with the annual salary to each of the fortresses of one hundred thousand maravedís, which you shall enjoy from the time they be severally built and finished and enclosed, in the opinion of our said officers; to be done at your own cost, without our being obliged, or any of the kings who shall come after us, to pay you what you may expend on those fortresses.

Again, inasmuch as you have petitioned us to bestow on you some portion of the land and vassals in said province you would conquer and populate, considering that you have served us, and the expenditure you will meet from this time in making said conquest and pacification, we receive the petitions favourably: hence we promise to bestow on you, and by these presents we do, twelve leagues of land in square in the said two hundred leagues you shall designate to hold in government in the said territories and provinces before declared, which we command our officers of the said province to assign, after you shall have designated the said two hundred leagues, to include no sea-port, nor the principal town, and that with the jurisdiction and title we shall confer at the time we give you the deeds.

Again, as has been said, you have petitioned us, that for the better governing and providing of all the principal and important matters for the conquest and settlement of said territories and provinces, I should order that there be given to you with them the government of the said Island of Cuba, which, to that end, we deem well, and is our pleasure, for the time it shall be our will, that you hold the government of said island; and for this much we will order to be given you our provision by which you will be obliged to have a Chief-Justice, who shall be a lawyer, to whom we shall require you to pay yearly on that Island the salary of two hundred pesos of gold; and we give to you five hundred ducats annual gratuity for the government of said Island, while you hold the same, to be paid from the duties and profits we may have from the province you have thus to conquer, pacify, and hold in government; and if there be none there, we will not be obliged to pay you that, nor any other thing more than the two hundred pesos of the said Chief-Justice.

Also, we give you liberty and right that you from these our kingdoms and lordships, or from the Kingdom of Portugal, or

Islands of Cabo Verde, of Guinea, do and may pass, or whosoever may exercise your power, to the said Island of Cuba fifty negro slaves, not less than one-third of them to be female, free of the import duties that of right may belong to us at said island, upon paying the license of two ducats on each to Diego de la Haya, which sum by our order he is charged to collect.

Again, also we promise that upon your arrival in that country of your government, which you have thus to conquer and settle, we give liberty and right to whomsoever shall have your power, that you may take thither from these our said kingdoms, or from Portugal, or the Islands of Cabo Verde, another fifty negro slaves, the third part of them females, free from all duties.

Also, we concede to those who shall go to settle in that country within six years first following, to be reckoned forward from the day of the date of these presents, that of the gold which may be taken from the mines shall be paid us the tenth, and the said six years being ended, shall pay us the ninth, and thus annually declining to the fifth part; but from the gold and other things that may be got by barter, or is spoil got by incursions, or in any other manner, shall be paid us thereupon one-fifth of all.

Also we give, free of import duty, to the inhabitants of that country for the said six years, and as much longer as shall be our will, all they may take for the furnishing and provision of their houses, the same not being to sell; and whatsoever they or any other, merchants or traffickers, sell, shall go free of duty for two years, and not longer.

Likewise, we promise that for the term of ten years, and until we command otherwise, we will not impose on the inhabitants of those countries any excise duty, or any other tribute whatsoever.

Likewise, we grant that to said inhabitants may be given through you the lots and grounds proper to their conditions, as has been done, and is doing, in the Island of Española; and we also give you license, in our name, during the time of your government, that you take the bestowal of the Indians of that land, observing therein the instructions and provisions that will be given to you.

Again, we bestow on the hospital that may be built in that country, to assist the relief of the poor who may go thither, the charity of one hundred thousand maravedís from the fines imposed by the tribunal of that country.

Again, also, according to your petition and consent, and of the settlers of that country, we promise to give to its hospital, and by these presents we do give, the duties of escobilla *and* relabes, *existing in the foundries that may there be made; and as respects that, we will order our provision to be issued to you in form.*

Also, likewise we will order, and by the present command and defend, that from these our kingdoms do not pass into said country, nor go, any one of the persons prohibited from going into those parts, under the penalties contained in the laws and ordinances of our letters, upon which subject this by us and by the Catholic Kings are given, nor any counsellors nor attorneys to exercise their callings.

The which, all that is said, and each thing and part thereof, we concede to you, conditioned that you, the said Don Hernando de Soto, be held and obliged to go from these our realms in person to make the conquest within one year next following, to be reckoned from the day of the date of this charter.

Again, on condition that when you go out of these our said kingdoms, and arrive in said country, you will carry and have with you the officers of our exchequer, who may by us be named; and likewise also the persons, religious and ecclesiastical, who shall be appointed by us for the instruction of the natives of that Province in our Holy Catholic Faith, to whom you are to give and pay the passage, stores, and the other necessary subsistence for them, according to their condition, all at your cost, receiving nothing from them during the said entire voyage; with which matter we gravely charge you, that you do and comply with, as a thing for the service of God and our own, and any thing otherwise we shall deem contrary to our service.

Again, whensoever, according to right and the laws of our kingdoms, the people and captains of our armaments take prisoner any prince or lord of the countries where, by our command, they make war, the ransom of such lord or cacique belongs to us, with all the other things movable found or belonging to him; but considering the great toils and perils that our subjects undergo in the conquest of the Indias, as some recompense, and to favour them, we make known and command, that if in your said conquest and government any cacique or principal lord be captured or seized, all the treasures, gold, silver, stones, and pearls that may be got from him by way of redemption, or in any other manner whatsoever, we award you the seventh part thereof, and the remainder shall be divided among the conquerors, first taking out our fifth; and in case the said cacique or lord should be slain in battle, or afterward by course of justice, or in any other manner whatsoever, in such case, of the treasurers and goods aforesaid obtained of him justly we have the half, which, before any thing else, our officers shall take, after having first reserved our fifth.

Again, since our said officers of said Provinces might have some doubt in making the collection of our duties, especially on gold and silver, stones and pearls, as well those that may be found in sepulchres, and other places where they may be hidden, as those got by ransom and incursion, or other way, our pleasure and will is, that, until some change, the following order be observed.

First, we order that of the gold and silver, stones and pearls that may be won in battle, or on entering towns, or by barter with the Indians, should and must be paid us one-fifth of all.

Likewise, that all the gold and silver, stones, pearls, and other things that may be found and taken, as well in the graves, sepulchres, ocues, *or temples of the Indians, as in other places where they were accustomed to offer sacrifices to their idols, or in other concealed religious precincts, or buried in house, or patrimonial soil, or in the ground, or in some other public place, whether belonging to the community or an individual, be his state or dignity what it may, of the whole, and of all other, of the character that may be and is found, whether finding it by accident or discovering it by search, shall pay us the half, without diminution of any sort, the other half remaining to the person who has found or made the discovery; and should any person or persons have gold, silver, stones, or pearls, taken or found, as well in the said graves, sepulchres,* ocues, *or Indian temples, as in the other places where they were accustomed to offer sacrifices, or other concealed religious places, or interred as before said, and do not make it known, that they may receive, in conformity with this chapter, what may belong to them, they have forfeited all the gold and silver, stones and pearls, besides the half of their goods, to our tribunal and exchequer.*

And we, having been informed of the evils and disorders which occur in making discoverings and new settlements, for the redress thereof, and that we may be enabled to give you license to make them, with the accord of the members of our Council and of our consultation, a general provision of chapters is ordained and dispatched, respecting what you will have to observe in the said settlement and conquest, and we command it here to be incorporated in tenor as follows:

As Smith (1866:272) notes, this "general provision" was an ordinance, first incorporated in the royal charter of Francisco de Montejo, granting him the conquest of Yucatan; Montejo's charter was dated December 7, 1526. The contents of this ordinance, which were not included in the copy of de Soto's charter that Smith translated, but which are known from other charters, are given below, following this last section of de Soto's *asiento.*

Hence, by these presents, you, the said Captain Hernando de Soto, doing as aforesaid at your cost, according to and in the manner before contained, observing and complying with the said provision here incorporated, and all the other instructions we shall henceforth command you to obey, and to give with regard to that country, and for the good treatment and conversion to our Holy Catholic Faith of the natives of it, we promise and declare that to you will be kept these terms, and whatever therein is contained, in and through all; and you doing otherwise, and not complying therewith, we shall not be obliged to keep with you and comply with the aforesaid, nor any matter of it; on the contrary, we will order that you be punished, and proceed against you as against one who keeps not nor complies with, but acts counter to, the commands of his natural king and lord. In confirmation whereof we order that the present be given, signed by my name, and witnessed by my undersigned Secretary. Done at the town of Valladolid, the twentieth day of the month of April, of the year one thousand five hundred and thirty seven.

I The King.

De Soto's charter followed a set form, one developed by the crown based on experience with other New World expeditions. Likewise, the ordinance referred to above was originally drawn up (and dated November 17, 1526) by the crown in consultation with various Spanish governmental and church officials. The ordinance, which evolved as a part of Spain's New World policy, set forth the ideology and basis of conquest and the role of church and state vis-à-vis the native inhabitants of the New World. The purpose of conquest was to bring the native peoples to the true faith and establish their allegiance to the Spanish crown. Indians were free people who were to be afforded the protection of the crown and the church and could not be used as laborers against their will (Chamberlain 1948:22–23).

The ordinance required that at least two members of the clergy accompany each expedition. These clergymen were further commanded to try to convert the natives to Christianity and to report to the crown any violations of the rights of the native peoples. A further requirement was that each expedition read a lengthy statement, the *requerimiento*, to the natives, outlining the desire of the Spanish monarchy that the natives pledge allegiance to the crown and accept Catholicism. The *requerimiento* was supposed to make known to the Indians that they and their lands now belonged to the Spanish crown. It was to be read three times by the leader of the Spanish expedition or a representative (using an interpreter, if needed) and explained to the Indians so that they understood its meaning. The event was to be witnessed by a member of the clergy and duly recorded.

On the one hand, it is easy to visualize the ceremony and pomp that accompanied the mandatory reading of the *requerimiento* when de Soto or another conquistador encountered a new native society. It is also easy to visualize the result. The *requerimiento* incorporated Catholic ideology with legal and political complexities based on European models. It is highly unlikely that it was immediately understood by New World peoples whose ideology and political organization was based on very different concepts.

The failure of a native person to obey the *requerimiento* meant disaster for that individual, since such failure meant that the Spaniards could use force to enslave that individual. In essence, the *requerimiento* offered the Spanish expeditions, such as that of de Soto, a legal excuse to wage war against the people of La

Florida as necessary to further the Spanish empire in the New World. Excerpts of the *requerimiento* in use when de Soto first came to the New World in 1514 illustrate the complex nature of this document and the threat it implied (from Chamberlain 1948:24–25):

> *On behalf of the king . . . and the queen . . . , subjugators of barbarous peoples, we, their servants, notify and make known to you as best we are able, that God, Our Lord, living and eternal, created the heavens and the earth, and a man and a woman, of whom you and we and all other people of the world were, and are, the descendants. . . . Because of the great numbers of people who have come from the union of these two in the five thousand years which have run their course since the world was created, it became necessary that some should go in one direction and that others should go in another. Thus they became divided into many kingdoms and many provinces, since they could not all remain or sustain themselves in one place.*
>
> *Of all these people God, Our Lord, chose one, who was called Saint Peter, to be the lord and the one who was to be superior to all the other people of the world, whom all should obey. He was to be the head of the entire human race, wherever men might exist. . . . God gave him the world for his kingdom and jurisdiction. . . . God also permitted him to be and establish himself in any other part of the world to judge and govern all peoples, whether Christian, Moors, Jew, Gentiles, or those of any other sects and beliefs that there might be. He was called the Pope. . . .*
>
> *One of the past Popes who succeeded Saint Peter . . . , as Lord of the Earth gave these islands and mainlands of the Ocean Sea [the Atlantic Ocean] to the said King and Queen and to their successors . . . , with everything that there is in them, as is set forth in certain documents which were drawn up regarding this donation in the manner described, which you may see if you so desire.*
>
> *In consequence, Their Highnesses are Kings and Lords of these islands and mainland by virtue of said donation. Certain other isles and almost all [the native peoples] to whom this summons has been read have accepted Their Highnesses*

as such Kings and Lords, and have served, and serve, them as their subjects as they should, and must, do, with good will and without offering any resistance.... You are constrained and obliged to do the same as they.

Consequently, as we best may, we beseech and demand that you understand fully this that we have said to you and ponder it, so that you may understand and deliberate upon it for a just and fair period and that you accept the Church and Superior Organization of the whole world and recognize the Supreme Pontiff, called the Pope, and that in his name, you acknowledge the King and Queen ..., as the lords and superior authorities of these islands and mainlands by virtue of the said donation....

If you do not do this, however, or resort maliciously to delay, we warn you that, with the aid of God, we will enter your land against you with force and will make war in every place and by every means we can and are able, and we will then subject you to the yoke and authority of the Church and Their Highnesses. We will take you and your wives and children and make them slaves, and as such we will sell them, and will dispose of you and them as Their Highnesses order. And we will take your property and will do to you all the harm and evil we can, as is done to vassals who will not obey their lord or who do not wish to accept him, or who resist and defy him. We avow that the deaths and harm which you will receive thereby will be your own blame, and not that of Their Highnesses, nor ours, nor of the gentlemen who come with us....

As representatives of God, the pope, and their sovereign, and armed with weapons from another world, de Soto and his army sailed to the New World from Spain in April 1538 (Elvas 1922:11). After a stop in the Canary Islands, the fleet arrived in Santiago, Cuba. De Soto sent a portion of his expedition on to Havana via the sea while he and 150 of his men went overland on horseback. Forty days later, they too arrived in Havana (Elvas 1922:18, 20).

In Havana, de Soto, who had been given the governorship of Cuba, took control of the colony and began to finalize plans for his La Florida expedition. On May 18, 1539 he and his army departed for the mainland "to conquer and settle and reduce to peaceful life those provinces which his Majesty has bestowed upon him ..." (Ranjel 1922:50–51). The La Florida expedition had begun.

One week later, de Soto's fleet sighted the western coast of Florida and dropped anchor near the mouth of the harbor they had sought. Over the next few days they would make their way into the harbor and unload more than 600 people (including 2 women, tailors, shoemakers, a stocking-maker, a notary, a farrier, a trumpeter, servants, priests, cavalry, and infantry), 220 horses, a drove of pigs, and their supplies. The exact number of people who accompanied de Soto is uncertain. Biedma (1922:3) says 620 men, while Ranjel (1922:52) says 570 men plus 130 sailors totaling "fully 700."

Over the next four years the expedition would travel through much of the Southeast, going as far north as the Appalachian Mountains in North Carolina and Tennessee. De Soto and his army with their Indian bearers would cross the Mississippi River into Arkansas before heading back eastward to once again reach the Mississippi River. There de Soto would die.

Under new leadership the Spaniards would try to reach New Spain (Mexico) by walking overland, but after traveling well into Texas they would abandon the effort and retrace their steps to the Mississippi River. There they would spend the winter of 1542–1543 constructing seven keeled boats. In June, the survivors would row southward with the Mississippi River current, eventually reaching the Gulf of Mexico and then working their way westward along the coast. The incredible odyssey ended in September 1543, when the ragged survivors, numbering slightly more than 300, reached a Spanish settlement on the Panuco River near Tampico, Mexico.

CHAPTER III

THE LANDING

There is no part of Hernando de Soto's route of exploration in the southeastern United States that has not been controversial. And this holds for the very first segment of the route: where he made his landfall, where he established his base camp, and the route he followed northward to Apalachee, the place where he spent his first winter, that of 1539–1540.

THE HARBOR

While de Soto was in Cuba making preparations for his expedition, he sent Juan de Añasco with fifty men in a caravel with two pinnaces to explore the harbor in La Florida where the army expected to make its landing (Elvas 1922:20). Unfortunately, little is known about what Añasco discovered. He did bring back some Indians captured during his exploration who were to be used as guides and interpreters. From signs that these Indians made, de Soto and his men expected to find much gold and a very rich land.

Even before Añasco carried out this exploration, it is very likely that de Soto knew that there were at least two good harbors on the west coast of Florida. De Soto, or his chief pilot, Alonso Martín, must surely have had access to the information in Alonso de Chaves's *Espejo de Navigantes*, a guide for navigators, compiled by 1537. In this guide two good harbors are located on the Gulf coast of the Florida peninsula: the Bahía de Juan Ponce to the south and the Bahía Honda to the north (Ranjel 1922:54;

Figure 8

The Florida Gulf coast.

Castañeda, Cuesta, and Hernández 1983:364–365, 366). Bahía de Juan Ponce was presumably visited by Juan Ponce de León on his first voyage in 1513, while both must have been seen by Alonso Alvarez de Pineda, who sailed along the entire Gulf of Mexico coast in 1519 (Weddle 1985:38–54, 95–108). A drawing showing Pineda's discoveries clearly shows two harbors on Florida's Gulf coast at the relative locations of Tampa Bay and Charlotte Harbor (see Weddle 1985:101). Both harbors are also shown in the 1524 "Cortes map," whose authorship is uncertain, but which is almost certainly based on information from Pineda's voyage (Weddle 1985:148, 159–160; Winsor 1884–1889 (2):403). The harbors are also shown on the 1542 map by Jean Rotz, a Frenchman who prepared it for King Henry VIII of England (Portinaro and Knirsch 1987:68–69). By the time of the de Soto expedition, the coastal geography of eastern North America was established and Tampa Bay (Bahía Honda) and Charlotte Harbor (Bahía de Juan Ponce) were known locations.

De Soto also benefited from the knowledge of Alvar Núñez Cabeza de Vaca, a survivor of the Pánfilo de Narváez expedition that had located one of these two harbors in 1528. It is likely that de Soto intended to land at the same harbor. Upon sighting the Florida coast, de Soto renamed the harbor where he was to land the Port of Espíritu Santo (de Soto 1866:287; Elvas 1922:21; Ranjel 1922:164; Varner and Varner 1951:59).

But which harbor was it? Serious arguments have been made for three different landing places on the west coast of Florida: San Carlos Bay and the mouth of the Caloosahatchee River (Wilkinson 1954; Schell 1966), Charlotte Harbor (Williams 1986, 1989), and Tampa Bay (Swanton 1939).

San Carlos Bay can be ruled out on the grounds that it was far too shallow to have accommodated de Soto's ships. In a description of this bay written around 1576, Juan López de Velasco, a contemporary of de Soto describes San Carlos Bay as follows: "Its entrance is very narrow so that one cannot enter except with boats [i.e., small craft], within it is spacious, of four or five leagues in circumference although entirely marshy . . ." (Boyd 1938b: 208–209).

The unsuitability of the mouth of the Caloosahatchee River for large ships is confirmed by the initial survey by the Corps of Engineers done in March and April 1879 (Meigs 1880a). The engineer in charge of the survey noted that: "No vessel exceeding

5.25 feet in draught can pass from the mouth of the river to Fort Myers at mean low-water. The range of the tides, however, between mean low-water and mean high-water being here 2.2 feet, vessels drawing from 6 to 7 feet are enabled by taking advantage of tides to reach Fort Myers" (Meigs 1880a:869).

A later, more extensive report makes it clear that the channel of the Caloosahatchee River was obstructed by oyster bars for some distance above its mouth (Black 1889:1337). San Carlos Bay and the Caloosahatchee River were not navigable by ships until after the dredging that began in 1881–1885. Clearly such a shallow bay could not have accommodated the large ships (*navios*) in de Soto's fleet.

Deciding between Charlotte Harbor and Tampa Bay is not nearly so easy because of the extraordinary confusion in sixteenth-century maps and navigational aids describing the west coast of Florida. Apalachee Bay, Tampa Bay, and Charlotte Harbor are confused with each other both with respect to name and geographical location.

This confusion is present in book IV of Alonso de Chaves's *Espejo de Navigantes* (Castañeda, Cuesta, and Hernández 1983: 364–368). For information on the west coast of Florida and the Gulf coast, Chaves evidently drew on at least two, perhaps three, firsthand sources. He made no discernible attempt to iron out discrepancies among these reports. For example, he gives the distance from the Río del Espíritu Santo (the Mississippi River) to the Río de Flores (Mobile Bay) variously as sixty-eight leagues, sixty leagues, and sixty-four leagues, presumably citing information from three separate accounts.

Some of Chaves's descriptions and locations are reasonably accurate. His Río de Canoas is at 26.67 degrees, and it is clearly the Caloosahatchee River (its actual location is closer to 26.5 degrees). He locates it at 6 leagues south-southeast of the Bahía de Juan Ponce (i.e., Charlotte Harbor). Using a nautical league of 3.67 miles to the league, the actual distance is 5.5 leagues. [In all measurements of distance by water we have used a nautical league of 3.67 miles. For Spanish travel on land we have used the *legua commún* of 3.46 miles and for French travel on land the *lieu commune* of 2.76 miles; see Roland Chardon's "The Linear League in North America" (1980).]

Chaves locates the Bahía de Juan Ponce at 27.25 degrees, whereas the entrance to Charlotte Harbor is closer to 26.67

degrees, an error of a little over .5 degree. He says that the Bahía de Juan Ponce is 32 leagues north-northwest of the point of Florida, whereas the actual distance is 36 nautical leagues. In his *Espejo,* Chaves places the Bahía de Miruelo—his name for Apalachee Bay—70 leagues north-northwest of the Bahía de Juan Ponce. The actual distance is 70.6 nautical leagues. The name "Bahía de Miruelo" probably derives from Diego de Miruelo, the pilot who served Pánfilo de Narváez in 1528 (Weddle 1985:187, 204). Narváez is commonly thought to have located Tampa Bay, from whence he marched northward to Apalachee. After his expedition fell apart in Apalachee, the survivors built flatboats at Apalachee Bay and attempted to sail from there to Mexico.

It is clear from Chaves's description that Bahía Honda ("deep bay") is Tampa Bay. He describes it as being 10 leagues long and 5 leagues wide at the mouth. In fact, Tampa Bay is about 10 leagues long but closer to 4 leagues wide at the mouth. It has, Chaves says, three small barren islands (*isolotes*) in its mouth—Passage Key, Egmont Key, and the north end of Anna Maria Key. Inside, the bay is said to be clear, quite deep, and safe for all large ships. From the mouth of the bay, running along the coast to the south, Chaves describes two large barrier islands, the Islas de San Clemente, said to be 4 leagues long. These were Anna Maria Key and Longboat Key, and, using the 3.67 mile nautical league, their actual combined length is about 5.1 leagues. Between these islands, Chaves goes on to say, one could find passage to the mainland, i.e., to the area now occupied by Sarasota.

To the north of the mouth of the Bahía Honda, according to Chaves, there were three similar islands—the San Gines—the combined length of which was 6 leagues. Chaves's San Gines islands were perhaps the group that includes Mullet Key, St. Jean Key, Madeline Key, and Cabbage Key, all of which might have been perceived as one island, along with Long Key and Sand Key. The actual length of all of these is about 7.1 leagues from one end to the other. It is possible that "St. Jean" is an Anglicization of "San Gines."

Beyond this, there is much inaccuracy and confusion in Chaves's *Espejo.* He says that Bahía Honda is located at 29 degrees, whereas the mouth of Tampa Bay is at 27.5 degrees, an error of 1.5 degrees. This same error in latitude, 1.5 degrees too far north, is also found in the sightings recorded by Anton de Alaminos, pilot on Juan Ponce de León's first voyage to La

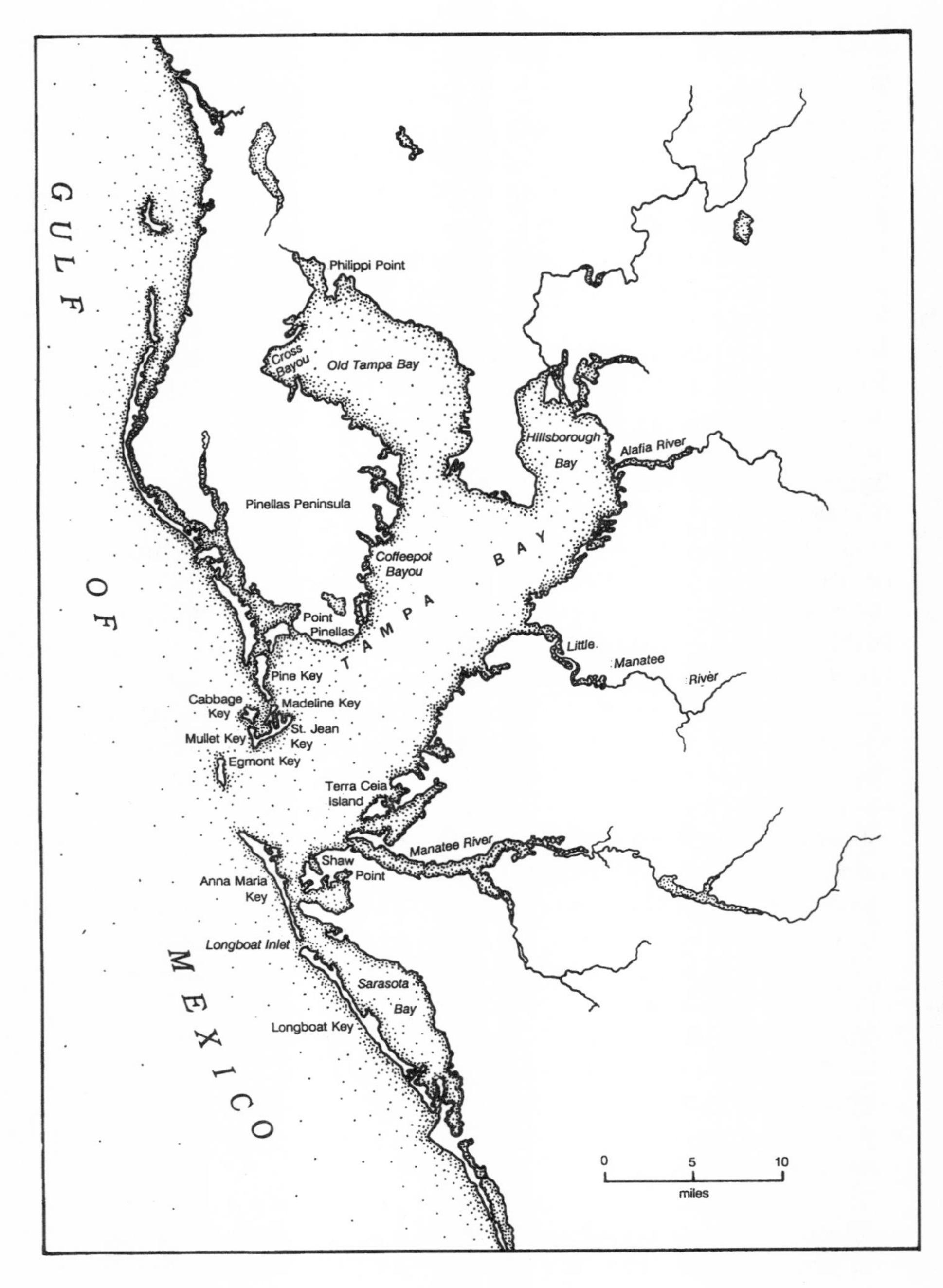

Figure 9

Tampa Bay.

Florida in 1513. Weddle (1985:41) suggests the error is so regular in Ponce's account of his 1513 expedition that it might be due to faulty tables or a faulty astrolabe. It is not impossible that some of Alaminos's or another pilot's erroneous readings found their way into the *Espejo.* An error of 1.5 degrees latitude at the longitude of the Bahamas and Florida computes to about 104 miles or about thirty leagues.

Chaves says that Bahía Honda is thirty-six or thirty-eight leagues north northwest of Bahía de Juan Ponce, whereas the actual distance is about nineteen leagues, only about half the distance given by Chaves. Chaves also says that Bahía de Honda is twenty-six leagues south southeast of Bahía de Miruelo, whereas the actual distance is fifty-two leagues, almost twice as far as the distance given in the *Espejo.* Perhaps these erroneous locations for Tampa Bay relative to Bahía de Juan Ponce and Bahía de Miruelo are both the result of the 1.5 degree error (too far north) recorded in the *Espejo.*

While the Bahía Honda is accurately described by Chaves but inaccurately located, the Bahía de Miruelo is accurately located but inaccurately described. Chaves says that the Bahía de Miruelo (i.e., Apalachee Bay) is 70 leagues north northwest of the Bahía de Juan Ponce, and the actual distance is 70.6 nautical leagues. But he describes the bay as being 10 leagues long, with its channel lying in an east-west direction, and he says that it was 8 leagues wide. An inlet full of shoals—Ancón Bay—was said to lie 5 leagues to the south of Bahía de Miruelo and was separated from it by a point of land going out into the sea (Castañeda, Cuesta, and Hernández 1983:366).

This description in no way resembles Apalachee Bay, which is wider than it is long. It does not run to the east-northeast nor does it have an inlet to the south. While it is impossible to be sure why Chaves described the Bahía de Miruelo so inaccurately, one suspects that, in fact, he is again describing Tampa Bay. The compass orientation of the bay and its dimensions are approximately those of Tampa Bay, and "Ancón Bay" may be Sarasota Bay. Chaves, who apparently never visited the New World, must have made use of descriptions and latitude readings provided by several pilots. In attempting to reconcile discrepancies in such information, he made interpretive errors and perhaps duplicated descriptions of some bays.

But however these inaccuracies are to be explained, it is clear enough that Chaves's Bahía Honda was Tampa Bay, and Luys Hernández de Biedma states that de Soto landed in Bahía Honda (1922:3). A Tampa Bay landing is confirmed in the documentation of an incident that occurred in 1612—seventy-three years after de Soto landed. Juan Fernández de Olivera, governor of Florida, sent a detachment of soldiers from St. Augustine to punish the Indians of South Florida, who had been attacking Indians in northern Florida. Commanded by Ensign Juan Rodríguez de Cortaya, this detachment consisted of a pilot and twenty soldiers who apparently went down the Suwannee River in a longboat (*lancha*). They anchored at the mouth of the Suwannee River and continued down the coast in dugout canoes to the province of Pojoy (also spelled "Pooy" and "Pojoi") located on a large bay at 27.3 degrees—the actual latitude of the mouth of Tampa Bay. The bay is described as free of shoals, and so deep a fleet of ships could enter it. The Tocopaca (the "Tocobaga" encountered by Pedro Menéndez de Avilés in Tampa Bay in 1566) are also said to reside at the bay. Moreover, the Indians of Pojoy told Rodríguez that this was where Hernando de Soto had landed (Swanton 1934:336–337; Quinn 1976:137).

Two other pieces of evidence also place both de Soto and the Pojoy at Tampa Bay. First, "Pohoy" has a probable variant in "Capaloey," named (along with Uzita) by Ranjel (1922:57–58) as one of the chiefs living along the Tampa Bay coast. And in a report on the early Franciscan missionary efforts in La Florida that was published after 1617, Father Luis Gerónimo de Oré confirms that de Soto's Bahía del Espíritu Santo was the place the Indians called Pojoy (Oré 1936:6).

Early United States Corps of Engineers' surveys leave no doubt that Tampa Bay had a large, deep, and clear channel. The initial survey states: "Schooners and steamers are employed in the navigation of Tampa Bay, the former drawing from 5 to 7 feet, and the latter from 7 to 12 feet of water. These vessels find no difficulty at the lowest stage of the tide in the navigation between the entrance to Tampa Bay at Egmont Key and buoy No. 9, which is located about 7,300 yards nearly due south of the pier at Tampa" (Meigs 1880b:871).

A detailed map of Tampa Bay published somewhat later than 1880 shows that the Tampa Bay Southwest Channel, which passes southwest of Egmont Key, had a minimum depth of 25.5 feet (the map accompanies Benyaurd 1897). Two nineteenth-century guides for pilots both support Tampa Bay as the landing site and indicate that Charlotte Harbor was not suitable for larger ships. Both of these accounts predate the dredging of the harbors by the Corps of Engineers. In *The American Coast Pilot* (Blunt 1822:279) Tampa Bay is described as follows:

> *The entrance of Tampa Bay is obstructed by various sand shoals, upon which are raised some islands. Between these shoals there are three channels to enter, called the West, South West, and South East; the first two have plenty of water on their bars; on the first [at low water] there are 23 feet, and in the second 18 feet. The channels are frank, and to take them there is not necessity of advise, as, at high water, the shoals shew [sic] themselves, and at low water are dry.*

Charlotte Harbor is described as being less navigable, at least for ships drawing more than eight feet of water:

> *Carlos Bay is a large entrance made in the coast in which are emptied various rivers, whose mouths are covered by many keys and shoals, which leave between them channels more or less wide: the northernmost is called Friar Gaspar, and has 6 feet of water; the next, called Boca Grande, is the deepest, having 14 feet of water. This bay is only good for vessels of 8 feet draught, by the little shelter which it affords in gales in winter; and although the holding ground is good, you are obliged to look for the bends of the bay to shelter you from the wind which blows. The tide rises 2 feet, and when the wind is off shore it runs with great velocity.* (Blunt 1822:280)

The second set of sailing instructions comes from *The West Indian Pilot* (Barnett 1861:466). Tampa Bay is again described as very navigable:

> *The outer part of the estuary [Tampa Bay] is greatly obstructed by a Middle-ground of hard sand, with depth from 8–12 feet, which stretches two-thirds of the way across from the western shore. Vessels of 18 feet draught, however, can pass round the east and north sides, and thence down a lane of deep water on the west side of it, to secure anchorage in 4 to 5 fathoms within only a short distance of Piney Point.*

In contrast, the guide notes that, "Charlotte Harbor, on San Carlos Bay, [is] an extensive bight, with only 8 to 12 feet of water" (Barnett 1861:468).

Further evidence that favors Tampa Bay over Charlotte Harbor is that both the geography and location of Indian polities encountered by de Soto in his march to the north fits Tampa Bay as a starting point far better than does Charlotte Harbor. This evidence is discussed later in this chapter.

THE LANDING AND THE CAMP

Deciding on Tampa Bay as the bay in which de Soto anchored his fleet is only a part of the problem. The next task is to locate the areas in which de Soto and his men first landed and where they established their camp. Two interpretations have been proposed. One is that de Soto landed on the western side of Tampa Bay, and the second is that he landed on the eastern side of the bay. Mark F. Boyd made the most forceful argument for a landing on the western side, arguing that they landed on Pinellas Peninsula at Cross Bayou or even south of Coffeepot Bayou, and that their camp was at Philippi Point (Boyd 1938b:214–215). Swanton (1938, 1939:135–137, 1952) has made the most forceful argument for a landing on the eastern side of the bay, arguing that de Soto put his horses and men ashore at Shaw Point and that the camp was established on Terra Ceia Island.

In choosing between these two interpretations, or indeed deciding on a third, let us proceed by first examining the course of events in which the landing and establishment of the camp occurred, and beyond this, we must pay attention to some of the events that occurred when de Soto began to march inland. We can then place this sequence of events against the geography and archaeology of Tampa Bay and attempt to find a fit that has the smallest number of inconsistencies.

Immediately after arriving in Cuba, de Soto sent Juan de Añasco with fifty men in small ships to reconnoiter the coast of Florida. Añasco reported having found a suitable landing place at seventy-five to eighty leagues from Cuba. This distance is consistent with Chaves, who says that it was sixty-four or sixty-six leagues from Havana to the Bahía de Juan Ponce (Charlotte Harbor). That is, Tampa Bay was farther north. Along with this information, Añasco also brought back to Cuba four Indians whom he captured to serve as interpreters and as guides (Gaytan, Añasco, and Biedma 1866).

De Soto departed from Havana on Sunday, May 18, 1539. His fleet consisted of nine vessels: five ships, two caravels, and two brigantines (Ranjel 1922:51). Ranjel says that they sailed from the Tortugas due north. A channel ten leagues wide between the Tortugas and the Martires is described in Chaves's *Espejo* (Castañeda, Cuesta, and Hernández 1983:368), and it is reasonable to assume that de Soto sailed through this channel. De Soto's pilots knew that the mouth of Tampa Bay was almost due north from the easternmost of the Tortugas. Ranjel also says that the bay where they landed was ten leagues west of the Bay of Juan Ponce. Using a longitudinal measurement, the mouth of Tampa Bay is approximately nine nautical leagues to the west of the mouth of Charlotte Harbor.

They made landfall seven days later. They evidently drifted very slightly east of due north because they cast anchor some four or five leagues (14.4 to 18 miles) south of the mouth of Tampa Bay (de Soto 1866:284), and one or two leagues from land (3.6 to 7.2 miles), in four fathoms or less of water (Elvas 1922:21; Ranjel 1922:51). This location places them off the coast of Longboat Key. Modern navigation charts show that at a point 16 miles southeast of the north end of Anna Maria Island (marking the south side of the entrance to Tampa Bay) and 5.4 miles west of the mainland (modern Sarasota), the water depth is approximately four fathoms deep today (the tidal range is about 2.3 ft). This location is about 2 miles off the southern part of Longboat Key. Similar water depth, six fathoms, is also found northward off Anna Maria Island.

After they cast anchor, presumably on the afternoon of May 25, they could not see an entrance to the bay from their location off the coast of Longboat Key. Hence, de Soto, Juan de Añasco, and Alonso Martín, the chief pilot, sailed in one of two brigantines that went in search of the entrance. De Soto and the others failed to find the channel into the harbor, and when it began to grow dark, they turned around and attempted to sail back to the fleet. But the wind was contrary, so they had to cast anchor and went on shore, where they found an Indian village that they were later told was one of the villages of Uzita (de Soto 1866:284; Ranjel 1922:51–52).

De Soto may have sailed his brigantine through Longboat Pass and into northern Sarasota Bay. The Indian village he mentions could have been at one of the several archaeological sites located on the mainland directly on Sarasota Bay. Several Safety Harbor period sites are recorded for that locality (in Manatee County, e.g., Burger 1982:83, 189–190).

The next morning, de Soto tried to sail back to where his fleet was anchored, but again the wind was contrary. Baltasar de Gallegos shouted to the admiral's ship, now commanded by Vasco Porcallo, that he should go and give assistance to de Soto. But either Porcallo and his shipmates did not hear, or they chose not to go. Then Gallegos took a large caravel and sailed over to a point near de Soto's brigantine (Ranjel 1922:52–53).

In the meantime, the other brigantine found the entrance to the bay. Perhaps when de Soto sailed back through Longboat Pass the other brigantine sailed northward. It may even have done so by remaining within Sarasota Bay and sailing through Sarasota Pass.

Then de Soto's brigantine and the caravel sailed to join the brigantine that had found the entrance. De Soto anchored the brigantine on one side of the channel and the caravel on the other side, so that the other ships could pass between them. Then he evidently used the brigantine he was in as a pilot ship to guide his fleet through the passage and into the bay (Ranjel 1922:53).

The fleet probably entered Tampa Bay through Egmont Channel or the Southwest Channel, the latter being the more likely of the two. It is probable that the five large ships entered the bay one by one, with the brigantine leading them. De Soto (1866:284) says that it took them three days to find the entrance and get all of the ships inside the mouth of the bay. This implies that it was accomplished by May 28. From this point onward, an exact reconstruction of what happened is crucial for determining the location of where de Soto put his men and horses ashore and where they established their camp.

As the ships began moving up the channel of the bay, the Spaniards found it to be shallow, and as they moved they constantly sounded the lead. De Soto (1866:284) explicitly says that they had no knowledge of this channel. The ships sometimes scraped bottom, but because the channel was sandy no harm was done (Ranjel 1922:53).

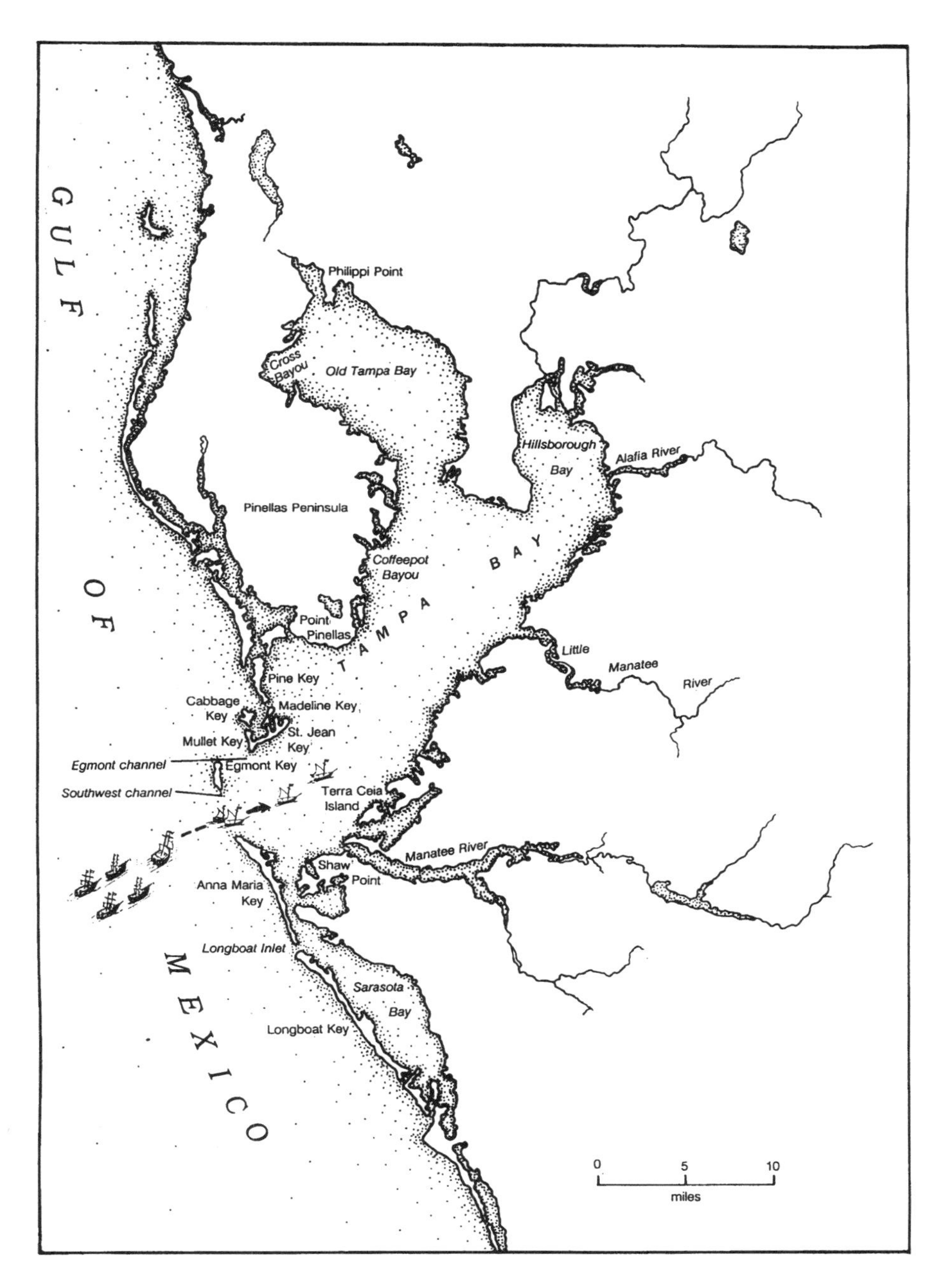

Figure 10

The route of de Soto's fleet into Tampa Bay.

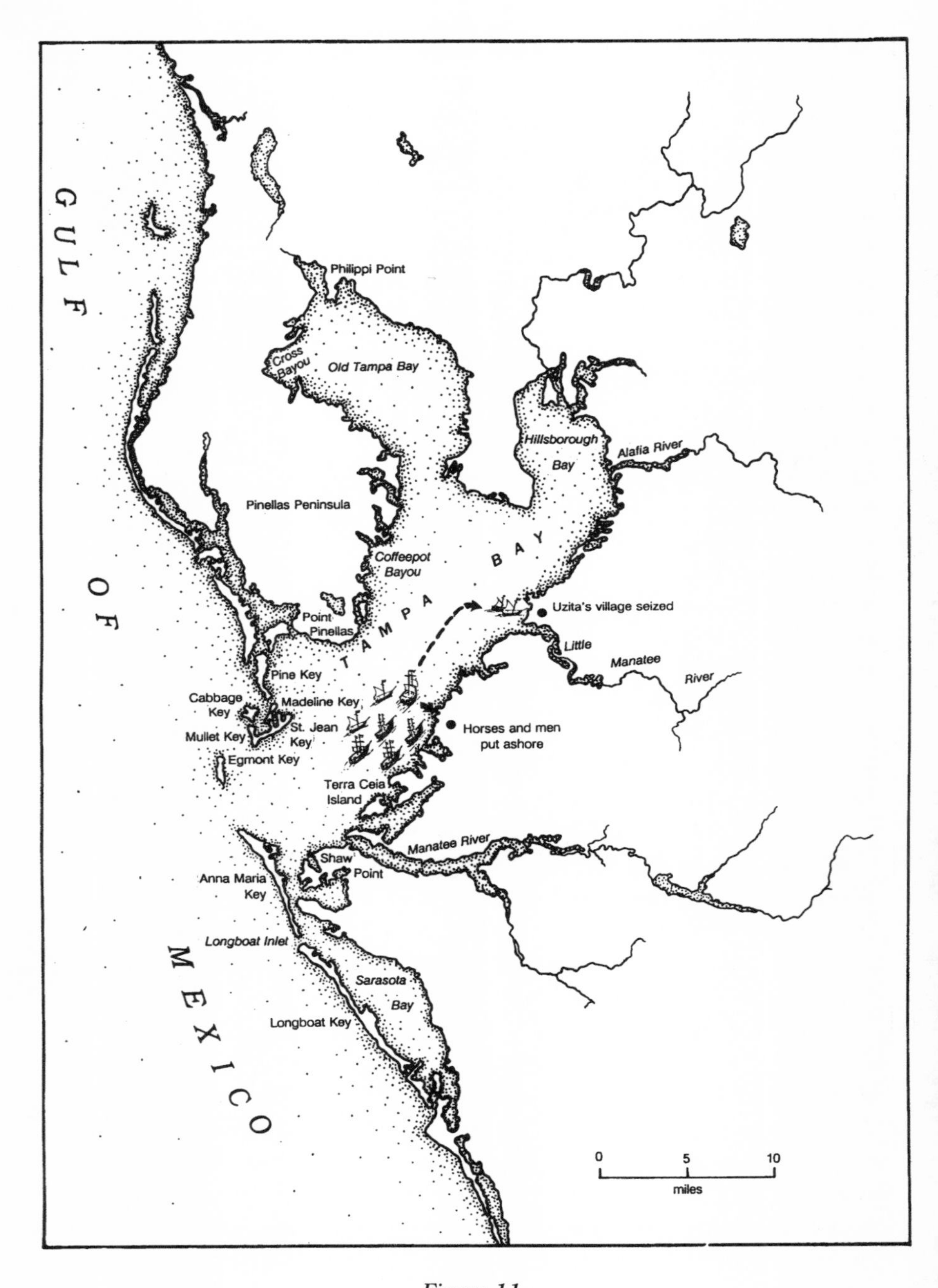

Figure 11

Unloading the horses and men and seizing the village of Uzita near the mouth of the Little Manatee River.

On May 30, two days after all the ships were inside the mouth of the bay, the horses and the men were unloaded in order to lighten the ships. According to Elvas, the place where the horses and men came ashore was two leagues (6.9 to 7.2 miles) from the Indian village where they would build their camp (1922:22). But according to Ranjel, the ships were anchored about four leagues from this village (1922:34). Up until this time, the only men who went ashore were those who went to get water and forage for the horses (Ranjel 1922:54). According to Ranjel, they started out with 243 horses, but 19 or 20 died en route, so that they put 223 or 224 ashore (Ranjel 1922:55). Elvas sets the number of horses at 213 (1922:22).

Because entering the bay and unloading took so much time, de Soto sent his lieutenant, Vasco Porcallo de Figueroa, ahead with some men in the brigantines to seize a town that lay "at the head of the bay." When they got there they found that the Indians had abandoned that town, as well as others, for a distance of thirty leagues, and had fled (de Soto 1866:284). After they occupied the village, Gómez Arias returned in one of the brigantines and reported to de Soto (Ranjel 1922:55).

On Sunday, June 1, the horses and men began marching toward the village. They used as guides the four Indians whom Juan de Añasco had captured, but these guides either lost their bearings, or the Spaniards could not understand them, or they deliberately misled the Spaniards, leading them into swamps.

De Soto went ahead of the army with some horsemen, but they tired out their horses when they chased after deer and foundered in swamps. They had to travel around many large creeks that ran into the bay, and they had to travel for twelve leagues before finding themselves beside an inlet with the village on the opposite side (Elvas 1922:23; Ranjel 1922:55). It was an inlet that was too large for them to easily go around (*el ancón del puerto en medio, de manera que no pudieron doblar el ancón* [Fernández de Oviedo 1851:546]). Because the men were exhausted, they slept scattered about in an undisciplined way (Ranjel 1922:55–56). The twelve leagues mentioned by Elvas is evidently an exaggeration of the distance they actually traveled. While the army was traveling by land to the village, the ships were gradually approaching it by water and were constantly being unloaded by boats that ferried clothing and provisions ashore (Ranjel 1922:55–56).

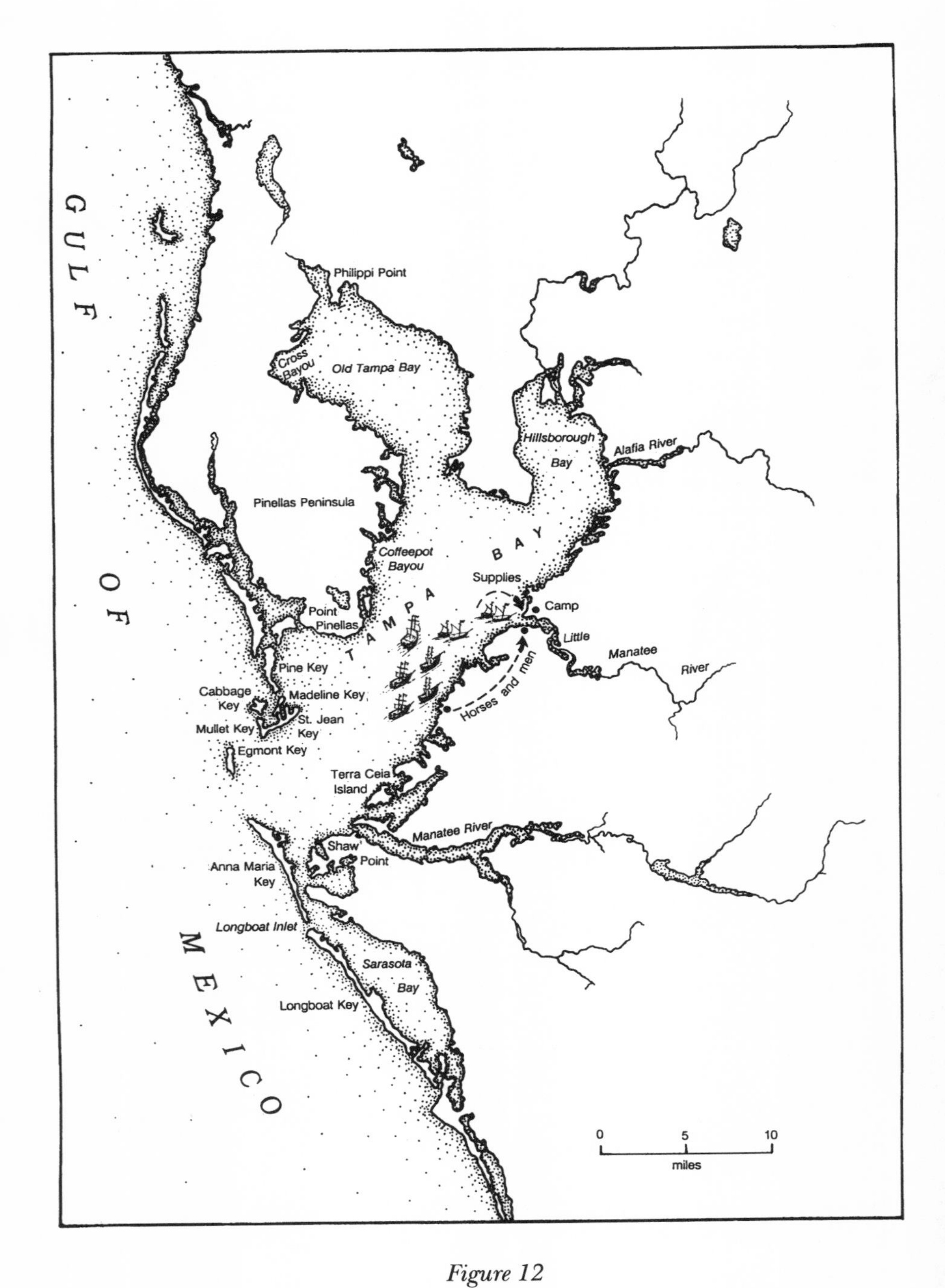

Figure 12

Unloading supplies and moving horses and the army to the camp established at Uzita's village.

Though none of the documents explicitly says so, on the day after reaching the inlet, Monday, June 2, the army must have been ferried to the other side, or they marched around the inlet and arrived at the village where their camp was to be. This village contained seven or eight houses, which were built of timber and covered with palmetto leaves. The chief's house stood near the beach, built on a very high artificially made mound. De Soto, Vasco Porcallo, and Luis de Moscoso were housed in the chief's dwelling. Across from the chief's house, on the opposite side of the town, stood a temple. Inside this temple the Spaniards found some pearls that had been drilled through for use as beads. Baltasar de Gallegos was lodged in a house in the center of the town, and some other houses were used for storing equipment and supplies. The remaining houses were torn down, and the soldiers, in groups of three or four, built small cabins in which they were quartered (Elvas 1922:23). The land around this village of Uzita was fenny, with dense thickets and high trees, and many places were marshy (Elvas 1922:23–24).

Before examining certain crucial events that occurred after de Soto marched his army northward, let us briefly review some of the requirements that the landing place and campsite must meet.

1. It took the ships at least two days to go from the mouth of the bay to where the horses and men were unloaded. Hence, the site must be at some distance from the mouth of the bay. Also, it had to be relatively free of mangrove so that the men and horses could get ashore.

2. The place where the horses and men were put ashore was, by water, two leagues distant from the camp site. That is, it was 6.9 miles (using the *legua común*) to 7.3 miles (the nautical league) distant from it.

3. But by land this landing place was two days' travel from the camp. One day of travel was required for them to reach the inlet which lay alongside the camp site. The second day was required for them to cross over the inlet or to march around it. In this distance there were many marshes and creeks which ran into the bay.

4. The village where they built their camp appears to have not been very large—seven to eight houses—though each of the houses may have been large. But it had a large artificial

mound that stood near the beach, and on the opposite side of the town stood a temple. Though the sources do not say so, this temple could also have stood on a mound.

Just as events leading up to the debarkation and establishment of the camp help narrow the possibilities of where de Soto and his men could be located, so do some of the events that occurred after the camp was established. On Wednesday, June 4, de Soto sent out Baltasar de Gallegos with forty cavalry and eighty infantry to look for Indians and towns. When the scouts did so, they encountered a group of Indians. Among them was Juan Ortiz, who had been captured by the Indians in the aftermath of the Narváez expedition and had been held captive for eleven years (Ranjel 1922:56–57). With Ortiz, de Soto gained the services of someone who could translate from an Indian language into Spanish. But it turned out that Ortiz's actual knowledge of the area was limited. Beyond twenty leagues, he knew nothing from actual experience or even from hearsay (Biedma 1922:4).

At first Ortiz had been held captive by the chief of Uzita, but when Ortiz learned that this chief was about to have him killed, he escaped into the territory of an Indian chief, Mocoso, a two-day journey from where he had been held captive (Elvas 1922:29–31). According to Garcilaso, the chief of Uzita was named Hirrihigua (Varner and Varner 1951:60), but this may be an error because Ranjel mentions a chief "Orriygua" who was a neighbor of Uzita (Ranjel 1922:57–58). By traveling all night, Ortiz reached the River of Mocoso. The languages of Uzita and Mocoso were apparently mutually unintelligible. The first of Mocoso's villagers encountered by Ortiz could not understand him. Later, an Indian who did speak the Uzita language translated for them.

On Saturday, June 7, de Soto went with Ortiz to Mocoso's village to meet with the chief. When he did, Mocoso complained that four nearby chiefs—"Orriygua, Neguarete, Capaloey, and Ecita"—were angry at him because he was friendly with the Spaniards and had given Ortiz to them to serve as an interpreter (Ranjel 1922:57–58).

Unfortunately, Ranjel gives no itinerary for this journey to Chief Mocoso's territory. Later, when de Soto marched his army inland from the camp, it took one day to reach the River of Mocoso, and they had to build bridges to cross it (Ranjel

1922:63). Elvas says that Mocoso came to visit de Soto, though this visit may have occurred after de Soto visited him (1922:33).

On the same day, Captain Juan Ruiz Lobillo went out with about forty or fifty infantry, and they captured several Indian women (Ranjel says two; Elvas says four). He went out in a different direction than that taken by Gallegos, marching over swampy ground, where horses could not travel (Elvas 1922:25). Ruiz found some Indian houses only a half league from the camp, near a river. But nine Indians followed them, attacking, and they killed one Spaniard and wounded three to five others. This means that at least one of de Soto's men was buried at or near the camp (Ranjel 1922:58).

At some point, de Soto ordered General Vasco Porcallo de Figueroa to go to Uzita because he had heard that Indians had assembled there. Presumably, Porcallo went by boat and sailed toward the mouth of the bay, where de Soto had encountered a town that belonged to Uzita. But when they arrived, the village had been abandoned.

On another occasion, de Soto sent Juan de Añasco with some infantry in the ship's boats along the shore to disperse some Indians who had gathered on an island. Añasco killed nine or ten Indians with small cannons, but as many of his own men were killed or wounded by the Indians.

Añasco sent some of his men back to camp (hence, he had more than one boat) for horsemen as reinforcements to prevent the Indians from escaping to the mainland. De Soto sent Vasco Porcallo with forty cavalry and some infantry, but when they got to where Añasco was the Indians had already fled. When they failed to find Indians on the island, the Spaniards spread out and conducted raids, capturing some women (Ranjel 1922:60–61). This particular action would seem to have occurred in a relatively short time, perhaps a single day. This means that an island had to have been located quite near the camp, and it could not have been located on the opposite side of the inlet.

On June 20, de Soto sent Baltasar de Gallegos with 80 cavalry and 100 infantry to Urriparacoxi, who lived inland (Ranjel 1922:60; Elvas [1922:34] says 50 cavalry and 30 to 40 infantry). The Spaniards had decided that the land near camp was barren and not a good place for settlement. (Cabeza de Vaca had made a similar observation about Tampa Bay.) This probably means that the Indians in this area did not cultivate corn.

On July 15, de Soto took most of his army and started out from the camp heading toward Urriparacoxi. On the sixth day of travel they reached the territory of Urriparacoxi and rendezvoused with Baltasar de Gallegos (Ranjel 1922:64–65). Biedma (1922:5) says that they went west from their camp and then northwest. (We will later argue that the first of these directions has to be an error.) When they departed from the rendezvous in Urriparacoxi's territory it took them four days to reach the River of Ocale, which was broad and had a swift current. If Tampa Bay is where de Soto landed, then no matter on which side of the bay they landed, the River of Ocale had to have been the Withlacoochee River.

According to Biedma, Urriparacoxi lived about twenty leagues from the coast (1922:5). But Elvas says that, according to Juan Ortiz, Urriparacoxi lived thirty leagues away, that his land was more fertile than that near the camp, and that Urriparacoxi was said to have had plenty of corn (1922:32–33).

Let us again extract from these events key elements that will help pinpoint the location of the landing place and camp.

5. Juan Ortiz was first made captive by the chief of Uzita, who, as already seen, commanded territory near the mouth of the bay. This means that Mocoso held territory toward the head of the bay. The two territories were separated by a river.

6. Both from the time it took Ortiz to escape from Uzita to Mocoso and the time it took de Soto's army to reach this river, it was one day's travel away. De Soto and his men had to build a bridge to get across this river.

7. From their camp all the way to the Withlacoochee River, the River of Mocoso was the *only* stream they crossed that required them to build a bridge. In fact, for some reason they built *two* bridges.

8. Biedma says that they first went west (though it must, as already indicated, have been east), and then they went toward the northwest.

Let us now fit this information to a map, trying first a landing on the west coast of Tampa Bay. De Soto could have put his men and horses ashore south of Coffeepot Bayou, as Boyd suggested (1938b:214). A day of circuitous travel, allowing a little less than five leagues, would have put them in the vicinity of present-day

High Point, on the shore of an inlet of Old Tampa Bay. Since the camp clearly occupied a village with a mound that could be seen from where they encamped, we have to ask where the nearest mound site was. It was on Philippi Point, about four miles away, straight-line distance. From here de Soto and his men could have seen smoke from fires in the camp and they could have seen brigantines anchored offshore.

Boyd argued that de Soto and his entourage encamped on Cooper's Point at the end of the first day of travel. This is dubious because it would have required them to travel about six leagues through swampy, difficult terrain. But, if they had been able to do so, the camp could have been, as Boyd thought, located at the mound site at Philippi Point, a distance of about two miles from where they would have encamped after their first day of travel. Thus far everything fits, but beyond this there are serious discrepancies. First, the distance to the camp from the place where the men and horses were put ashore would have been 5.5 nautical leagues, and not 2 leagues, as Elvas said it was.

Another discrepancy is that on departing from the camp to go to Urriparacoxi from Philippi Point, the group would have had to travel six leagues over difficult terrain in order to reach a river large enough to require a bridge—the Hillsborough River. It would have been difficult to travel this distance in a day, though not impossible.

A third problem is that, had the men encamped at Philippi Point, they could have traveled to Urriparacoxi without crossing Hillsborough River. That is, they could have gone northeast to about the present town of Drexel and then continued on to the present towns of Dade City and Lacoochee, which were probably west of the territory of Urriparacoxi. De Soto had Ortiz as a guide, and it is unlikely that Ortiz would have taken a trail requiring a river crossing if he could have avoided it.

Another problem is that if the Spaniards had established their camp in this area, surely they would have heard of Tocobaga, the people who lived around Philippi Point when Pedro Menéndez de Avilés visited the area in 1567.

Finally, when de Soto spent his first night on land, it was at a village under the control of the chief of Uzita. This village was almost certainly south of the mouth of the bay, and it is extremely unlikely that the chief of Uzita would have controlled both sides of Tampa Bay.

We must conclude, therefore, that this landing on the west coast of Tampa Bay presents serious evidentiary problems. Let us now see how a landing on the east coast fits the lay of the land.

According to Swanton's scenario, de Soto put his men and horses ashore at Shaw's Point, west of Bradenton, at the mouth of the Manatee River. The day's march was spent going around the mouth of the Manatee River and coming to Terra Ceia Bay. The camp was at the Terra Ceia Mound site. The next day they could have quickly gone around Terra Ceia Bay to join the men in the camp. This scenario fits the landing in several respects. Shaw's Point is about two nautical leagues from the Terra Ceia site. Also, Terra Ceia Bay would have been an *ancón* like the one described in the documents.

But in almost every other respect Swanton's scenario fails to fit the information in the documents. For one thing, this landing place would require us to throw out Ranjel's statement that the ships were anchored four leagues away from the camp when they put the men and horses ashore. Four nautical leagues from Terra Ceia would have placed the ships barely inside the barrier keys. And, even if we lessen Ranjel's distance somewhat, surely they could have gone further than Shaw's Point in two or more days of easing their way up the channel.

Another difficulty with Swanton's scenario is that if the men had gone around the mouth of the Manatee River, they would have had to travel almost ten leagues in one day. This might have been possible for the cavalry, but would have been well nigh impossible for the foot soldiers.

A final difficulty, as Swanton himself recognized, is that if de Soto's camp had been at Terra Ceia he would have had to cross not one river but two—the Little Manatee and the Alafia (1938:173). In fact, Swanton, not realizing that the men could bypass the Hillsborough River, said that they would have had to cross three rivers.

We can construct a scenario for the east side of the bay, however, that fits all of the information better than does Swanton's. Namely, after entering the bay de Soto moved his ships along a natural channel that lies near the eastern shore. He anchored his ships somewhat southwest of Piney Point, which at that time was a mangrove-free beach that lay close to the channel. At about 0.5 miles offshore from Piney Point the water is nine ft deep, but it shallows rapidly as one moves toward the shore. This is one of the few places on the eastern side of the bay where deep water came this close to shore (prior to modern dredging), and it must be where de Soto put his men and horses ashore. The location is also consistent with Ranjel's placing the anchorage at about four leagues from the base camp.

When the men and horses set out from Piney Point to go to the camp, the inlet that finally stopped them was the mouth of the Little Manatee River, because the camp was on the northern side of this inlet. The mouth of the Little Manatee River is another location on the eastern side of the bay that lies close to the channel. The channel is about 1.5 miles from the mouth of the river, but for the entire distance there is a lesser channel with a minimum depth of eight to nine ft, and this is substantially deeper than areas on either side of the mouth of the Little Manatee River. This lesser channel coming out from the mouth of the Little Manatee River is the avenue that was used by the smaller boats in unloading de Soto's ships. Allowing for circuitous travel, from Piney Point to the Little Manatee River would have been an overland distance of about four leagues, a distance the foot soldiers could have traveled in a day. They lay down to sleep, then, on the shore opposite the camp. The next day some or all of the infantry could have been ferried across in the boats and brigantines. The cavalry would have had to go around the mouth of the river—a distance of 4.5 to 5 leagues—an easy day's travel for cavalry.

By water, the straight-line distance from Piney Point to the mouth of the Little Manatee River is about two nautical leagues. Moreover, when de Soto departed from camp on his way to Urriparacoxi, he would have encountered the Alafia River after about five leagues of travel. Hence, the Alafia was the River of Mocoso, where the Spaniards had to build bridges to get to the other side. From this crossing they headed northeasterly, eventually circling around the headwaters of the Hillsborough River.

ARCHAEOLOGICAL EVIDENCE

The location of the base camp on the north side of the mouth of the Little Manatee River on Tampa Bay is consistent with available archaeological evidence, both in terms of the overall distribution of archaeological cultures and in terms of the location of specific sites. However, although this evidence certainly strongly supports Tampa Bay as the Bahía Honda where de Soto landed, we still do not have archaeological evidence from the Little Manatee River locale that positively confirms the presence of the Spaniards' campsite. Unfortunately, such evidence may never be forthcoming; the destruction of archaeological sites around Tampa Bay has been severe. The archaeological sites in the area where we postulate the camp was located have been mined for oyster shells since the late nineteenth century. The shells are the remains of millions of oysters eaten by the Tampa Bay Indians, including the Uzita and the other groups and their ancestors who resided there in the early sixteenth century and before. Other sites have been bulldozed as twentieth-century development has occurred. First, we will review archaeological evidence that supports the east side of Tampa Bay as the landing-camp area, then we will look specifically at the Little Manatee River locality.

Archaeological investigations in the Tampa Bay region began more than a century ago and have continued to the present (e.g., Stearns 1870, 1872; Walker 1880; Moore 1900, 1903; Fewkes 1924; Stirling 1930, 1931; Willey 1949; Griffin and Bullen 1950; Bullen 1951, 1952b; Luer and Almy 1981). As a result, more than 100 archaeological sites have been located, and the pre-Columbian archaeology of the bay is quite well understood.

At the time of both the Pánfilo de Narváez (1528) and de Soto expeditions, the Safety Harbor archaeological culture occupied the Tampa Bay region (Willey 1949:475–488; Bullen 1952a, 1955, 1978; Milanich and Fairbanks 1980:204–210; Luer and Almy 1981; Mitchem 1989b). Safety Harbor temple mounds, burial mounds, and midden sites are well documented for Manatee, Hillsborough, and Pinellas counties surrounding the bay. Inland Safety Harbor sites also extend northward at least to the mouth of the Withlacoochee River and southward to Charlotte Harbor.

Archaeological evidence of the Safety Harbor culture is consistent with the information gleaned from the de Soto narratives regarding the general pattern of settlement around the bay—small clusters of villages, each controlled by a chief. Clusters of Safety Harbor period sites are found near the mouth of the Little Manatee River. Similar clusters of sites can be found elsewhere around the eastern and southern edges of Tampa Bay at the mouths of the Manatee and Alafia rivers and at Cockroach Key and Bishop's Harbor. The natural resources of the bay and the estuaries at the mouths of rivers were the focus of aboriginal subsistence efforts, accounting for the clusters of sites. We might suppose that the various clusters around estuaries correspond to the political groups mentioned in the de Soto narratives. The Uzita probably controlled the Little Manatee and Manatee rivers, the Mocoso the Alafia River, and so forth.

The archaeological evidence is also consistent with the description of the Indian village where de Soto placed his camp that is provided by the Gentleman of Elvas (1922:23):

> *The town was of seven or eight houses, built of timber, and covered with palm-leaves. The Chief's house stood near the beach, upon a very high mount made by hand for defense; at the other end of the town was a temple, on the top of which perched a wooden fowl with gilded eyes.... The Governor [de Soto] lodged in the house of the Chief. . . . The rest of the dwellings, with the temple, were thrown down, and every mess of three to four soldiers made a cabin, wherein they lodged.*

From the data available from other Safety Harbor sites, we would expect that the "high mount" on which the chief's house was placed was a temple mound. Such mounds are present at many Safety Harbor sites around Tampa Bay (Milanich and Fairbanks 1980:205–206; Luer and Almy 1981). The "temple" mentioned by Elvas was probably a charnel house placed on a low mound. Indians of the Safety Harbor culture placed the bodies of the dead within these charnel houses. After the bodies had been defleshed, they were bound up in bundles and stored in the "temples." Periodically, the charnel houses were torn down and the bundled bones were placed on the mound and covered over with a layer of sand. Then a new charnel house was erected on the summit of this burial mound. (When Juan Ortiz had been a prisoner of Uzita, one of his tasks had been to guard the corpses in a charnel house.)

Along with temple mounds and burial mounds, Safety Harbor period sites around Tampa Bay also have middens composed of garbage, mainly shells, discarded by the villagers who had lived at the site. These middens mark the locations of the houses described by the Gentleman of Elvas. Thus, both the settlement pattern of Safety Harbor period sites around Tampa Bay and the pattern of individual village sites are consistent with the information in the de Soto narratives.

Are there de Soto–period Spanish artifacts at any of the sites around Tampa Bay? Three archaeological sites with early sixteenth-century Spanish artifacts are known from the inland area on the east side of Tampa Bay between the Manatee River and the Little Manatee River drainages. A fourth site in that locality also contained European artifacts, but their ages are uncertain. That site, Parrish Mound #2 located six miles inland from Tampa Bay and one-half mile south of the Little Manatee River, was excavated in the 1930s. Archaeologists uncovered a low platform mound on which a charnel house had been built. The platform mound covered a large crematory pit dug by the aborigines into the old ground surface. Other cremations were placed in the fill of the mound and a number were contained within the structure. The charnel structure was destroyed by fire, and the remains, along with the mound, were covered with earth to form a larger mound. Found in the mound were three glass seed beads, a brass pendant (which appears to be hardware of some type), and a bone or tortoiseshell comb (Willey 1949:146–152, plate 59).

The other three sites all contained artifacts diagnostic of the early sixteenth century and the de Soto expedition. The first, Parrish Mound #1, was located in Manatee County about sixteen miles east-northeast of the settlement of Parrish on the South Fork of the Little Manatee River. The burial mound contained green glazed ceramics (Spanish olive jar fragments?); several hundred blue, white, and yellow glass seed beads; several hundred other small glass beads; several large glass beads; one pentagonal green glass bead; a glass pendant; three tubular rolled silver beads; one rolled gold cone; one copper ear ornament; and two fragments of a bone or tortoise-shell comb (which may be of aboriginal manufacture) (Willey 1949:142–146, plate 58). One bead from the site—a red, olive-shaped variety with spiral white stripes—is similar to examples recovered from the Tatham Mound in Citrus County, a de Soto–era site discussed in the next chapter (Mitchem and Leader 1988:47) There is also a faceted Nueva Cadiz Plain bead from the site, again a very good marker for the de Soto expedition (Mitchem and Hutchinson 1987).

Parrish Mound #3, another burial mound excavated in the 1930s like the other Parrish mounds, was located about two miles east of Parrish on Gambel Creek, which empties into the Little Manatee River. The mound contained 211 bundled burials (probably from a charnel house) and a small amount of European artifacts (Willey 1949:152–156). The latter included glass

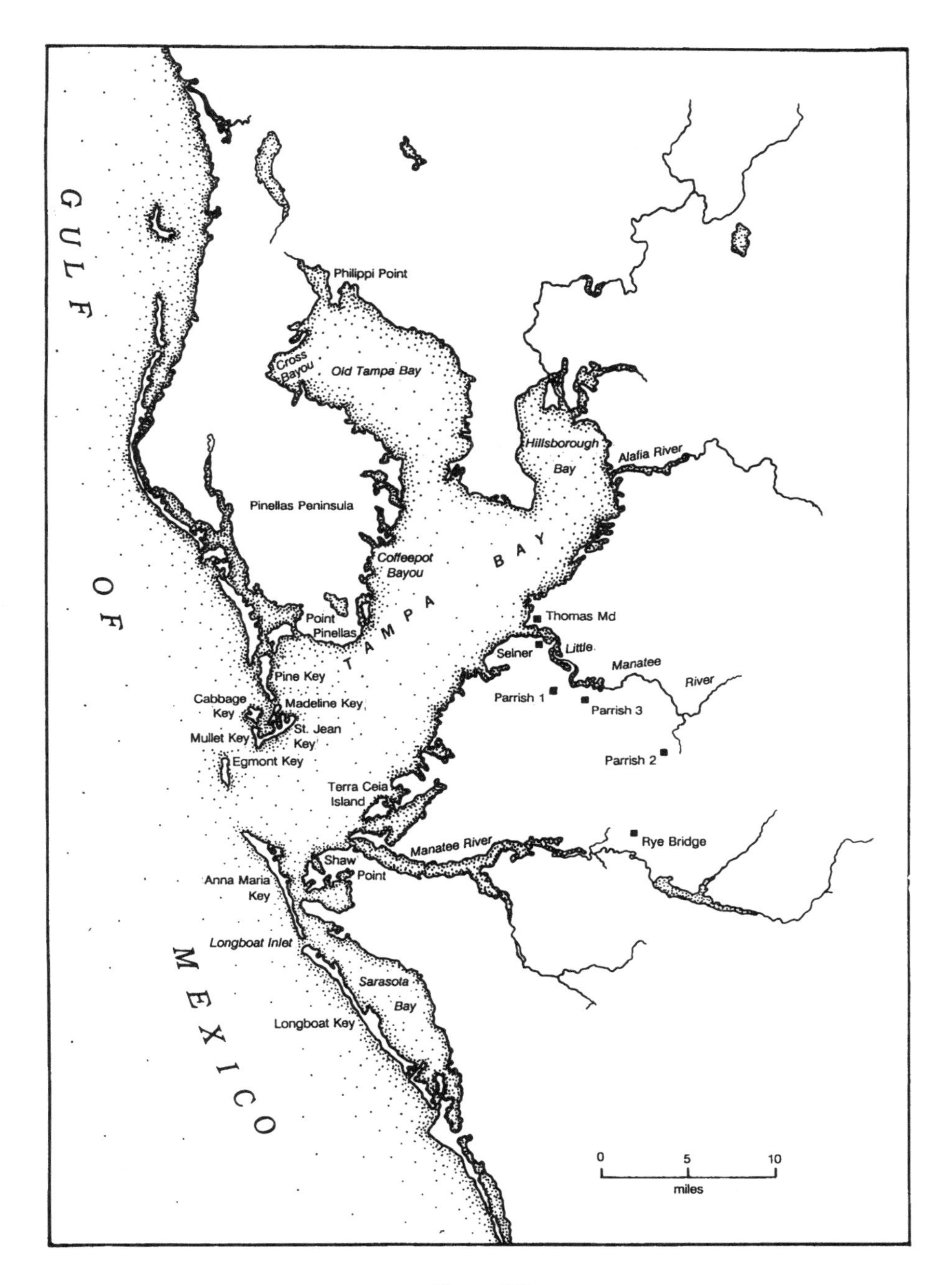

Figure 13

Archaeological sites mentioned in the text in the Little Manatee and Manatee river drainages just east of Tampa Bay.

beads, two iron chisels, a knife or sword blade, iron fragments, and what might be a rolled iron bead (Mitchem 1989b:157–158). The geographical locations of the three Parrish Mounds suggest that all three were under the political control of Uzita.

The third site with diagnostic Spanish artifacts is the Rye Bridge Mound (8MA715), located about thirteen miles east of the town of Palmetto on a small creek that empties into the Manatee River. Mitchem (1989b:194–196) studied a portion of the glass and silver beads from the mound. Included in the collection were four Nueva Cadiz Plain beads—good de Soto–period markers. The site possibly was a village controlled by Uzita.

Several other sites containing Spanish artifacts are also known for the east side of Tampa Bay. They are from sites north of the Little Manatee River and are discussed in the next chapter.

How does the archaeological evidence from the mouth of the Little Manatee River fit with the information provided in the de Soto narratives? Seven archaeological sites have previously been recorded for the locale from the mouth of the river extending inland to the town of Ruskin (8HI1, 23, 27, 29, 30, 93, 94), a distance of about three miles. It is likely that these sites represent only the remnants of shell middens and mounds that once blanketed both banks of the river. Many of the shell middens were mined for material to pave roads beginning about the turn of the century.

At the end of the nineteenth century, before extensive destruction had taken place, a Philadelphia archaeologist, Clarence B. Moore, undertook excavations at one of the largest of the sites, the complex known as the Thomas Mound (8HI1; Moore 1900:358–359). It was located on the north side of the river near where the de Soto campsite must have been situated. Later, under the auspices of the Works Progress Administration (WPA) and the Florida State Board of Conservation (Simpson 1937, 1939; Willey 1949:31, 103–105, 113–135; Bullen 1952b:1–2, 7–20), excavations were carried out at the Thomas Mound and at shell middens on the opposite side of the Little Manatee River. Since that time the Thomas Mound has been destroyed.

A sketch map of the Thomas site made in the 1930s combined with Moore's descriptions indicate that the site consisted of a large burial mound (six ft high and sixty ft in diameter) and several other mounds, as well as an extensive village midden. The site layout and mounds fits the Gentleman of Elvas's descriptions

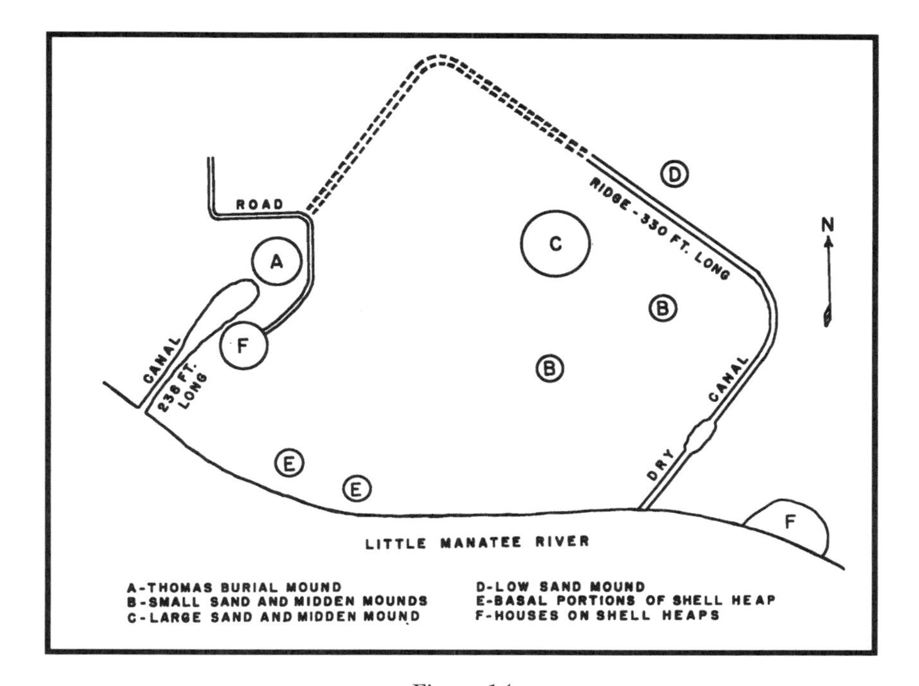

Figure 14

Ripley Bullen's sketch map of the Thomas site, showing what could be parts of three sides of an earthwork (Bullen 1952b:8). The missing northwest corner has been added here.

of a high mound, temple, and village.

What appears to be a linear ridge 330 ft long borders the northeast side of the site, but it is undescribed on the map. The ridge borders one leg of a dry canal that ran from the Little Manatee River northeast and then turned 90 degrees northwest; it was this latter leg of the canal that was bordered by the ridge. A portion of a second canal was also present, running from the Little Manatee River northeast to the large burial mound. It was west of and parallel to the first leg of the dry canal. Together these earthworks form parts of three sides of a square ca. 500 ft on a side, with the river as the fourth side. The western canal apparently intersected the borrow pit used by the site's occupants to excavate the soil for the burial mound. According to information collected by

Moore, high tides entered the canal in the 1870s when the first settlers entered the area.

Bullen (1952a:9), who examined the evidence, agreed with Moore that this western canal was "aboriginal" in origin, but he states, "Examination of the site in 1952 strongly suggested both canals [the two forming an L] were drainage ditches dug by early settlers for farming purposes." We can only wish that the site were still extant so the earthworks could be excavated and thus determine whether they were first constructed by de Soto's army as a part of a fortification around the camp, where a part of the army would live for at least four months.

The de Soto narratives are unclear as to whether the Spaniards fortified the village of Uzita where they established their camp. Several clues suggesting they did, however, are found in the account of Garcilaso de la Vega (Varner and Varner 1951:224, 233). When Juan de Añasco and other cavalrymen, returning to the landing camp from the winter camp at Apalachee, approached the town "a mounted patrol came out two by two with their lances and bucklers to watch over and guard the camp in the night." This vaguely suggests that some sort of enclosure was present through which the patrol rode. On their return journey northward to Apalachee the Spanish encountered Chief Mocoso, who referred to their camp as a "fortress." Although Mocoso's speech was undoubtedly recalled from the memory of a Spaniard many years after the fact, that Spaniard seems to have thought of the camp as being fortified.

Moore's report (1900:359) mentions "a number of blue glass beads and two bits of looking glass" from the burial mound at the Thomas site. This may be significant because looking glasses are among the objects that de Soto traded and bartered to the Indians (Ranjel 1922:113). The later WPA and Florida Board of Conservation excavations produced "about 200 more glass beads, a triangular piece of sheet copper, measuring three inches on each side, a tubular silver bead, a brass pendant or tablet, and a larger silver pendant" (Bullen 1952a:17). The tablet displays a spider effigy. Such spider effigy tablets are well known from a variety of south Florida mound sites of the early historic period (Allerton, Luer, and Carr 1984), but they probably postdate de Soto. Moore recovered 112 burials from the mound, most of which were bundle burials (1900:358–359). Probably, the mound served as the base for one or more Safety Harbor period charnel houses while it was in use.

Additional European artifacts were excavated from the Selner shell mounds that extend "about a half mile along the south bank of the Little Manatee River, opposite the Thomas mound" (Bullen 1952a:71). European artifacts reported by Bullen (1952a:72–73) included a "copper penny, a copper punch, modern iron and brass, lead weights, a long glass bead, and bones of a pig and of a horse or of a cow." Although Bullen considers the materials to be of recent origin, the long glass bead may be a Nueva Cadiz Plain bead, a type known to date from the de Soto era (Smith and Good 1982:27–28). The Selner shell middens are located approximately where de Soto's men camped at the end of their day's march after being put ashore at Piney Point.

As a part of the Florida de Soto project, an archaeological survey of the Little Manatee River locality was carried out in 1987–1988 by William Burger, aided by Arthur M. Miller, Melanie Hubbard, and students from New College, University of South Florida. The goal of their research was to determine what was left of the sites previously known to have existed and to look for new, unrecorded sites. If it was feasible, sites would be tested to recover evidence of the de Soto camp.

There is no doubt that such evidence—Spanish artifacts—would have been left at the camp. De Soto's entire army stayed there for six weeks after landing, and a hundred men continued to live there until about November 1 of that same year, when they marched northward to join de Soto and the rest of the expedition in Apalachee.

The archaeological search was not successful. The destruction of sites along the Little Manatee River has been too severe. Burger and his team located only remnants of the village middens adjacent to the Thomas site (at two locations on Goat Island and at Cedar Grove); the burial mound itself had long since been totally destroyed, although its former location was ascertained from maps. Several sand mounds that Moore observed at the site are also gone.

Approximately one mile to the west, closer to Tampa Bay, is another large site, Shell Point (8HI27). Burger visited this site and, using archival information and interviews with local residents, he ascertained that in the past the site consisted of two large shell mounds.

On the south side of the Little Manatee River, opposite the Thomas site complex and Goat Island, Burger also relocated the Selner site (and the adjacent Ruskin shell mound, 8HI94). The two probably formed one long linear shell midden, about seventy ft wide and a half mile long. A great deal of the midden still remains. Several test excavations were placed in the midden, but they failed to produce any Spanish materials.

Absolute archaeological proof that the de Soto expedition camp was located on the north side of the Little Manatee River, most likely at the Thomas site or in the immediate vicinity, is not available. However, the archaeological information that we *do* have from past excavations in the Thomas Mound certainly supports that locality as the site where the camp was located. And interpretation of the geographical data from the de Soto narratives indicates that the Little Manatee location is the only location that satisfies all of the locational requirements.

CHAPTER IV

NORTH TO OCALE

Hernando de Soto had not been long in Florida before he began to make plans to move his army into the interior to fulfill his royal mandate to conquer the land. It was also probably necessary to move inland to find sufficient cultivated food to feed his army. The soil near their camp at the mouth of the Little Manatee River was barren (*esteril*), and the local aboriginal peoples evidently lived primarily by hunting and fishing. There is no evidence that the Indians who lived in the vicinity of their camp cultivated corn. Juan Ortiz, who had been held prisoner by Indians around Tampa Bay for eleven years, told de Soto about a chief named Urriparacoxi, who lived some twenty to thirty leagues away and who had plenty of corn. Ortiz said that "Mocoso, Uzita, and all they that dwell along the coast paid tribute" to Urriparacoxi (Elvas 1922:32), the location of whose territory is discussed later in this chapter.

It appears that it was the barrenness of the land and the sparse population around Tampa Bay that led Vasco Porcallo de Figueroa to abandon the expedition and return to Cuba (Elvas 1922:34–35; Ranjel 1922:61–62). There may also have been a personality clash between Porcallo and de Soto. In particular, they quarreled after Porcallo returned from a foray in which he captured some Indian women to be slaves.

Soon after gaining intelligence about Urriparacoxi from Ortiz, de Soto sent an Indian messenger to the chief, but the man never returned (Ranjel 1922:60). Then, on June 20, de Soto sent Baltasar de Gallegos with 80 cavalry and 100 infantry to Urriparacoxi (de Soto 1866:285; Ranjel 1922:60).[1]

Gallegos reached the territory of Urriparacoxi, but he found that the people had abandoned their town and fled to the forests (Varner and Varner 1951:95). The chief dealt with Gallegos through intermediaries, claiming to be too ill to come to see him in person. When Gallegos asked these intermediaries whether gold or silver could be obtained in this country, they told him that toward the west was a province called Ocale where people waged war with a people who lived "where the greater portion of the year was summer," i.e., presumably, far to the south (Elvas 1922:35). These people, perhaps the Calusa, possessed so much gold that when they came on a raid against Ocale they were said to wear hats made of gold. Because Gallegos feared that if he let these messengers go they would not return, he seized them and put them in chains (Elvas 1922:36). According to de Soto, Gallegos seized about seventeen men, some of whom were old principal men, i.e., respected elders.

Gallegos sent eight cavalry to the camp at Tampa Bay to carry the news of his discovery to de Soto. Garcilaso says the distance to camp was twenty-five leagues and the horsemen covered it in two days, which would be an extraordinary pace unless they traveled straight through (Varner and Varner 1951:96). Gallegos sent word to de Soto that he had found large fields of corn, beans, and pumpkins at Urriparacoxi. Moreover, at a three-day journey from Urriparacoxi there was said to be a large town, Acuera, with plenty of corn, and two days further on there was said to be the town of Ocale, also very large (de Soto 1866:285).

Presumably on the basis of Gallegos's information, de Soto (1866) reported that the Indians of Ocale had many turkeys kept in pens as well as herds of tame deer. Further, there were said to be tradesmen among the people of Ocale and much gold, silver, and pearls. Even though de Soto threatened to kill his Indian informants if they lied to him, de Soto indicated in his letter that he did not know whether he could believe their information. This information is especially difficult to interpret because there is evidence that the Indians of Urriparacoxi were not the only ones who distorted or misrepresented the truth. According to Ranjel (1922:62), de Soto ordered Gallegos to send back to him two letters from Urriparacoxi: one giving a good report of what he found and the other letter telling the truth. De Soto told his men that the secret letter contained information that he would reveal to them later. In this way, de Soto gave them hope of great things to come, without promising them anything in particular. Biedma (1922:5) was persuaded that Ocale was such a wonderful place that the natives there could shout at birds on the wing and cause them to drop to the ground.

With this rumor of wealth, de Soto's men clamored to invade the land, and those who were ordered to remain behind at the base camp did so reluctantly. While still at his Tampa Bay camp, de Soto made plans to spend the winter at Ocale. This, in any case, is what he wrote in his letter (de Soto 1866:286).

THE LOCATION OF URRIPARACOXI

The de Soto narratives provide a number of clues to the location of Urriparacoxi. Juan Ortiz told de Soto that "Paracoxi" lived thirty leagues distant from the Tampa Bay camp (Elvas 1922:32). Biedma (1922:5) places the distance to "Hurriparacoxi" at about twenty leagues, while Garcilaso (Varner and Varner 1951:25) says it was twenty-five leagues. Garcilaso's account also suggests that Urriparacoxi was northeast from the Tampa Bay camp. De Soto's letter provides the additional information that Acuera was three days' travel beyond Urriparacoxi (ca. fifty-one miles) and that it took two days to journey from Acuera to Ocale (ca. thirty-four miles) (1866:285).

It seems certain that de Soto's army never actually reached Urriparacoxi's village, but instead rendezvoused with Gallegos and the soldiers who had accompanied him at the village of Luca. That rendezvous was at the end of the army's sixth day of travel after leaving Tampa Bay. Ranjel (1922:64–65) writes, ". . . they [the main army] came to Luca, a little village, and there Baltasar de Gallegos came to meet the governor. The Monday following, July 21, they were joined by the soldiers that Baltasar de Gallegos has, and the Governor [de Soto] sent a messenger to Urriparacoxi, but no reply was received." De Soto arrived at Luca on July 19, met Gallegos the next day, and remained at the village until July 23, waiting for the messenger to Urriparacoxi to return. This suggests that Urriparacoxi's village was some distance away from Luca; it was not on the route taken by de Soto and his army.

Using this information, we can surmise that Urriparacoxi's village was about twenty-five leagues (eighty-six miles) from the Tampa Bay camp (probably to the northeast), two days' rapid travel from Luca (roughly thirty-four miles). We will argue below that Luca is near Lacoochee, Florida, and three days' travel from Acuera (roughly fifty-one miles). Our arguments for placing Acuera in the Lake Weir–Lake Griffin vicinity also are presented below). Plotting these data provides a location for Urriparacoxi in southeastern Lake and southwestern Orange counties, the locality around Lake Louisa, Lake Butler, Lake Tibet, and Big Sand Lake.

Evidence for the presence of sixteenth-century native peoples and Spaniards in this locality does exist. In the State of Florida Archaeological Site Files, John Goggin, a University of Florida archaeologist, recorded mounds near Lake Butler that contained Spanish artifacts. At least two mounds and probably more existed in the same locality (see, e.g., Featherstonhaugh 1897, 1899). One mound (8OR11) recorded by Goggin was located on the east side of the lake and contained a gold and silver disc (Kunz 1887).

A second mound (8OR12), possibly west of the lake near Gotha, was excavated in the late nineteenth century by Adolph Meinecke, a trustee of the Milwaukee Public Museum, who donated his collection to the museum. Goggin examined the collection in 1961 and brought part of it to the University of Florida. That portion is now curated at the Florida Museum of Natural History, where it was restudied by Jeffrey Mitchem as part of his dissertation research. Mitchem has also examined the portion of the collection that remains at the Milwaukee Public Museum.

Mitchem (1989b:32–38) believes that the Meinecke artifacts are from at least two mounds, one of which may have also been excavated by Featherstonhaugh (1897, 1899). Mitchem notes that Hale Smith probably drew on Goggin's notes when he described the site (Smith 1956:52). The Milwaukee collection includes Weeden Island pottery (too early to be associated with the Spanish in Florida) as well as a Nueva Cadiz bead and an oblate transparent purple bead, both early sixteenth-century types. Other beads and a Seminole Indian pottery vessel suggest that the collection represents an occupation in later centuries as well. Metal artifacts include a rolled silver bead, a brass disc, brass fragments, two iron "awls" (possibly raw material for blacksmiths), a copper disc, a tanged knife blade, an iron celt, an iron chisel, a possible sword fragment, an iron adze, and parts of two

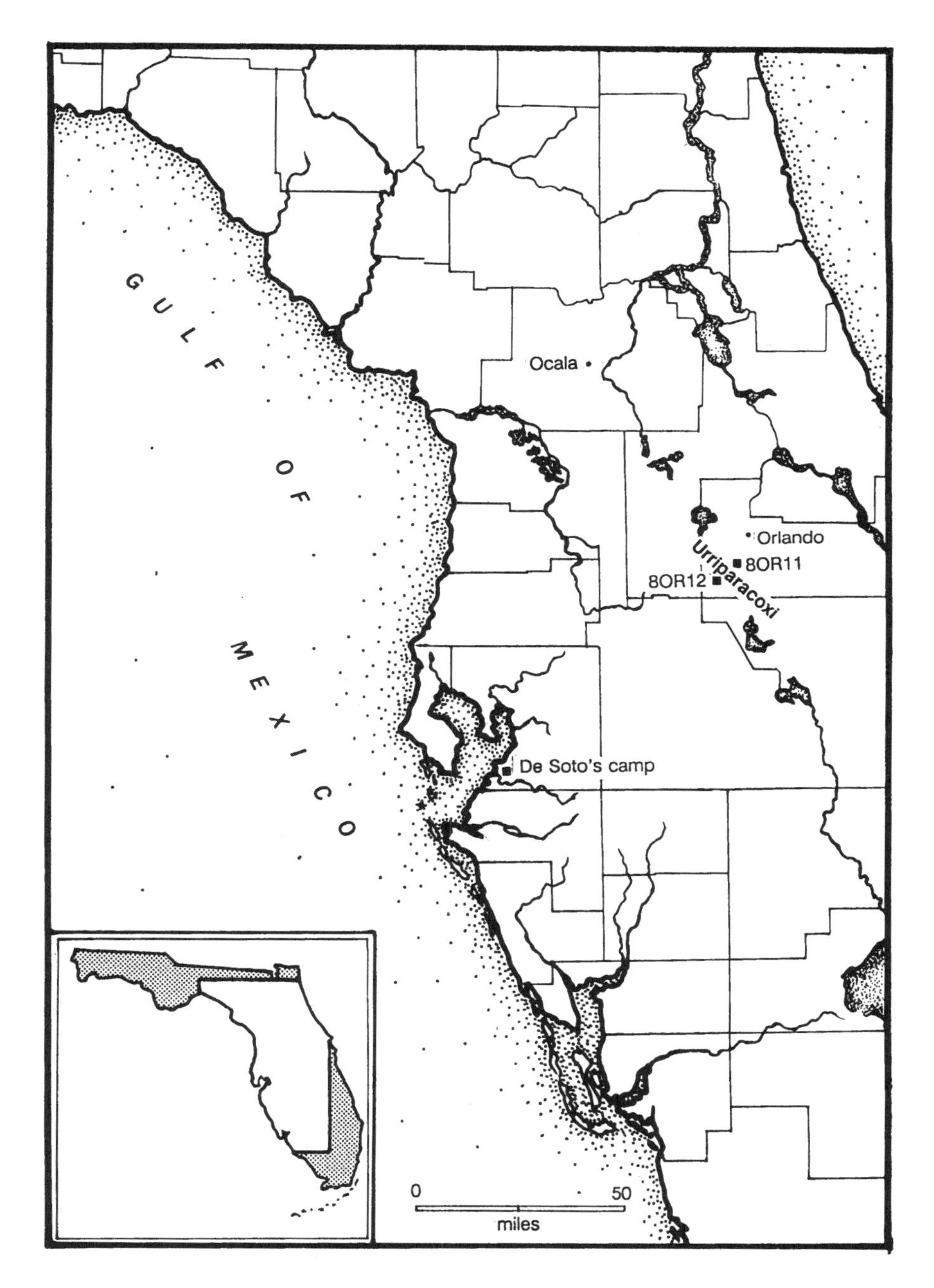

Figure 15

Archaeological sites and Urriparacoxi's territory southwest of Orlando.

pairs of scissors. The early sixteenth-century beads, iron awls, chisel, and scissors could be from the de Soto expedition.

"Urriparacoxi" was not the name of a Florida Indian group. It is a Timucuan word used to designate a war chief, probably the head war chief for one group. According to Julian Granberry (1989:171, 179), *paracusi* means "prince or war-prince," while *iri* can mean "war-counselor, war-prince, or warrior." There were probably many war chiefs or *paracusi* among native peoples in Florida, but it is uncertain if all *paracusi* were Timucuans, since leadership titles were often borrowed. The territory of this particular war chief included at least the lake region southwest of Orlando, as delineated above.

THE RIVER OF MOCOSO

On July 15, de Soto departed from his Tampa Bay camp, leaving behind forty cavalry and sixty infantry under the command of Captain Calderón (Ranjel 1922:63).[2] They were to guard the supplies left behind as well as the caravels and the two brigantines left in the harbor (Varner and Varner 1951:101–102).[3] The larger ships that had brought the army to Florida had already been sent back to Cuba (Ranjel 1922:63).

When departing from Tampa Bay, the army must have numbered about 500 Spaniards with additional Indian bearers. Garcilaso (Varner and Varner 1951:103) correctly notes that they departed from the base camp heading in a generally northeasterly direction, evidently toward the territory of Urriparacoxi. Biedma (1922:5) says that they traveled west, but this is obviously an error.

At the end of the first day of travel, they reached the River of Mocoso, the Alafia River. Their crossing may have been between Buckhorn Creek and present Bell Shoals bridge; the precise location of the crossing may have been at Bell Shoals. A military map published in 1856 shows a crossing at this location (Ives 1856). Such fords were placed at locations where rivers are shallow and, consequently, often broad. Modern bridges, however, generally span rivers at narrow locations without concern for water depth. As a result, highway bridges and traditional fords rarely coincide. To cross the Alafia River, the Spaniards built two bridges (Ranjel 1922:63). Why they found it necessary to build *two* bridges is not clear. Perhaps they built one bridge—possibly little more than a

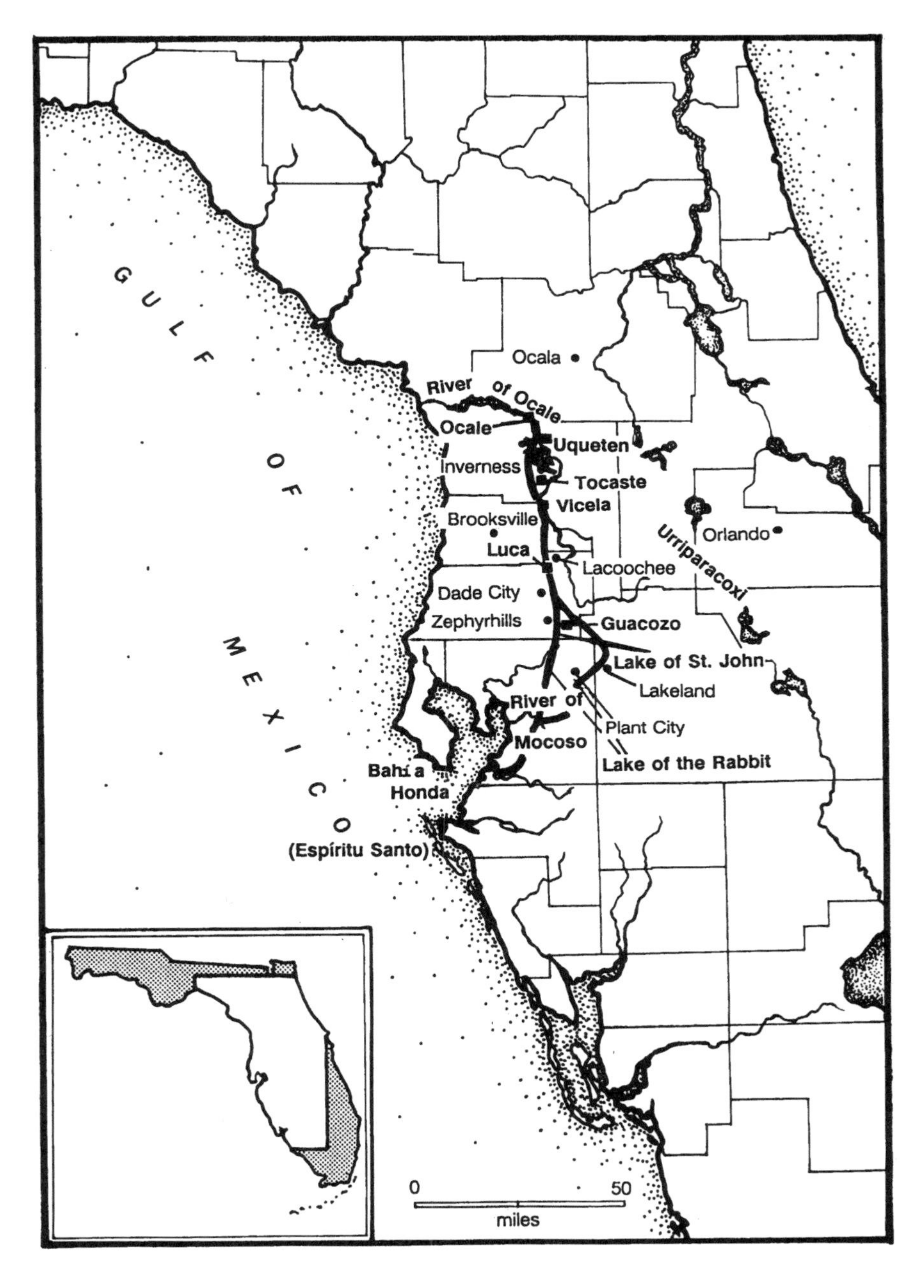

Figure 16

Route of the de Soto expedition from the camp on Tampa Bay to Ocale. The two alternative routes from the Alafia River to the vicinity of Dade City are shown. De Soto names are in bold.

felled tree—from the near bank to an island or a shoal in the middle of the river, and then another bridge from the island or shoal to the bank on the other side.

Adjacent to the Bell Shoals crossing point on the south side of the Alafia River is a Safety Harbor period archaeological site (8HI79). A surface collection from this site contains aboriginal Safety Harbor pottery, six Spanish olive jar sherds, and two fragments of Spanish majolica (the Spanish pottery does not appear to date from the sixteenth century, however). This site may have been the general location of de Soto's camp on the night of July 15, 1539.

There is no evidence that de Soto passed through Mocoso's main town. Because Juan Ortiz (in Elvas 1922:30) specifically said that he had to cross the River of Mocoso when he fled from Uzita, we should expect to find Mocoso's main town on the north side of the river. A site that could be one of Mocoso's towns, and perhaps the main town, is the Mill Point village/mound complex (8HI16/20), located about one-half mile above the mouth of the river on the north bank. It is about one mile west of Bell Shoals.

Moore (1900:356–358) carried out limited excavations in several of the mounds at the Mill Point site. Shell middens were present along the bank of the river on the south side. According to Moore's map, the middens were about 1000 ft long, and he gives the maximum height as 8 ft. At the eastern end of the site was a large temple mound with a borrow pit to the north. The rectangular mound measured 148 by 62 ft and was 11 ft high, with a ramp extending out toward the village plaza. On the opposite side of what was probably the plaza was a burial mound. Two other low sand mounds, perhaps the bases of other structures, were to the north. The site was one of the largest Safety Harbor mound and village complexes on Tampa Bay. It has been destroyed by modern development activities.

Inland, near a tributary of the Alafia River, is the Picnic Mound (8HI3), which might have been a town subject to Mocoso. The site, located about fourteen miles from the bay, is adjacent to Hurrah Creek, near the South Prong of the Alafia River, about seven miles below where the river splits into a north and south prong. At the time of its excavation by WPA and Florida Board of Conservation archaeologists in the 1930s (Bullen 1952b:61–71), the upper portion of the burial mound was badly disturbed by looters.

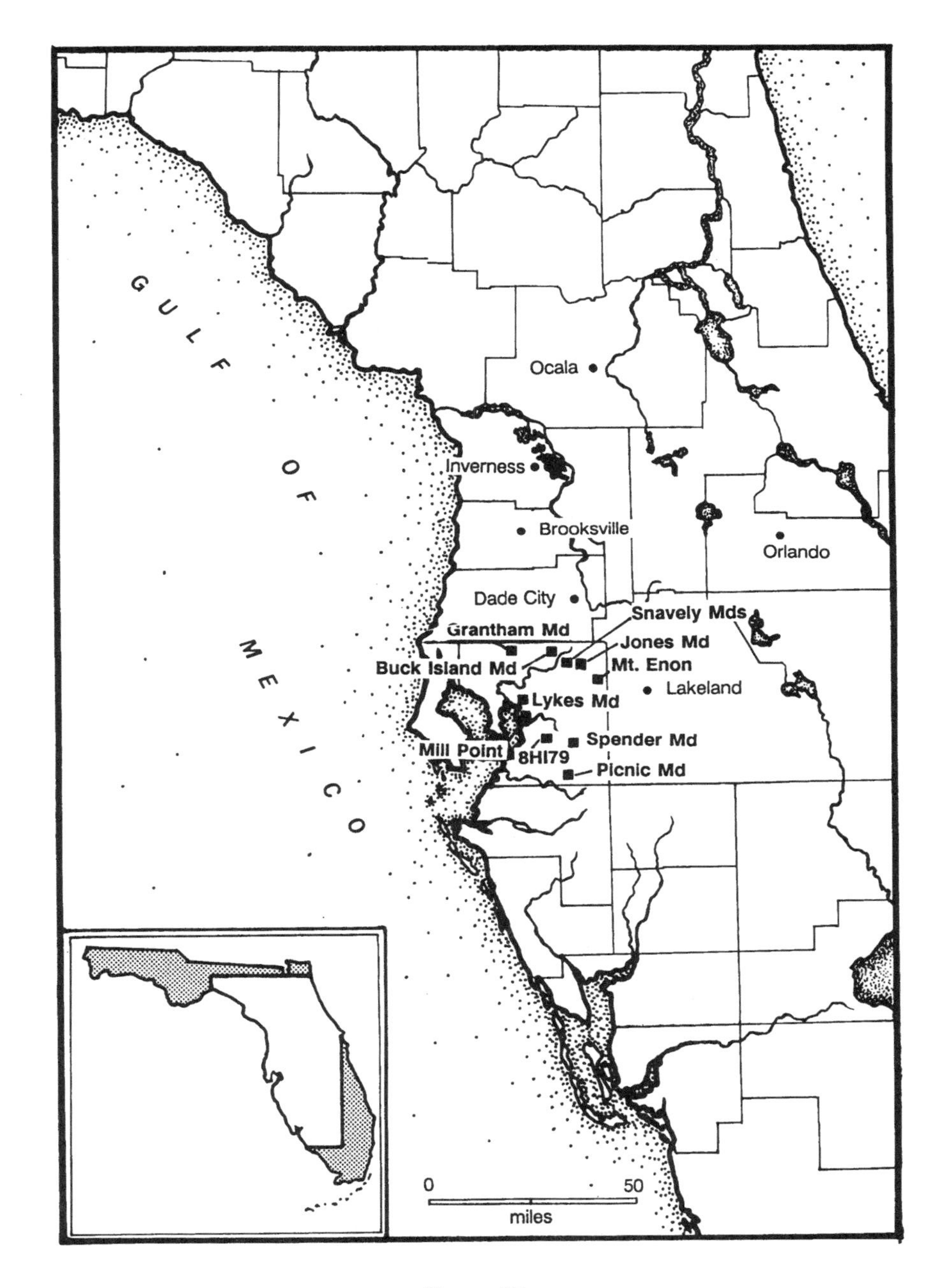

Figure 17

Archaeological sites north and northeast of Tampa Bay. Sites are in bold.

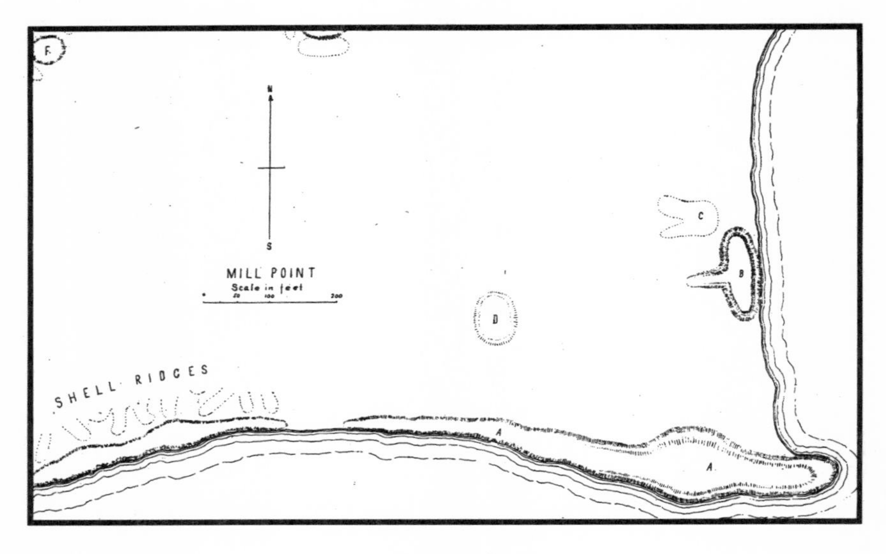

Figure 18

C. B. Moore's sketch map of the Mill Point site (Moore 1900:357). B, D, E, and F are mounds; A is a part of the extensive shell middens that bordered the Alafia River.

According to Bullen (1952b:63) the disturbed portion of the mound, a portion of a mound stratum placed on top an earlier mound, "[o]riginally . . . contained burials and many post-Columbian objects. Screening of this disturbed dirt produced fragmentary skeletal material, objects of European origin, including many glass beads of various types, and nearly 100 narrow triangular arrow points." And, "A large number of glass beads and post-Columbian metal objects were found, particularly in the upper or secondary mound, both during the WPA excavation and previously. . . . An iron celtiform axe came from disturbed dirt. . . . Silver objects included a small claw- or fang-like object, a perforated disc, a decorated pendant, an undescribed pendant, . . ." (Bullen 1952b:69). We know nothing about the village site associated with this burial mound, if one existed. The large quantity of Spanish artifacts associated with the mound makes it a leading candidate for one of Mocoso's towns. According to Garcilaso (Varner and Varner 1951:227–228), when the last of de Soto's men departed from the base camp at Tampa Bay in the fall of 1539, they gave all of the supplies that they could not carry to Mocoso.

Other mound sites at the head of Tampa Bay could have been within Mocoso's territory. These include the Spender Mound, a domiciliary mound between Fishhawk and Bell creeks, both tributaries of the Alafia River (Bullen 1952b:25–26); perhaps the Lykes mound, about a half mile northeast of the head of McKay Bay, in which "mule" and horse bones were interred (Bullen 1952b:33–38); and the Snavely Mounds (8HI5 and 42) and the Jones Mound (8HI4) near Lake Thonotosassa (Bullen 1952b: 39–61). Several European objects were recovered from the Jones Mound, including a broken green glass bead and pieces of sheet copper. One Nueva Cadiz bead and two faceted chevron beads, good indicators of the de Soto expedition, were taken from the Buck Island Mound (8HI6) on the north side of Tampa, and a Nueva Cadiz twisted bead, also early sixteenth century, came from the Grantham Mound (8HI14) near Lutz (Smith and Good 1982:49; Mitchem 1989b:109–111, 116).

FROM THE RIVER OF MOCOSO TO OCALE

Building bridges to cross the River of Mocoso appears to have posed no difficulties. De Soto's men evidently built the bridges, probably little more than trees cut down to span the river, in the afternoon of July 15 (Ranjel 1922:63). The next day they traveled eastward to the "Lake of the Rabbit," so called because at this place a rabbit suddenly jumped up and startled the horses, stampeding them (Ranjel 1922:63–64). If they traveled a full day, this lake was probably one of the lakes in the vicinity of present Plant City (if they were traveling east), or even Lake Thonotosassa (a northerly route). The easterly route seems the best choice because the narratives suggest that the army was headed toward Urriparacoxi's village where Gallegos had gone. The Mt. Enon Mound east-northeast of Plant City has produced glass beads, although the age of the beads is uncertain (Mitchem 1989b: 117–118). If one could succeed in reconstructing old roads and trails in this vicinity, one might be able to decide which lake was the likely camping place.

On July 17, the expedition traveled to a place they called St. John's Lake (Ranjel 1922:64). A day's travel continuing in an easterly direction from Lake of the Rabbit would place St. John's Lake near present Lakeland, perhaps Lake Parker or Lake Gibson.

If, on the contrary, they were following the more northerly route, St. John's Lake would be in the vicinity of Zephyrhills. A major north-south trail passes about three miles west of that town, although it is unlikely the army was that far west. Nothing in any of the narratives suggests that at either the Lake of the Rabbit or at St. John's Lake did the Spaniards camp at a native village, nor is a trail specifically mentioned.

During the first days of the army's journey we might expect that the main body of the army, the foot soldiers and porters, traveled at a slower pace than it did later along the route when as a whole it averaged about five leagues per day—about seventeen miles. Also, we know from descriptions in the narratives that the various parts of the expedition did not all travel at the same speed. Infantry and porters often lagged behind cavalry, while mounted advance parties, sometimes accompanied by infantry (e.g., Gallegos's trip to Urriparacoxi), went ahead to reconnoiter.

The army, dependent on taking stored food from native peoples in order to feed itself, had to continually scout ahead to locate villages with food that could be commandeered. Deciding where to camp, therefore, might depend on finding a suitable village rather than basing the decision on distance traveled. Scout parties also sought intelligence about routes and wealth.

Thus, although the main body of the army followed a single route, members of the expedition occasionally ranged far and wide over a considerable area. We may never be able to determine the exact route taken in some regions. Instead, what we can reconstruct in such places is a corridor of possibilities, based on the narratives and archaeological evidence. This is especially true for the route just north of the Alafia River. We simply do not have enough information to pinpoint the Lake of the Rabbit and St. John's Lake, although we can determine the corridor in which they must lie and through which the army and its advance and scout parties traveled.

The unusual events of July 18 are particularly notable, and any reconstruction of this portion of de Soto's route must be able to account for them. What happened is that the men traveled this day under a very hot sun and they were unable to get drinking water, so that one of de Soto's stewards died of thirst (*murió de sed*), and other men would have died had they not been able to ride on horses (Ranjel 1922:64; Ranjel in Fernández de Oviedo 1851:549). Their plight ended when they came to a plain or grassland (*sabana*) where they found water. According to our route, this waterless area must have been the string of sandhills that are located in the vicinity of Zephyrhills and Lumberton and that are so distinctive on the 1975 United States Geological Survey *Zephyrhills* 7.5 minute quadrangle map of the area. The Atlantic Coast Line Railroad and highway U.S. 98 adjacent to the railroad both go north-south through the heart of the region. Both may follow an old trail.

Among these sandhills, there is no standing water, springs, or streams. Similar sandhills north-northwest of Lake Parker are clearly indicated on a topographical map of Florida that accompanies the *Official Records of the Union and Confederate Armies, 1861–1865* (General Topographic Map Sheet XI, in Bien and Co. n.d.). Bernard Romans, who traveled from Tampa Bay to St. Augustine in the summer of 1769 gives us some idea of how dangerous these sandhills could be: "My Indian guide had the precaution to carry water for ourselves and horses, which proved very serviceable as it was a very hot day, no growth of trees to shade us, and such a burning sand for the sun to reflect on; I leave the reader to judge what we suffered, though it was but short distance over, both ourselves and beasts often experienced the necessity of carrying water; what must traveling over this place be in a hot day, where it is forty or more miles wide?" (Romans 1962:36).

The location reached at the end of July 18 must be several miles southeast of Dade City, at the northerly edge of the sandhills. Such a location would be less than a normal full day's travel from the previous night's camp if the northerly route from the Alafia River were taken, but not if the more easterly route (toward Lakeland and Lake Parker or Lake Gibson) were. The railroad and U.S. 98 both exit the sandhill ridge at a point several miles southeast of Dade City, suggesting old trails in that locale.

On July 19 the army traveled to the savannah of Guacozo, where it found cornfields. This is the first corn it reports having seen. The army again may not have traveled a full day, choosing instead to stop to take advantage of the availability of food. The plain of Guacozo was probably in the vicinity of present-day Dade City. It is in this area that one first encounters the band of mixed hardwoods and loamy soils that continue to the north and that are good for agriculture. A number of village and mound sites are known to exist in the area, including the Pottery Hill site, a previously unrecorded mound and village with a Safety Harbor period component. Several other mounds located close by were destroyed in 1946 (Mitchem 1989b:48–49). Wilfred Neill (1978:224–225) mentions three Safety Harbor period cemeteries in Pasco County, and he notes that Safety Harbor sites are abundant in inland areas. He also says that Spanish majolica has been found at several of the large village sites.

The next day, July 20, de Soto arrived at Luca, a small village where Baltasar de Gallegos, who had led the advance party to Urriparacoxi, came to meet him the following day. Probably they were traveling along a north-south Indian trail that became a major military road during the Second Seminole War. Again, it is not clear that de Soto traveled a full five leagues on July 20, so it is not possible to determine precisely where Luca was. However, one is tempted to place it near the present town of Lacoochee, near a bend of the Withlacoochee River, where there is a remarkable convergence of modern roads and railroads. The nineteenth-century topographical map cited earlier also shows a number of trails in this area. One leads up the western side of the Withlacoochee River—the one de Soto followed—and another crosses the Withlacoochee and goes north past Lake Weir through the area in which Acuera was probably located. It is possible, in fact, that the resemblance of the names Luca and Lacoochee is more than coincidental.

This location is due west of Lake Butler, our location for Urriparacoxi's village. Urriparacoxi's territory might have extended all the way to Luca, but the evidence is not in the documents. Nor is it clear how de Soto knew to wait for Gallegos at Luca. Apparently messengers were traveling back and forth, and the Spaniards had a good idea of their relative locations. A blue glass bead from a mound, 8HE14, west of Lacoochee is recorded. A second mound very close to the town has been excavated, but the information in the brief report published on the research gives no details (Stirling 1931:171).

De Soto camped at Luca apparently to wait for Gallegos, who had been at Urriparacoxi's village. Gallegos arrived two days later, and the remainder of his men arrived the day after that. If Urriparacoxi's main town was located in the vicinity of Lake Butler, the distance to it from Luca would have been about forty

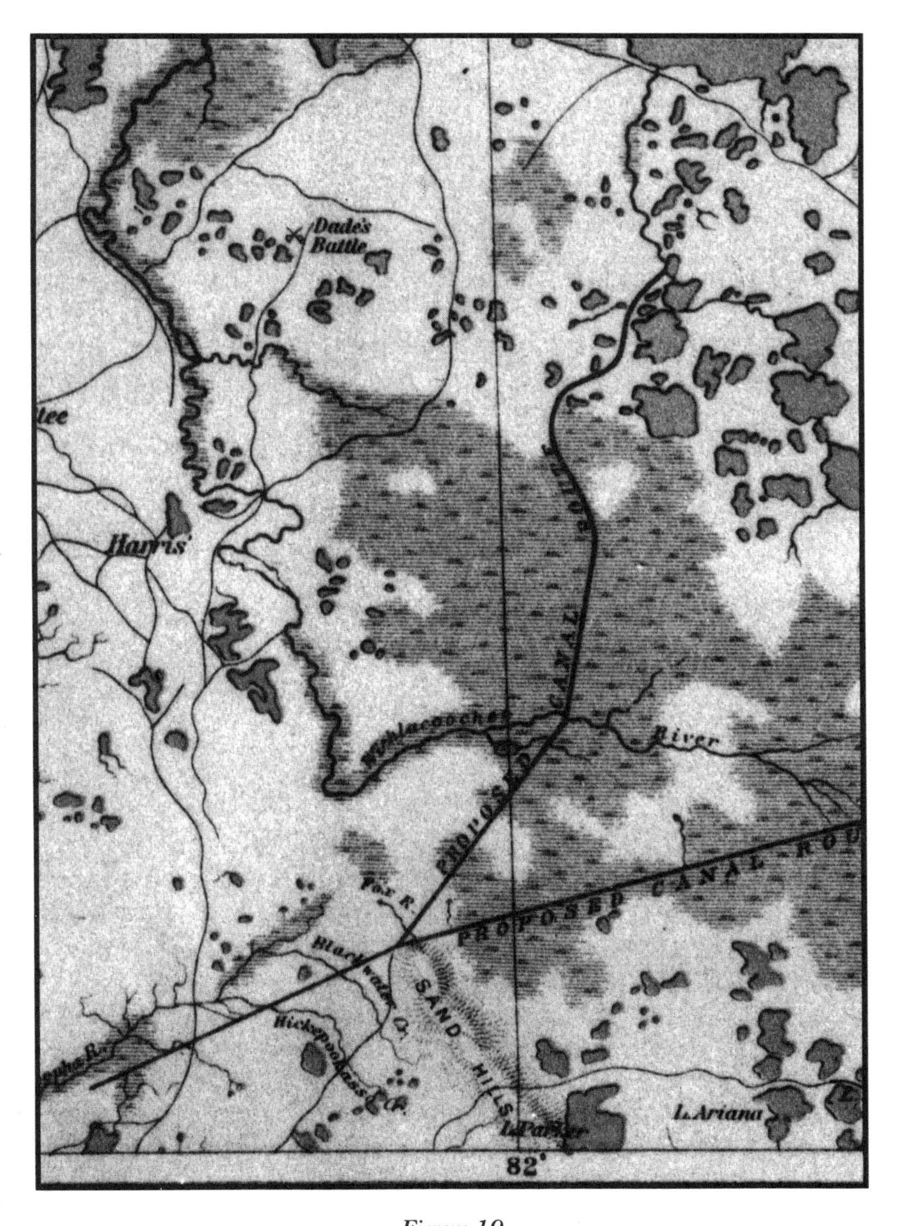

Figure 19

This Civil War period map (Bien n.d.) shows sandhills northwest of Lake Parker, which is northwest of Lakeland.

miles, not an unreasonable two-day journey for the advance party.

The same day that Gallegos's men arrived at Luca (July 21), de Soto sent a messenger to Chief Urriparacoxi, but he received no answer, although he waited until July 23 (Ranjel 1922:64–65). On that day de Soto broke camp and continued on to a small village called Vicela.[4]

If the Spaniards traveled a full day, Vicela would have been located in the vicinity of present-day Istachatta in northeastern Hernando County. On July 24 the men continued northward, reaching the village of Tocaste, which was on a large lake. Here the army camped, but de Soto continued on with a small party of about eleven cavalry, going toward Ocale (Elvas 1922:36; Ranjel 1922:65). This would imply that the entire party traveled less than five leagues on this day, and it may mean that Tocaste was located in the vicinity of present Floral City. The large lake must have been Lake Tsala Apopka. A probable location for Tocaste is the Duval Island site, 8CI5, a Safety Harbor culture archaeological site adjacent to the lake and east of Floral City (Mitchem and Weisman 1987:156–158; Mitchem 1989b:18–20). Collections from this site include a metal axe head.

Traveling on with his small party, de Soto encountered "broad roads," an indication, he felt, that he was close to a wealthy province. He sent Ranjel back to the camp at Tocaste to get reinforcements, and Master of Camp Luis de Moscoso immediately sent forward fourteen horsemen, increasing de Soto's contingent to twenty-six cavalry (Ranjel 1922:66).

The next day, July 25, the main body of the army moved forward to join de Soto. However, it soon met two messengers sent to tell it to return to Tocaste because de Soto had been attacked by Indians. One horse had been killed and several of de Soto's men had been wounded (Ranjel 1922:67).

Evidently de Soto and the advance party were scouting the area to find Ocale, but the going was rough because Ocale was on the opposite side of the Cove of the Withlacoochee, a wetlands area in eastern Citrus County of which Lake Tsala-Apopka is a part. The cove measures about twenty-four miles long and six miles wide, and it is bounded on the east by the Withlacoochee River. The Duval Island site, possibly the village of Tocaste, is located at the southern end of this wetland. Finding a way through the cove was not an easy task. Because the army had to remain at Tocaste, the men soon began to suffer from lack of food (Ranjel 1922:67) and had to eat green corn whose kernels had not filled out.

The following day, July 26, de Soto again sent two messengers back to Tocaste, this time ordering an additional thirty cavalry to move up and the army to follow. These two horsemen appear to have been Gonzalo Silvestre and Juan López Cacho, the latter being one of de Soto's pages (Varner and Varner 1951:107–113). At some point, de Soto passed through an abandoned town and then spotted some Indians on a lake. Through Ortiz, the Spaniards persuaded one of the Indians to serve as a guide, presumably to show them the way across the cove to Ocale (Elvas 1922:36).

The locality where de Soto and the cavalry encountered the "broad roads" was probably near present Inverness. One can look at a modern map and see why the trail may have widened here. Along this western side of Lake Tsala-Apopka, two railroads and a highway run parallel to each other, suggesting that the corridor through which trails could run was constricted here because of topography. As a result, this trail would have been much more heavily traveled and therefore broader than in less constricted areas, where multiple trails existed. Had de Soto marched his army from Tampa Bay to Urriparacoxi's village and then north to Ocale, he would have avoided the cove and its extensive wetlands, passing east of it, i.e., traveling north from Urriparacoxi to Ocale approximately along a trail paralleling present-day highway U.S. 27 past Acuera and into Ocale. His captive Indian guides may have deliberately led him the more difficult way.

THE CROSSING OF THE SWAMP AND RIVER OF OCALE

De Soto and his horsemen crossed the cove on Saturday, July 26, followed the next day by the thirty horsemen under the command of Nuño de Tovar (Ranjel 1922:67). The rest of the army, mostly on foot, was not so fortunate. It took these men from Saturday, the day they left Tocaste, until Tuesday to march northward to the crossing and then make their way through the swamp (Ranjel 1922:68)

The narratives of Elvas and Ranjel and later testimony recorded in Spain (at Jeréz de los Caballeros on June 12, 1560;

Oribe 1866) give us valuable clues to the nature of the crossing, making it clear that the army did indeed travel through the wetlands and across the Withlacoochee River to reach Ocale. It did not bypass the cove on its north side and cross the river at Stokes Ferry—called Camp Izard Ferry in the Second Seminole War—a traditional ford, nor did it cross the Withlacoochee River near the modern U.S. 41 bridge even farther north at Dunnellon. Instead, led by Indian guides, the army waded and walked directly across the swamps of the cove, and then bridged and waded the Withlacoochee River and its backswamp before reaching high ground and the town of Ocale.

Ranjel only briefly describes the river crossing of de Soto and the mounted advance party: "The Governor . . . reached the river or swamp of Ocale. The current was strong and broad and they crossed with great difficulty, and where there was no need of a bridge they waded through the water up to their necks" (1922:67). On the following day, one of the horses was swept away by the current and drowned. Elvas (1922:36) corroborates Ranjel, calling the river current "powerful."

The expedition members who were on foot, however, had a much harder time. "[T]hey traveled hungry and on bad roads; the country being very thin of maize, low, very wet, pondy, and thickly covered with trees" (Elvas 1922:37). De Soto sent men and mules carrying food back to those who trailed behind. "[T]hey found them in that swamp eating herbs and roots roasted and others boiled with salt, and what was worse, without knowing what they were" (Ranjel 1922:68).

In his secondhand account, Garcilaso provides a colorful description of the crossing of what he calls the "great swamp," although he confuses the name Acuera with Ocale (Varner and Varner 1951:103–117). Garcilasco recounts that one attempt to cross by de Soto and his cavalry ended when they reached high ground, but could not advance further because of the marshy conditions beyond. They were forced to retreat and spend considerable effort in finding a better way through. Along the way they were harassed by Indians and misled by guides. Garcilaso says it took the main body of the army three days to cross.

That the crossing was a difficult one is confirmed in official testimony recorded in Spain in 1560, more than twenty years later. One of the survivors, Alonso Vázquez, filed a petition to the crown seeking compensation for hardships he suffered in La

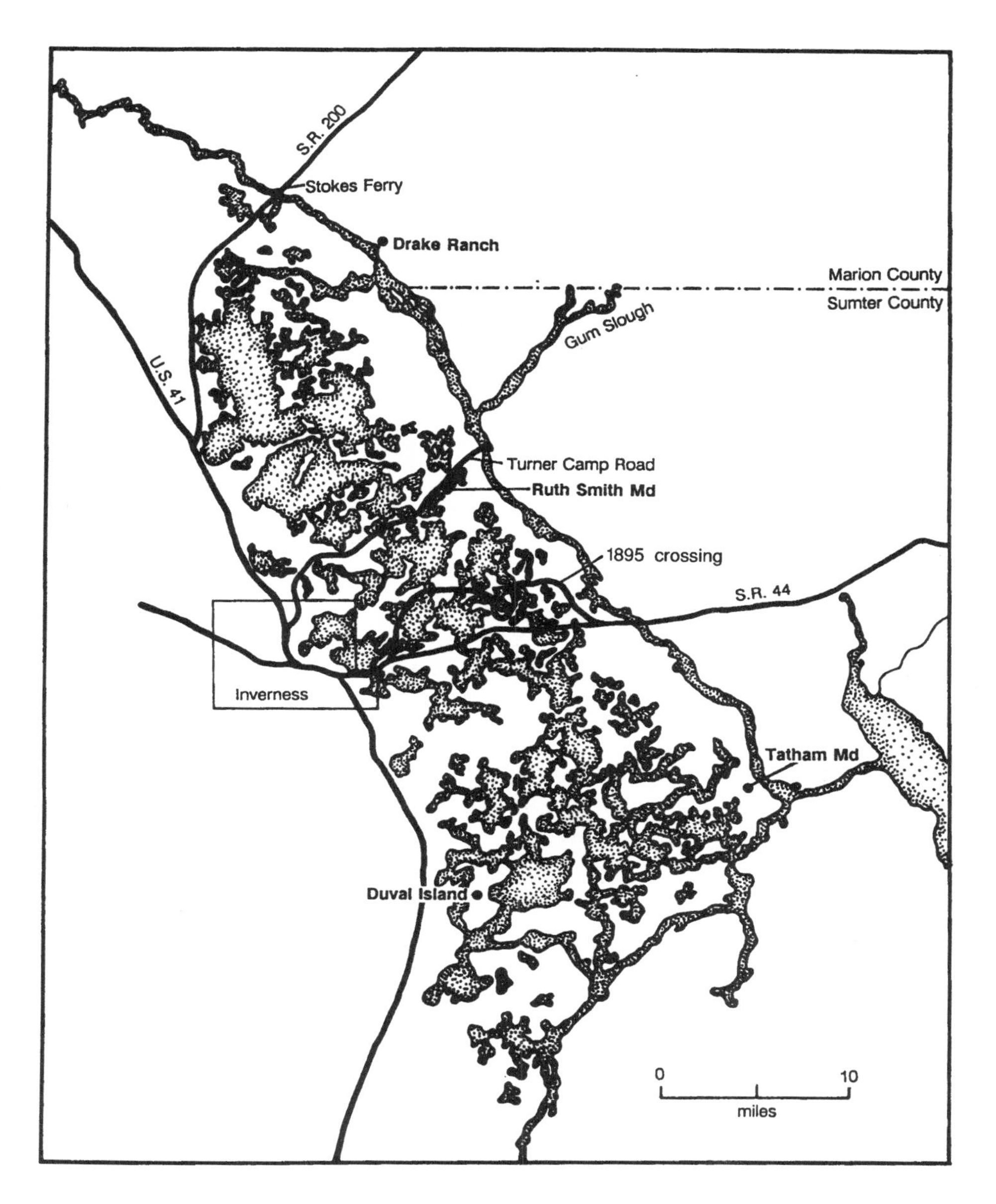

Figure 20

The Cove of the Withlacoochee. Archaeological sites are in bold.

Florida (Oribe 1866:301–312). He sought to prove that a part of his suffering consisted of "marching through that country [La Florida] with great toil and hunger," and arriving "at a marsh, where they remained three days without eating, until, getting through it and coming out, they arrived at a province called Ocal, where there was some food" (Oribe 1866:304).

One of the most remarkable stories of the expedition is that of Ana Méndez, one of two Spanish women who accompanied the army, and the only one to survive. She gave verbal testimony on behalf of Vázquez, confirming his hardships. At the time of her testimony, her age is given as about thirty-one, meaning she may have been only ten at the start of the expedition. Méndez "remembers crossing that swamp, there being much water in it, in places reaching to the knee, in others to the waist and thence over the head, which they went through with much labor in three days" (Oribe 1866:310).

These descriptions accurately depict the Cove of the Withlacoochee, with its wet prairies and ponds, palmettos (mentioned by Elvas [1922:37]), stands of higher ground with scrub vegetation and oaks, the Withlacoochee River, and the heavily wooded river backswamp. Today, the timbered-out stumps of huge cypress trees can still be seen. The higher, drier land the men came to when they reached the east side of the river also accurately portrays the topography of western Marion and Sumter counties, part of the province of Ocale.

Where exactly did de Soto and his army finally cross the Cove of the Withlacoochee? In the past, before modern highway construction, there were at least three crossings. Highway S.R. 44 approximately follows one of these trails, running east from Inverness across the wetlands and over the river. The modern roadbed is, of course, built up to keep it above high water. The 1895 USGS quadrangle map (Tsala-Apopka Sheet) shows a second cover crossing several miles north of present S.R. 44. That second crossing turned south and intersected the S.R. 44 route just east of the Withlacoochee River. Still another way through the swamp to the river is shown on the 1895 map; today that crossing is approximated by Turner Camp Road, which leads northeasterly from Inverness.

All of these routes would have been difficult, especially in times of heavy rain. Trying to decide which one the army took is difficult, especially without knowing exactly where on the east

Figure 21

The Cove of the Withlacoochee, typical terrain.

side of the Withlacoochee River the town of Ocale was located. At this time, however, the Turner Camp Road crossing, the most northerly, seems most likely. Let us look at the evidence for the location of Ocale.

OCALE

After crossing the Withlacoochee River, the first village within Ocale that de Soto came upon was Uqueten. Two Indians were captured and food was sent back from there to the main body of the army still in the swamp (Ranjel 1922:68). Unfortunately, none of the chroniclers tells precisely when de Soto got to Uqueten or how far it was from the river. Presumably the Spaniards arrived on Saturday, the same day they crossed the swamp, but this is not certain. By Tuesday, when the main army had caught up to him, de Soto and the advance party had moved on and set up camp in the town of Ocale itself, a "good region for corn" (Ranjel 1922:68). The inhabitants had abandoned their town, but the maize fields were abundant and de Soto "ordered all of the ripe grain, enough for three months, to be secured" (Elvas 1922:37).[5] Apparently de Soto was still planning to winter at Ocale.

Despite providing food for the hungry army, Ocale contained none of the wealth that the Spaniards had hoped to find based on information gathered while they were at Tampa Bay. Biedma's (1922:5) account notes, "On arrival there we found it to be a small town. . . . We got some maize, beans, and small dogs, which were no small relief to people who came perishing with hunger."

Locating Ocale, a key native town along de Soto's route through Florida, is difficult because none of the three firsthand accounts specify in detail the movements of de Soto and the advance party after they moved on from Uqueten. If the advance party—de Soto and twenty-six horsemen (Ranjel 1922:67)—arrived at Uqueten on Saturday, July 26, and was in Ocale on Tuesday, it could have traveled a considerable distance on horseback in the intervening days, as much as twelve leagues a day. Hence, on the days after the party crossed the river it could have ridden at least as far as modern Ocala, or even to Orange Lake.

But such long distances are not likely. When we plot the movement of the main body of the army, it seems probable that Ocale was located at least within one day's march—five leagues—from the crossing of the Withlacoochee River. The last of the army reached de Soto at Ocale on July 29, three days after he had crossed the swamp and river. It would have taken the army at least two days to reach the river (July 26 and 27) and a third day (July 28) to make the crossing. On the next day it marched to Ocale. This suggests that Ocale was not more than about five leagues from the crossing.

If the crossing was near the intersection of modern Turner Camp Road and the river, probably about two and one-half miles south of the mouth of Gum Slough (Dead River on some maps) at Cotton's Landing (on the 1895 map), where the river is relatively wider and shallower, the army would have reached higher, dry ground in the northwest corner of Sumter County. If the army marched a full five leagues from that point before reaching Ocale, the town could have been as far east as Belleview, almost to modern Ocala to the northwest, or into west-central Marion County to the north.

But two sources of information suggest that Ocale was in southwest Marion County near the Withlacoochee River. Relative distances between Urriparacoxi, Acuera, and Ocale, taken together with archaeological information, suggest Ocale to be near the river, and not more than several leagues from the Turner Fish Road crossing.

The first piece of evidence is contained in the letter de Soto sent back to Cuba from Tampa Bay. Apparently based on information Gallegos gathered from Indians on his foray to Urriparacoxi, de Soto says the distance from Urriparacoxi to Acuera was three days' travel (ca. fifty-one miles) and from Acuera to Ocale two days (ca. thirty-four miles) (de Soto 1866:285). Garcilaso, who confuses Ocale with Acuera, says de Soto's camp (at Ocale) was "some twenty leagues" from Urriparacoxi (Varner and Varner 1951:116). If Urriparacoxi's territory was in the locality west of Orlando as suggested above, these pieces of evidence would be consistent with Acuera being in the Lake Weir–Lake Griffin locale near the headwaters of the Oklawaha River (discussed below), with Ocale west situated in southwestern Marion County.

A location for Ocale in southwestern Marion County not more than several leagues from the Withlacoochee River is also consistent with our reconstruction of the route north through Marion and Alachua counties to the Santa Fe River. The locations of subsequent towns encountered by the Spaniards fits best with Ocale being within a few leagues of the Withlacoochee River. This location is also consistent with the Withlacoochee River being called the "river or swamp of Ocale" (Ranjel 1922:67), which suggests that the people of Ocale lived on or near it and controlled both the wetland and adjacent territory along the river.

Finally, Elvas (1922:35) says that Ocale is "towards the sunset" (i.e., northwest in June) from Urriparacoxi, while Garcilaso (Varner and Varner 1951:116) says that Ocale (his Acuera) is "on a line running more or less north and south" from Urriparacoxi. These two approximations support a location for Ocale near the Withlacoochee River.

What archaeological evidence exists for the province and town of Ocale? Led by Johnson (1987) and by Mitchem and Weisman (1987), archaeological teams from the Florida Museum of Natural History carried out archaeological surveys on the eastern side of the Withlacoochee River to search for potential sites. For several hundred yards back from the river proper there is a swamp containing stands of cypress and other water-tolerant trees. Unlike the west side of the river, however, once the backswamp on the east side is crossed, dry ground is reached.

The archaeologists found a number of small archaeological sites where the high ground and swamp meet. Most, such as the eight sites on the Drake Ranch property north of Gum Slough, in northwesternmost Sumter County and southwesternmost Marion County, contain snail and other freshwater mollusk shell middens (sites 8SM68, 69, 70, and 71; 8MR53, 54, 1111, and 1112). The nearby Marion Oaks (8MR1110) and Indian Mounds Spring (8SM64) sites are similar.

Uqueten, the first town in the province of Ocale encountered by the advance party of Spaniards, could correspond to the northernmost cluster of shell middens on the Drake Ranch property (Drake Ranch shell middens E, F, G, and H; 8MR53, 54, 1111, 1112). Tests in various of these middens, however, failed to produce any aboriginal or Spanish artifacts diagnostic of the sixteenth century. The aboriginal pottery found was mainly the type Pasco Plain, the same ware most prevalent at sites throughout the Cove of the Withlacoochee.

No large sites that might correspond to Ocale were found immediately adjacent to the river backswamp. But this is not surprising. We would expect the town of Ocale to be farther back from the river, where better agricultural soils could be found. Such soils, with a few exceptions, begin about ten to twelve miles from the river (ca. three leagues), and they extend northward through the central portion of the Florida peninsula.

Johnson (1987) has also carried out archaeological surveys back from the river, near and within areas of good agricultural soils. Many small sites were found (e.g., 8MR1113–1118, 1126), but none of them are likely candidates for Ocale.

Our best archaeological evidence for Ocale originally comes from a 1965 survey of the proposed route of the Cross Florida Barge Canal. Florida State Museum archaeologist Ripley P. Bullen recorded the remnants of three archaeological sites about six miles from the Withlacoochee River and the Cowhead Flats crossing.[6] The sites were around the edges of Ross Prairie, an area of nearly two square miles of marshes and other wetlands. The prairie had been severely impacted in the 1930s by construction of a portion of the proposed Gulf Atlantic Ship Canal, the forerunner of the later Cross State Barge Canal. More recent construction of S.R. 200 also impacted the prairie and its archaeological sites. One site, 8MR101, was described by Bullen as a small village, ca. 100 by 700 ft, that had been destroyed by the excavation of the canal many years previously. A second small village also had been previously destroyed. A third site was recorded, but the survey team found only chert chips. The site had been destroyed by the construction of S.R. 200.

In 1987, Johnson resurveyed the northern portion of Ross Prairie (Johnson 1987:91–94), locating eight separate sites (8MR1119–1125, 1865). None of the sites, however, could be tied definitively to either the sixteenth century or to the de Soto expedition. The exact location of Ocale remains a mystery, although the Ross Prairie locality seems the most likely candidate at this time.

There is also documentary evidence pertinent to Ocale. On the 1560s map of Florida drawn by Frenchman Jacques Le Moyne, the aboriginal town of Eloquale (akin to Biedma's Etocale) is located in the central part of the peninsula west of the St. Johns River and west of Aquouena (probably Acuera; see the discussion of Acuera below). D'Escalante Fontaneda, a Spaniard shipwrecked in southern Florida in 1545, mentions Olagale, a "separate kingdom," that is located (vaguely) south of Apalachee

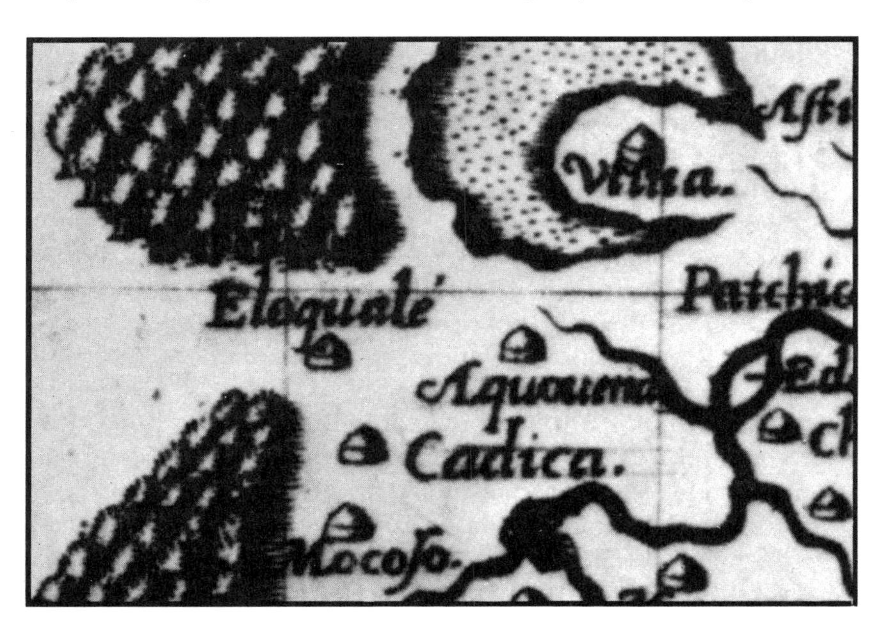

Figure 22

"Eloquale" (Ocale) and "Aquouena" (Acuera) are shown in the interior of Florida on Le Moyne's map.

(True 1945:29, 30). A 1630 petition to the Spanish king from a Franciscan priest names San Luis de Eloquale as one of the missions in the interior of La Florida where a horse was a necessity for priests working in the area (Hann 1990:469–470). This implies that the mission could not be reached by canoe. The location of Ocale at some distance from the St. Johns–Oklawaha, used for river transportation in the mission era, would be consistent with the priest's request.

ACUERA

De Soto's army needed to continually commandeer food from the natives. Corn and other crops and food were taken from the fields and stores of the villagers encountered along the route. As long as the army was in motion, a new village to raid could be reached almost every day, and food supplies replenished. If the army were going to winter at Ocale, as de Soto wrote in his letter sent from Tampa Bay back to Cuba (de Soto 1866:286), large quantities of food, especially corn, had to be collected and stored. During the two weeks the entire army remained at Ocale, de Soto evidently sought to amass enough corn to last the army three months (Elvas 1922:37). In order to do that, soldiers (and Indian bearers?) were "sent to Acuera for provisions" (Ranjel 1922:68). As many as two trips were made.

Where was Acuera? We know from de Soto's letter (1866:285) that Acuera was a two-day journey from Ocale. The best location, then, seems to be in the Lake Weir–Lake Griffin vicinity, north of Leesburg near or on the Oklawaha River, a tributary of the St. Johns River. As argued above in this chapter, that placement is consistent with our interpretations of the locations of Ocale and Urriparacoxi.

Other documentation hints at this location for Acuera. An aboriginal town called Aquouena is shown on the Le Moyne map a short distance east of Ocale and adjacent to a tributary of the St. Johns River (in Lorant 1946:34–35). Aquouena may be Acuera, and the tributary could represent the Oklawaha River. Acquera is also mentioned in a 1564 French account as one of the more than forty chiefs vassal to Chief Utina (see chapter 7). These vassal chiefs probably all were within the St. Johns drainage or nearby, and during the mission period were a part of the district called Agua Dulce (or Freshwater) by the Spaniards.

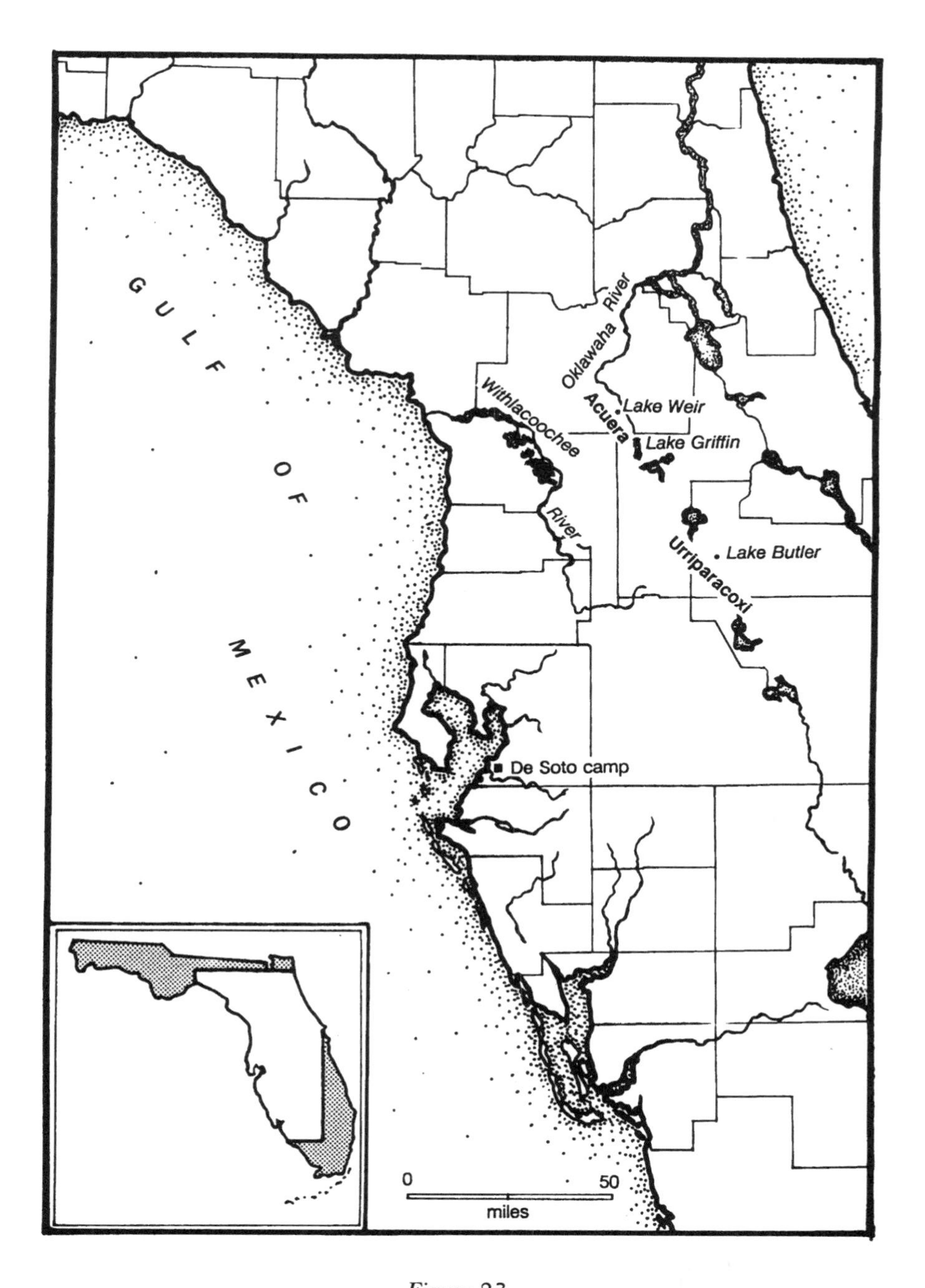

Figure 23

Locations in central Florida mentioned in the text. De Soto names are in bold.

On an early map of Florida by John Lee Williams, Lake Weir is labeled Lake Ware, perhaps an Anglicization of Acuera (Williams 1837). Bloodworth and Morris (1978:159) say that "Lake Weir was named for Dr. Weir (or Ware), whose home was near the lake." It is highly unlikely that any settlers were living around the lake by 1837, however.

Acuera must have been an important aboriginal province, because Spanish Franciscan missionaries established missions there by the midseventeenth century and probably visited the region earlier. Father Francisco Pareja, in a catechism he prepared by 1627 for use at the Florida Timucuan missions (Pareja 1627:36-37), mentions Santa Lucia de Acuera as a dialect of the Timucuan language. And by the midseventeenth century two Franciscan missions had been established in the province, San Luis de Acuera and Santa Lucia de Acuera (Hann 1990:460, 487). Both names appear on a 1655 list of missions, which states that the two missions were thirty-two and forty-three leagues, respectively, from St. Augustine. These measurements, roughly 115 miles, mirror the distance from St. Augustine west to the St. Johns River, and then west and south along the Oklawaha to the Lake Weir–Lake Griffin locale. Both missions were probably in existence at the time Pareja wrote his catechism. John Hann (1990:460) notes an assertion by Maynard J. Geiger (in Oré 1936:133–134, n. 7) that the mission of Avino, mentioned by Father Luis Gerónimo de Oré in 1616, was the same as San Luis de Acuera, and Pareja's mention of a Santa Lucia dialect suggests that the mission of that name had been established among the Acuera at that time.

ARCHAEOLOGY IN THE COVE OF THE WITHLACOOCHEE AND OCALE

Despite our failure to pinpoint the principal town of Ocale, archaeological research in the Cove of the Withlacoochee and on the east side of the river, in what must be the province of Ocale, has produced new information on the presence of the de Soto expedition and its encounters with the native peoples. Research has also raised important questions concerning previous interpretations of the archaeological culture associated with the province of Ocale.

Previous interpretations, based on the assumption that Ocale was located quite near Ocala in central Marion County, have equated the sixteenth- and seventeenth-century Ocale with the same archaeological culture that was associated with the Potano Indians to the north, in Alachua County (e.g., Milanich 1978:62, 69). That culture, called the Alachua tradition by archaeologists, consisted of an assemblage of certain kinds of pottery and stone tools along with a strong correlation between village locations, good agricultural soils, and lakes. When de Soto and his army crossed the Withlacoochee River into Ocale, it was previously thought they were entering a new aboriginal province, one whose archaeological assemblage contrasted sharply with that found west of the river.

This does not seem to be the case, however. It is now known that the archaeological assemblage found in the Cove of the Withlacoochee in precolumbian times—including snail and other mollusk middens and an association between swamp-marsh-riverine locations and the presence of Pasco pottery in villages—also extends for a short distance east of the river (Mitchem and Weisman 1984, 1987; Mitchem and Hutchinson 1986, 1987; Weisman 1986; Johnson 1987; Mitchem and Leader 1988; Mitchem 1989b). For example, the sites around Ross Prairie are characterized by Pasco pottery, not by Alachua tradition pottery. This suggests that the province of Ocale might have included a portion of the wetlands of the Cove of the Withlacoochee west of the Withlacoochee River itself. The area east of the river, the main part of Ocale, also included some wetlands, such as Ross Prairie.

The material culture of Ocale, at least in pre-Columbian times, was more like that found in Citrus, Hernando, and Pasco counties than like the Alachua tradition found in central Marion and Alachua counties. We will return to this point in chapter 5.

Research in the Cove of the Withlacoochee has also provided some of the best archaeological evidence for the presence of the de Soto expedition. The army camped at Ocale for two weeks (July 29 to August 11) before de Soto and an advance party marched on ahead. About two-thirds of the Spaniards remained at Ocale for an additional two and one-half weeks, probably until about August 28. The largest part of the army was at Ocale for a month, the longest time the Spaniards camped at any location along the route from Tampa Bay to Apalachee in northwest Florida, where they would ultimately winter.

These three locations—Tampa Bay, Ocale, Apalachee—should provide our best opportunity for finding artifacts from the expedition because the Spaniards were at those locations for relatively long periods of time. Just as we would expect to find evidence for the presence of the army—items such as European beads—in aboriginal sites around southern and eastern Tampa Bay (which is indeed the case, as we saw in chapter 3), similar Spanish-derived artifacts should be found in the province of Ocale as well as in Apalachee. This has turned out to be true, and it greatly strengthens our interpretation of the route.

Evidence for the de Soto expedition in Ocale comes from two sites in the Cove of the Withlacoochee, both located near the river. The first is Ruth Smith Mound (8CI200) located beside Turner Camp Road northeast of Inverness (Mitchem and Weisman 1984; Mitchem, Smith, et al. 1985; Mitchem 1989b:25–26), immediately adjacent to the route the army may have taken in crossing the cove. Local collectors had dug in the mound for many years, destroying it. However, archaeologists were able to examine private collections that contained artifacts taken from the mound. The collections included aboriginal pottery and other artifacts, as well as a number of metal and glass beads and other objects of European manufacture. All of the glass beads that could be dated by style are from the early sixteenth century.

Thirty-two glass beads were studied, including nine faceted chevron beads and twenty-one Nueva Cadiz Plain beads. As we saw in chapter 3, similar beads have been found in sites around Tampa Bay. Other European-derived artifacts include fifty-one small silver beads, two gold beads, an iron chisel, two large rolled iron beads, a smaller iron bead, three small brass rings (possibly fragments of chain mail), and a potsherd of Spanish coarse earthenware pottery called Green Bacín ware. The chisel is like those found at other early contact sites in Florida and the southeastern United States, a Spanish trade item that was highly valued by the native peoples (Smith 1987:35–36, 44–45). Such chisels were distributed by the 1560s Juan Pardo expedition in the Carolinas and Tennessee (Hudson 1990:136–137).

The second site, Tatham Mound (8CI203), is several miles south of the Ruth Smith Mound in a small hammock on high ground just west of the Withlacoochee River. It was discovered by

Brent Weisman (then a University of Florida graduate student) and members of the Withlacoochee River Archaeological Council in 1984 as a part of an ongoing survey of the Cove of the Withlacoochee. Weisman's test indicated that the mound was probably associated with the Safety Harbor culture, the focus of doctoral research by Mitchem, another University of Florida graduate student. The undisturbed nature of the site and its location relative to two nearby village-type sites (Wild Hog Scrub and Bayonet Field, 8CI197 and 198, respectively; see Mitchem, Weisman, et al. 1985:44–47 and Mitchem 1989b:23–24) led to a long-term field project in 1985 and 1986. The field excavations were directed by Mitchem and the results were reported in several field reports and in his dissertation (Mitchem, Weisman, et al. 1985; Mitchem and Hutchinson 1986, 1987; Mitchem 1989b: 306–549). The human remains from the site have been studied and reported in a dissertation by bioanthropologist Dale Hutchinson of the University of Illinois (1991).

Tatham Mound, a small site tucked away in the Cove of the Withlacoochee River, provides some of our best information on the types of artifacts that the native peoples of the Southeast obtained from the de Soto expedition and on the impact of Europeans on the native peoples themselves. The events played out in Ocale probably took place all along the route, not only in Florida, but across the entire southeastern United States. Let us look first at the de Soto accounts for hints of what took place in Ocale during that 1539 encounter between native Floridians and the Spanish invaders.

While the army was still camped at Tocaste, on the southern side of Lake Tsala-Apopka, de Soto and a small contingent of cavalry explored northward along the west side of the cove. Rodrigo Ranjel was sent back to camp for reinforcements, apparently at one point having to fight his way past Indians "that were on the trail of the Governor" (Ranjel 1922:66). The next day, Friday, July 25, de Soto, still searching for a way across the cove, had a skirmish with the Indians in which a horse was killed and several of the Spaniards wounded (Ranjel 1922:67). During the journey to the town of Ocale "some soldiers . . . had been wounded and a crossbow-man named Mendoza slain (Ranjel 1922:68). On the excursions to Acuera to gather provisions, skirmishes occurred and three soldiers were killed and others wounded (Ranjel 1922:68). Although the chroniclers were careful to record the casualties suffered by the members of the expedition, they tell us nothing about the effect of these seemingly minor skirmishes on the native peoples of Ocale (or Acuera). One might surmise that the effect was relatively minor.

But this is not the case. If the archaeological evidence from Tatham Mound is any indication, the encounters between the soldiers and Indians were very serious for the natives. Skirmishes and, later, the effects of disease wreaked havoc. Military engagements and epidemics clearly caused the deaths of many people in Ocale, more than seventy of whom were interred in Tatham Mound, some accompanied by numerous European artifacts, including metal and glass beads and hardware. Most of this collection of artifacts—especially types of beads and metal tools—are typical of those thought to be associated with the de Soto expedition and also found elsewhere along the route.

Mitchem's careful investigation of the site indicates that sometime between A.D. 1200 and 1450 the pre-Columbian ancestors of the Ocale built a low mound. In the mound they buried the remains of nineteen individuals (Hutchinson 1991:96). Several people wore shell beads and had crushed galena, a shiny grey mineral, sprinkled on them. Objects made of native copper also were placed with some of the burials. That this episode of construction occurred in the late precolumbian times is confirmed by radiocarbon dating and by the style of the copper artifacts and pottery found in the mound. An earthen ramp was constructed on the east side of the low mound.

The mound was then either left unused, or a charnel structure in which the bones of dead relatives were stored was erected on top of it. Perhaps as a result of the decomposition of bodies, a thick layer of black soil accumulated on the mound. At one point a portion of the stratum was scraped away and clean sand was deposited. Mitchem (1989b:529) suggests that this might have been done at a time when a charnel structure, if one existed, was rebuilt or refurbished. After this period of construction, the dark soil layer continued to accumulate.

In July 1539, members of the de Soto expedition passed near the site, undoubtedly coming into contact with the Ocale peoples, whose ancestors were responsible for the original pre-

Columbian mound. At least one native person was killed, and the body, with an arm severed probably by a sword cut, was stored in a charnel house, perhaps the one on the mound. A severed shoulder blade was found in the mound, although it could not be determined whether it belonged to the individual with the severed arm or a second person. Ten other bones (six femurs, two tibias, and two humeri) displayed probable sword wounds, each the result of an oblique blow (Hutchinson 1991:118–121).

As we shall see in chapter 8, members of the expedition passed through the Cove of the Withlacoochee not one time, but three: in July, at the time of the original crossing; in the fall, when cavalry were sent from the winter camp at Apalachee in northwest Florida south to the camp at Tampa Bay; and when the soldiers at the camp at Tampa Bay marched north to rendezvous with de Soto and the army in Apalachee. The injuries to the natives, whose remains were placed in the mound, may have been a result of battles fought with members of de Soto's army on any of these trips.

Although some of the Ocale peoples suffered from the military encounters, the most devastating impact of the passage of de Soto's expedition was a probable epidemic that killed at least the seventy people interred in the mound in the same burial episode. The germs could have been introduced directly by the Spanish on any of their three trips through the region, or they could have been introduced weeks or months later from Indians who had been in contact with the Spaniards.

When the epidemic struck, the survivors cleaned off the top of the mound, removed the charnel house (if one existed), and scraped away a part of the dark soil stratum. Sand was added to the top and the flanks of the mound, covering the dark soil that remained. The bodies of the more than 70 people were then laid down on the sand, some in parallel rows. Around, under, and atop these individuals were placed the disarticulated bones of at least 240 additional individuals. These remains, mainly long bones and skulls, had apparently been stored in a charnel house. All twelve of the bones displaying sword wounds were included among the disarticulated remains.

After the remains of all the individuals were laid down, a cap of sand was placed over all of the bones, burying them. Then a sand ramp was built on the west side of the mound and at least one ceremony was held, probably to ritually cleanse the survivors who had participated in the burial rites. We would expect that the rites included imbibing black drink, a ceremonial beverage brewed from the parched leaves of yaupon holly, *Ilex vomitoria* (see Hudson 1979). The drink was typically brewed in large pottery vessels and then drunk out of shell cups made from large *Busycon* shells. Mitchem found many of the shell cups and broken pottery vessels on top of the mound, where they had been left when the ceremony was completed. As humus built up on the mound, the cups and pottery vessels were gradually covered by a thin layer of soil.

That the people whose remains were laid to rest in the mound had been in contact with the de Soto expedition is confirmed by the numerous European artifacts found in the mound, many in direct association with the interred individuals. Most of these objects were perhaps given to the people by members of the de Soto expedition. The Gentleman of Elvas specifically says that such gifts were made (Elvas 1922:87, 149). Others may have been obtained from Spanish camps in the area. All of the materials were carefully recorded and studied by Mitchem (1989b: 436–468; also see Mitchem 1989a).

A total of 153 European glass beads were found, most of which had been worn by the native peoples as necklaces or ear ornaments or in some other fashion. Sixty-five were Nueva Cadiz beads (either plain or twisted) and twenty-two were faceted chevron beads. Other early sixteenth-century beads were also found.

Studies by Mitchem (1989a) have shown that some of the subtypes of Nueva Cadiz beads found at Tatham Mound have only been found additionally at the nearby Ruth Smith Mound and at the Weeki Wachee Mound, a site southwest of the Cove of the Withlacoochee, discussed below. One subtype of faceted chevron bead has only been found at those three sites and at the Poarch Farm site in northwest Georgia (believed to be a de Soto contact site), the St. Marks Wildlife Refuge Cemetery site on the coast of northwest Florida (thought to be near Aute, the coastal town visited by de Soto, see chapter 8), and the Fountain of Youth site in St. Augustine (thought to be the site of Pedro Menéndez de Avilés's first St. Augustine encampment). Still another variety of faceted chevron bead has come only from Tatham Mound, the St.

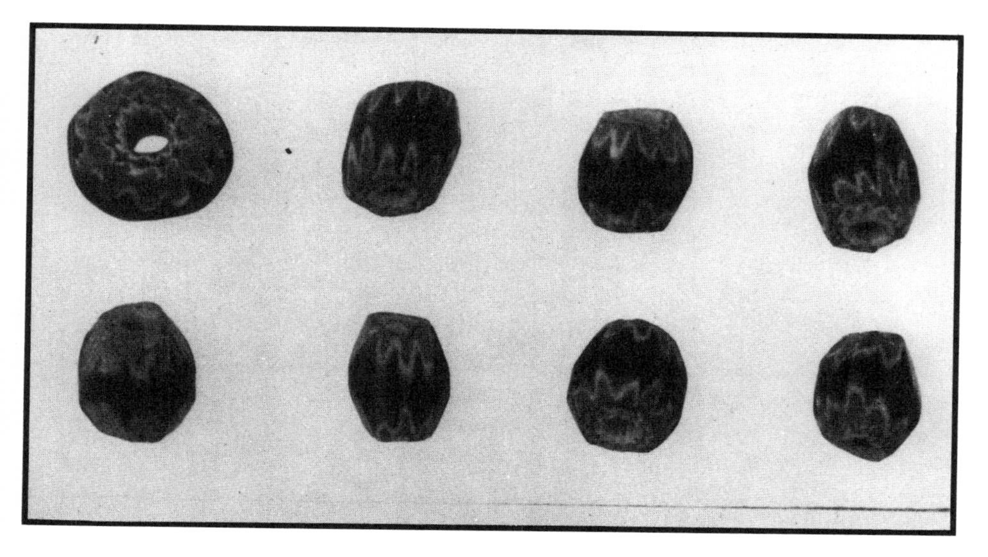

Figure 24

Faceted chevron glass beads from the Tatham Mound (courtesy Jeffrey Mitchem). The beads are less than half an inch long.

Marks site, and the Governor Martin site (location of Iniahica, de Soto's winter camp among the Apalachee; see chapter 8). Such evidence strongly ties these sites together as de Soto contact locations. The giving of beads as gifts to native peoples is mentioned by Elvas (1922:87, 149).

Many other European artifacts also were recovered by Mitchem from the Tatham Mound (1989b:452–468). Of the 298 metal beads from the site, 209 were associated with human burials, many with the same burials that had glass beads with them. The largest number of metal beads were fashioned by aboriginal artisans from Spanish silver. As Mitchem notes, the silver could have been salvaged from coastal shipwrecks, but it could also have been obtained from horse trappings or clothing decoration. Some beads were probably made from coins. Ranjel does note that chiefs were given gifts, including silver items (1922:90).

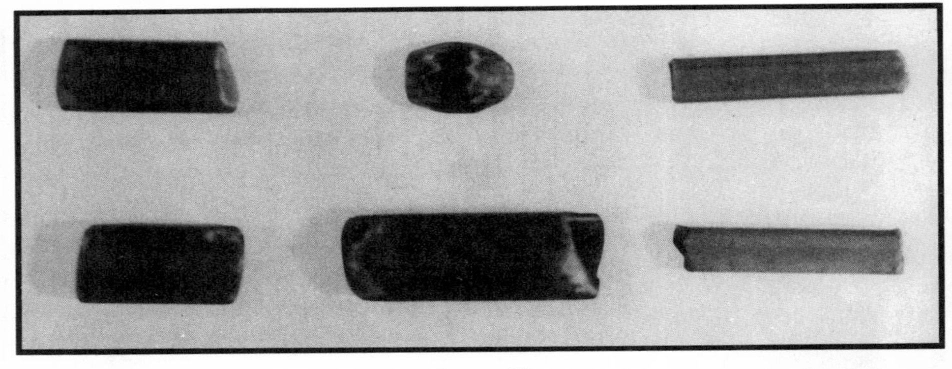

Figure 25

Five Nueva Cadiz Plain glass beads and one faceted chevron bead from Tatham Mound (courtesy Jeffrey Mitchem). The chevron bead is about half an inch long.

Included among the beads were several that were made from rolled pieces of gold. Brass or bronze items were also found in the mound.

One of the most interesting iron objects was a piece of Spanish armor found in the right hand of an elderly woman, one of the more than seventy probable epidemic victims. An iron plate, about two by four inches, was identified as either a piece of brigandine, a type of armor consisting of overlapping iron plates that were riveted to canvas material and worn, or a piece of jack armor. Jack plates were generally sewn on the inside of fabric rather than riveted (Mitchem 1989b:464–465).

The Tatham plate is most likely brigandine (Mitchem notes that both types of armor were worn by European infantry in the fifteenth and sixteenth centuries). A rivet hole and an intact rivet were present on one end of the specimen. Mitchem also noted evidence that the plate was tinned, a common practice to help prevent the formation of rust. The curvature of the plate indicates it is probably from one of the arms of a set of upper body (vest) brigandine.

The same woman had an iron bead around her neck. The bead had been made by breaking off one end of the same or another brigandine plate and rolling it lengthwise. A second rivet and holes were present in the bead. The rolled iron bead was very similar to the two large rolled iron beads noted above from the nearby Ruth Smith Mound.

Figure 26

The piece of armor, probably brigandine (top) from Tatham Mound, with the rolled iron bead (lower left) thought to have been made from a piece broken off the brigandine. The section of armor has a squash seed adhering to it.

Still other European metal objects came from the mound. Radiographs of an encrusted and rusty small mass of iron showed two small (about one-quarter inch in diameter) iron rings, one of which appeared to have a small rivet in it. The rings are probably from chain mail (Mitchem 1989b:456); similar rings have been found at the Governor Martin site in Tallahassee (chapter 8). Two iron chisels and a piece of a spike or nail were also recovered, along with fragments of what were probably other spikes or nails. One of the chisels, which was four and three-fourths inches long and five-eighths inches in diameter, was similar to a round cross-sectioned chisel from the Ruth Smith Mound. As a whole, the Tatham Mound represents perhaps one of the best-documented collections of de Soto expedition-related artifacts from anywhere on the entire route.

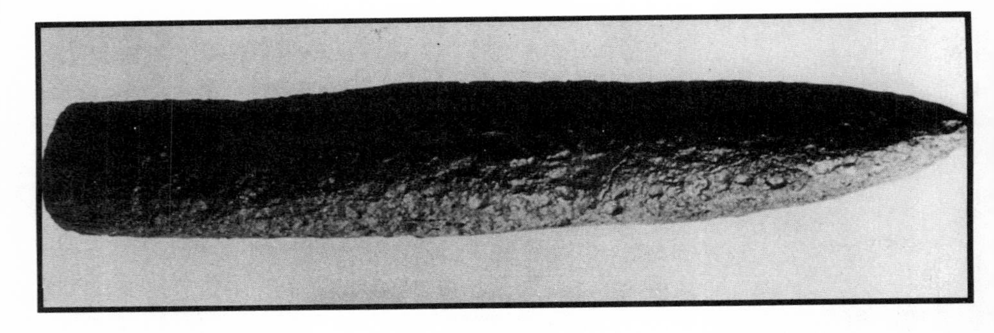

Figure 27

An iron chisel from Tatham Mound (courtesy Jeffrey Mitchem). It is just under six inches in length.

A third west-central Florida archaeological site containing evidence of early sixteenth-century Spanish contact should also be mentioned. The Weeki Wachee Mound (8HE12), located in eastern Hernando County, is off our reconstructed expedition route (it is about twenty-five miles easterly from our placement of Luca and Vicela), but it contains European artifacts similar to the Tatham and Ruth Smith mounds. Excavations at the site were carried out in 1970 by Robert Allen, then a University of Florida anthropology student (Mitchem, Smith, et al. 1985:181, 184–195, 200–211; Mitchem 1989b:41–42).

Like the Ruth Smith and Tatham mounds, Weeki Wachee was built by people associated with the Safety Harbor archaeological culture. It contained Safety Harbor pottery, along with human interments, both primary, flexed burials and secondary deposits of bones, as at Tatham Mound. And, as at Tatham, *Busycon* shell dippers had been placed on top of the final mound cap. The mound also contained more than 120 glass beads, all sixteenth-century types, including Nueva Cadiz, faceted-chevron, and striped beads; 151 silver beads; and 1 amber bead.

The variety and subtypes of beads are extremely similar to the two collections from the Cove of the Withlacoochee sites, sug-

Figure 28

Nueva Cadiz Plain glass beads from the Weeki Wachee Mound (courtesy Robert Allen). The largest are slightly more than an inch long.

gesting all three collections came from the same source. If indeed all three came from the de Soto expedition, why is the Weeki Wachee site so far removed from our reconstructed route? We are not certain why. Perhaps the region was contacted by de Soto's cavalry, scouting a day's ride to the side of the main army's march, or perhaps the people responsible for the mound were refugees, fleeing to the coastal region away from the aftermath of the de Soto expedition.

The Tatham Mound and, to a lesser extent, the Ruth Smith and Weeki Wachee sites are extraordinary time capsules containing actual evidence of that tragic encounter in 1539 between Indians and Spaniards. It offers us a poignant glimpse into the consequences of that encounter. On the one hand, the native peoples of Ocale must have been eager to obtain the metal objects brought by the Spaniards, items that were highly valued and quickly fashioned into jewelry. The decorative metal and glass beads were exotic goods brought from another world. They must have seemed wondrous to the native peoples. But along with the exotic objects came unknown diseases and military strife, battles in which new weapons and tactics triumphed. It is remarkable that despite the wholesale destruction of archaeological sites by modern construction and land-use activities, dramatic evidence of those events of 450 years ago can still be found in the Florida landscape.

CHAPTER V

NATIVE PEOPLES OF SOUTHERN AND CENTRAL FLORIDA

When a detailed reconstruction of de Soto's landing and the route he followed northward to Ocale is supplemented with documentary evidence from other sixteenth-century Spanish and French sources, it becomes possible to gain considerable insight into the locations of native groups. We also can learn something about their political interrelationships and their culture.

Using sketchy information from Juan Ponce de León's initial voyage (1513) and the Pánfilo de Narváez expedition (1528), as well as fuller information from the de Soto expedition (1539), the French excursions in the early 1560s, the activities of the Spaniards under Pedro Menéndez de Avilés (beginning in 1565), and the missionary activities of the Jesuits and the early Franciscans, we can begin putting together a historical account of at least some of Florida's native cultures. This can then be coupled with the later seventeenth-century record of the mission period to further chart the history of specific native groups and their experience with Europeans. It does not make for pleasant reading, because none of these native groups survived for very long.

The documentary information becomes even more valuable when it is combined with data garnered from archaeological research. Increasingly, we are able to correlate archaeological assemblages of the late pre-Columbian, early contact, and mission periods for specific named native groups. Such correlations allow the histories of specific native societies to be traced back in time hundreds of years prior to written records.

The information on the Florida native peoples during the colonial period also may be used in comparative studies. When the specific histories of the Florida natives are compared among themselves and with other New World native groups, we can begin to gain some understanding of the nature of the population reductions and the social and cultural changes that took place after 1492. Although anthropologists and others might agree on generalities concerning the impact of European contact and colonization on New World peoples, the specifics of the tragic events that took place are still very much debated. Were there pandemics affecting entire regions, or were there a series of local epidemics? Did depopulation occur in many areas even before the first European observers entered and recorded their observations? Did changes in Native American social structure occur immediately on contact with Europeans as a result of depopulation, or did they occur more gradually over many generations? Was the demographic impact of Old World diseases more severe among dense farming societies than it was among less demographically dense nonfarmers? Such questions are hard to answer, but they are crucially important if we are to explain the early historic period.

Two native societies in southern Florida illustrate how we can begin to build histories of Florida's native peoples in the early colonial period. The Tequesta and Calusa are perhaps the first two southeastern United States native societies to have come in contact with Europeans, and both are mentioned in the historical account of Juan Ponce's initial voyage to La Florida (Davis 1935). Both occupied territories south of Tampa Bay, south of the route of the de Soto expedition, and their names do not appear in the de Soto–related narratives. Nevertheless, they were important peoples whose colonial histories were intimately entwined with the early history of Spanish colonization in La Florida. Both peoples were also nonagriculturists, and it is instructive to compare their response to the European presence with that of the natives of central and northern Florida, nearly all of whom were agriculturists.

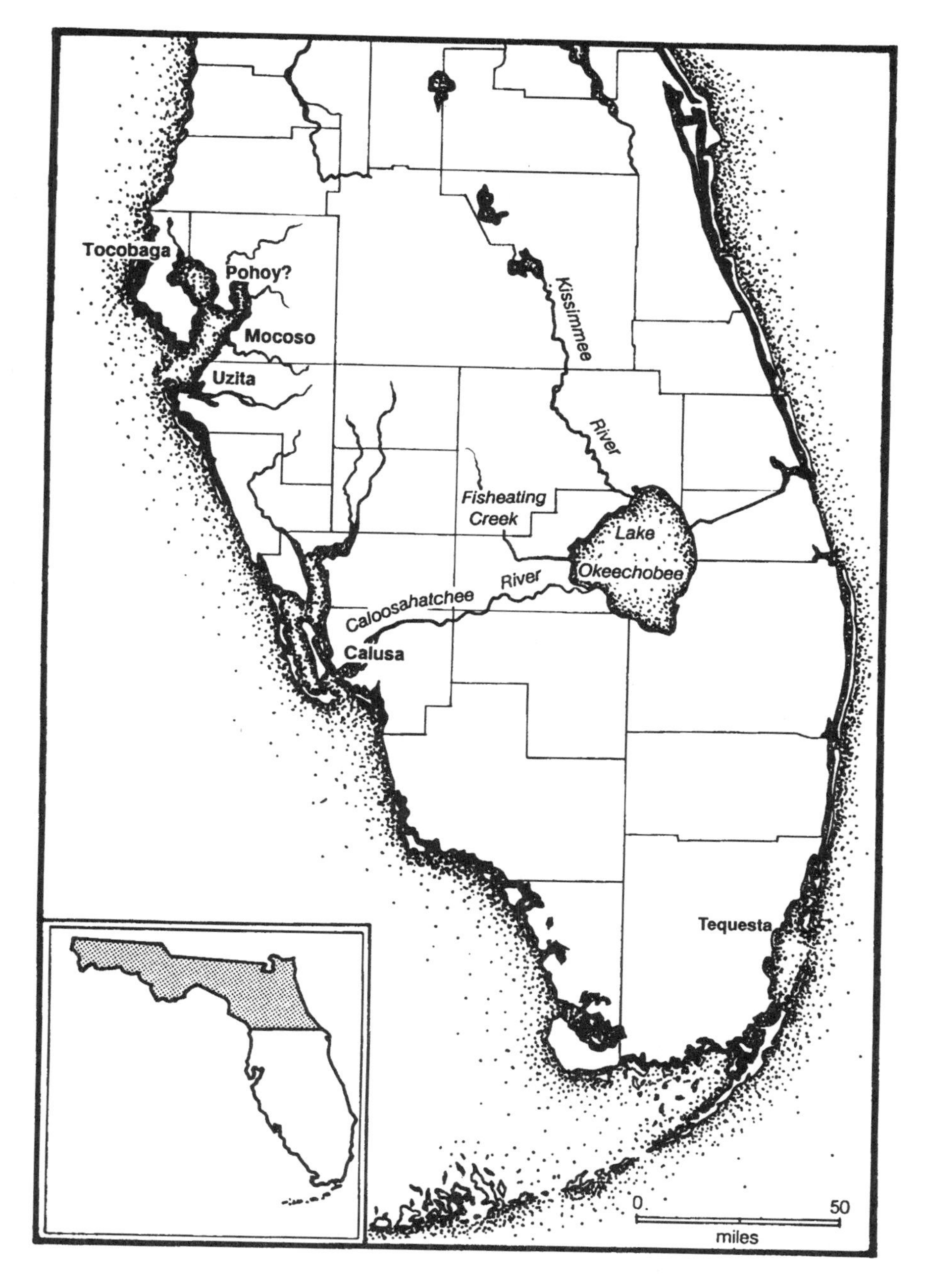

Figure 29

Native groups in south Florida and the Tampa Bay region (in bold).

THE TEQUESTA OF SOUTHEAST FLORIDA

The Tequesta Indians of the Miami area first were encountered by Juan Ponce in 1513, on his return voyage from the Gulf coast of Florida to the Caribbean. Hernando d'Escalante Fontaneda, a Spaniard shipwrecked in south Florida in 1545 for seventeen years, also mentions the Tequesta. According to Fontaneda, the Tequesta lived at the north end of the Keys on the bank of a river, probably the Miami River, that extended into the interior fifteen leagues (True 1945:27). This is the same location given by Juan Ponce and verified by Juan López de Velasco, writing in the early 1570s, and by other early Spanish historians (see True 1945:42; for ethnographic information, see Goggin 1940; McNicoll 1941). Mutinous members of the Menéndez expedition reached Tequesta in 1566, and in March 1567 a Jesuit missionary was placed there along with a garrison of thirty soldiers and a few carpenters (Solís de Merás 1964:232; Hann 1990:428). Twenty-eight houses and a small church were built, but both the mission and garrison (with only eighteen surviving soldiers) were abandoned the next year. In 1568 Spaniards returned to the site, but they left again in 1570. The Spaniards were aided in their return by a Christianized native leader who had been taken to Spain by Pedro Menéndez de Avilés in 1567 (see chapter 7). These early accounts all refer to a chief called Tequesta, said to be a relative of Chief Carlos of the Calusa and in the past subject to him (Solís de Merás 1964:222, 224). Apparently Tequesta had opted for independence, and a state of war existed between Carlos and him.

The same documents that mention Chief Tequesta also refer to a province or land of the same name. As Garcilaso de la Vega noted, based on interviews with survivors of the de Soto expedition, the native peoples of La Florida used the same name for their "lord and his lands as well as his principal village" (Varner and Varner 1951:93). Modern researchers have applied the same name to the people themselves. Thus, we write about the Tequesta or Potano or Calusa peoples. Just how the natives referred to themselves is uncertain, but some evidence indicates that when asked by the Europeans what a location was called, the natives responded "our land." This is the case with Uti-na, the name of a north Florida chief visited by the French and by

Menéndez in the 1560s, which literally means "my land" in the Timucuan language (Granberry 1989:187).

It is perhaps significant that in 1568 a letter written by Francisco de Villareal, a Jesuit missionary lay brother stationed at Tequesta, states that several of the villagers—an infant, several children, and an old woman—were sick and that the infant and old woman both died. The letter recounts happenings over an eight-month period, during which time the two deaths were extraordinary events that received special attention in Villareal's letter to his superior. Evidently the lay brother did not witness any epidemics in the short time he was at Tequesta. Following the demise of the Jesuit mission, the name Tequesta only occasionally appears in contemporary Spanish documents or accounts of south Florida, the only exception being documents dealing with the reasons for the failure of the mission and garrison. What happened? Can we assume the Tequesta were wiped out by disease, perhaps by an epidemic after the Spanish pulled out? That seems unlikely, and the reason is germane to a history of other southern Florida groups, who, like the Tequesta, were nonagricultural and presumably less sedentary than northern Florida agriculturists. As noted above, the name Tequesta, first recorded by Juan Ponce, was a place name that the Spanish used to refer to a locale and to the people who lived there. If, in later times, the Tequesta moved to a new location, the Spanish might well refer to them by the name of the new place, often designated by a European word. Thus, from the late sixteenth century well into the eighteenth, groups mentioned for southeast Florida include the Cayos (Keys), Boca Ratones, Santaluces, and Vizcayanos (see Sturtevant 1978). Clearly, all of these are Spanish place-names used to refer to native groups. Apparently the Spanish collectively called such people "Indios de la Costa." It is likely that some of these people were descendants of the Tequesta or were related to them. This was clear to the Spanish. In 1765 the Spanish cosmographer Hernán de Martínez noted that the "Indians of the Tequesta Nation, . . . today are called Costas" (Parks 1985:51).

In 1743 the site of Tequesta was again the scene of an attempt by the Spanish to establish a Jesuit mission and a fort (Sturtevant 1978). Among the 180 aborigines at the mission were remnants of people from three "nations": the Keys Indians, the Calusa, and the Boca Ratones. The latter are possibly descendants of the sixteenth-century Tequesta because a map accompanying the mission report assigns the name Boca Raton to Miami Beach, across Biscayne Bay from the original site of Tequesta at the mouth of the Miami River. Earlier, in 1675, the aborigines at the exact same rivermouth location were called Vizcayanos, from which modern Biscayne Bay receives its name. A great deal of archaeology has been done at the Granada site located at the mouth of the Miami River, and there is no evidence of any material culture changes in the historic period (Griffin 1975:380). The archaeological assemblages of the Tequesta, Vizcayanos, and Boca Ratones are the same, suggesting that they are the same or closely related groups.

What can be learned from this exercise? First, descendants of the aborigines in southeast Florida first contacted by Europeans in 1513 were still living in approximately the same location in 1743. Apparently, the massive epidemics that struck the Caribbean peoples immediately after contact did not take place in south Florida or were not as severe. An epidemiologist might suggest that one reason is that the native populations in southeast Florida were not as dense as those of the Taino or other Caribbean agriculturists. Another possibility is that European activities in southeast Florida were more sporadic and involved fewer people than in the Caribbean. And the Florida Indians were not enslaved for work in mines or otherwise maltreated, as were the Taino on Hispaniola.

Another observation is that when the name Tequesta disappears from Spanish documents, reference to a dominant Tequesta chief or leader who politically interacts with other native chiefs or the Spanish also disappears. Does this reflect the demise of the fragile Tequesta chiefdom, one that probably originated and was maintained in response to interaction with the powerful Calusa? Probably it does. Tequesta political structure could not be sustained in the face of a declining population, even if the rate of demographic decline was less than for agricultural groups. The Tequesta population, not as large as the Calusa or north Florida groups to begin with, grew too small to maintain. As the chiefdom broke apart, the surviving Tequesta moved about and amalgamated with other survivors, forming small groups that the Spanish later called by place-names, such as the Boca Ratones.

As we shall see, the experience of the Tequesta, a small nonagricultural group, was different from that of the larger Calusa chiefdom, another nonagricultural people, as well as from the farming chiefdoms of north Florida. But, as discussed below in this chapter, the Tequesta did share some experiences with the small, nonagricultural groups of Tampa Bay among whom de Soto landed. But before looking at those Tampa Bay societies, such as the Uzita and Mocoso, let us briefly recount the history of the Calusa, another of the southern peoples contacted in 1513 by Juan Ponce.

THE CALUSA OF SOUTHWEST FLORIDA

Another south Florida society, the Calusa, inhabited coastal southwest Florida, especially the many offshore islands with their rich, adjacent estuaries. The Calusa developed a large chiefdom based on the collection of wild foods from those estuaries rather than from farming (Widmer 1988). A great deal of archaeological and ethnohistorical work has been done on the colonial period and pre-Columbian Calusa (see Goggin and Sturtevant 1964; Lewis 1978; Marquardt 1987, 1988).

The account of Juan Ponce de León's initial voyage to southwest Florida mentions Chief Calos of the Calusa (the Spaniards called him Carlos). There is no doubt that Calos, whose territory extended from Charlotte Harbor to the Ten Thousand Islands, was the most powerful chief in south Florida. For whatever motive, he made himself felt far and wide, and he is named in many Spanish accounts of the sixteenth century.

It is thus noteworthy that the Calusa are not mentioned in the de Soto narratives. Except for the Indians of Urriparacoxi, who told the Spaniards about warfare between Ocale and Indians far to the south, who supposedly wore golden helmets, perhaps a reference to the Calusa, there is no specific mention of Chief Calos or of the Calusa in the de Soto documents. This has been taken by some as evidence that de Soto did not land at Charlotte Harbor, for if he had, so the argument goes, he would have at least heard of Chief Calos (see, e.g., Swanton 1939:21).

According to Hernando d'Escalante Fontaneda, Calos controlled a large territory—some fifty towns in all—along the southwest coast and in the interior of south Florida around Lake Okeechobee (True 1945:30–31). Fontaneda, whose secondhand knowledge of the geography of La Florida is somewhat confused, also claims Calos controlled two towns in the "Lucayos," the

Bahama Islands, but from other things said in his narrative it is clear enough that his "Lucayos" are actually part of the Florida Keys or other south Florida barrier islands. He also says that Calos had at least partial control over the Tequesta, the Ais, and the Jeaga (on the coast north of the Tequesta) and over some of the interior south Florida groups north of Lake Okeechobee (True 1945:35). When any of the south Florida natives salvaged wrecked Spanish ships, Calos was apparently able to demand that he be paid a portion of the goods in tribute.

The extent of Calos's power and renown is illustrated by an incident involving René de Laudonnière, who, in the early 1560s, was the commander of the French Huguenots at Fort Caroline, near the mouth of the St. Johns River. Some Indians were sent to Laudonnière by Chief Marracou, whose territory was probably near Ponce de León Inlet (Laudonnière 1975:109). They told Laudonnière about two Europeans who were living among Indians. One of these was living with Chief Mathiaca, whose territory, according to the Le Moyne map (Lorant 1946:34–35), was on the upper St. Johns River near Lake George. Mathiaca possibly means "freshwater town" in Timucua. Chief Mathiaca's people may have been one of the groups speaking the Agua Dulce (Freshwater) dialect of Timucuan (Pareja 1627:36–37), and are probably a distinct group from the more southerly dwelling Mayaca (see chapter 7). The second European, a man whom the Indians called Barbu, lived with Chief Oathchaqua, whose domain the Le Moyne map shows at Cape Kennedy, but who, as we shall see, must have lived farther south.

Laudonnière offered a reward for these men, and the Indians brought them to him. Both of the men were naked like Indians and wore their hair long, down to their loins. They were so thoroughly acculturated to Indian ways that at first they found the manners of the French to be strange. The two men were Spaniards who had been on a fleet of three ships which wrecked fifteen years earlier in the Florida Keys. Along with others, they had been captured by Calos, who also salvaged the greater part of the riches that the ships carried. Each year Calos would sacrificially kill one of the male Spaniards he had captured. The castaways included three or four young women who had married Indians and had children. The two rescued men told Laudonnière that in one of his villages Calos had a store of gold and silver sufficient to fill a hole in the ground as deep as a man's height and as big around as a barrel (Laudonnière 1975:110). Calos got most of this precious metal from shipwrecks, but also from trade with other Indians, who in turn probably got it from shipwrecks.

Barbu told Laudonnière that he had served Calos as a messenger for a long time and that on several occasions he had been ordered to go visit Chief Oathchaqua who lived four or five days away. Between Calos and Oathchaqua there was a large freshwater lake. On the Le Moyne map (Lorant 1946:34–35) Oathchaqua is shown at Cape Canaveral, but from Calos to Cape Canaveral it is about 185 miles. To travel this distance in five days Barbu would have had to go 37 miles per day—not likely. Oathchaqua was probably closer to present Melbourne or Fort Pierce, at 168 and 120 miles respectively from Calos, a distance that Barbu could have traveled in five days at 34 miles per day for the former and at 24 miles per day for the latter.

In the freshwater lake there was a large "island" called Serrope that was said to be five leagues from side to side. The freshwater lake could have been Lake Okeechobee and the wet prairies surrounding it. The "island" was probably the higher ground between Fisheating Creek and the Kissimmee River on the northwesterly side of the lake. This area is about seventeen miles from side to side, about five leagues in all. According to Barbu, this area abounded in fruits, especially palms that bore dates. The Indians of Serrope traded these dates to other Indians, and they also traded bread that they made from the root of a plant which grew there. Other Indians greatly desired this bread.

Moreover, according to Barbu the Indians of Serrope had the reputation of being exceedingly belligerent. As an example, Barbu told Laudonnière of an incident in which Calos was trying to form a marriage alliance with Oathchaqua. But when Oathchaqua was en route with his daughter, who was to be married to Calos, the Indians of Serrope learned about the coming marriage, and they laid an ambush. The ambush was successful, and they captured the bride-to-be along with her attendants. These captured women were taken as wives by men of Serrope. This capture was considered by the Serrope to have been a great victory and it could only have been thus regarded by people for whom marriage alliance was a major part of their political life. After this defeat, Barbu escaped from Calos and went to live with Oathchaqua (Laudonnière 1975:111–112).

After defeating the French at Fort Caroline in 1565, Pedro Menéndez sought to establish missions and garrisons along both coasts of La Florida. One such outpost was at Tequesta, as we have already seen, and in 1566 another was at Calos, the main town of the Calusa, thought to be on Mound Key in Estero Bay, south of Fort Myers (see Lewis 1978). As at Tequesta, houses for the Spanish soldiers were built along with a chapel. The Jesuit mission and garrison were removed in 1569 (Hann 1990:427), but Calusa-Spanish contacts continued, albeit sporadically, throughout the seventeenth century, as Spanish slavers, traders, and fishermen all traveled to the southwest Florida coast.

In 1697 the Franciscans tried unsuccessfully to establish a mission among the Calusa. At that time the Calusa chiefdom still was functioning, and the Calusa still inhabited their traditional lands (Hann 1991b). Almost two centuries after Juan Ponce first landed among them, the Calusa apparently were maintaining their way of life.

Like the Tequesta, the Calusa were not immediately decimated by sixteenth-century epidemics. We have more than 600 printed pages of correspondence from the Jesuits involved in the mission efforts in La Florida during the 1560s and much of it deals with the Calusa (Zubillaga 1946; Hann 1991b). Those letters contain no references to epidemics and almost none to illness. This is in stark contrast to midsixteenth-century Jesuit letters from missions in eastern Brazil. Those documents record the epidemics that follow one after the other, killing thousands of people at a time (Hemming 1978). Such epidemics did not occur among the Calusa during the time the Jesuits were attempting to establish their mission. Epidemics may have taken place in the sixteenth and seventeenth centuries, but if they did, the Calusa population continued to rebound, staying at a level that allowed the Calusa to maintain their way of life.

But neither that way of life nor the Calusa population continued into the eighteenth century. By 1743, when the Jesuits attempted to reestablish a mission at the mouth of the Miami River to serve remnant south Florida native groups, the Calusa had been decimated, their way of life had been destroyed, and they no longer were residing in their traditional lands. The cause of this relatively rapid change was probably twofold. First, as early as 1704, Indians allied with the English began raiding into Florida, even as far as the south end of the peninsula. One priest said that by 1743 the "Uchises" (i.e., Creeks) were raiding all of the way to the Florida Keys (Sturtevant 1978:145) and were instrumental in reducing the "nation" of the aboriginal inhabitants to only a few families. Second, the growth of the Cuban-based fishing industry, which used south Florida Indians for labor, apparently enticed people to move to the Keys and other locations.

Sturtevant (1978) has used contemporary Spanish documents to chronicle the demise of the Calusa and other south Florida aborigines in the period ca. 1700–1748. During that time, some of the Calusa and other peoples were removed to Cuba where most died of disease. By 1743 only a few hundred natives remained.

That the Calusa survived and prospered as long as they did may be a product of several factors. (1) Their initial population may have been large enough to rebound from disease epidemics. (2) Because their population was not as dense of that of agriculturists, epidemics may have been less severe. (3) The Calusa were not crowded into missions, thus increasing the opportunities for disease vectors, nor were they enslaved for work in mines or on plantations, nor were they subjected to military encounters by the de Soto expedition. (4) Although the Calusa were in contact with Europeans for a long period, that contact involved fewer people and was more sporadic than was the case with other Florida natives. The Calusa were finally brought down as a result of military engagements with northern Indians who raided them and changes brought by the Cuban fishing industry. Interacting with Cuban fishermen and other native groups also may have exposed them to Old World diseases.

INDIANS OF THE TAMPA BAY REGION

What can we learn about the Uzita, Mocoso, and other native groups around Tampa Bay who were in contact with the de Soto and other Spanish expeditions? Did they undergo patterns of depopulation and change similar to those of the Tequesta and Calusa in southern Florida?

Hernando de Soto's landing in Tampa Bay had been preceded eleven years earlier in 1528 by the Pánfilo de Narváez expedition. However, the one account of the Narváez trek through La Florida provides no information on the east and south Tampa Bay aborigines (although, according to Garcilaso, de Soto's expedition cited evidence that Narváez had shown great cruelty toward Uzita [Varner and Varner 1951:60–61, 68]). Our history of those peoples begins in 1539 with de Soto and his army, a portion of which camped at Tampa Bay interacting on an almost daily basis with the Uzita for about five months. The de Soto expedition also came into contact with the Mocoso and heard of still more native groups, e.g., the Neguarete and the Capaloey, said by Mocoso to be led by chiefs who threatened him because he had befriended de Soto (Ranjel 1922:57–58). Other chiefs were Ecita (Uzita) and the Orriygua (Hirrihigua).

The impact of de Soto's army on the Uzita and Mocoso was quite different from that of the other Spaniards on the south Florida natives. De Soto had many more Spaniards with him than were with Menéndez. And de Soto's army routinely enslaved aboriginal women for sexual favors and men as porters. When the expedition traveled north from Tampa Bay a number of Indians were shackled and forcibly made to accompany the expedition all the way to Apalachee. De Soto did not hesitate to use force, even excessive force, fighting pitched battles. As a consequence, the Tampa Bay peoples suffered more severely from the early Spanish presence than did the Tequesta or the Calusa.

Archaeologists have long noted the presence of true temple mounds in the Tampa Bay region, mounds similar to those found among pre-Columbian chiefdoms in the interior of the southeastern United States (see Bullen 1955:60–63; Luer and Almy 1981). The mounds and other archaeological attributes, along with the descriptions from the de Soto narratives, make it clear that the native peoples around Tampa Bay either were organized as chiefdoms or that they had leaders who acted in a chiefly fashion in response to military and political initiatives brought by other native groups, such as the Urriparacoxi. All of the de Soto chroniclers refer to caciques, or chiefs, among the Tampa Bay groups (Biedma 1922:1; Elvas 1922:22; Ranjel 1922:54, 57). Cacique is an Arawakan word common in the Caribbean and brought to La Florida by the Spanish. One of Garcilaso's informants remembered that the chief was entitled to a special "salute" or greeting, and a kinship tie between Mocoso and Urriparacoxi is mentioned (Varner and Varner 1951:71, 93), although this may have been a political relationship symbolized as fictive kinship. It is clear that the chief of Uzita had a special house (Elvas 1922:23), and Ranjel (1922:57) refers to a chief's *wives*, suggesting that the chief practiced polygyny.

Villages contained both huts and a large building (a council house?), said to be like those seen in the West Indies. Isolated huts or groups of huts were also noted (Elvas 1922:25; Ranjel 1922:52, 58). Mocoso's town had a structure for the storage of human remains. In his captivity, Juan Ortiz had been made to guard the charnel house, and on one occasion his life was jeopardized when a large carnivore entered the building and took the body of the son of a principal man (Elvas 1922:28–29). This suggests that the charnel house or temple was for the deposition of the remains of relatives of the high-ranking or chiefly kin group. Such a practice, tied to an ancestor cult, would be typical of a chiefdom (see Brown 1985).

The Tampa Bay aborigines (and all the native peoples encountered by de Soto's army) were expert archers. Their bows, as tall as a man, shot cane arrows tipped with fishbones or spines and stone points (Elvas 1922:22, 26; Ranjel 1922:54–55, 69). The latter undoubtedly were the arrowheads called Pinellas Points by archaeologists (Bullen 1975:8). Warriors were agile enough to avoid arrows which were shot at them (Elvas 1922:25).

Other traits that are mentioned in the de Soto accounts are tattooing on arms, the wearing of red paint (ocher?) and feathers, beads made from pearls, possibly shell beads made from nacre (the iridescent inner layer of some mollusks), and the use of smoke to signal over long distances (Elvas 1922:22, 23, 26; Ranjel 1922:56).

Although the Uzita and Mocoso were independent political units, perhaps chiefdoms or bigman societies, their territories and presumably their populations were much smaller than those de Soto's army encountered in the southeastern interior. The territory of Uzita appears to have extended from the mouth of the Little Manatee River southward to Sarasota Bay. It would have included a number of mound and village archaeological sites, including Harbor Key, the Bickel Mound, Snead Island, Pillsbury Mound site, Whitaker Mound, and the Thomas Mound and adjacent village areas. The territory of Uzita may also have included inland sites, such as some of the Parrish mounds and the Old Myakka site (Luer and Almy 1981:128).

The Indians whom General Vasco Porcallo de Figueroa attacked on an island were probably people of Uzita, and the island could have been Harbor Key, the Bickel site (actually on a peninsula), or Snead Island. The natives whom captain Juan Ruiz Lobillo captured on June 7 were probably living in a small village up the Little Manatee River. And the Indians whom Juan de Añasco attacked on an island were probably on one of the islands in the channel of the Little Manatee River, or else along the edge of Tampa Bay near the mouth of the Little Manatee River. Again, all of these were probably Indians of Uzita.

The territory of Mocoso lay around Hillsborough Bay and on the Alafia and Hillsborough rivers. Mocoso's territory would have included the Mill Point site, the Fort Brooke mound site, and possibly the Bull Frog Creek and Picnic Mound sites. It may have included the Jones Mound southeast of Lake Thonotosassa. The people of Uzita and Mocoso spoke mutually unintelligible languages, which seems odd, though perhaps both were dialects of Timucuan. Given the level of hostility that existed between Uzita and Mocoso, it would make sense that the area between the Little Manatee and Alafia rivers was an uninhabited or sparsely inhabited buffer zone. Juan Ortiz traveled through this area when he escaped from Uzita to Mocoso, reaching the Alafia River, the boundary of Mocoso's territory (Elvas 1922:32).

After the de Soto army left Tampa Bay, the names of the Uzita and the Mocoso appear to have never again been mentioned specifically in written records. Fontaneda, writing in 1575 about his experiences in southern Florida in 1545–1562, does mention the separate "kingdom" of Mogoso (True 1945:30, 31, 38). But whether this is the Mocoso of de Soto is uncertain. On his map of La Florida, Jacques Le Moyne places "Mocosso" south (inland?) of Ocale in the St. Johns drainage. He also places "Mocossou" on the east coast, south of Cape Canaveral (Lorant 1946:34–35). If, as some historians think, Fontaneda was rescued in 1562 by the French and then returned to Spain, it is possible that his geographical knowledge was influential to the Frenchmen's knowledge of Florida geography and Le Moyne's map. On the other hand, Fontaneda's knowledge might have come from the French, who traveled southward up the St. Johns River on several occasions. On one trip they were told about a chief named "Moquoso," who, like the "Acquera," apparently lived somewhere within the St. Johns drainage (Laudonnière 1975:76). The situation is further complicated by Solís de Merás's (1964:204) account of Menéndez's voyage up the St. Johns River in 1566 that reached the territory of Chief Macoya, thought to be a corruption of Mayaca, a group that Fontaneda also mentions (True 1945:34). It seems likely that the St. Johns–region Mogoso and the Tampa Bay Mocoso were different people.

The Uzita, like the Mocoso, receive no mention in post–de Soto sixteenth- and seventeenth-century documents. No additional expeditions were sent to either group; no missionaries ever arrived to administer to them. What happened? Did these small groups and their populations also disappear? Clearly, the Uzita and the Mocoso were flourishing in late spring 1539 when de Soto and his army landed among them, although the extent of the impact of the Narváez expedition on them is unknown. But that state of well-being did not continue. The military actions of de Soto's army and the enslavement of many of the native peoples must have been devastating. If epidemics occurred, they would have been even more potent among populations shrunken by battle, forced servitude, and enslavement. Unlike the Tequesta and the Calusa, the Uzita and the Mocoso may not have survived long as viable political units.

What of the other Tampa Bay peoples who were not so severely impacted by de Soto? The "Capaloey," whom Chief Mocoso mentioned, are most likely the same group called Pohoy, Pooy, and Pojoi in various Spanish documents. The Pohoy were residing on the same bay as the Tocobaga (Tocopaca) when they were visited in 1612 by the detachment of Spanish soldiers who traveled from the mouth of the Suwannee River down the coast and around Pinellas Peninsula into Tampa Bay (called the "Bay of Pohoy") in dugout canoes (Quinn 1976:137). It is likely that the people of Pohoy inhabited some part of upper Tampa Bay or the region surrounding it. Some of the Pohoy were in northwest Florida ca. 1718–1719 when they raided a group of Tocobaga living at St. Marks (Hann 1989b:193, 198). In the 1730s, Antonio Pojoi was said to be the chief of the Alafaias Costas group of Indians, residing near St. Augustine.

Another group mentioned by Chief Mocoso, the Neguarete, do not appear again in any known documentary records. Perhaps they also lived on or around Tampa Bay, but their fate is unknown.

It is striking that the name "Tocobaga" does not show up in any of the de Soto documents. By the Menéndez era the Tocobaga, who lived on the north side of Tampa Bay, probably in

Old Tampa Bay, were the most important group in the region (Zubillaga 1946:272–277, 291–297, 303–304; Solís de Merás 1964:223–230, 242). A number of archaeological sites in the locality of the town of Safety Harbor on the bay contain Spanish artifacts, some of which probably came from the Menéndez excursion into the area in 1567.[1]

Of all the people who lived around Tampa Bay the Tocobaga appear to have been the only ones who cultivated corn. Some of Pánfilo de Narváez's men apparently found corn here, as well as another field of corn ten or twelve leagues away (Bandelier 1905:12–13). But compared with locales further north on de Soto's route, one gets the impression that there was not a great quantity of corn at this place.

Chief Tocobaga met with Menéndez and told him that he had known for a long time about the Spaniards and their treatment of the native peoples, including their raiding for maize. The chief spoke of his principal men and of other chiefs who were vassals to him and who apparently lived up to two days away. In a show of their support for him, Tocobaga assembled twenty-nine of these vassal chiefs at his village. Tocobaga also maintained a temple (Solís de Merás 1964:226–228).

Menéndez left thirty soldiers to establish a garrison among the Tocobaga and to teach them the Christian doctrine. When the Jesuit priest Father Juan Rogel visited the outpost several months later, it was "in good health and spirits," although Chief Tocobaga, who attended a Mass celebrated by Father Rogel, had threatened that if their idols were burned, he and his family would immolate themselves in the fire (Lyon 1976:202).

In January 1568 the Spaniards again returned to Tocobaga, but this time they did not find a flourishing Spanish-Indian village and garrison. All of the Spaniards had been killed and the bodies of only two soldiers could be found. The village itself was abandoned; the Indians had withdrawn beyond the reach of Spanish retribution. All the Spanish commander of the expedition could do was to burn the village and withdraw (Zubillaga 1946:274–311; Lyon 1976:203).

During his sojourn in south Florida, Fontaneda had also heard of Tocobaga. He reports that Chief Tocobaga was the "chief cacique" of his Gulf-coast region, an "independent king" with "many vassals," who controlled the regional pearl trade (True 1945:29). Fontaneda's knowledge cannot always be trusted, because much of it was based on hearsay. He states that Tocobaga was located on a large river where de Soto had been (and where he died, which, of course, he did not). Fontaneda also advanced the idea of a cross-state river passage, believing that the St. Johns River connected with a river or led into a river that in turn flowed to Tampa Bay and the Tocobaga (True 1945:36). Pedro Menéndez sought such a route, and for this reason he was interested in the Calusa and Tocobaga and establishing settlements among them (Lyon 1976:141–142, 176, 1989:159). (With higher water levels in the past, it may have been possible to traverse Florida from the Gulf to the St. Johns River, employing some land portages.)

How could Tocobaga have been so powerful by the 1560s, yet not even have been mentioned in the de Soto narratives, despite being only forty miles away from de Soto's landing site? One suggestion is that after 1539 and the probable demise of Uzita's and Mocoso's power (and Urriparacoxi's?), due to the impact of de Soto's expedition, Tocobaga, located on the northern end of the bay away from the landing site and the region reconnoitered by the Spaniards, was able to consolidate political power at the expense of those other Tampa Bay–region chiefs. He may not have been able to do so in 1539.

The Tocobaga were still living on Tampa Bay in 1612 when the Spanish military expedition to the Bay of Pohoy took place (Quinn 1976), but there is no information by which one can gauge their political might. The Tocobaga continued to exist as a distinct group for another century. By 1677, a number of Tocobaga men, women, and children were living as non-Christians under Spanish protection at Wacissa in the province of Apalachee (Hann 1988:41–42). In 1718 two small groups of Tocobaga were living near Fort San Marcos—one on the Gulf coast proper, near the mouth of the St. Marks River, and one upstream a short distance (Hann 1988:407–408). It was the St. Marks group that was raided by the Pohoy. Reasons for the Tocobaga's initial move to northwest Florida are not clear. The Tocobaga may have been the victims of raids by Alabama or Georgia Indians and may have sought protection from the Spanish, or the Tocobaga may have been a population that the Spanish moved from Tampa Bay to use as a labor force.

INLAND NATIVE GROUPS

Another central Florida group contacted by the de Soto expedition was the Urriparacoxi, located twenty to thirty leagues inland from the bay. In contrast to the Uzita and Mocoso, who were said not to cultivate corn, the Urriparacoxi were said to cultivate large fields of corn, beans, and pumpkins (de Soto 1866:161). De Soto may have been exaggerating somewhat in order to impress some of the financial backers of his expedition. Elvas (1922:32–33) does state that Urriparacoxi was in a fertile area with maize, a contrast to Ranjel's description of Tampa Bay as having poor quality soils (Ranjel 1922:60).

Urriparacoxi, living in the interior, clearly was the most powerful chief in the region. Uzita, Mocoso, and the other chiefs around Tampa Bay were subsidiary to Urriparacoxi and paid tribute to him (Biedma 1922:5; Ranjel 1922:32–33). This pattern—villages of people who were primarily coastal or riverine fishers being subsidiary to agriculturalists—is found also, as we have seen, among the Tocobaga and Tampa Bay–region groups in the 1560s. And the same pattern was present on the eastern side of the Florida peninsula. In the 1560s, when visited by the French and then the Spanish, a number of towns within the St. Johns River drainage were subject to a chief named Utina. His main town lay five leagues west of the river and his people practiced agriculture (Solís de Merás 1964:206–208; Laudonnière 1975:76,132–133). The Utina will be discussed more fully in chapter 7.

Urriparacoxi, Tocobaga, and Utina were apparently located on better agricultural soil than were the towns which were subject to them. This would seem to confirm what southeastern archaeologists have long thought. That is, agricultural production conferred a competitive or military advantage, and this was one of the principal ingredients in the chiefdom societies that dominated the late pre-Columbian Southeast. Ironically, it is in peninsular Florida, on the margin of the large Mississippian chiefdoms, that these economic realities are most clearly seen.

The portions of the narratives recounting the trek of de Soto's army northward from Tampa Bay to Ocale provide little information on the native societies or their political affiliations. The Spaniards saw the first cornfields four days north of their Tampa Bay camp, around present Dade City. Elvas (1922:37, 38), however, notes that the Cove of the Withlacoochee was "thin of maize," in contrast to Ocale proper and Acuera. He also mentions that the maize was pounded in log mortars with a hand-held pestle. From the narratives, we are left with the impression that the town of Luca may be on the western edge of territory controlled by Urriparacoxi, while a portion of the Cove of the Withlacoochee may have been controlled by Ocale, who lived on the eastern side.

After de Soto, the Spaniards apparently never again penetrated these interior portions of Florida north and east of Tampa Bay. Nothing is known of the fate of Urriparacoxi, the mighty interior war chief, or of Guacozo, Luca, or Vicela. As we have seen in chapter 4, both Ocale and Acuera existed in the midseventeenth century when they were the focus of Franciscan missionary efforts. Hann's study of a document from ca. 1678 indicates that at least some non-Christian Acuera still existed at that time (1991b, and see chapter 7).

ARCHAEOLOGICAL CORRELATIONS

The Uzita on the southern side of Tampa Bay, the Mocoso on the eastern side of the bay, and the Tocobaga around Old Tampa Bay all are associated with the Safety Harbor archaeological culture. Variants of that culture extend northward into the Cove of the Withlacoochee, encompassing the Withlacoochee River itself (Mitchem 1989b). The Ocale may have been associated with one of these geographical variants, as are all of the sixteenth-century groups in the region between Mocoso's territory and the Ocale. Although pottery found in village sites in Ocale, east of the Withlacoochee River, is like that found in Safety Harbor sites, as yet no Safety Harbor mounds have been located east of that river.

The Safety Harbor culture and its variants are quite distinct from the Alachua tradition archaeological culture found along the route de Soto followed north from Ocale as he marched toward the Santa Fe River. Safety Harbor culture is also distinct from the archaeological culture found south of Tampa Bay in the Caloosahatchee/southwest Florida coastal region believed to be associated with the Calusa Indians and their pre-Columbian ancestors.

The archaeological culture of the Urriparacoxi is less certain. Artifact collections examined by Mitchem from mounds and col-

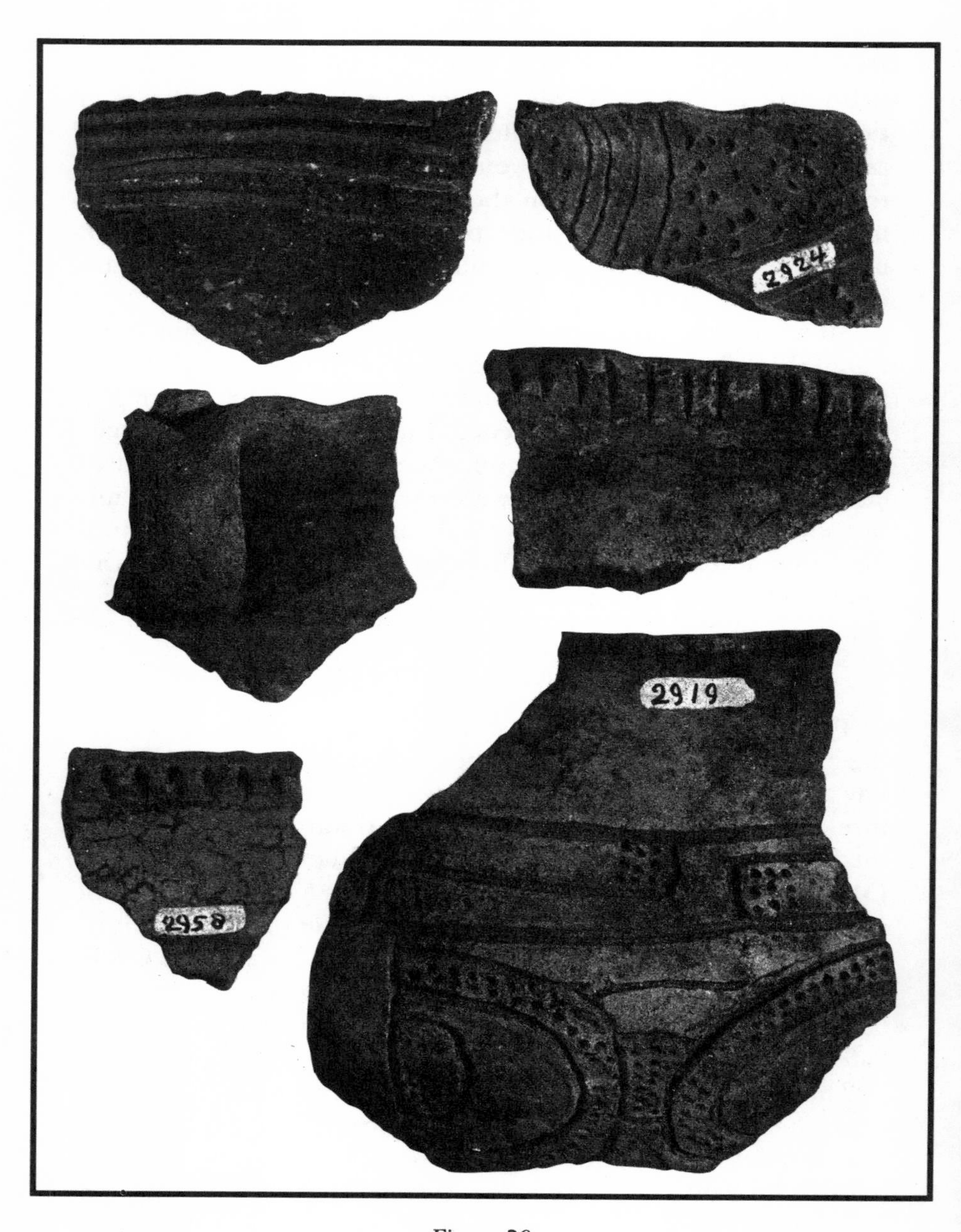

Figure 30

Pottery of the Safety Harbor archaeological culture (from Milanich and Fairbanks 1980).

lections that have come from the present location of Disney World west of Orlando (made by Bullen and others) suggest that both Safety Harbor and St. Johns culture ceramics are present in Urriparacoxi's region. The St. Johns archaeological culture is typical of the large region from Orlando northward into the St. Johns River drainage and east Florida. More research is needed to further correlate the Urriparacoxi with an archaeological assemblage.

Much better known is the region of the Acuera, where the St. Johns archaeological assemblage is well documented. That distinctive assemblage can easily be distinguished from those of the peninsular Gulf coast and the Alachua tradition north of Ocale. Thus, some of the ethnic distinctions among sixteenth-century native groups in Florida are reflected in their material culture assemblages.

CHAPTER VI

OCALE TO AGILE

While at the Tampa Bay camp, de Soto had outlined in a letter his plan to march inland to Ocale and to spend his first winter there (de Soto 1866). Information he obtained apparently had led him to believe that in Ocale he would find sufficient food to feed his army for several months. But, as we have seen, Ocale turned out to be disappointing in this regard. Stored food supplies apparently were less than anticipated, and at least one and perhaps two parties were sent east to Acuera to collect food. De Soto's intention to winter in Ocale must have weakened as the true situation became known.

The calendar also might have led de Soto to consider changing his plan. His army arrived in Ocale July 29 and remained there into early August. Anyone who has experienced late July and early August in central Florida can attest to the hot weather at that time; the Spaniards may have realized that winter and cold weather were farther off than they had originally thought.

This, and the none-too-abundant food, must have led de Soto to consider moving farther north into the interior of La Florida. But where? The army needed to find an area with sufficient food to carry it through the winter, but which could be reached before the onset of winter. The province of Apalachee, described by the Indians as being of "great fame," "populous," and "abounding in maize" (Biedma 1922:5; Elvas 1922:39; Ranjel 1922:69) seemed to be such a place. In addition, two Indians taken captive in Ocale said that Apalachee was only a seven-day journey from Ocale (Elvas 1922:39).

De Soto opted to take a contingent of his army and move rapidly northward to Apalachee to see if it were a better location for a winter camp. Accordingly, de Soto, with a force of fifty cavalry and sixty infantry, left Ocale on August 11, 1539 (Elvas 1922:39).[1] Luis de Moscoso was left in charge at Ocale with the bulk of the army. He was to wait until word was sent to him on "how the advance section got on" (Ranjel 1922:69). Presumably, if Apalachee proved to be all it was said to be, the army could winter there, and word would be sent back to Moscoso to march forward. If Apalachee did not prove to be better than Ocale, de Soto and his smaller force could return.

TO THE RIVER OF DISCORDS

De Soto, his cavalry, and foot soldiers left Ocale on August 11. All three chroniclers—Biedma, Elvas, and Ranjel—accompanied the advance party. But none of them provide any significant clues that help establish the route taken for the next five days. Almost the only information given is a litany of names of the Indian towns where the Spaniards stayed.

Apparently, for at least several days, the advance party moved very rapidly, staying in a new town each night (Ranjel 1922:70–71): first Itaraholata, then Potano, then Utinamocharra, then Malapaz (Spanish for "Bad Peace"), and then a "fair-sized village," which Elvas (1922:39) says was called Cholupaha. The latter was renamed "Villafarta" by the Spaniards, which translates as "Village of Plenty."[2] Just north of Cholupaha the Spaniards came to a river, an important geographical clue, because it is the first river they came to north of the Withlacoochee.

Although only scant information is provided in the narratives, we can gain considerable insights into the possible routes of the army from Ocale northward to the river when we compare the village names from the narratives with information provided by later sixteenth-century French and Spanish documents and information from Spanish sources of the seventeenth-century mission period. It is also easy to determine that the river located just north of Cholupaha is the Santa Fe River, providing a firm geographical marker. The river, however, does run east-west a considerable distance, some fifty miles, forming the northern boundaries of present Alachua and Gilchrist counties and offering not

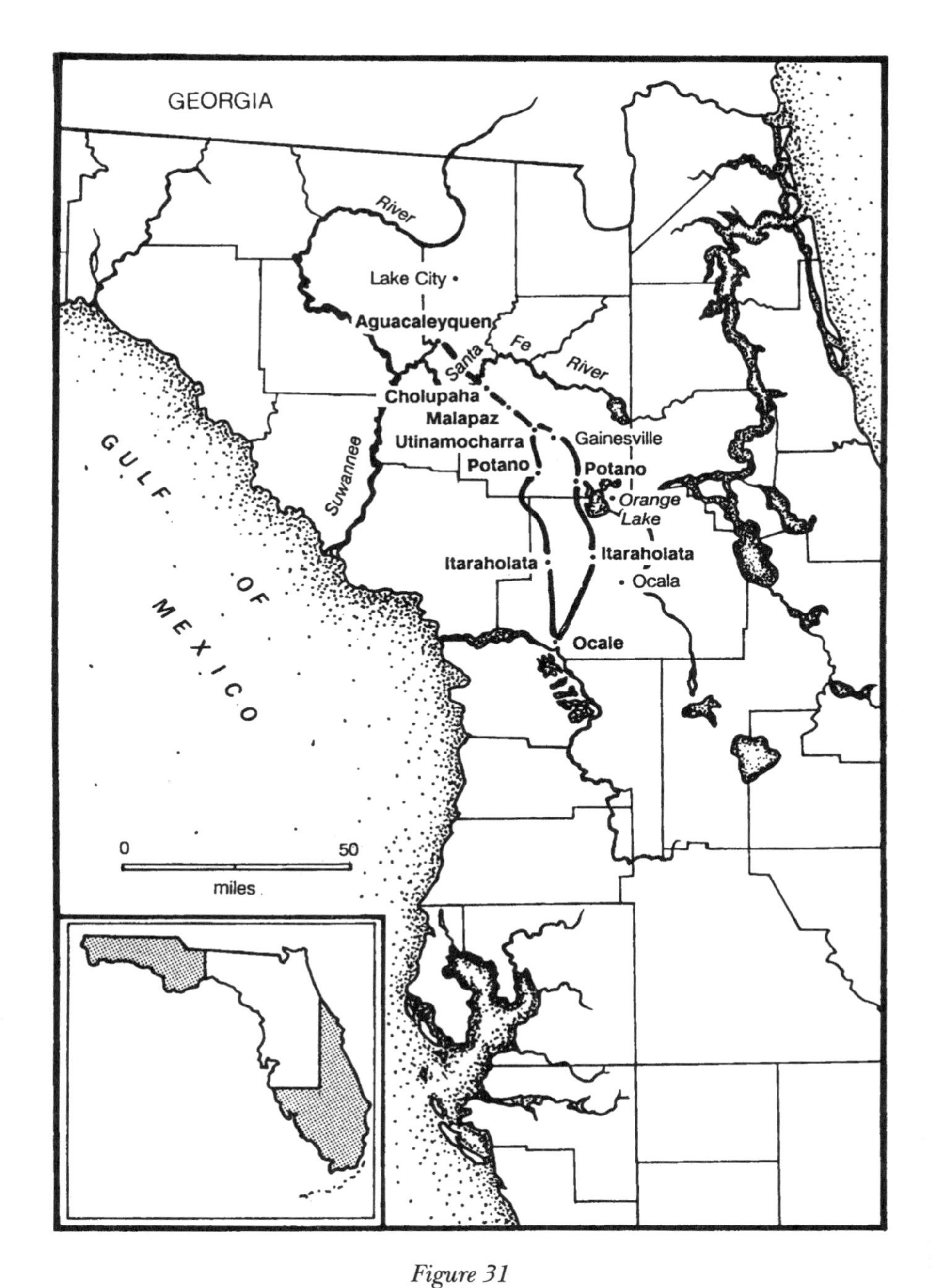

Figure 31

Route of the de Soto expedition from Ocale to Aguacaleyquen. The alternative routes are shown. De Soto names are in bold.

one but several possibilities for the spot where de Soto made his crossing.

Reconstructing this portion of the route—from Ocale to the Santa Fe River—does become easier when the documentary sources are examined in the context of the excellent archaeological site survey data and analysis provided by Kenneth Johnson (1991). Johnson's analysis, carried out as a part of the Florida Museum of Natural History's de Soto project (Johnson 1986, 1987; Johnson, Nelson, and Terry 1988), includes a reconstruction of old trails in the region and identifies the location of contact and mission period aboriginal sites (Johnson 1991:chap. 6). When all of these sources of information are combined, our reconstructions of this portion of the route take on a higher degree of certainty than when we began this project in 1983.

At the end of the first day's travel, de Soto and the advance party reached Itaraholata, a "small town" with "plenty of corn" (Elvas 1922:38; Ranjel 1922:69). In the Timucuan language "holata" is "chief" (Granberry 1989:168). Cognates of this word are found in Muskhogean languages, and they, too, refer to a chiefly official, e.g., *orata* recorded by the Juan Pardo expedition in 1566–1568 in the Carolinas and Tennessee, and meaning "village chief" or "headman" (Hudson 1989). We would expect Itaraholata to be on a trail about seventeen miles north of Ocale. From our presumed location for Ocale in southwestern Marion County, de Soto and his men could have moved northward on either of two trails. The first, which we will call the western option, led almost due north through the western portion of Marion County paralleling (but several miles east of) highway U.S. 41.

That trail goes north through Heidtville, Cotton Plant, and Elmwood and then swung westward through northeastern Levy County and the area of Wacahoota, where the trail is approximated by highway S.R. 121. In his analysis, Johnson (1991:chap. 6) calls this portion of the trail the Florida Santa Fe Trail and traces it from the vicinity west of Micanopy northward around the west ends of Levy Lake and Paynes Prairie, past Moon Lake and the west side of San Felasco Hammock, and north to the town of Alachua, where it intersected the east-west Mission Trail from St. Augustine to Tallahassee.

The Mission Trail evidently followed an old aboriginal trail. It was mapped by the British in 1778 (the Stuart-Purcell map, see

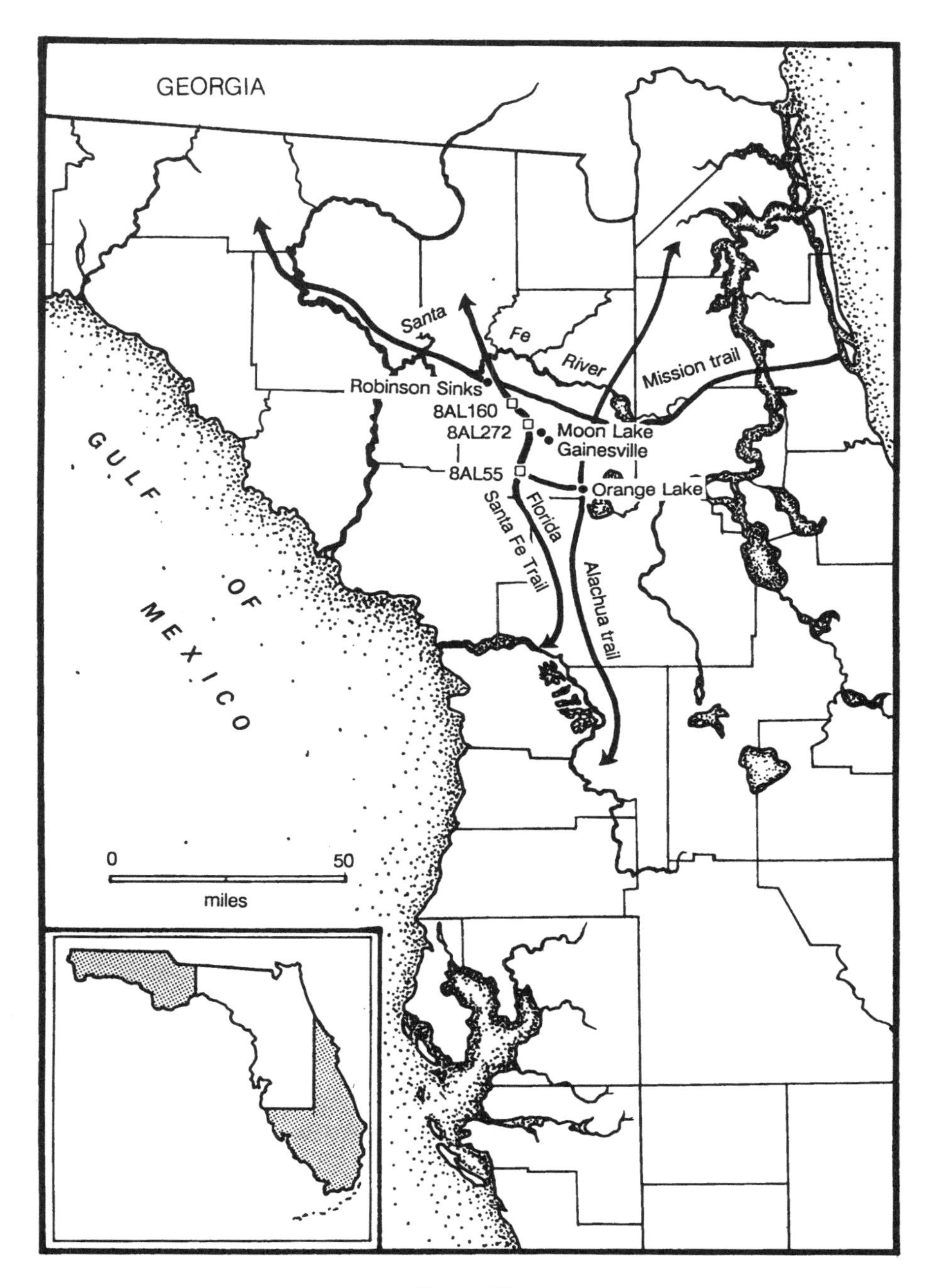

Figure 32

Trails and archaeological sites and site clusters in the region just south of the Santa Fe River.

Boyd 1938a and Johnson 1991). Later, in the early nineteenth century after Florida became a territory, large portions of the Mission Trail shown in the Stuart-Purcell map became the Bellamy Road. Johnson located the intersections of the Florida Santa Fe Trail and the Bellamy Road and Mission Trail in the vicinity of Alachua. Portions of the Florida Santa Fe Trail still exist in Marion County, e.g., in the vicinity of Cotton Plant, and Johnson found traces of the route farther north in Alachua County, where nineteenth-century maps label it "Ray's Road."

The Florida Santa Fe Trail connects with another north-south trail, the Alachua Trail, near Micanopy. That trail, which leads south to Tampa Bay, goes north past Micanopy, then east of Paynes Prairie and Newnan's Lake, ultimately reaching eastern Georgia (see Vanderhill 1977; Johnson 1991). At various times after having left the Tampa Bay camp, de Soto's army probably followed portions of the Alachua Trail. However, the necessity of continually finding food and the desire to locate Ocale probably caused the Spaniards to take the route they did across the Cove of the Withlacoochee into southwestern Marion County, rather than following the Alachua Trail all the way from Tampa Bay.

If the advance party took the western option—the trail north from Ocale through Cotton Plant and west of Micanopy (where it became the Florida Santa Fe Trail)—we would expect Itaraholata to be located west or west-southwest of present Morriston and Lake Stafford, near the border of Marion and Sumter counties (southward of Williston).

Archaeology is not much help in locating Itaraholata in this locality; no de Soto-era artifacts have been found in the Lake Stafford area, although archaeological sites, presumably villages, exist nearby. While archaeology does not help us pinpoint the exact location of the town, it is known that the same archaeological assemblage—the Alachua tradition—is present from central Marion County and western Levy County through Alachua County almost to the Santa Fe River (Milanich 1971; Milanich and Fairbanks 1980:169–180; Johnson 1991). As pointed out in the preceding chapter, this archaeological culture is distinctive from the Safety Harbor culture associated with Ocale and found in the Cove of the Withlacoochee and further south to Tampa Bay.

The Alachua tradition archaeological culture correlates quite well with that portion of the Middle Florida Hammock Belt that extends in a north-south band through the central portion of

Figure 33

Pottery of the Alachua tradition archaeological culture (from Milanich and Fairbanks 1980). The practice of impressing the soft clay surface of the clay pots with dried corn cobs (the top five specimens) was common in the late pre-Columbian period and into the seventeenth century. The three lower objects are sherd discs—each a piece of pottery ground into a round shape and probably used in playing a game.

north-central Florida southward to Belleview in Marion County. The forests of this zone are characterized by loamy soils that are well suited for agriculture. When de Soto and his men reached Itaraholata, they entered a physiographic and cultural setting quite unlike what they had experienced before. Although the narratives offer us little information about the route the Spaniards took (or, for that matter, the people encountered on those first five days beyond Ocale), they do comment several times on the agricultural plenty they observed.

On August 12 the advance party continued on from Itaraholata to the town of Potano. Continuing on the western-option route, the Florida Santa Fe Trail, a day's travel would place Potano either on the western side of Levy Lake or the southwestern end of Paynes Prairie in Alachua County. Here both documentary and archaeological evidence help us. Johnson's research has located a possible village site, 8AL55, on the western end of Paynes Prairie, potentially the village of Potano. Again, however, we do not have any de Soto–era artifacts to substantiate that possibility.

Even though the de Soto narratives tell us nothing beyond the fact that Potano was another village (Elvas 1922:38), a host of later documents leave no doubt that Chief Potano and his people (and the later Spanish province of Potano) were located in the Alachua County area. In 1564 the French traveled into the region from their settlement at Fort Caroline. Later, Potano became an early focus of the Franciscan mission system. There are a great number of documentary references to Potano, and its location in north-central Florida is secure (e.g., see Milanich 1978:75–79). Here, for the first time, we have independent documentary confirmation for the location of a de Soto place-name in Florida.

Using those documentary data, three generations of archaeologists have convincingly correlated the Alachua tradition culture with the Potano Indians and their pre-Columbian ancestors (Goggin 1953; Milanich 1971; Johnson 1991). There is no doubt that the Potano peoples were associated with the Alachua tradition, which has been well documented in Alachua County and portions of adjacent counties to the south and west.

One early map, that of Jacques Le Moyne in 1564 (later engraved by Theodore de Bry), shows "Potanou" located on the northwestern side of an inland lake in northern Florida (Lorant 1946:34–35), perhaps the Alachua Lake (Paynes Prairie).

Figure 34

On the Le Moyne map Potano is shown on the northwest side of a large lake, which could be either Paynes Prairie or Orange Lake.

Whether the village of Potano in 1539 was in the same location in 1564 is uncertain, but the map does hint that at one time the village of Potano was on or near a lake.

The third day out from Ocale, August 13, de Soto and his advance party arrived at Utinamocharra. Still following the Florida Santa Fe Trail, the Spaniards would have found the village somewhere near Gainesville. The most likely location, one practically on the trail, is the very dense cluster of sites immediately east of Moon Lake. Found originally by Goggin and his students, sites 8AL327, 331, and 334 all contain aboriginal materials dating from the time of de Soto (see Johnson 1991:chap. 5). There are a number of earlier Alachua tradition sites in the same cluster, including 8AL325–326,328–330, 333, 335–337. Spanish ceramics

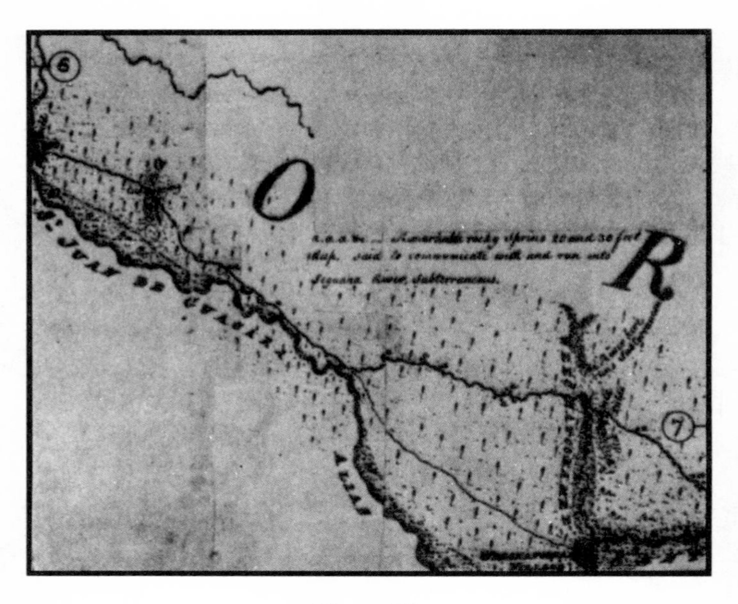

Figure 35

These two connecting portions of the Stuart-Purcell map show the Mission Trail across northern Florida as well as intersecting trails (see Boyd 1938a). The portion above shows the trail from Charles Spring on the Suwannee River (location of mission San Juan de Guacara) east (to the right) across the Ichetucknee River (Weechatookamee). At that river crossing, near the modern head springs, the map says "the river here runs subterranean."

have been picked up in this locale that might have been the site of a later Spanish mission village. The Moon Lake cluster of sites has largely been destroyed by modern development, including Buchholz High School. The cluster extended from N.W. 16th Boulevard in Gainesville north to N.W. 39th Avenue. Only a short distance farther north (west of the Devil's Millhopper) was the later mission of San Francisco de Potano, site 8AL272, and a late pre-Columbian site, 8AL273. San Felasco Hammock, just north of the mission, is a corruption of "San Francisco."

Another day's travel on the same trail brought the expedition to the town the Spaniards called Malapaz, Bad Peace, in reference to an incident in which an Indian attempted to deceive them (Elvas 1922:39; Ranjel 1922:70). A large site previously discovered near the town of Alachua, 8AL166, could have been Malapaz. Like the sites near Moon Lake, aboriginal pottery, with the distinctive corncob impressions so common in late pre-

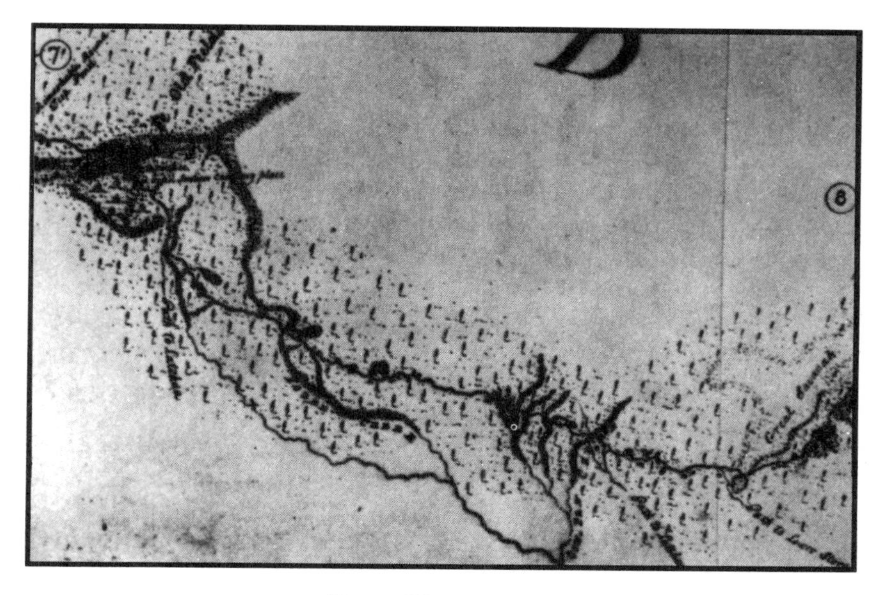

Figure 35 (continued)

The portion above traces the route further east, across the natural bridge of the Santa Fe River, past Santa Fe Old Fields (location of mission Santa Fe), and on across Alachua County. The two side trails south to "Latchua" are marked.

Columbian Alachua tradition sites, has been found here in large quantities. Spanish pottery has also been found, suggesting that a later Spanish mission or visita may have been at the same location. Among the Potano (and Aguacaleyquen, Uzachile, and Apalachee to the north) the correlation between sixteenth-century archaeological sites and seventeenth-century aboriginal /Spanish missions is extraordinary, and it strongly suggests that the major towns visited by de Soto were still in place 70 to 100 years later when missions were placed in or near them.

It was probably at Malapaz that the Mission Trail, later shown on the Stuart-Purcell map, and the Florida Santa Fe Trail (Ray's Road) intersected. This intersection is labeled "first path to Latchua" on that map (see Boyd 1938a; Johnson 1991). At Malapaz, as elsewhere on the trek north of Tampa Bay, de Soto and his army were apparently presented with a choice of directions and trails to take. They chose to continue northward, reaching the village of Cholupaha in another day. A glance at a map of Florida shows that the expedition was following a course almost due north from Tampa Bay, deviating only to cross the

Cove of the Withlacoochee to reach Ocale. It is likely that the exact route must have wavered a bit as villages with stored food were sought. But the general course seems to have been to head north until the expedition found or learned something that would cause it to change direction.

On the fifth day out from Ocale, on August 15, a Friday (Ranjel [1922:70] noted they reached Utinamocharra on a Wednesday), the Spaniards came to the town of Cholupaha, "a pretty village" with an "abundance of maize" that was located just before a river (the Santa Fe River) (Elvas 1922:39; Hann 1989a). The ending *-paha* is Timucuan, meaning "house, dwelling, habitation" (Granberry 1989:170). Here they found plenty of corn and a great quantity of dried chinkapins that had prickly burrs on the nut pods (Ranjel 1922:70–71; Hann 1989a).

A likely location for Cholupaha is on or near the northern extension of the Florida Santa Fe Trail, north of its intersection with the Mission Trail, within the very dense and large cluster of archaeological sites near the Robinson Sinks locality in northwest Alachua County. These sites are on high ground south of the Santa Fe River and east of the Natural Bridge at Oleno State Park. Again, many of these sites were originally found by Goggin and his students. As a part of the Florida Museum of Natural History's de Soto project, Johnson relocated Goggin's sites and found a number of additional ones, including pre-Columbian, contact-period, and mission-period sites in the same cluster (Johnson 1986, 1987, 1991). The Robinson Sinks and the Moon Lake clusters are both large and dense.

The archaeological evidence gathered by Johnson leaves no doubt that the Robinson Sinks cluster of sites represents a major focus of aboriginal settlement. Johnson's research indicates that the contact-period and pre-Columbian archaeological assemblage in this locality is not the Alachua tradition found south among the Potano Indians. Rather, it is an assemblage recently identified as being associated with the native peoples who lived to the north, the people in the de Soto documents referred to as the Aguacaleyquen, but who later are referred to as the Utina (Johnson 1991). Both early Weeden Island (ca. A.D. 200–750) and Suwannee Valley (ca. A.D. 750–early mission period) archaeological assemblages are present in the Robinson Sinks site cluster. This evidence suggests that Cholupaha and the Santa Fe River were controlled by or affiliated with the Aguacaleyquen-Utina, not the Potano. A similar pattern was true of the Withlacoochee River and

Ocale. Rivers, important sources of food and routes of travel by dugout canoe, were incorporated into powerful groups' territories rather than being boundaries and buffers between groups, as was sometimes the case in the interior of the Southeast.

Even before Goggin and his students recorded some of the sites in the Robinson Sinks area, the Simpson family of High Springs, Florida excavated in several burial mounds found within the cluster of village sites. Their notes, on file at the Florida Museum of Natural History, state that one mound contained beads, presumably glass beads. Johnson's field surveys located a crescent-shaped village area just north of that mound's former location. The village, which measures ca. 340 by 450 ft, dates from the early contact period and could be Cholupaha (Johnson 1991:chap. 7).

Like some of the clusters of Potano sites to the south, the Robinson Sinks locale continued to be an important settlement area into the seventeenth century. Johnson's survey found the Spanish mission of Santa Fe just south of the contact village described above (Milanich and Johnson 1989). The mission, founded by Father Martín Prieto in the early seventeenth century, was in existence until the early eighteenth century. It is easy to see why this location was important. It was near a major river (the Santa Fe) as well as the crossing of several trails.

Both the Ranjel (1922:71) and Elvas (1922:39–40) accounts agree that the next day (it would have been Saturday, August 16, according to Ranjel) the advance party built a bridge spanning the river near Cholupaha. Apparently, some disagreement or argument occurred at this time, causing the Spaniards to name the Santa Fe River "the River of Discords." Nothing in the narratives sheds any light on the cause of the discord.

Let us for the moment leave the advance party on the south side of the Santa Fe River and examine the other possible route northward from Ocale—what we will call the eastern option. From Ocale in southwest Marion County, the advance party could have traveled northeast on a trail that is approximated by S.R. 200 toward modern Ocala. They would have intersected the Alachua Trail that runs north-south from Tampa Bay past Ocala and continuing north. If de Soto and his soldiers took this route, they would have gone north through present Kendrick, Martin, Lowell, Reddick, Orange Lake, Boardman, Evinston (past the west side of Orange Lake), and past the east side of Paynes Prairie. Near Micanopy they also could have connected with the Florida Santa Fe Trail (our western option) and taken it around the west side of Paynes Prairie, rather than continuing on the Alachua Trail east of the prairie.

If the Spaniards took the Alachua Trail past Ocala through Marion County to Orange Lake and the vicinity of Micanopy, Itaraholata would have been around Kendrick or just south of it. A number of Alachua tradition archaeological sites are known to exist in this area. Indeed, the density of Alachua tradition sites is greater in this central portion of Marion County than it is on our western-option route in western Marion County (paralleling U.S. 41). This eastern route through Kendrick is approximated by the old Seaboard Coastline Railroad that leads from Ocala (and south) north to Rochelle in Alachua County where it branches, the eastern branch to Hawthorne and Palatka and the western branch curving around the northern edge of Paynes Prairie into Gainesville and then northwest to the town of Alachua. Both of these railroad beds apparently follow old trails.

Although the railroad did not continue north from Rochelle, the Alachua Trail did. It passed east of Newnan's Lake and Hatchett Creek and continued north. Like the Florida Santa Fe Trail to the west, the Alachua Trail also intersected the Mission Trail. According to Johnson (1991), that intersection was west of Orange Heights. The Stuart-Purcell map labels this intersection the "second path to Latchua." Johnson correlates the Hatchett Creek drainage (on the north side of Newnan's Lake) with the creeks in that locale shown on the Stuart-Purcell map.

If Itaraholata were near Kendrick, then Potano, the second village reached, would be in the vicinity of northern Orange Lake, near or on the Alachua Trail. We do have an excellent candidate for Potano, the Richardson site (8AL100), located on the northwest shore of Orange Lake just north of Evinston. The site is one of a cluster of several Alachua tradition sites in that general region (including 8AL101 and a mound, 8MR48). Goggin first found the site in the 1950s (see Goggin 1953, 1968) and it was excavated in 1970 (Milanich 1972). Both sixteenth- and seventeenth-century Spanish ceramics have come from the site (Goggin 1960, 1968). The Richardson site's location on Orange Lake fits with the position of Potanou shown on the Le Moyne–de Bry map of La Florida as being on a lake (Lorant 1946:34–35).

If Potano were on Orange Lake, and if the Spaniards continued north on the Alachua Trail, then the third village encountered from Ocale, Utinamocharra, would be somewhere on the east side of Newnan's Lake. Here again Johnson's research has revealed a cluster of sites, one of which could have been visited by de Soto. North of Newnan's Lake the advance party would have intersected the Mission Trail and could have taken it, marching west across northern Alachua County. If they did that, the next town, Malapaz, would have been roughly in the vicinity of Hague. Continuing on they would have intersected the Florida Santa Fe Trail and taken it north to the Robinson Sinks locale and Cholupaha just south of the Santa Fe River. Certainly that is possible, but it assumes a much more circuitous route than the western option. That latter route is more likely because it takes the expedition through the densest distribution of Alachua tradition sites that runs from Paynes Prairie past Bivens Arm, Moon Lake, and the Millhopper north to the town of Alachua and then to the large cluster of sites near Robinson Sinks.

The correct route could just as easily be a combination of the two options we have presented. If the army took the eastern route through Kendrick (Itaraholata) and past Orange Lake (Potano) to Rochelle, it could then have branched off the Alachua Trail and followed the northern rim of Paynes Prairie into Gainesville to Moon Lake (Utinamocharra), then north along the Florida Santa Fe Trail. Still another possibility is after leaving Potano on Orange Lake, the army took the western Florida Santa Fe Trail, passing Paynes Prairie on the west side, rather than continuing on the Alachua Trail and passing it on the east. In some ways, this combination route is best because it is consistent with the northerly route of the expedition and it brings the Spaniards to the major archaeological site clusters that are the best candidates for de Soto–era major villages: the Orange Lake cluster (Potano), the Moon Lake cluster (Utinamocharra), site 8AL166 near Alachua (Malapaz), and the Robinson Sinks cluster (Cholupaha). Perhaps future archaeologists will be able to find artifacts from the expedition that would help to pinpoint the exact route.

What is undisputable is that on its way northward from Ocale, the advance party, and later the rest of the army, passed through the central portion of Alachua County and the territory of the Potano Indians before reaching Cholupaha just south and east of the Santa Fe River in northwestern Alachua County. There is no other archaeological candidate for Cholupaha farther east in northern Alachua County. And, as we shall see below, the Santa Fe River crossing had to have been west of the New River–Santa Fe River intersection, and probably was west of the Olustee Creek–Santa Fe River intersection, meaning Cholupaha could only have been in northwest Alachua County. The Robinson Sinks cluster of sites offers the best location.

There is another piece of evidence linking the de Soto expedition to the Potano region. When the Franciscan father Martín Prieto sought to establish missions among the Potano in the early seventeenth century, the chief of one village (named Santa Ana by the Spaniards) refused. This old man still remembered the mistreatment he had suffered at the hands of de Soto more than sixty years earlier (Oré 1936:113).

TRAILS AND SITES IN NORTH FLORIDA

Our reconstruction of the de Soto route through Potano to Cholupaha and the Santa Fe River was enhanced by knowledge of old trails through the region and by the distribution of late pre-Columbian and later archaeological sites, information provided by Kenneth Johnson. His work has demonstrated that in northern Florida, late-period archaeological sites tend to occur in clusters that generally are no more than about two miles across. He also showed that these clusters are not randomly scattered across the landscape. They are on established trails—trails that can be traced today. The clusters are located within the Middle Florida Hammock Belt, a region of hardwood forests and good agricultural soils with lake or wetland resources nearby.

Fortunately, Johnson's research also extended north of the region of the Potano Indians, from the Santa Fe River drainage into large parts of Union, Columbia, Suwannee, and Madison counties, as well as portions of adjacent counties, such as Bradford. His work revealed that the same pattern of trails and site clusters found in the Potano region also is present north of the Santa Fe River. Again, these data provide us with important clues to the distribution of the native population in the sixteenth century and the potential routes taken by de Soto and his army. As in Potano, Johnson found that many of the late precolumbian and contact-period site clusters north of the Santa Fe River also contained seventeenth-century Spanish artifacts, and, in at least several instances, seventeenth-century Spanish Franciscan missions were present within these clusters (Johnson 1991:chap. 5).

Prior to Johnson's work, we had almost no information on the archaeological assemblage(s) that dated to the late pre-Columbian–contact and mission periods in Florida north of

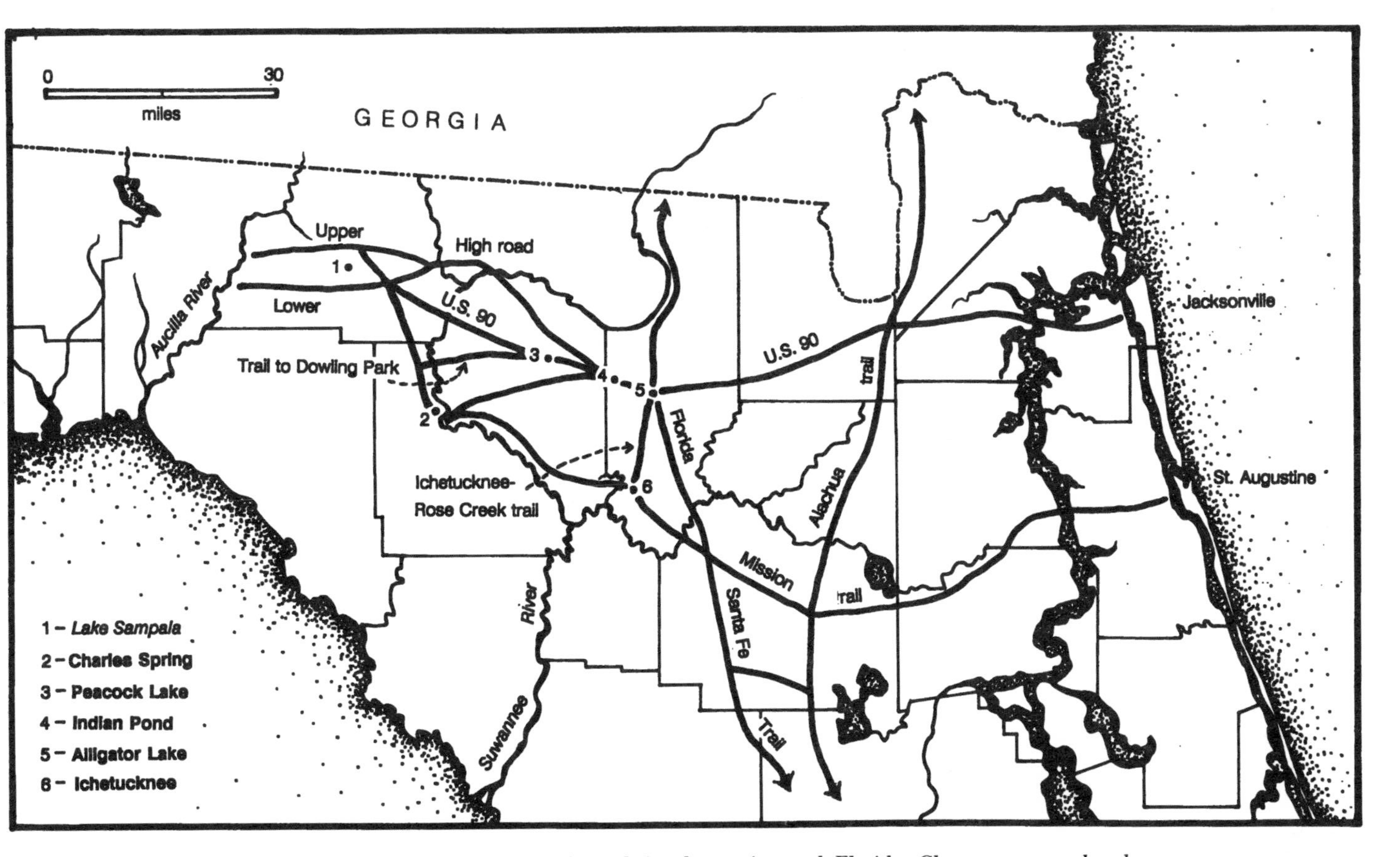

Figure 36. Trails and archaeological site clusters in north Florida. Clusters are numbered.

Potano. Now it is known that the archaeological assemblage associated with the de Soto–period people of Aguacaleyquen, Uriutina, and Napituca was the Suwannee Valley complex found in the region from the Santa Fe to the Suwannee River (largely Columbia and Suwannee counties) (Johnson 1991:chap. 4). The early sixteenth-century manifestation of this complex is called the Indian Pond culture.

Johnson's work has also clarified another vexing problem: that of the relationship between the Aguacaleyquen and other north Florida groups and the Utina Indians. Many researchers have applied the name Utina to the native peoples of Columbia and Suwannee counties, thereby confusing them with another group called "Utina" living just inland (i.e., west) of the St. Johns River. It is now clear that the Aguacaleyquen, Uriutina, etc., and the Utina were separate and different groups (Johnson 1991:chap. 3). Johnson suggests using the term "eastern Utina" to refer to the St. Johns–area group. The use of "Utina" to refer to the north Florida people is too firmly entrenched in the literature to remove it, so we will follow Johnson's suggestion and refer to these north Florida people as the northern Utina, recognizing that the name includes the Aguacaleyquen and other peoples encountered by de Soto north of the Santa Fe River (see chapter 7).

Utina is a common Timucuan word for chief. All of the north peninsular Florida native peoples east of the Aucilla River, including the Ocale, Acuera, Potano, Aguacaleyquen, and eastern Utina were Timucuan speakers. *Utina* appears in several de Soto–era titles and place-names: *Utina*mocharra or *Utina*ma in Potano, Uri*utina* and Guat*utima* in Aguacaleyquen, and *Utina* among the eastern Utina. It also means "our land."

In order to reconstruct de Soto's route from Cholupaha and the Santa Fe River north to the next town, Aguacaleyquen, let us first examine the system of old trails in north Florida and their relation to the clusters of sites found and identified by Johnson. We have already mentioned the Mission Trail that, in the seventeenth century, would become the major route from Spanish St. Augustine across northern Florida to the province of Apalachee. Franciscan missions were often built on or near this trail, or on side trails that led to it. As we have seen, in Potano the Mission Trail intersected both the Alachua Trail and the Florida Santa Fe Trail. It is also the trail that is mapped in the eighteenth-century

Figure 37

Pottery of the Suwannee Valley ceramic assemblage.

Stuart-Purcell map and that served as the base trail for the nineteenth-century Bellamy Road.

From St. Augustine the Mission Trail went almost due west to Picolata on the east bank of the St. Johns River. On the opposite side, after one crossed the river by canoe or boat, the trail continued southwest across the corner of Clay County and then past Georges Lake, forming the present west half of the boundary between Clay and Putnam counties and passing south of Lake Santa Fe. The trail continued west across northern Alachua County, intersecting the Alachua Trail near the Hatchett Creek drainage north and east of Newnan's Lake, past Fairbanks, southeast of Hague, and then past Alachua, where it intersected the north-south Florida Santa Fe Trail south of the Robinson Sinks locale. Continuing west, the Mission Trail crossed the natural bridge of the Santa Fe River (now in Oleno State Park) and, heading more northwest, passed just north of the head springs of the Ichetucknee River, near several archaeological sites, including the seventeenth-century mission of San Martin.

The trail continued across southeastern Suwannee County and reached the Suwannee River southwest of O'Brien, probably near Little River Springs in the vicinity of the mission of Santa Cruz de Tarihica, the precise location of which has not been found. Paralleling the Suwannee River, the trail passed by Baptizing Spring, location of another cluster of sites, including what may be a Spanish mission, all located west of Luraville, and then reached Charles Spring on the Suwannee, still another site cluster, that included mission San Juan de Guacara. San Juan has been corrupted to "San Juanee" and then to "Suwannee." Both Santa Cruz and San Juan were probably moved to these locations from elsewhere following the mission Indian rebellion of 1656.

After crossing the Suwannee River, the road turned north to avoid the wet lowlands in Lafayette County and southern Madison County known as San Pedro Bay, named for a Spanish mission, San Pedro, located north of the bay in Madison County. This north-running portion of the Mission Trail parallels the western side of the Suwannee River and, in Lafayette County, is approximated by S.R. 53. Along the trail there still exist natural road signs, such as a pond called Tenmile Pond (ten miles from the Suwannee River and Charles Spring).

Once the road was far enough north to avoid the wetlands of San Pedro Bay, it turned west through Hopewell and past Lake Sampala, location of mission San Pedro y San Pablo de Potohiriba, which gave its name both to San Pedro Bay and Lake Sampala, a corruption of San Pablo. Near where that mission was located, the Mission Trail connected with another east-west trail, called by Johnson (1991) the "High Road." That trail follows a course about fifteen to twenty miles north of and parallel to the Mission Trail and leads from the St. Johns River to the vicinity of Lake Sampala. From Lake Sampala the Mission Trail continued west, reaching the Aucilla River at roughly the U.S. 27 crossing, the location of another site cluster, as well as the mission of San Miguel de Asile, from which the Aucilla River derives its name.

Although the Mission Trail is well documented and was much used in the last half of the seventeenth century (when it was the major east-west route to the Spanish missions), it is not at all certain that it was the major trail across Columbia and Suwannee counties at the time of de Soto or even in the early mission period. One Spanish document dating from 1597 describes the location of the future site of the San Martin mission—near the

Ichetucknee head spring and on the Mission Trail—as "off the beaten path" (*desviado*) from St. Augustine (Hann in Milanich 1990), suggesting at that time the Mission Trail was not the major trail it would become in the late seventeenth century. Evidence from the early seventeenth century, when the first missions were established among the northern Utina, suggests another, more northerly route was more in use (Milanich, in press). A portion of that route is the High Road Trail mentioned above. Johnson's reconstruction, based on Bernard Romans's map and other maps, traces the High Road from the west bank of the St. Johns River where it diverges from the Mission Trail (Romans 1962). Rather than heading southwest as the Mission Trail does, the High Road Trail goes west, southwest of Kingsley Lake to Starke where it intersected two other trails: the north-south Alachua Trail, which led from Tampa Bay north through the eastern Potano region and into Georgia, and the Black Creek Trail, which led northeast to near Middleburg and the Black Creek drainage.

Past Starke, the High Road lies near the course of S.R. 100. The High Road crossed the New River, then Olustee Creek, where it probably intersected the north-south Florida Santa Fe Trail, both continuing on to Alligator Lake south of Lake City. Continuing, the High Road swung northwest to Mineral Springs on the Suwannee River in northwest Suwannee County, on or near S.R. 249. Side trails, unnamed, led west from Alligator Lake and/or the High Road to traditional crossings on the Suwannee, such as at Charles Spring, Dowling Park, and Ellaville (U.S. 90).

From Mineral Springs the High Road continued west, crossed the Suwannee River just below the mouth of the Alapaha River, crossed a portion of Hamilton County, forded the Withlacoochee River, and then it or a side trail connected with the Mission Trail near Lake Sampala.

Major clusters of late pre-Columbian, contact-, and mission-period sites were found by Johnson near Alligator Lake (a major intersection of several trails), east of Wellborn in western Columbia County near both the High Road and the unnamed trail from Alligator Lake to Charles Spring (the Indian Pond cluster), and at Peacock and White lakes southeast of Live Oak and north of the unnamed trail to Charles Spring.

One additional trail should be mentioned. From the area of the head springs of the Ichetucknee River, a trail led north from the Mission Trail to Alligator Lake, intersecting the High Road and the unnamed trail to Charles Spring. It is approximated by S.R. 47, which is one to two miles to the east, however. Johnson (1991) calls this the Ichetucknee/Rose Creek/Alligator Trail and says it also can be traced south from the Ichetucknee to the Santa Fe River south of present-day Fort White. North of the Ichetucknee the trail turns slightly north-northeast and crosses the old bed of the Ichetucknee River about six miles north of the present Ichetucknee head spring. Johnson found cartographic and hydrological evidence that in the past, including at least some portion of the nineteenth century, the Ichetucknee River did not have its present head spring as its origin. A network of creeks, including Cannon Creek, Clay Hole Creek, and Rose Creek, drained a large portion of central Columbia County and even parts of Union County and formed an Ichetucknee–Rose Creek River, which extended far to the north and east of the present Ichetucknee head spring (and see Meyer 1962:12). An 1829 map shows the river and the trails crossing it (Anonymous 1829).

North Florida was criss-crossed by a system of east-west and north-south trails, with still other trails that connected as needed. Indian villages tended to be on or near these trails and their intersections. This web of trails and clusters of archaeological sites provides the framework within which the de Soto route must be reconstructed in north Florida.

AGUACALEYQUEN

On August 16 the Spanish advance party departed from Cholupaha and arrived at the River of Discords, the Santa Fe River. The men built a bridge that they crossed the next day. Ranjel (1922:71) notes that the crossing of this river was as difficult as was the crossing of the Withlacoochee. This is a puzzling statement because the Santa Fe normally is a relatively small stream. But it is only so in dry weather. After a hard rain, the river becomes turbulent. When it gets out of its banks, in places it can be nearly half a mile wide, flooding the adjacent woods, as it did, for example, in the summer of 1984.

The next day, after crossing the river, the Spaniards arrived at Aguacaleyquen, a moderately large town that lay near a second river (Biedma 1922:5; Ranjel 1922:70–71).[3] There is a discrepancy between Elvas and Ranjel on the exact sequence of events

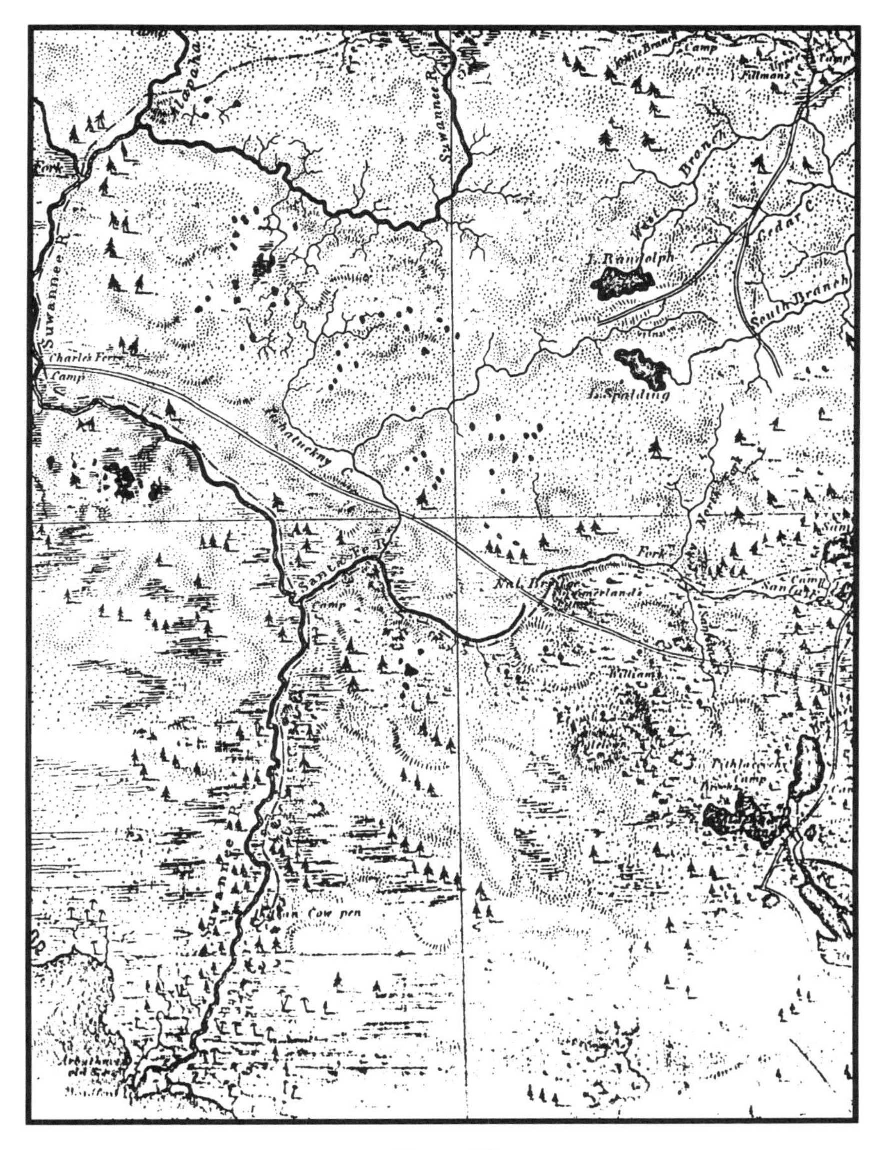

Figure 38

The 1829 map showing the Ichetucknee River extending north and connecting with Rose Creek and other creek systems. The Mission Trail crosses the river near the present head spring.

that transpired on the way from the river crossing to Aguacaleyquen. Both agree on the date the party left Ocale (August 11) and on the number of days it took to reach Cholupaha (five), meaning Cholupaha was reached on August 15. Elvas and Ranjel both note that the Spaniards reached the river and built the bridge the next day. But Elvas says they then traveled two days through uninhabited territory before reaching Aguacaleyquen on August 17. Ranjel, on the other hand, says they crossed the river and the next day reached the village, which would be August 18. Elvas's account appears to be in error, unless his two days included both the day the river was crossed and the next day when they reached the village; but his date would still be in error. Biedma's account is very sketchy; he simply says it took five to six days to get from Ocale to Aguacaleyquen.[4]

Aguacaleyquen, citing either account, would be one to two days' travel from the Santa Fe River. At this time, the most likely location is one of the sites just east of the Ichetucknee River and immediately south of the mission of San Martin (8CO1). The archaeological assemblage associated with these premission sites, one of which produced a faceted chevron bead in a surface collection, is the Suwannee Valley archaeological complex. The early sixteenth-century manifestation of that complex has been correlated with the northern Utina (Johnson 1991). Moreover, when the San Martin mission was established there in the early seventeenth century, the founding priest, Martín Prieto, noted that he was establishing the mission in the major town in that mission province (Oré 1936:114).

If this is the correct location for Aguacaleyquen, it suggests that the Spaniards chose not to continue north from Cholupaha on the Florida Santa Fe Trail, where they would have crossed the Santa Fe River approximately where the S.R. 241 bridge crosses. Instead they opted to turn west and cross the river at the natural bridge at Oleno, where the Mission Trail crossed. Why did they have to bridge the river if they crossed at the natural bridge? The reason is that at high water the natural bridge is flooded, and crossing it is as difficult as other crossings (perhaps more difficult because of the flooded trees and vegetation). If they crossed there, they could have followed the Mission Trail to the village on the Ichetucknee, slightly more than a day's travel away.

If this interpretation is incorrect and the advance party did continue north from Cholupaha on the Florida Santa Fe Trail, crossing the Santa Fe River near the present S.R. 241 bridge, then we would expect Aguacaleyquen to be in western Union County, probably near the intersection of the Santa Fe Trail and the High Road east of Olustee Creek. Archaeological surveys in this region, however, have failed to locate any potential sites for Aguacaleyquen here, although the area around Palestine Lake appears to be a likely location for sites.

De Soto and his army rested at Aguacaleyquen for several days. The town had been abandoned, but two natives were captured who showed the Spaniards where maize had been hidden. Apparently the native peoples were well aware of the army's need to locate and commandeer food (Biedma 1922:5–6; Elvas 1922:40; Ranjel 1922:71–72). Seventeen Indians were captured, including the chief's daughter. The Spaniards used her as a hostage to demand obedience from her father, who was then also taken prisoner. The Indians told de Soto that they had heard of Narváez's having been in Apalachee, and they painted a dismal picture of what he had found. They said Narváez had withdrawn because there were no roads or towns beyond Apalachee, there were no other settlements, and there was water all around. The Spaniards were all too familiar with Narváez's fate, and the men tried to talk de Soto into aborting the expedition and returning to the camp at Tampa Bay, but he refused.

On August 22 "a great multitude of Indians appeared," which caused de Soto to rethink his militarily precarious position. Eight horsemen were dispatched back to Ocale to tell Moscoso to move forward to Aguacaleyquen. The army arrived in Aguacaleyquen on September 4, meaning it took the horsemen probably six to seven days to reach Ocale, and the army took about the same time to march north. On the march, Moscoso's men suffered because the country was devastated from de Soto's previous travels through it, and there was little corn to be had.

Before leaving Ocale, Moscoso "buried . . . some iron implements with other things" (Elvas 1922:40).[5] This apparently allowed Moscoso and his men to travel lighter and reach de Soto more quickly. It also provided a cache of supplies that might prove useful if the expedition had to return to Tampa Bay, where some Spaniards were still encamped.

There is no indication in any of the narratives that this hardware was ever recovered by the Spaniards. We might guess that the Indians got possession of them, and, as noted in chapter 4, it is possible that it was some of these supplies that were found in the Tatham Mound and Ruth Smith Mound in the Cove of the Withlacoochee near Ocale.

Garcilaso de la Vega provides some information on Aguacaleyquen, although he confuses the name of the village, calling it "Ocali" (Varner and Varner 1951:121–122, 124–126). However, his distance and direction of travel from Ocale are approximately correct. He says that the men left the swamp (near Ocale), they traveled toward the north, but turned a little to the northeast (the eastern option through Kendrick?), and traveled for about twenty leagues. Moreover, Garcilaso says that the region they passed through was largely uninhabited and covered with a vast forest of "walnut" and pine trees spaced widely apart, so that the horses could safely run between them, and they encountered fewer swamps.

Also, like the other chroniclers, Garcilaso notes that the population was denser in Aguacaleyquen than it had been to the south, and this meant that there was more food to be had from the Indians of Aguacaleyquen. In fact, Garcilaso says that for seven leagues before reaching Aguacaleyquen, they encountered only small towns and homesteads (Varner and Varner 1951:122). It was Garcilaso's impression that Aguacaleyquen was the dominant chief of this area.

Other portions of Garcilaso's account are not very useful, because, for instance, he confuses the Suwannee River with the River of Aguacaleyquen. In the early stages of our research, Garcilaso's transposition of these two rivers posed a formidable stumbling block. It was Joyce Hudson, Charles Hudson's wife, who finally realized that Garcilaso had transposed the Suwannee River with the River of Aguacaleyquen (i.e., the Ichetucknee–Rose Creek).

TO THE RIVER OF THE DEER

On September 9 de Soto's army departed from Aguacaleyquen, taking the chief and his daughter as hostages. They immediately came to the River of Aguacaleyquen, where they built a bridge out of pine logs (Elvas 1922:40-41; Ranjel 1922:72). Also taken hostage was a high ranking individual named Guatutima, who served as guide. (*Gua-utima* may mean "honored chief" [Granberry 1989:182, 187].) They may have crossed the river on

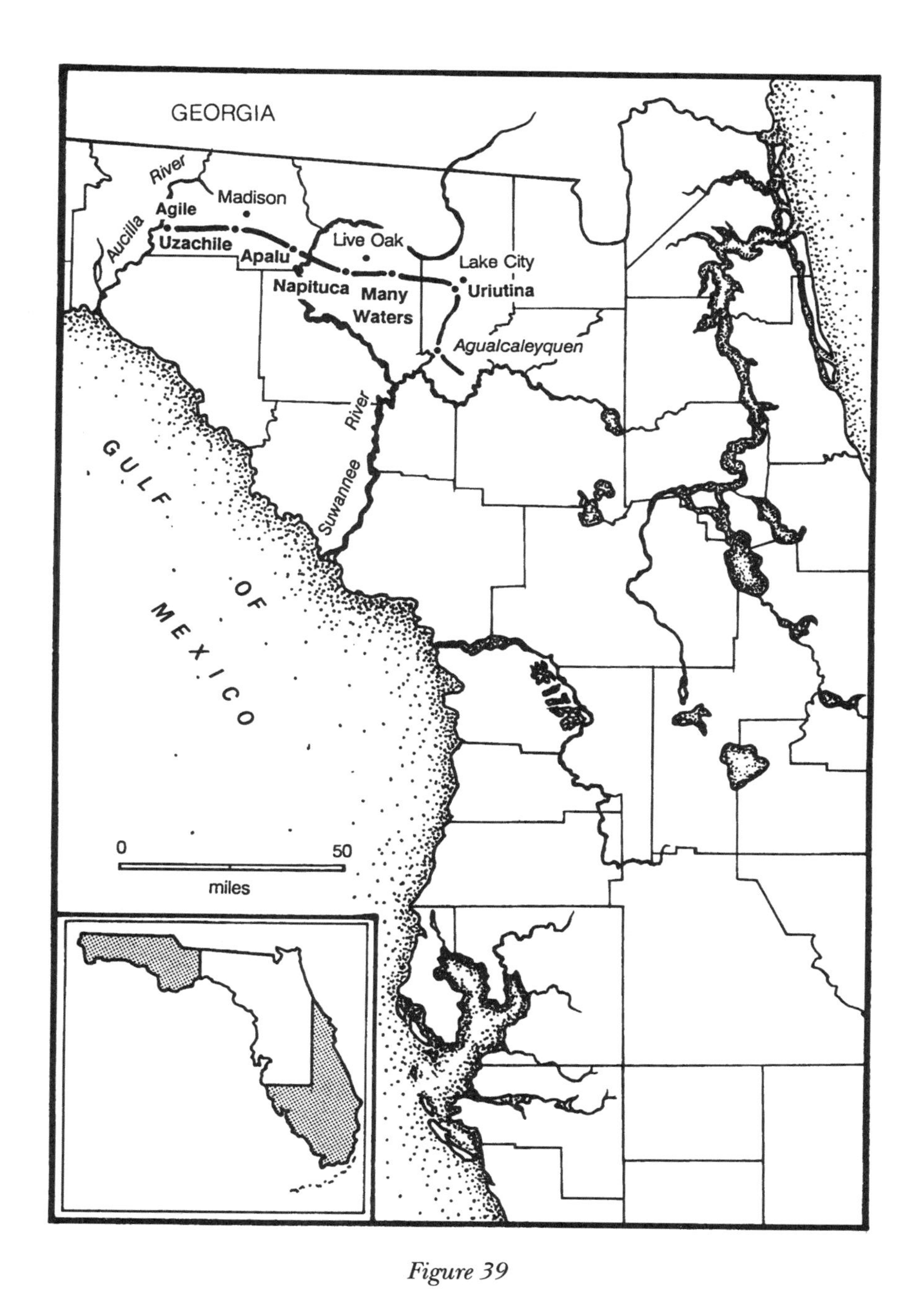

Figure 39

Route of the de Soto expedition from Aguacaleyquen to Agile. De Soto names are in bold.

that same day or the next, and they reached a small village where they spent the night.

If Aguacaleyquen were near the present Ichetucknee head spring, then they marched north on the Ichetucknee–Rose Creek–Alligator Trail, and the river they crossed was the Ichetucknee–Rose Creek River, today normally a dry bed. The small village probably would be near Alligator Lake in the cluster of sites documented by Johnson (1991), close to the intersection of the several trails in that locale.

Another possibility is that the army continued west along the Mission Trail. If that were the correct route, then the river crossed would also be the Ichetucknee–Rose Creek River. However, the events of the next several days do not fit with what lay along the Mission Trail from the Ichetucknee River to that trail's crossing of the Suwannee River at Charles Spring. We have carefully considered the Mission Trail as de Soto's route across Suwannee County, and it does not work. In addition, the archaeological evidence is clear that the largest late pre-Columbian native populations in the region were across the central portion of Columbia and Suwannee counties, not in southern Suwannee County. The route de Soto took passed through that populated region, on or near that portion of the High Road west from Alligator Lake and then on one of the connecting trails leading to the Suwannee River.

If an Ichetucknee River locale for Aguacaleyquen is incorrect, and that village is actually in western Union County near Palestine Lake, then the route beyond that village would probably have been on the High Road westward across Olustee Creek (the river after Aguacaleyquen) to Alligator Lake and the small village where the Spaniards spent the night. Any reconstruction of the route that has de Soto crossing both the New River and Olustee Creek, however, is incorrect. The accounts are clear that after the Aguacaleyquen, the expedition crossed only one river, not two. That river must be either the Ichetucknee–Rose Creek River or Olustee Creek.

The next day, either September 10 or September 11, depending on the time spent bridging the river after Aguacaleyquen, the army reached the village of Uriutina, where they found abundant food.[6] This village had a large council house (*buhio*) with a great deal of space in the center (Ranjel 1922:72; Hann 1989a). Garcilaso may be describing this same structure, or one like it, when he describes a building that was more than 120 ft long and 40 ft wide. It had four doors, one in each of the cardinal directions (Varner and Varner 1951:130). The army spent either one or two nights in Uriutina.

Along the route the Spaniards were met by native messengers sent to de Soto by Chief Uzachile, a great chief who lived to the west and was said to be a kinsman of the chief of Aguacaleyquen. It is possible that the relationship was actually a political alliance symbolized in terms of fictive kin terminology. The messengers, who played "flutes," sought the hostage chief's release (Elvas 1922:41; Ranjel 1922:72–73).

It is likely that Uriutina was one of the villages in the cluster of sites near Indian Pond in westernmost Columbia County, west of I-75 and south of I-10. This cluster, surveyed by Johnson (1991), is quite close to a pre-Columbian Weeden Island archaeological site (the McKeithen site) and a number of other early Weeden Island sites. Johnson's work at Indian Pond (and follow-up testing by Samuel Chapman of the Florida Museum of Natural History) has documented both contact-period occupations and a seventeenth-century Spanish-Indian occupation. The latter might be the mission of San Augustin de Urica. In the Timucuan language, Uriutina (*Iri-utina*) could be translated as "warchief." Similarly, Urica (*Iri-ca*) could be "place of the warchief" (Granberry 1989:160, 171, 187). San Augustin de Urica is known to have been established by 1630 and still existed in 1655 (Geiger 1940:125–126; Hann 1990:470).

On September 12 (a Friday) the army traveled to the Village of Many Waters, so called because it rained heavily and the Spaniards were forced to stay in this place on September 13 and 14 (Ranjel 1922:73). For the first time since leaving the camp at Tampa Bay, the route had changed from a generally northerly heading to a westerly one. The reason is simple: the guides must have indicated that Apalachee was to the west, which it is. This change in direction occurred after the army left the small village at Alligator Lake. The Spaniards probably followed the High Road west from that village, or they could have taken a combination of the High Road and then one of the unnamed trails that led west to the Suwannee River.

The Village of Many Waters was probably one of the sites in the cluster found by Johnson (1991) in the Peacock–White Lake locale just south of U.S. 90, between Wellborn and Live Oak.

Johnson's archaeological tests at these sites revealed both late Suwannee Valley pottery and mission-period Spanish ceramics. The latter suggest that this cluster may be the location of still another Spanish mission. Slightly more than one mile north, a second survey by Keith Terry of the Florida Museum of Natural History located two additional sites that are a part of this cluster (Terry 1990). The combination route mentioned above would have taken the army from the vicinity of Alligator Lake to the Indian Pond site cluster, and then to the Peacock–White Lake site cluster.

On September 15 the army continued west, crossing a bad marsh or swamp where travel was difficult, and it reached Napituca, a fine village with plenty of food (Ranjel 1922:73; Hann 1989a; Elvas [1922:41] says Napetaca). *Na-api-taca* could mean something like "this ash, fire," in the sense of a revered fire. In Timucuan, *taca* also means charcoal, however. The swampy wetland must have been Gum Slough or another of the wetlands southeast of Live Oak. Napituca, in travel time, would have been farther west than Live Oak, perhaps somewhere along the edge of the north-south escarpment marking the western edge of the Middle Florida Hammock Belt. From this escarpment, which roughly parallels S.R. 129, to the Suwannee River there are more karst surface features and fewer archaeological sites.

De Soto remained in Napituca for more than a week. During this time, an alliance of Indians attempted to attack de Soto and free his hostage, the chief of Aguacaleyquen. De Soto was warned of the plot and he easily defeated the Indians. When the Spanish advantage became plain in the battle that ensued, many of the Indians fled to two ponds, swimming out toward the centers and treading water for many hours. One pond was apparently small enough for the Spaniards to surround, and both were guarded all night. The next day the northern Utinas began to surrender or they were pulled out by the Indian bearers who had been forced to accompany the army from Tampa Bay. The other pond, some distance removed from the first, was either too large to surround, or else de Soto did not have enough men to surround both of them. These "ponds" were no doubt two of the many limestone sinkholes found in the karst topography of western Suwannee County.

The 300 Indian tribespeople and five or six Indian chiefs captured in this fashion were tied and taken to a council house, where they quickly rebelled. Another horrible battle ensued before the Indians again were subdued. Those who survived were either put in chains or slain by arrows shot by the enslaved Indians from Tampa Bay (called Paracoxi, by Elvas) (Biedma 1922:6; Elvas 1922:41–44; Ranjel 1922:73–77; Hann 1989a).

Garcilaso erroneously calls Napituca "Vitachuco," evidently confusing it with Ivitachuco, an important town of Apalachee (Varner and Varner 1951:134–168). His description of the shape of the ponds is like that of the other chroniclers, specifying that one was small enough so that the Spaniards could surround it, while the other was large. He adds that the small one was so deep that the water was over a man's head only three or four steps from the bank. This further implies that it was a limestone sinkhole.

On September 23 de Soto and his army departed Napituca and traveled to the River of the Deer—the Suwannee. As mentioned above, Napituca must have been just west of present Live Oak. Our best guess would place it west-southwest a few miles or less.

The Spaniards marched to the river, probably to the vicinity of what is now Dowling Park, where they camped (Elvas 1922:45). On September 24, they built a bridge that was three great pine trees in length and four in breadth (Ranjel 1922:77). They named the Suwannee the River of the Deer because the messengers from Chief Uzachile brought them some deer, possibly as offerings of good intentions.

Garcilaso confuses the River of the Deer with the River of Discords, but his description makes it plain that he is talking about the Suwannee River. He says that where the Spaniards built their bridge the banks on both sides were twenty-eight ft high, and they were as sheer as a wall—a good description of the deeply entrenched Suwannee River near Dowling Park (but less so of the river at Charles Spring or Ellaville). It was not a huge river, because as the Spaniards were building the bridge, Indians appeared on the opposite bank of the river and shot arrows across it (Varner and Varner 1951:123). This also is the place where the Indians shot and killed one of de Soto's dogs when it broke away from its handler and began swimming across the river to attack the Indians.

After de Soto reached Apalachee, he sent a detachment of men back to the base camp at Tampa along the same trail they had followed previously. They returned to the same crossing place on the Suwannee River, though on this occasion the river was in flood. Garcilaso again specifies that the banks were twenty-eight ft high and very steep (Varner and Varner 1951:201).

If the crossing was at Dowling Park, then the army was not on the High Road that crossed the Suwannee farther north, whence it crossed a second river, the Withlacoochee. Our placement of Uriutina and Many Waters suggests that the Spaniards were following a connecting trail that led from the High Road west of Alligator Lake to the Suwannee. If they crossed the river at Dowling Park, a portion of that unnamed trail would be approximated by highway S.R. 250 and the old Live Oak, Perry, and Gulf Railroad. They were not on another of the westward connecting trails, one that led to Ellaville or Charles Spring.

The Spaniards crossed their bridge over the Suwannee on September 25 and traveled through several towns of Uzachile, including one large one, Apalu. By nightfall they came to the main town of Uzachile, which had been abandoned by its people (Ranjel 1922:77–78).[7] *Apalu*, in Timucuan, is "fort" or "stockade" (Granberry 1989:158). Unfortunately, none of the chroniclers tell us whether Apalu was fortified.

According to Garcilaso, the army encountered the first agricultural fields of "Osachile" two leagues from where they built their bridge. Then they encountered fields and small households over the next four leagues until they came to the principal town, where they found plenty of corn, beans, and squash, but from which the inhabitants had all fled. Garcilaso says there were 200 houses in the main town, probably an exaggeration (Varner and Varner 1951:169). Ranjel also says there was an abundance of food—maize, beans, and pumpkins—in the main town.

While discussing Uzachile Garcilaso describes what he felt was a typical southeastern Indian town. He tells how earthen mounds were built, and he describes buildings up on top of the mounds. He tells of a plaza in the town around which the principal men built their houses (Varner and Varner 1951:170–171; see also Hann 1989a). But one must always be skeptical of Garcilaso. It is quite possible that he is here describing a town of Apalachee or presenting a generic view of the types of towns encountered in Apalachee and among other peoples in the interior of the Southeast encountered later on in the expedition. Such mounds were not found in Potano, northern Utina, or Uzachile, nor are there archaeological sites in those regions that are the remains of such mounds.

Once it crossed the Suwannee River near Dowling Park, the Spanish army would have intersected the Mission Trail, south of Tenmile Pond, south of the point where the trail turns west and passes around the northern end of San Pedro Bay. The High Road, or a trail from it, connected with the Mission Trail somewhat further north, as did the connecting trail that reached the river at Ellaville.

The Stuart-Purcell map indicates that beyond the Suwannee River, the Mission Trail divided into an upper road, which roughly follows highway U.S. 90 and reaches the Aucilla River west of Greenville at the U.S. 90 crossing, and a lower road, the Mission Trail described above in this chapter that passed close to the north end of San Pedro Bay, then through the present towns of Hopewell, Mosley Hall, and Ebb. This lower Mission Trail, probably the one the expedition was on (as we shall see below), passed by Lake Sampala and reached the Aucilla River near the highway U.S. 27 crossing.

The upper Mission Trail through Madison County connected with the High Road, continuing that route westward to the Aucilla (the two are the same trail through much of Madison County). The connecting trail mentioned above led from the upper Mission Trail to the lower Mission Trail, reaching the latter near Lake Sampala. The town of Uzachile is probably close to Lake Sampala in Madison County, south of the town of Madison, a location near both the lower Mission Trail and the connecting trail that led north to the upper Mission Trail. Lake Sampala is one day's travel from the Suwannee River. The seventeenth-century mission of San Pedro y San Pablo de Potohiriba was found by B. Calvin Jones of the Florida Bureau of Archaeological Research near Lake Sampala, and the Stuart-Purcell map labels the general area near the lake "San Pedro Old Fields," indicating extensive old agricultural fields and remains of settlements.

Surveys by Kenneth Johnson and Claudine Payne have located two small sites between the general Lake Sampala area and the Suwannee River (8MD20–21), which may be related to the towns and settlements the army passed through on the way to the main town of Uzachile. It is clear from the de Soto accounts that Uzachile was a major area of settlement, and a number of large and small late pre-Columbian sites should exist between the Suwannee River west to Lake Sampala. One such site has been recorded several miles north of the east end of the lake on the east side of Hixtown Swamp (Terry 1990).

AGILE

After remaining in Uzachile for several days, de Soto and his army departed on Monday, September 29, heading west toward Apalachee (Elvas 1922:46; Ranjel 1922:78). They traveled through a large woods and came to a pine grove where they spent the night, ". . . é passado un gran monte, fueron á dormir á un pinar . . ." (Fernández de Oviedo 1851:553). Buckingham Smith's translation of *monte* as "mountain" is in error (see Hann 1989a). The great forest was probably a hardwood forest in the uplands, and the *pinar* was a stand of pine trees. The men were traveling through a wilderness or buffer zone between Uzachile and the Apalachee Indians to the west. Garcilaso says this "wilderness" was twelve leagues across—an accurate measure (Varner and Varner 1951:175)—and Elvas (1922:46) indicates that it took them two days to cross it (September 29 and 30).

Traveling on the lower Mission Trail, the Spaniards would have skirted the northern margin of San Pedro Bay, approximately following the small road that today passes through Hopewell, Mosley Hall, and Ebb and leading to the Aucilla River near the U.S. 27 crossing east of Lamont. At the end of the second day of travel through the uninhabited area they reached Agile, the first town that was subject to Apalachee (Ranjel 1922:78).[8] The people of this town had no warning that de Soto was coming, an indication of just how deep the social division was between the Apalachee and the Timucuans in northern Florida. Agile, which must have been on or near the Aucilla River, is the Indian place-name from which "Aucilla" is derived.

That the lower Mission Road route to the river is the correct one is supported by the presence of a cluster of archaeological sites, including the seventeenth-century mission, San Miguel de Asile, located on the eastern side of the river near U.S. 27. The mission, 8MD5, is close to several other late precolumbian sites, including 8MD6, any of which could be the town where de Soto and his expedition camped. The archaeological assemblage associated with the pre-Columbian sites is the Fort Walton culture, the same as that found to the west in Apalachee and one very different from the Suwannee Valley ceramic complex. This cluster of sites, including a Spanish mission, is the same pattern seen in Potano, Aguacaleyquen, and Uzachile. This pattern also continues into eastern Apalachee (see chapter 8).

It is abundantly clear that the chiefdom of Apalachee was at war with the people to the east. While the army was at Napituca, seven chiefs who were subjects of Chief Uzachile sent word to de Soto that they wished to enlist the Spaniards' help in fighting the Apalachee, "a mighty province hostile to Uzachile and to themselves" (Ranjel 1922:73). Although Uzachile was a powerful chief exerting influence across northern Florida all of the way to Aguacaleyquen, he was apparently no match for the power of the Apalachee.

CHAPTER VII

NATIVE PEOPLES OF NORTHERN FLORIDA

The route of the de Soto expedition north from Tampa Bay took the Spaniards from small, seemingly nonagricultural groups, such as the Uzita and Mocoso, to the Ocale, who cultivated maize. Along that portion of their march, the Spaniards encountered the first maize fields at about Dade City. Some of the soldiers traveled to the main town of Urriparacoxi, the chief of a dominant agricultural group in central Florida, and others went to Acuera, another agricultural region. All of these native peoples are thought to have been Timucuan speakers, although they may have spoken different dialects of that language.

When the advance party departed Ocale and proceeded rapidly to Aguacaleyquen north of the Santa Fe River, the descriptions in the narratives indicate that the Spaniards were passing through a region of greater agricultural bounty than they had seen before. And from Aguacaleyquen into Uzachile, there was even more abundance. Other comments in the narratives make it clear the regions of Aguacaleyquen, Uriutina, Napituca, and Uzachile had larger and denser populations than any encountered previously on the march from Tampa Bay. In addition, the political complexity found in north Florida appears to have been greater than that seen previously.

These observations are what might be expected based on knowledge of the Florida environment and the archaeology of the aboriginal societies. As the expedition traveled through the Middle Florida Hammock Belt, which extends down about as far south as Belleview, it was in a region of good agricultural soils. It is no surprise that farming populations inhabited that region. Also, as the Spaniards neared Apalachee, it is no surprise that they began to encounter even more complex polities. In order to survive military engagements with the Apalachee, it is reasonable to think that people like the Uzachile had to develop and maintain competitive social and political structures. Apalachee was a densely populated agricultural chiefdom whose archaeological remains, the Fort Walton culture, leave no doubt that it was a full participant in the complex pre-Columbian cultural developments that typified the interior of the Southeast after about A.D. 1000. It is no wonder that a wilderness lay to the west side of Uzachile as a buffer against Apalachee military initiatives.

Let us look at the three groups or regions through which the expedition passed after leaving Ocale on its way to Apalachee. For each region—Potano, Aguacaleyquen, and Uzachile—we will see what we can learn from the de Soto narratives and later European accounts.

POTANO

Although scholars have traditionally listed the five towns through which the de Soto expedition traveled on the way from Ocale to the Santa Fe River as affiliated with Potano, there is nothing in the de Soto narratives to indicate that this was so. We cannot be certain that the towns, each probably with its own chief, were united under a single paramount chief. Was the region that was later known by Spanish missionaries as Potano a single polity with several village chiefs vassal to a paramount chief? Although such a level of organization is not in evidence in the de Soto accounts, it does seem there was a paramount chief twenty-five years later during the period of French and Indian interaction, and one may very well have been present at the time of the de Soto expedition.

As we have seen, the region of four of the Potano region towns—Itaraholata, Potano, Utinamocharra, and Malapaz—is included in the area of the Alachua archaeological culture, suggesting cultural ties within the region if not political ties. Cholupaha, often listed as a fifth Potano town, is on the border of the

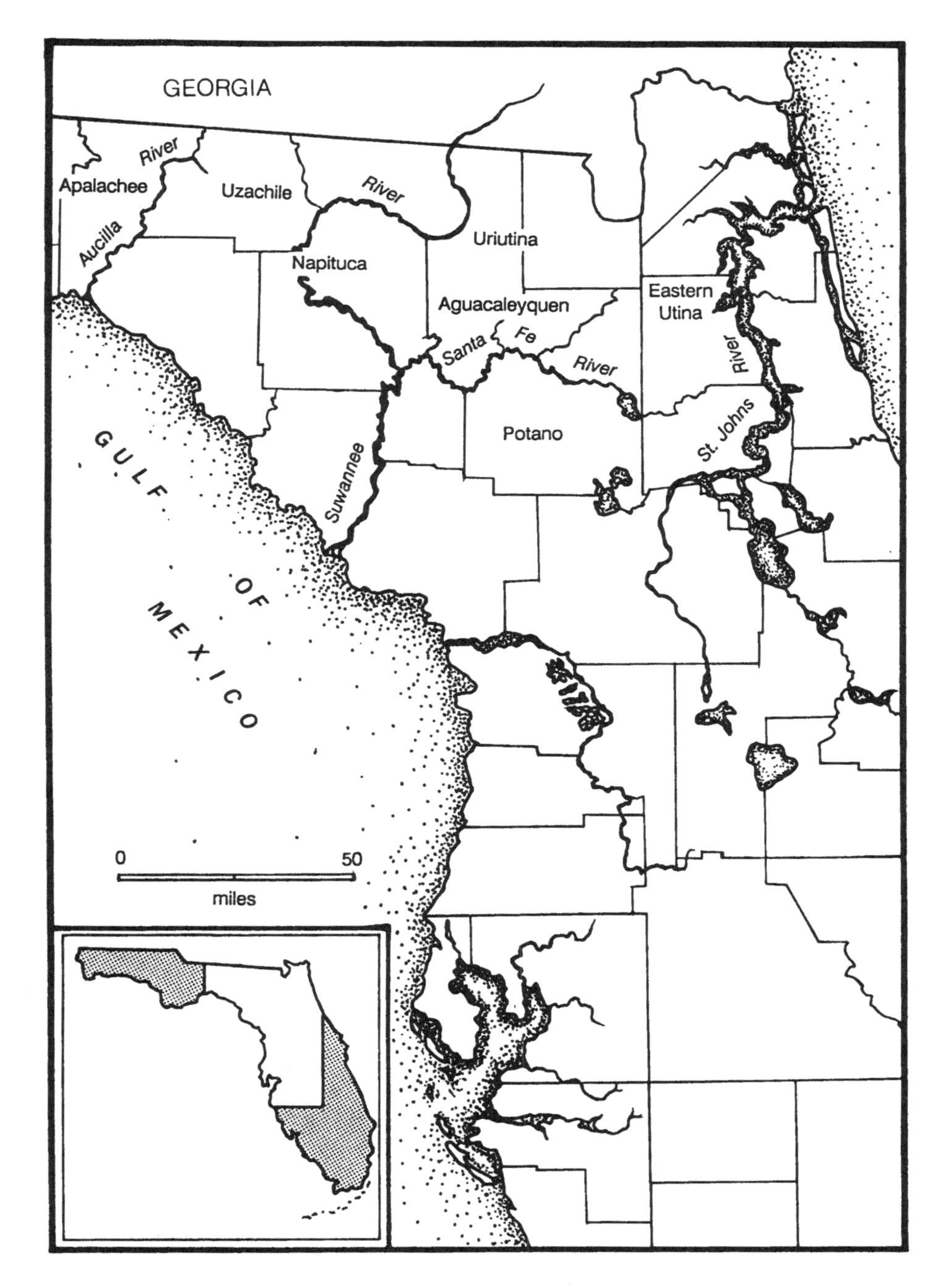

Figure 40

Native groups in northern Florida at the time of the de Soto expedition.

Alachua and Suwannee Valley archaeological assemblages, and it may actually have been associated with Aguacaleyquen and the people to the north. Some activities and documents from the late sixteenth century and the seventeenth-century mission period suggest that the Potano were a unified group at that time (e.g., see Milanich 1978; Johnson 1991), but the evidence is ambiguous.

At the time of de Soto, the Potano were farmers, and impressions of dried corncobs as well as rows of corn kernels are common on Alachua tradition pottery from the period. Ranjel (1922:69) notes that there was plenty of maize at Itaraholata, and both he and Elvas commented on the abundance of food at Cholupaha (Elvas 1922:39; Ranjel 1922:70). Each village in the region apparently had a chief. Indeed, the names Itaraholata, Utinamocharra, and Potano all are related to Timucuan names for chiefs, e.g., *holata*, *utina*, and *potano*. Could village chiefs have been arranged in a hierarchy, with each playing different traditional roles within a large Potano chiefdom?

At Utinamocharra, the Spaniards captured twenty-eight to thirty men and women. When they arrived at Malapaz (the native name of which is not given), a man who said he was the chief approached the Spaniards, saying that if the captives were released, he would provide provisions and a guide. The prisoners were set free and the man was held. The next day, a group of his people came to the camp and he went to talk with them, to give them instructions. But as soon as he got near them, he abruptly fled. He did not escape, however, for the Spaniards released a bloodhound to run him down, and he was recaptured (Elvas 1922:39). Ranjel (1922:70) indicates that the man was not the chief, but someone who had sought to deceive the Spaniards.

In 1564, the French, who had established a settlement at the mouth of the St. Johns River, became involved in the political affairs of the native peoples who resided nearby, as well as with native groups living near the St. Johns River, especially the eastern Utina. In an attempt to curry favor with Chief Utina, the most powerful native individual in that region, the French agreed to help him in his military exploits against his enemy, Chief Potano, who lived in the interior of northern Florida.

The alliance began when René de Laudonnière, leader of the forces at Fort Caroline in 1564–1565, sent Captain le Vasseur up the St. Johns River. There he met Chief Molona, who said he was a vassal of Utina. Molona told Vasseur about Utina's enemies, one of whom was "Pota[n]ou," who lived a two-day journey from Utina and made war with him regularly (Laudonnière 1975:76–77). Potano was said to oppose Utina because Utina and his allies came and took "hard stone" from his land to make arrow points. This must be a reference to the chert outcroppings found in north-central Florida.

Molona and the other allies of the French referred to their enemies as "Thimogona" (Laudonnière 1975:66), and the French soon began to use this name as a geographical reference. "Thimogona" was the word from which the Spanish derived "Timucua," the name they assigned to north Florida and the mission province established there. Modern scholars use "Timucua" as the name of a language as well as the people who spoke that language. It is highly unlikely that any of the Timucuan speakers ever referred to themselves as Timucuans.

In September 1564, Vasseur and ten to twelve French soldiers took another trip up the St. Johns River, traveling to Utina's main village to return some of his people who had been captured by another chief and who were later recovered by the French. Utina, who probably realized that the French sought his friendship, convinced the small party to send six or seven of their number, armed with guns (probably arquebuses), to accompany him and 200 of his warriors on a raid against Potano. The raiders traveled the twenty-five leagues to Potano's village and attacked without warning. The French guns carried the day, and Utina took Potano men, women, and children as prisoners. Apparently, a number of the Potano were slain, as was one of Utina's men (Laudonnière 1975:88, 90–91).

The next year Utina asked the French to send him twelve or fifteen soldiers so he could again raid Potano. In return he promised the French he would allow them access to the "mountains," which the French believed were in Apalachee, and where it was thought, at least by the French, that gold and silver could be mined. Utina quickly learned what to promise the French in order to gain their help.

Laudonnière, not fully trusting Utina, sent him thirty soldiers under the command of Lieutenant d'Ottigni, thinking that this larger number would be safe from an attack by Utina. The French soldiers stayed at Utina's town for two days while preparations for the raid were made. The war party numbered thirty

French soldiers, 300 Utina warriors, as well as women, children, and berdaches who carried the supplies. At the end of one day of travel they had not gone quite halfway, thus it was more than two days from Utina's village to that of Potano. Our placement of Utina's village near Lake Grandin west of the St. Johns River would mean it was roughly forty to forty-five miles to Potano, no matter whether the town was located on the west end of Paynes Prairie or on Orange Lake. That distance could well have been slightly more than two days' travel for the war party (Laudonnière 1975:117, 199).

When the war party was within three leagues of Potano's town, scouts were sent on ahead. They observed several people fishing from a canoe in a lake several leagues from Potano's village (Alachua Lake or Orange Lake?). It was expected that other people armed with bows and arrows would be somewhere close by, guarding the people in the canoe, so the scouts returned to report. Utina sent them back with orders to surprise the fishermen to prevent warning Potano in any way. This was done, but two of Potano's people got away. The third, who tried to escape by swimming, was captured, killed, scalped, and dismembered (Laudonnière 1975:119).

At that point Utina sought advice from his diviner, who became possessed during a divination ritual in which he claimed to be able to see what would happen if Utina attacked. The diviner reported that Potano had 2000 warriors who were carrying cords with which to bind Utina's men who would be taken prisoner. Utina tried to abort the raid, but the French were furious and convinced Utina to go forward. In the three-hour battle that ensued, the French firearms again routed Potano's forces, but Utina withdrew, again to the disgust of the French. Once back home, Utina immediately posted guards in anticipation of a retaliatory raid by Potano (Laudonnière 1975:119–121).

One of the de Bry engravings of a Jacques Le Moyne painting depicts the battle between Utina and Potano. The opposing forces are shown in European battle formation, and the engraving probably is not very accurate. Close examination shows that the individual who should be Potano is actually labeled "Saturiwa," evidently a mistake (Lorant 1946:61). Following the ouster of the French from Fort Caroline in 1565, the Potano also suffered at the hands of the Spaniards. In retaliation for their killing of Captain Andrade and thirty other soldiers in 1567, the

Figure 41

This 1591 de Bry engraving based on Le Moyne portrays the battle between chiefs Utina and Potano. Potano, however, is mistakenly labeled Saturiwa. The engraving may bear little resemblance to the actual event.

Spanish raided Potano in 1585 (Lyon 1976:198). In 1597 the chief of Potano went to St. Augustine to render obedience. Fear of additional Spanish raids had caused him to live in the woods for more than a decade.

In 1600 the Franciscan priest Baltasar López visited the region. López, assigned to the San Pedro de Mocama mission on Cumberland Island, Georgia, had begun making frequent excursions to the native groups on the St. Johns River and to north Florida beginning in 1587 (Geiger 1940:68). He apparently began with the more easterly groups, such as the eastern Utina, and then expanded westward, making two trips into Potano between 1600 and 1602 (López 1933:28–32).

López met with success among the Potano. In 1602 he reported nine conversions at Yca Potano (*ica [hica]* in Timucuan is "village") and ten in Potano, both native villages. Beyond this he had a number of instructees who were learning the catechism.

As a result, a full-time resident priest was requested, and in 1606 Martín Prieto and Alonzo Serrano were sent to tend to the Potano.

In that year Prieto established San Francisco de Potano, which is probably the Fox Pond archaeological site (8AL272), located on or near the Florida Santa Fe Trail northwest of Gainesville. Prieto also built a house at San Miguel de Potano and administered to natives at Potano, Santa Ana (the one in Potano), and San Buenaventura de Potano, all native villages. It was at this latter location in 1585 that the Spaniards killed a number of people in retaliation for the Indians having killed Captain Andrade and his men in the summer of 1567 (Lyon 1976:198; Hann 1990:458–460). The chief of Santa Ana was the one who told Prieto about having been mistreated by de Soto in the past.

Prieto, in a single day, could walk from San Miguel, to Santa Ana, and to San Buenaventura (Oré 1936:112–114). We suspect that these towns and San Francisco were in the cluster of sites from Fox Pond south to the Moon Lake locale, the probable location of Utinamocharra. In the four towns Prieto baptized 800 people out of the total population of 1200 (Oré 1936:112–114).

In 1616, Father Luis Gerónimo de Oré made a visitation to the Timucuan missions. His journey took him by canoe up the St. Johns River to the mission of San Antonio de Enecape (Geiger 1936:257), thought to be north of Lake George and south of Palatka. He might have been wiser to disembark much sooner and take the Mission Trail into Potano. As it was, he had to "travel over flat and marshy ground studded with pine trees . . . at times impeded by lagoons [lakes]. After two and a half days on the road, he came to the mission station [visita] of Apalu and from there proceeded to Potano" (Geiger 1936:258).

Oré's account is a good description of the roughly forty-mile route from the St. Johns River west to the Orange Lake region and the Richardson site where Goggin placed the later mission visita of Apalu (1968:73). That site might have been the main town of Potano in 1539 and the 1560s, when de Soto first marched through it and the same village the French and the eastern Utina later decimated. By 1616 the village of Potano could have been reduced in status to a small village, the site of a Franciscan visita visited infrequently by priests.

San Francisco and other Potano towns and visitas continued to be mentioned in Spanish accounts throughout the seventeenth century, a time of epidemics, occasional rebellions, and dwindling native populations (Gannon 1965; Milanich 1972, 1978; Hann 1990; Johnson 1991:chap. 3). Only a few Potano survived into the early eighteenth century and they were moved to near St. Augustine. By 1728 the remnant population of San Francisco was living in a small village, a satellite to the Nombre de Dios mission. Of the forty-three people in the town, fourteen were men and only one is listed as Potano (Geiger 1940:134).

NORTHERN UTINA: AGUACALEYQUEN, URIUTINA, NAPITUCA

Like the Uzachile to the west, the Aguacaleyquen, Uriutina, Napituca, and other towns north of the Santa Fe River and east of the Suwannee have presented modern researchers with a taxonomic nightmare. Did these towns belong to a single polity or chiefdom? Are they the same people as the Utina of the 1560s encountered by the French and Spanish just west of the St. Johns River and in Bradford County and the vicinity? Are we justified, as many authors have done in the past, in referring to them and the region as "Utina"?

Johnson's research has done much to dispel the confusion (1991:chap. 3). He has argued convincingly that the Utina who lived near the St. Johns River and who formed an alliance with the French against the Potano were a different people from the people living north of the Santa Fe River in Union, Columbia, Hamilton, and Suwannee counties, whom scholars have also called "Utina." These latter people were associated with the de Soto–era towns of Cholupaha (probably), Aguacaleyquen, the small unnamed village we have placed near Alligator Lake, Uriutina, the Village of Many Waters, and Napituca.

These north Florida people were not the Utina. But there is some evidence to indicate that they themselves were united through alliances that also tied them to their western neighbor, Chief Uzachile, who lived west of the Suwannee River. It seems that Uzachile was the paramount chief—or at least was first among equals. Aguacaleyquen also seems to have been an important chief, although he did not possess the power that Uzachile did. Documents from the period of French interaction with the Florida Indians and documents and accounts from the mission period help to clarify the political relationships, which may have changed through time. The entire region north of the Santa Fe River and west across the Suwannee toward the Aucilla River thus seems to have been a region of chiefs, who were allied with one another and who may have been hierarchically arranged, with Uzachile being most powerful. This alliance or chiefdom might have been for mutual military benefit, protection against enemies to the east (Utina), west (Apalachee), and south (Potano?).

Both Elvas (1922:41) and Ranjel (1922:71) mention the chief of Aguacaleyquen, who, the Spaniards were told, was a kinsman of Uzachile. There was also a chief of Uriutina, and he, too, was taken hostage by the Spanish. Seven other chiefs, vassals, or allies of Uzachile also came forward and asked de Soto to free Aguacaleyquen and help them in fighting the Apalachee.

The initial battle at Napituca occurred when 400 warriors arrived and sought to free Chief Aguacaleyquen, diplomacy having failed. Through his interpreter, Juan Ortiz, de Soto had learned of the attempt ahead of time and was prepared to retaliate immediately. Thirty to 40 natives were killed outright, and the remainder jumped into two sinkhole ponds, treading water for hours to prevent capture. In the end, the natives who had been brought from the Tampa Bay region helped to defeat the swimmers. In a speech translated by Ortiz, Uriutina acknowledged that he and the natives of Uzachile were of the same "nation."

Uriutina then tried to kill de Soto, setting off still another battle. When the natives were subdued a second time, de Soto had all of the chiefs tied to stakes and killed with arrows (Elvas 1922:41–42; Ranjel 1922:73–76).

Garcilaso (Varner and Varner 1951:125–171) thoroughly confuses names and events. He calls the region north of the Santa Fe River the "Province of Vitachuco" and says it was governed by three brothers. The oldest, "Vitachuco," is said by Garcilaso to have ruled half the territory, the next younger brother (whose name is not given) three-tenths of the region, and the youngest (Chief "Ochile") the remaining two-tenths. Garcilaso also briefly describes the journey through the province of "Osachile" (Uzachile).

Garcilaso's Vitachuco may actually have been Uzachile, and his two younger brothers may have been chiefs Aguacaleyquen and Uriutina. If this is true, then Garcilaso may be describing a loose alliance or chiefdom. This fits well with the model we have derived from the other de Soto accounts, i.e., all of north Florida from the Santa Fe River north and west nearly to the Aucilla was a single polity, with villages and village chiefs being somewhat equal to one another, but, at least in 1539, all being subsidiary to or allied with Uzachile.

As among the Potano, most of the village names in this region seem to reflect the statuses of chiefs or revered persons or activities. In Aguacaleyquen we have *caley,* as in Ocale, the chief in central Florida, and *qua,* which means "exalted" or "venerated" in Timucua. *Utina* in Uriutina is a chiefly name, and Napituca, as noted above, may have something to do with a sacred fire, or the place where a sacred fire was kept burning. *Chile* in Uzachile may also be a chiefly name. In his account of what he learned while shipwrecked in Florida, d'Escalante Fontaneda refers to Chief Tocobaga of the Tampa Bay region as "Tocobaga-chile" (True 1945:29, 35).

Why are the names of these north Florida peoples not found in later documents, as is the case with the Potano? At least two of the names do appear in another form later. We have already mentioned the village of Uriutina and the later mission at Urica. Aguacaleyquen may also appear in the name of a later mission, San Francisco de Chuaquin, a mission listed in 1655 and mentioned in 1657 (Hann 1990:471), but located a great distance from Aguacaleyquen.

It is possible that de Soto and his army dealt such a harsh blow to the native groups in this area that political relationships were altered. At Napituca the Spaniards killed at least nine village chiefs and perhaps hundreds of warriors. By the time the French established their colony on the northeast Florida coast at the mouth of the St. Johns River, Uzachile and Aguacaleyquen may not have been the names of the major figures. In 1564 Chief Molona on the St. Johns River told the Frenchman Vasseur that in addition to Potano, two powerful interior chiefs, both enemies of Chief Utina, were Onatheaqua and Houstaqua. It is argued below that "Houstaqua" is Yustaga, the Apalachee name for Uzachile. Could "Onatheaqua" refer to Chief Aguacaleyquen or Chief Uriutina, or to another chief who rose to prominence in the region north of the Santa Fe River after 1539, filling the power vacuum created by the devastation inflicted by de Soto's army?

Johnson (1991:chap. 3) argues that this is the case. Onatheaqua, who, like Houstaqua, was said to live near the "mountains" of Apalachee, where gold and silver were mined, was described as painting his face black rather than red, as did Molona and others. Onatheaqua is shown on the Le Moyne–de Bry map as beyond Potano and on the way to Apalachee, which is the proper relative location (Lorant 1946:34–35). This position is consistent with an incident reported by Laudonnière. He once tried to persuade Saturiwa, who controlled the coast from the mouth of the St. Johns River to St. Augustine, to cease his warfare with Utina and form an alliance with him. With this alliance Saturiwa would be able to wage war against his ancient enemy, Onatheaqua (Laudonnière 1975:87). This means that Utina's territory, adjacent to the St. Johns River in Clay and Putnam counties, lay between the territories of Saturiwa and Onatheaqua, especially if one were using either the Mission Trail or the High Road to travel inland.

In the account that accompanied his paintings, Jacques Le Moyne noted that the three chiefs, Potano, Onatheaqua, and Oustaca (Houstaqua), were keeping Utina from being able to reach the "Apalatchy Mountains" where the gold and silver was mined (Lorant 1946:48), again placing Onatheaqua inland (west) from Utina. The *qua* in two of the chiefs' names may mean "revered"; however, if "Houstaqua" is actually "Oustaca," *taca* may refer to charcoal or the black paint mentioned to Vasseur. Both *qua* and *taca* can mean "reverence" or "revered" in Timucuan, and the latter can also be "fire" or "charcoal" (Granberry 1989:182–184). Could "theaqua" and "taca" be the same word in two different dialects, a word referring to black face paint (charcoal), a sign of reverence worn by the two powerful and wealthy chiefs?

The French references to the "mountains of Apalachee," which are said to contain gold and silver as well as hard stone that could be made into wedges to split wood, are puzzling. Less puzzling is the fact that the Florida Indians did have gold and silver, some of which was obtained by the French, whetting their appetites for more. Gold, which the French thought was from mountains in Apalachee, was salvaged by the Apalachee and other natives from wrecked Spanish ships on the Gulf coast, or they got it from other natives who were doing the salvaging. Artifacts made of such metals, ultimately from native societies in Mexico and Central and South America and en route to Spain in the holds of Spanish ships, have been found in post-Columbian

Figure 42

On the Le Moyne map "Apalatci" is placed near the "Montes Apalatci," the Appalachian Mountains, which are located well inland from the Atlantic coast of Florida.

archaeological sites on the panhandle coast of Florida (Mitchem 1989a). Often these metals were reworked by Florida Indians, but some items were clearly made by non-Florida native peoples. The wedges of hard stone may refer to greenstone celts, a stone that was indeed mined by native peoples in the Appalachian Mountains, as was copper.

The Apalachee "mountains" of the Tallahassee area are either an error of information or of translation. One possibility is that the Indians of Saturiwa and Utina exaggerated the size of the hills of the Tallahassee Red Hills area, or else the French interpreted the Indians' statement about these hills as mountains. Another more likely possibility is that the Indians of Saturiwa and Utina may have been referring to a trade route from the Gulf coast to the piedmont and the mountains, on which the chiefdom of Apalachee occupied the southernmost position. Thoroughly confused, the Le Moyne–de Bry map shows the towns of "Apalatci" far to the northwest, among the mountains, instead of to the west in the region of present Tallahassee. It was by this error of understanding and cartography that the Appalachian Mountains got their name.

As noted previously, the natives with whom the French interacted on the lower St. Johns River called their enemies Thimogona. The Thimogona included groups southward along the

St. Johns River as well as peoples who lived several days inland from the river (Laudonnière 1975:66, 75). The Spaniards picked up the word "Thimogona" and used it to refer to much of the inland region east of Apalachee, their province of Timucua of the mission period.

In 1597 Baltasar López, the Franciscan priest on Cumberland Island, Georgia, visited the main town in Timucua Province. The town, located north of the Santa Fe River, was fifty leagues from St. Augustine and ten from the district of Potano (Geiger 1940:120; Hann 1990:461). After founding the San Francisco de Potano mission, Martín Prieto also began to visit the region, reporting in 1607 that there were twenty principal villages subject to one chief (Oré 1936:117). By 1610 Prieto had established the mission of San Martin de Timucua (sometimes called San Martin de Ayacuto) in the principal village of the region. The mission, which had four satellite villages (Oré 1936:127–129), is probably the one that was located at Ichetucknee Springs, possibly near the site of Aguacaleyquen (Weisman 1988; Hann 1990:461; Johnson 1987). The town and its chief apparently still retained some of the importance they had at the time of the de Soto expedition, or else they had once again achieved that importance.

By the time of Father Oré's 1616 visitation two additional missions had been established along the Mission Trail to the west, Santa Cruz de Tarihica[1] and San Juan de Guacara (Hann 1990:462–463). A third, Santa Isabel de Utinahica ("Utina-village") was said to be fifty leagues to the north. Either this was an exaggeration or it was located in southern Georgia in what must have been the northernmost extent of Timucuan speakers (Oré 1936:129–130; Hann 1990:463). Over time, more missions were added: San Augustin de Urica, Santa Maria de Los Angeles de Arapaha,[2] San Francisco de Chuaquin,[3] Santa Catalina de Ajohica,[4] San Ildefonso de Chamile or Chamine,[5] and Santa Cruz de Cachipile.[6] All were probably located in or near Yustaga. A separate mission, also called Ajohica, was present and by 1678 it was the site of a cattle ranch. At that time the mission and its village were abandoned and the people moved to Santa Catalina (Hann 1990:470). Hann notes that Ajohica variously appears as Nihoica or Nihayca. *Niho-hica* is "burned village" (Granberry 1989:167, 177), perhaps a reference to the village or the mission having been burned.

If the number of missions is a reflection of aboriginal population densities, the area of northern Timucua north and especially northwest of the Santa Fe River must have had a much larger population relative to Potano. Potano had only one full-time mission, San Francisco (two, if Santa Fe is counted), while the region to the north and northwest had more than six by the midseventeenth century.

However, as in Potano, the native population of northern Timucua quickly fell in number. In the second quarter of the seventeenth century in the vicinity of Tarihica and its satellite villages, Father Antonio de Cuellar converted an incredible 4000 people. But in 1675 the three missions still in operation had a total population of only 230 people (de Salazar 1675:38).

A Yamassee Indian raid in 1685 destroyed Santa Catalina (Hann 1990:472). San Juan de Guacara and Santa Cruz were similarly destroyed in 1691. These were apparently the last two missions north of the Santa Fe River. Mission villagers were withdrawn to the mission of Santa Fe and to St. Augustine. In 1710 an Englishman, Thomas Nairne, who had traveled through northern Florida (probably along the Mission Trail), wrote, "There remains not now, so much as one village with ten houses in it, in all Florida, that is subject to the Spaniards; nor have they any horses or cattle left, but such as they can protect by the guns of their Castle of St. Augustine" (in Crane 1956:81).

UZACHILE/YUSTAGA

After crossing the Suwannee River, de Soto's army entered the province of Uzachile and marched on to Chief Uzachile's main village. The chief had heard of the depredations that de Soto had visited on his vassal chiefs after the battles at Napituca, and wisely abandoned his village, leaving it to the Spaniards who raided it for food.

De Soto sent his soldiers out and they captured a hundred women and men who were put in chains attached to collars. Garcilaso (Varner and Varner 1951:168–171) describes Uzachile as "small, although well populated." He also describes continual skirmishing with the natives as the army marched from the Suwannee River toward the town of Uzachile through maize fields. Neither Ranjel nor Elvas mentions this.

Uzachile, as discussed above, may have been a paramount chief, who had power over the other village chiefs north of the Santa Fe River, such as Aguacaleyquen and Uriutina, or they were allied with him. Uzachile survived the Spanish invasion, unlike many of the other chiefs north of the Santa Fe River, but his people must have paid a terrible price. Biedma, who renders Uzachile as "Veachile" (probably a mistranscription), provides the information that allows us to equate the Uzachile with the Yustaga. According to him, the Apalachees called the people through whose territory de Soto had just passed *Yustaga* (Biedma 1922:6–7). These people are no doubt the same as the Houstaqua described by Laudonnière (1975:116) and shown as the Oustaca, located east of "Apalatci," a correct location, on the Le Moyne map (Lorant 1946:34–35). This map was engraved in 1591 by Theodore de Bry, based, presumably, on a map that Jacques Le Moyne drew or painted; de Bry apparently tried to "Latinize" some of the names and others simply are mistranscribed.[7] The Houstaqua, along with the Onatheaqua, were said to live near the "mountains," which were the source of gold and other metals.

In 1564 Laudonnière sent La Roche Ferrière to stay with Chief Utina (of the eastern Utina) and to explore the countryside, which he did over the course of five or six months. Even though the Yustaga (Houstaqua) were enemies of Utina, La Roche Ferrière visited at least one of their villages (Laudonnière 1975: 95–96). The chief sent Laudonnière a peace offering consisting of a wolfskin quiver filled with arrows, several bows, four or five painted pelts, and a silver chain. The Frenchman reciprocated by sending clothes, cutting hooks, and axes.

Another Frenchman, Grotauld, also went to Yustaga. On his return he told Laudonnière that the chief of Houstaqua could field 3000 to 4000 warriors. He also said that the chief knew where the Appalachian Mountains were and he sent along to Laudonnière several copper plates from the chief. This copper was said to have been collected by the Indians in the mountains. Laudonnière seems to indicate that he thought the natives confused copper and gold. He did not realize that to the native peoples of the Southeast, copper, which could be mined in small nuggets from deposits in the Appalachian Mountains and cold-hammered, was a highly valued item. It is quite likely that it was the French who confused copper with tales of gold; they wanted desperately to confirm that gold could be mined in La Florida.

According to Grotauld, the mountains were only five or six days from Utina to the northwest (Laudonnière 1975:116). This makes sense if we assume that the French were badly confused about the ultimate source of the metals they saw. They believed metal came from the mountains, but indeed only the copper came from there. However, the Apalachee Indians probably were the source of the Florida copper, having obtained it through trade from more northerly peoples who mined it, and the gold and silver ultimately came from elsewhere in the Western Hemisphere and was salvaged from Spanish shipwrecks. The Yustaga and Onatheaqua could have controlled the trails from the St. Johns River and Fort Caroline to the Apalachee. Both the High Road and the Mission Trail, as well as others, passed through their territories. Seen in this light, Grotauld's statement makes sense. From Chief Utina's lands west of the St. Johns River to the Aucilla River, border of Apalachee, it is about 120 miles. This distance could have been traveled in six days at 20 miles per day, a rate of travel that Indians could sustain.

Even in southern Florida, Fontaneda, the shipwrecked Spaniard, may have heard stories of gold, mountains, the Apalachee, and two powerful chiefs who controlled the trails to the gold. He speaks of the mines of "Onagatano" located in the distant, snowy mountains. Onagatano is said to be vassal to "Abalachi" and "Olagatano" (True 1945:31). If Onagatano and Olagatano are equivalent to Onatheaqua and Houstaqua, the story bears remarkable resemblance to the information told to Laudonnière. The similarities could result from Fontaneda's having lived for a time among the French at Fort Caroline following his rescue from his Indian captors, a possibility about which some scholars have speculated (True 1945).

As already discussed, while at Fort Caroline Laudonnière had two shipwrecked Spaniards brought to him from the natives who had held them. Both had been shipwrecked fifteen years earlier on the south Florida coast (Laudonnière 1975:109–112). Their stories bear some remarkable similarities to Fontaneda's account, written after seventeen years in Florida. If Fontaneda were, in fact, one of the two Spaniards brought to Laudonnière, his often confused sense of the geographical positions of native peoples might account for the inaccurate depictions on the Le Moyne map.

As with the Potano and the other native peoples of north Florida, the Uzachile were a focus of Franciscan missionary efforts. The inland mission chain in Timucua expanded westward from the Potano across the Santa Fe River and west to the Suwannee (between 1612 and 1616). In the early 1630s the first doctrinas were established in Apalachee west of the Aucilla River. It is likely that prior to the Franciscan expansion into Apalachee, the first missions were established in Uzachile/Yustaga (i.e., from ca. 1616–1630s). Four missions were established: San Pedro y San Pablo de Potohiriba (near Lake Sampala),[8] Santa Helena de Machaba,[9] San Miguel de Asile (which may have been subject to Apalachee),[10] and San Matheo de Tolapatafi[11] (Hann 1990: 473–476).

Bishop Gabriel Díaz Vara Calderón visited the Yustagan missions in 1675 and described them as spaced two leagues (ca. five miles) apart, evidently on the Mission Trail (Wenhold 1936). Their relative position within Yustaga suggests something of a shift in settlement from east to west during the mission period, perhaps because Apalachee no longer posed a military threat. At least one rancho was established in Yustaga, near Asile. Calderón (Wenhold 1936:8) refers to the "Ustacanian" Province, an indication that the identity of the region was maintained a century and a half after de Soto and his army marched through it. The four missions were still operating in 1688 (Gatschet 1880:495–497), and a 1689 census lists 330 families for the four (Compostela in Milanich 1978:67).

The mission system in Yustaga was destroyed in 1704 by English slave raiders. But the remains of the Yustagan settlements were still evident in 1778 when the Stuart-Purcell map noted "San Pedro old fields" in the vicinity. Johnson (1991:chap. 6, Tables 8.1, 8.2) notes variations of Yustaga—"Woostooka," "Utoca," "Octoka," "Octoke"—that continued to appear on maps of the eighteenth and early nineteenth centuries, as late as 1821.

EASTERN UTINA AND THE ST. JOHNS RIVER

In the remainder of this chapter we will stray far from de Soto and his travels to examine native peoples in northeastern Florida whom he by-passed. But in the decades following the de Soto expedition, these native peoples were prominent in both French and Spanish colonial affairs. Moreover, at this later time the people of northeastern Florida had dealings with people who *had* been visited by de Soto, and thus their locations corroborate some of our de Soto locations. Hence, although we will be diverging from the de Soto expedition, we will be rounding out the picture of the social geography of sixteenth-century Florida, which, as we stated at the outset, is de Soto's principal bequest to us.

Both the French under Laudonnière and the Spanish under Pedro Menéndez de Avilés came in contact with the eastern Utina in the 1560s. As Johnson (1991) has shown, the accounts of those encounters provide a relatively precise location for the main village of Chief Utina, a location that fits well with cartographic evidence.[12] Johnson's research places the eastern Utina in portions of Putnam and Clay counties at the eastern end of the High Road and the Mission Trail, east of the Potano and the Aguacaleyquen and the villages subject to Uzachile in northern Florida. This means the Utina were too far east to have been in contact with the de Soto expedition in 1539. Let us look at some of the evidence for the location of the Utina.

The French described the journey to Utina from Fort Caroline as follows. After they went by boat up the St. Johns River forty to fifty leagues from the fort, they would tie up their boats and travel overland six leagues to the main town of Utina (Laudonnière 1975:127). Laudonnière several times mentions that when the French went to Utina, they would pull their boats into the mouth of a small river that emptied into the St. Johns River, and tie them up (1975:133, 134, 135). The channel of this creek was narrow enough so that on one occasion the Indians threatened to entrap the French by cutting down trees to block their escape down the lower course of the creek (Laudonnière 1975:136). Using the French league of 2.76 miles, this would mean the small river was 110 to 138 miles up the St. Johns River and Utina's village was 16.56 miles inland. Another French account places Utina just over two days' journey from Potano (Laudonnière 1975:119). Still another bit of information comes from the Le Moyne map, which shows Utina situated on the eastern side of a crescent-shaped lake west of the St. Johns River (Lorant 1946:34–35). However, none of the French or Spanish accounts mentions such a lake adjacent to Utina's main village.

The French visits to Utina took place in 1564 and 1565. In 1566, after having ousted the French from Fort Caroline and renaming it San Mateo, Pedro Menéndez and 100 soldiers and some sailors sailed up the St. Johns River in three brigantines.

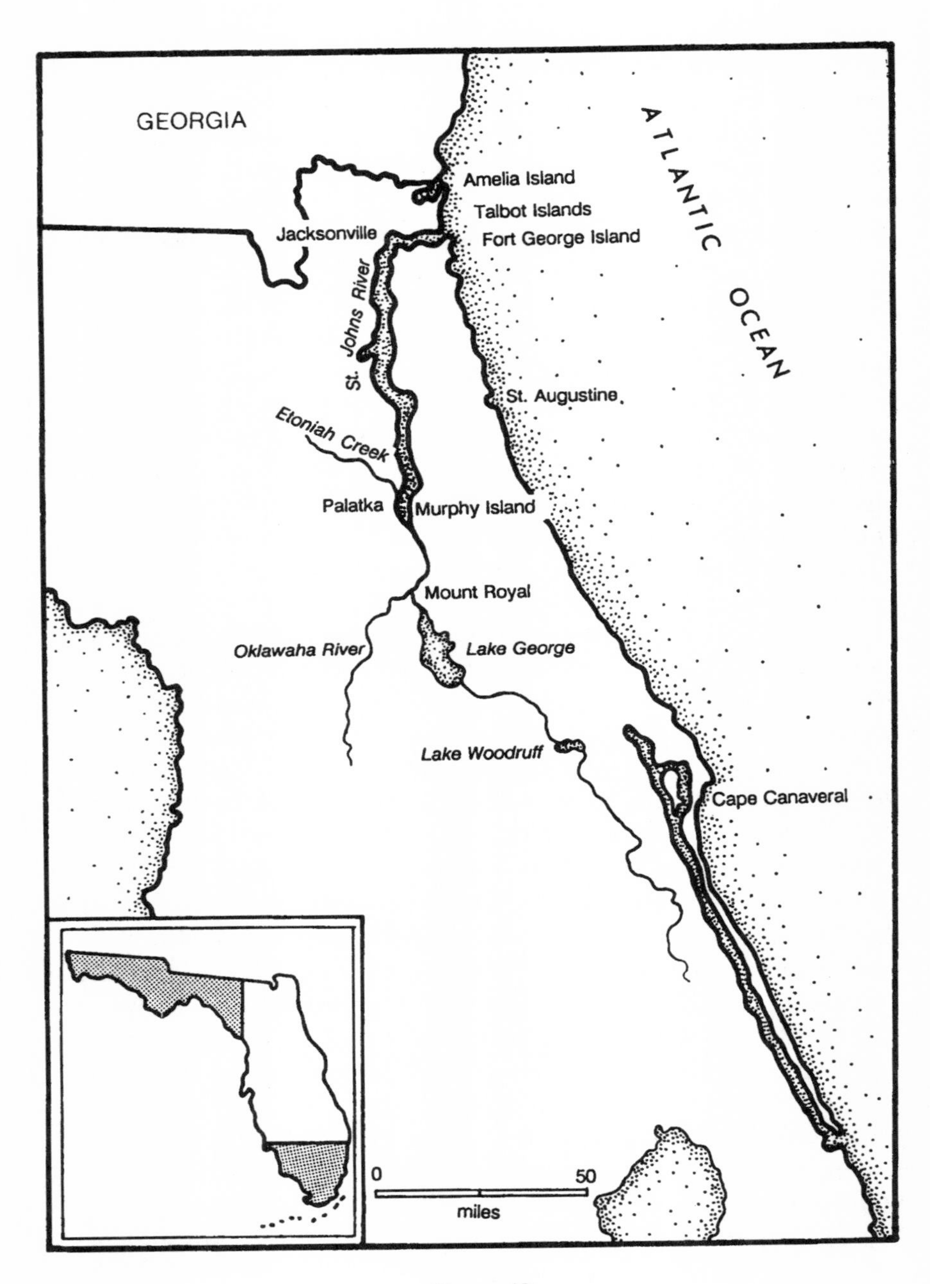

Figure 43

East Florida with locations mentioned in the text.

After having gone twenty leagues, he landed and marched five leagues "though good level lands" to Utina's village (Solís de Merás 1964:202). Using the Spanish league of 3.46 miles, this account would place Utina 70 miles upriver from the former Fort Caroline and 17.3 miles inland from the river. The 70 miles is about right. The distance up the St. Johns is at considerable variance with Laudonnière's estimate and may reflect Laudonnière's never actually having made the trip to Utina and having overestimated the distance. The two estimates of the distance of the village from the river are nearly identical.

Johnson's analysis of these sources, combined with his on-the-ground archaeological surveys, suggests that Utina's village was located in the vicinity of Lake Grandin in northwestern Putnam County, near its boundary with Clay County. That boundary coincides with the Bellamy Road, built atop or close to the Mission Trail shown in the Stuart-Purcell map. The lake shown in the Le Moyne map is an ancestral Lake Grandin, which today has much lower water levels and is composed of a number of smaller lakes and connecting wetlands, all part of the large depression known as the Florahome Trough. Ancestral Lake Grandin may have been at least partially drained when Etoniah Creek was channelized.

The small river or creek where the French and Spaniards tied up their boats and marched about seventeen miles to Utina's village was probably Clarkes Creek, almost directly across the St. Johns River from Picolata, where the Mission Trail reached the east bank of the St. Johns. The trail on the west bank picked up just north of the mouth of Clarkes Creek and went westward, passing by Utina's village. That is the trail the Europeans followed when they arrived from the north, having sailed up the St. Johns River. The distance from the mouth of the river, site of Fort Caroline/Fort Mateo to Clarkes Creek is about seventy miles, which fits well with the Spanish estimate.

One group of Frenchmen was sailing northward down the St. Johns River when they landed, tied up their boats in "a little branch of the river," rather than a small river, and marched to Utina's village (Laudonnière 1975:115). We suspect that this was not Clarkes Creek, but Etoniah Creek which flows southeast from the Lake Grandin locale and empties into the St. Johns River just north of Palatka. It has a wide mouth, and fallen trees could not have blocked canoes from escaping out of the creek, as may have been the case with Clarkes Creek. The aboriginal town of Coya may have been located near the start of this southerly route to Utina (Laudonnière 1975:115).

Etoniah is a corruption of Utina and appears in various forms on several nineteenth-century maps, including "It-tun-wah," "It-tun-ah," and "Etinni," as well as "Etoniah" Scrub (referring to vegetation?), "Itini" Ponds, and, simply, "Itina." On other maps, Etoniah (or "Etonniah") variously refers to a town, a stream, or an area of lakes and sandhills (Johnson 1991:chaps. 3, 5), all in the vicinity of Lake Grandin. The modern use of Etoniah is another example of a sixteenth-century Florida Indian name being retained to the present time. The correspondence of Utina and Etoniah offers strong support for Johnson's placement of Utina.

Utina's village was probably on the northeast side of ancestral Lake Grandin (comprising present-day Georges Lake, Long Lake, and Hall Lake), almost on the Mission Trail and near the upper part of Etoniah Creek. This locale is almost exactly seventeen miles from the St. Johns River along the Mission Trail.

For nearly two years the French and the Utina sought to manipulate each other for their own aims. Chief Utina wanted to enlist the military power of the French to aid him against his enemies. The French needed Utina's good will to enable them to deal with other natives so as to gain access to what they thought were gold and silver deposits. Much gift giving took place to forge ties of friendship, evidently a common native practice. Gifts were also exchanged between the Spanish and Utina. Menéndez gave Chief Utina, who was estimated to be twenty-five years old, a shirt, breeches, a green silk doublet, and a hat (Solís de Merás 1964:208). This may have been the standard gentleman's outfit of the time, for Menéndez gave the same clothes to the chief of the Calusa.

Utina's people grew maize and beans and ate a great deal of fish. They also harvested acorns and "water chinquapens" (Solís de Merás 1964:202–203; Laudonnière 1975:125, 128). When Menéndez first marched to Utina's village, it rained for the first time in six months, watering the maize fields and causing Utina to think that the Spanish governor possessed great supernatural power.

In 1565 the French at Fort Caroline were starving because they had not been resupplied and had run out of food. They tried

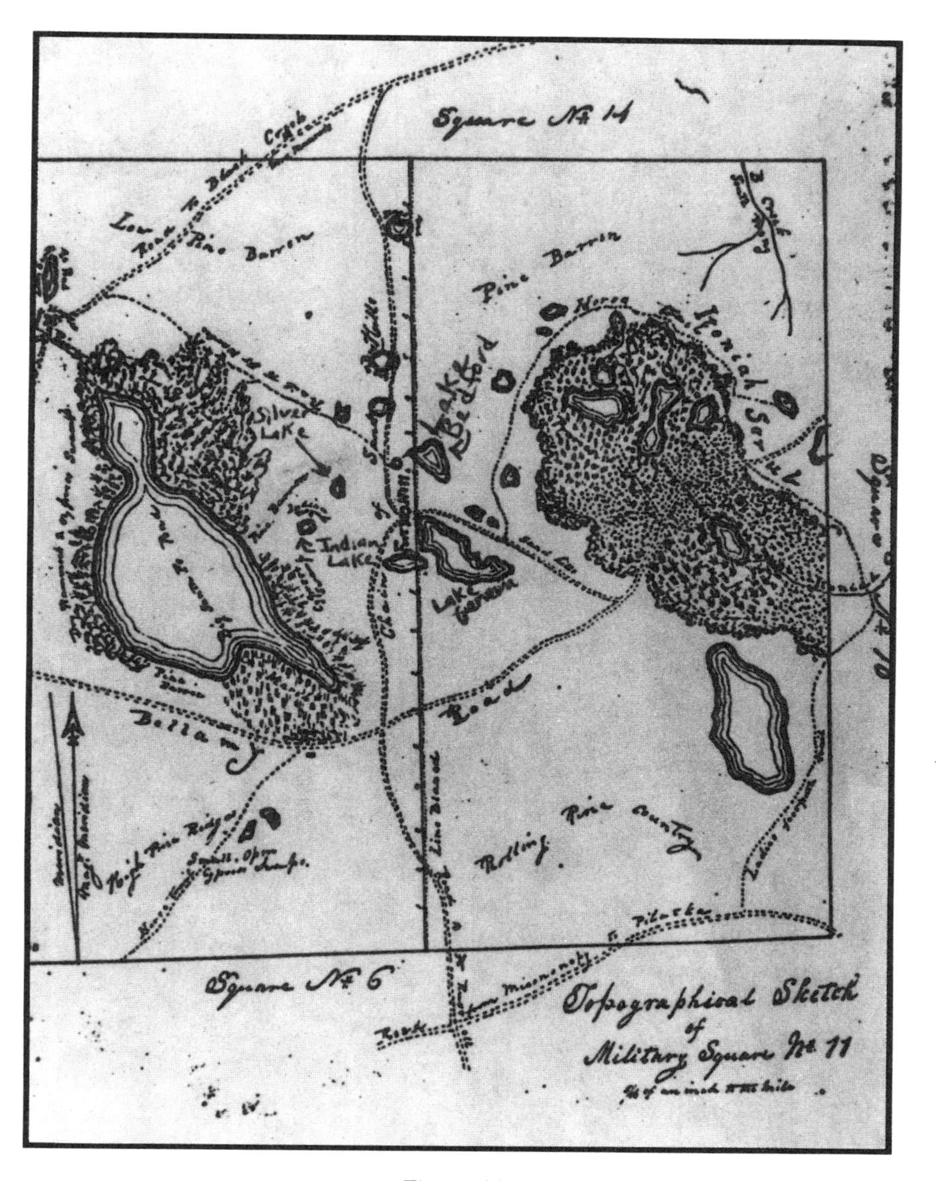

Figure 44

A Second Seminole War period map, which shows the Mission Trail (here the Bellamy Road) and the "Itoniah scrub." The names of Silver Lake, Indian Lake, Lake Bedford, and Lake Geneva have been written on the map recently. [The map is from the U.S. National Archives, Record Group 77, Civil Works Map File, L247–91. This copy was provided by Kenneth Johnson.]

desperately to force Utina to provide them with maize and other foods but were rebuffed, even after they took Chief Utina hostage. The natives apparently thought they could wait out the situation, eventually getting what they desired from the French. At one point, in May, the French lamented that Utina did not yet have maize or beans to give them, because planting had only recently taken place and there were no crops to harvest. In June the French heard that maize was being harvested upriver, south of Utina at Enecaque, but that apparently proved to be untrue, or, more likely, the natives only told the French they did not yet have corn.

Along the St. Johns fish were taken in large quantities in weirs. Menéndez threatened to burn villages, canoes, and weirs belonging to native groups who tried to flee from him and his men when they sailed upriver (Solís de Merás 1964:203). Apparently, the loss of canoes and weirs would have been a severe economic blow to the natives.

Solís de Merás (1964:184) describes the guerillalike military tactics of the natives and says it was difficult to fight them. To defeat them, the Spaniards would go to the village of the Indians; cut down their crops; burn their property, houses, and weirs; and take their canoes, thus destroying "all the property they have, so that they must leave the land." They used this same tactic to put down native rebellions in the seventeenth century as well.

The people living along and near the St. Johns River must have used canoes a great deal. The lowering of ground water and droughtlike conditions over the last decade have uncovered a very large number of aboriginal dugout canoes in the various ponds and lakes (remnants of ancestral Lake Grandin) in the Utina region. Research by Barbara Purdy of the University of Florida has shown that more dugout canoes have come from that locale than from any other single locality in Florida (Purdy 1991).

The archaeology of the St. Johns River Valley has been well described (Goggin 1951; Milanich and Fairbanks 1980:145–166). The St. Johns ceramic assemblage is distinctive and is present at many sites, including huge shell middens and villages that have been found along the river from its mouth to Lake George and beyond. Some of the sites dating from the late pre-Columbian period have burial mounds and mounds built as bases for temples and other structures.

Less well known is the archaeological assemblage found in the Lake Grandin–Florahome region, thought to be the eastern Utina region. Johnson's surveys in the area turned up sixteen sites on the northeast edge of the Florahome Trough, near Hall Lake and practically on top of the Mission Trail in southwestern Clay County (Johnson 1987:62–66). Other pre-Columbian sites have been recorded for the northern end of the trough. The aboriginal pottery at these sites includes types associated with the St. Johns archaeological culture; the Cades Pond culture, found before ca. A.D. 750 at sites on the southern end of the Florahome Trough and around the east side of Lochloosa Lake; and the Alachua tradition or the Indian Pond complex. At the northern Florahome Trough sites Johnson also found seventeenth-century, and possibly later, Spanish ceramics along with pottery known to be associated with people living on the Georgia coast. Perhaps the Spanish were moving natives from Georgia into Utina in the seventeenth century. The Cades Pond and St. Johns archaeological assemblages are quite distinct from the Alachua tradition and Indian Pond assemblages found to the west among the Potano and the Aguacaleyquen and related native groups north of the Santa Fe River.

From the efforts of the French to befriend him, it seems apparent that Utina, called "Olata [Holata] Ouae Outina" by the French and referred to as a "great king," was the most powerful chief along the St. Johns River north of Lake George and south of the natives around Fort Caroline, the latter of whom were his enemies. Utina's power and importance is verified by Chief Molona, one of his vassals, who told the French that Utina had more than forty vassal chiefs, although Molona could only name nine—ten with himself. An eleventh, Astina, was named by Utina as a vassal (Laudonnière 1975:76, 125). In his narrative, Fontaneda also mentions Utina, calling him "lord of his land" and stating that he was located sixty leagues inland along the San Mateo River, i.e., the St. Johns River. Fontaneda adds that Utina had the Saravai (Calanay or Calabay?) and Moloa (Molona?) as vassals, two of the ten listed by Molona (True 1945:35–36). This account, however, might well be derived from information Fontaneda received from the French, as suggested above.

Le Moyne (or de Bry), using Laudonnière's account that contained Chief Molona's recounting of Utina's vassals, placed the names of all eleven on his map (Lorant 1946:34–35). Trying to use that map, however, to pinpoint the locations of the Utina vassals is difficult because the map, rather than being an accurate geographical representation, is more of a schematic plan, summarizing knowledge and showing relative locations. It is based on information that Le Moyne got from Laudonnière and other French (also Spanish and Indian?) sources. Some information is undoubtedly hearsay, and other information must have suffered from bad translations. The French did not have a translator with skills like those of Juan Ortiz, who accompanied the de Soto expedition. Consequently, many distances and compass directions are in error, while general relative positions may be correct, e.g., one village is shown as being farther away from Fort Caroline than another. In at least one instance where we have independent information on exact locations, it can be shown that Le Moyne is incorrect. The locations around Port Royal (South Carolina), for which we have information from the Juan Pardo expeditions of the later 1560s, are clearly erroneous on Le Moyne's map: Le Moyne has Adusta (i.e., Orista) to the west of Port Royal Island while it actually lay to the north of Port Royal Island.

On the other hand, the map does appear to show the bends in the St. Johns River accurately. For example, the big bend beside and just north of Palatka seems to be shown along with other bends in the river from about Jacksonville to Lake George. The river from Jacksonville to its mouth appears also to be reasonably correct, except that the distance is much too long relative to the river distance south to Lake George. The accuracy that does exist, however, may be deceiving. Le Moyne's (or de Bry's) placement of native groups along the river is not totally consistent with their relative positions given in the French accounts, such as the sequence of towns recorded by the French on their return trip north down the St. Johns River from Lake George. This may be an artifact of the engraver, however, who had to get all the names on the map.

But all is not lost. In August 1566 Pedro Menéndez sailed with a small expedition up the St. Johns to explore, make friends with the natives, and determine whether the river flowed into the Gulf of Mexico (Solís de Merás 1964:202). This is the trip on which Menéndez visited Utina on his return downriver. Some of the information from the account of the Spaniards' trip up the St. Johns River can be correlated with the French account of their similar trip, as well as with later mission-period documents (e.g.,

Figure 45

Le Moyne's map showing the St. Johns River drainage and many of the Timucuan groups mentioned in the 1562–1564 French accounts.

Hann 1990) to provide clearer information on the eleven Utina vassals and other of the sixteenth-century native groups who lived along the central St. Johns River from Lake George northward to Utina's territory.

The Spaniards sailed up the St. Johns River and, apparently, across Lake George. They then rowed a short distance further, into the narrow, braided river system just south of the south end of the lake (present-day Hitchins Creek, Blue Creek, and the river's main channel). They said the point they reached was two leagues (about seven miles) farther than the French had gone. Menéndez knew this because he had with him two of the same guides who had accompanied the French. Laudonnière's men apparently had turned back when they reached the north end of Lake George. Possibly the French halted at Dayton Island, which is actually about ten miles from the lake's other end.

The French were told by natives that even if one climbed up in a tree the lake was so large one could not see to the other side (Laudonnière 1975:115). Some of Menéndez's men duplicated his 1566 trip to Lake George in 1567, but we have little information on what occurred (Solís de Merás 1964:233).

One of the guides with Menéndez on the 1566 journey up the St. Johns had been shipwrecked among the Ais Indians. It could not have been Fontaneda, who said that he "spoke four languages, but not the language of Ais and Jeaga, which is a country I never travelled into" (True 1945:31). The guide who accompanied Menéndez had been in Ais, and he offered this account of what lay beyond Lake George. In some respects it is remarkably like Fontaneda's account of south Florida:

> *The guide and interpreter the Adelantado [Menéndez] brought with him had been a slave of a cacique of Ays [Ais on the lower Atlantic coast of Florida] . . ., who lived 20 leagues up [south of Lake George] the river [the St. Johns] . . .; he told the Adelantado that he ought to return [down river], for there were many and very warlike Indians in that land, and that they told him that the river became very narrow from there inland [south] for more than 30 leagues, until it emptied into a large lagoon they call Maymi, which they say has a circuit of more than 30 leagues, and which gathers into itself many streams from the hill range; and that (a branch of) this lagoon discharged itself in the country of Cacique Carlos, which is on the coast of [toward] New Spain, and that another branch drained the land of Tequesta, which is at Los Martires. (Solís de Merás 1964:205)*

Listed below are the eleven known vassals of Utina and a discussion of the other groups mentioned in the French and Spanish accounts of the 1560s. The first nine listed are those given by Chief Molona.

1. ***Cadecha.*** The Le Moyne map shows "Cadica" well west of the St. Johns, near Ocale and Acuera. In Timucuan *ca-hica* means "that town"; Molona may have referred to one of the other towns he listed, but the translator for the French may not have realized it. In other words, the Cadecha may not be a people or town at all.

2. ***Chilili.*** The Le Moyne map shows Chilili on the east side of the St. Johns beside the island town of Edelano. This is in error, because a firsthand French account places it north of both Edelano and Enequape (Laudonnière 1975:115). Chilili (once given as "Chilily") may be related to "Chile," a chiefly term.

3. ***Eclavou.*** On the map "Eclanou" is shown well east of the river.

4. ***Euacappe.*** This is certainly the same as "Enequape," which was north of the island town of Edelano and south of Chilili (also "Enecaque"; see Laudonnière 1975:115, 131). The Le Moyne map shows "Enecappa(?)," but it is much too far north, although it may have been on the east side of the river, as it is depicted on the map. Laudonnière met a sister of Utina at the village of "Enecaque" and took maize from there to feed his soldiers.

The later mission of San Antonio de Enecape was established by 1587, presumably at the same town (Oré 1936; Hann 1990:439). The mission was possibly near Palatka or on Dunn's Creek, north of Murphy Island, identified below as the probable location of Edelano. In 1602 this might have been the town referred to as "Anacabila" (Deagan 1978:110–111). Documents at various times in the seventeenth century mention the mission. In 1680 mission San Antonio de "Anacape," apparently previously abandoned, was reestablished to serve Yamassee Indians. At that time it was said to be twenty leagues from St. Augustine (Hann 1990:439–440, 504–506).

5. ***Calanay.*** "Zaravay" (also Saravai) is also mentioned by Fontaneda as being a vassal of Utina. He says the village of Calanay was fifty to sixty leagues—an exaggeration—up the St. Johns River, and that if one left the river at that point and traveled from village to village on a westerly course, one could reach Canogacola, subjects of Tocobaga, and then Tocobaga itself (True 1945:46). Such a journey would actually have to be south-southwest. That a passage from the St. Johns River to Tampa Bay existed intrigued the Spanish, who sought it at both ends, i.e., from the Tocobaga at Tampa Bay and from the Macoya (described below) on the St. Johns River. Tocobaga cautioned Menéndez about traveling to Macoya from Tampa Bay because the Indians on the way were "numerous and warlike" (Solís de Merás 1964: 228–229, 233).

On their 1566 trip up the St. Johns River the Spaniards reached the Calanay seven to eight leagues downriver from the Macoya and the south end of Lake George. Calanay was said to be a vassal of Utina, and Menéndez was afraid he might attack, evidently because Menéndez was allied with Chief Saturiwa, who controlled the coast and adjacent interior around Fort Mateo and St. Augustine. To forestall such an attack, Menéndez pointed out that Calanay was only twelve leagues (41.5 miles) overland from St. Augustine, implying that he could retaliate quickly if provoked. Because it was so close, Menéndez agreed to Calanay's request to leave six soldiers there to give the Indians religious instruction. Three of the soldiers were to stay with Calanay and the other three were to go to another chief, Macoya, farther upriver. Menéndez said that if Calanay harmed the Spaniards, he would destroy the chief's canoes, houses, and weirs and cut off the heads of all the men, women, and children.

Later, when a jealous Chief Saturiwa heard that Calanay had resident Christians, he sent people to kill them or demand that they be brought to him. Calanay instead sent them back to San Mateo; he must have feared Menéndez more than Saturiwa. Using a nautical league of 3.67 miles, Calanay would have been 26 to 30 miles north of the north end of Lake George, possibly somewhere around Palatka and roughly 40 miles overland from St. Augustine, the distance estimated by Menéndez. The Le Moyne map shows Calanay east of the river on a tributary.

A deposition taken from Roberto Meleneche, a Spaniard who had sailed to Fort Caroline with Laudonnière in 1564, names "Carava" as one of four chiefs located closest to the fort (Saturiba was another; Bennett 1964:91). This Carava appears not to be the Caranay located much farther upriver. It is likely that it should be "Carana" and that is a variant of Saranay, a group located near the fort and probably subject to Saturiwa.

6. ***Onachaquara.*** The Le Moyne map shows Onachaquara well east of the river, beyond Calanay. This name may actually refer to the Oathchaqua, said to be at Cape Canaveral (Laudonnière 1975:112) and also shown on the Le Moyne map as "Oathkaqua." In other words, the map may have duplicated the name.

7. ***Omittaqua.*** "Omitaqua" is shown on the Le Moyne map well east of the St. Johns River.

8. ***Aquera.*** This group is probably the "Acuera" of the de Soto narratives, which we located on the Oklawaha River near Lake Weir (see chapter 4). This location would be fifty miles south of Utina. If indeed the Acuera were vassals of Utina, it may reflect an expansion of Utina's power following the devastation wrought in Acuera by the de Soto expedition.

In 1616 the friar from San Luis de Acuera went to Enacape to meet with Luis Gerónimo de Oré (Hann 1990:460). He could have traveled by canoe down the Oklawaha and the St. Johns rivers.

9. ***Moquoso.*** It is unlikely that these were the same Mocoso living at Tampa Bay (see chapters 4 and 5). As we noted in our

discussion of the Mocoso, the Le Moyne map shows a "Mocoso" west of the St. Johns River and south of Cadica; it also shows a "Mocossou" south of Cape Canaveral near the coast. The deposition from Meleneche, cited above, says that when the French journeyed up the St. Johns River to Lake George, they learned that three Spaniards they were seeking were being held by Chief Guajaca, and Mocoso was another chief nearby. The implication was that both were located somewhere farther south.

10. ***Astina.*** During the period when the French had run out of food, Utina tried to enlist their military help in capturing and punishing Astina, a vassal chief who had been disobedient. Utina promised the French they could get maize and acorns from Astina. Desperate for food, the French agreed, but soon learned that the clever Utina actually had led the French soldiers against one of his enemies, not a wayward vassal. The French were furious and retaliated by taking Utina hostage (Laudonnière 1975:127). The Le Moyne map shows Astina northward of Utina, west of the St. Johns River.

11. ***Molona.*** The Frenchman Le Vasseur met Chief Molona after having traveled up the St. Johns for two days (Laudonnière 1975:75–76). On his return to Fort Caroline, the incoming tide was so strong the French could not row against it, and they chose to land even though they were still three leagues from their goal. They went ashore and spent the night at the village of a second chief also named Molona (Laudonnière 1975:78). In the evening Le Vasseur, in order to go along with the entreaties of his host, fabricated a tale about how he had used his sword to kill some of Molona's enemies, the Thimogona, who lived upriver. Much to his surprise, one of Molona's men later pulled a dagger and stabbed one of Molona's sons. When asked for an explanation, Molona said it was a ceremony to remember the ways in which ancestral chiefs had been killed by the Thimogona, their enemies:

> *. . . [E]very time he or any of his friends or allies return from the Thimogona without bringing back the scalps of their enemies or without bringing home some prisoner, he ordered as a perpetual memorial to all his ancestors that the best beloved of all his children should be struck by the same weapon by which his ancestors had been killed. This was done to renew the wounds of their death so they would be lamented afresh. (Laudonnière 1975:81–82)*

This second Chief Molona, the one nearest Fort Caroline, may be the same individual as Chief "Emola," who gave the alarm to the French when the Spaniards landed to the south, at St. Augustine, prior to their raid on Fort Caroline (Laudonnière 1975:159). Chief "Emoloa" was later put in chains at Fort San Mateo by the Spaniards, in retaliation for the natives' killing Spanish cattle. Also, because it appeared that the people under Saturiwa were massing for a raid on the Spaniards, Emoloa and other captives, all apparently vassals of Saturiwa, served as hostages (Solís de Merás 1964:233). Roberto Meleneche listed "Molua" as one of the native groups close to Fort Caroline (Bennett 1964:91).

"Moloa" was also mentioned by Fontaneda as a vassal of Utina (True 1945:36), but which Molona is not specified. The Le Moyne map shows both: "Homoloua" near the mouth of the St. Johns and "Molona" farther upstream near the big bend where modern Jacksonville is located. In 1602 a "Molova" was listed as one of the Agua Dulce Province mission villages, apparently referring to the Molona that was farthest downriver (Deagan 1978:110–111). It was five leagues from San Juan del Puerto, a mission on Fort George Island north of Jacksonville (McMurray 1973; Hann 1990:454–455).

There are several additional native chiefs and towns in the St. Johns River Valley north of Lake George who are mentioned in the French and Spanish narratives and who are not said to have been vassals of Utina. Macoya was apparently the southernmost, located at the south end of Lake George (and beyond?). Menéndez's exploration of the St. Johns River was stopped in Macoya's territory, where he encountered a narrow channel, probably in the braided river system at the south end of the lake. The channel had a blockade of posts built across it by Macoya to prevent passage. The Spaniards broke through the blockade and began to row through the narrow channel, which was only two pike lengths wide, about 25.5 ft (a pike was a unit of measure about 12.75 ft in length; Hann 1989a). Eventually, however, their vulnerability to attack led Menéndez to withdraw. Macoya was seven to eight leagues south of Calanay.

On his voyage south from Fort San Mateo, Menéndez had stopped at Utina's village and demanded that the chief send word to his vassals farther upriver and along the Spaniards' route that they not flee when Menéndez and his soldiers approached.

Although Utina hid from Menéndez, he apparently did command his vassals to receive the Spaniards. As a consequence, from the Spaniards' point of view, all of the natives from Utina south to Macoya were cooperative. Macoya, however, did not answer to Utina. He was an independent and powerful chief who, along with Utina and Saturiwa, controlled a section of the St. Johns River.

The Macoya are probably the Mayaca associated with the seventeenth-century mission San Salvador de Mayaca, said to be thirty-six leagues from St. Augustine (Hann 1990:487, 506–507). A late seventeenth-century document reports that the Mayaca lived on islands and very large lakes (Hann 1990:507), an apt description of a location south of Lake George in a region encompassing Lake Dexter, Lake Woodruff, and the other lakes that are a part of the St. Johns River system there. The distance from St. Augustine also fits.

Hann's study of the Mayaca (1991a) presents additional documentary evidence from several sources that confirms the location of the Mayaca in this region. Those sources indicate that the Mayaca controlled a large territory that one scholar has summarized as: south of a line drawn from the southern end of Lake George to the Atlantic coast and north of a line drawn from the Orlando area to Cape Canaveral (Lyon 1982:168–169). Documents also indicate that the Mayaca spoke a language different from that of the Timucuans to the north (Hann 1991a). It could have been another dialect of Timucuan, or a different language entirely.

The name of the Mayaca continues to appear in Spanish documents into the early eighteenth century, and some of the groups were living in villages near St. Augustine (Hann 1991a). A 1735 letter written by the Franciscan priests in Florida said that the Mayaca had been annihilated (Deagan 1978:111). But this might not have been entirely true. In 1743 Mayacas (also "Maiacas") were said to be living four days north of Tequesta, which was at the mouth of the Miami River (Sturtevant 1978:147).

The Le Moyne map has several names on it that appear to be related to Mayaca, but which were most likely separate groups, all located north of Lake George. Mathiaca is placed just north of Lake George on the west bank of the river, and Mayarca is on the opposite bank slightly farther north. A third is Mayrra. After sailing about twenty leagues up the St. Johns River to reconnoiter, the Frenchman d'Ottigni met Indians who told him they could take him to Mayrra where there was gold and silver. One of his men left with the Indians, apparently going upriver.

D'Ottigni then traveled another ten leagues farther up the St. Johns and encountered the same man in a canoe. He said that the Indians had wanted to take him on a three-day journey to Mayrra, but that he did not want to go without permission (Laudonnière 1975:74–75). D'Ottigni gave permission and returned to Fort Caroline. Fifteen days later, the soldier met Vasseur at Chief Molona's village (the one farthest upriver) carrying five or six pounds of silver. This is the same incident that one of Laudonnière's men wrote home about. He says "d'Antigny" and Le Vasseur had discovered a gold and silver mine sixty leagues up the St. Johns River (Bennett 1964:70).

According to the deposition of Roberto Meleneche, the voyage the French made to Lake George took ten days (and covered sixty to seventy leagues), but only five days to return downstream to the fort (Bennett 1964:90). D'Ottigni must have been approximately half that distance when his man left on what was to be the three-day canoe trip to Mayrra, suggesting that Mayrra could have been at the north end of Lake George. The Le Moyne map shows Mayrra on the eastern side of the river north of Lake George.

A perhaps confused second French account of that trip to Lake George says that the French "were fully thirty leagues above a place called Mathiaqua, and there they discovered a lake so broad that the other side of it could not be seen" (Laudonnière 1975:114–115). It is uncertain exactly what is meant. Probably "Mathiaqua" refers to a group that were farther upriver, but whose territory the French never reached. Fontaneda (True 1945:36) mentions the "Mayaguaca," who are said not to be vassals of Utina and who live in the "land of Ais."

It is likely that in the Timucuan language, *my* or *mai* is "fresh water," and *hica* is certainly "village." Mayaca, Mathiaqua, Mayaguaca, Mathiaca, Mayarca, and Mayrra might all refer to people who lived on the freshwater St. Johns River and its lakes and tributaries or in adjacent wetland regions.

Another town mentioned in the French accounts is Edelano, located on a large island in the St. Johns River south of Enecape (Laudonnière 1975:115, 131). An island with Edelano on it is shown on the Le Moyne map, but it is much too far north relative to Chilili, which it was said to be south of. From Edelano to the river side of the island there was a walkway 300 paces long and 50 paces wide. Huge trees grew on both sides of the walkway, with their branches intertwined overhead. A walkway similar to this led from Utina's main town (Laudonnière 1975:115, 137), and the same kind of arrangement is archaeologically present at the Mt. Royal archaeological site. Naturalist William Bartram visited this site twice (in 1765 and 1774). His description was published in 1791 (in Van Doren 1928:101–102):

> *At about fifty yards distance from the landing place stands a magnificent Indian mount. About fifteen years ago [actually nine years] I visited this place, at which time there were no settlements of white people, but all appeared wild and savage; yet in that uncultivated state it possessed an almost inexpressible air of grandeur. . . . But what greatly contributed towards completing the magnificence of the scene, was a noble Indian highway, which led from the great mount, on a straight line, three quarters of a mile, first through a point or wing of the orange grove, and continuing thence through an awful forest of live oaks, it was terminated by palms and laurel magnolias, on the verge of an oblong lake, which was on the edge of an extensive green level savanna. This grand highway was about fifty yards wide, sunk a little below the common level, and the earth thrown up on each side, making a bank of about two feet high.*

The Indians of Edelano murdered Frenchman Pierre Gambaye, whom Laudonnière had sent to live with the Indians and to explore their country. Gambaye had collected a quantity of gold and silver from the Indians, and the chief of Edelano had him slain in order to get it back. Laudonnière went to capture and punish the chief, but when he arrived the chief had fled, abandoning his village, which the French burned (Laudonnière 1975:116–117, 131).

The island on which Edelano was located is probably Murphy Island, just south of Palatka. Aboriginal earthworks were observed on the island in the early twentieth century, but were indistinct (Goggin 1951:55). A bone European comb was recovered from one of the mounds on the island (8PU20; Goggin 1951:125).

Two other towns probably on the upper St. Johns north of Lake George were Patica and Coya. Both were visited by the French on their return to Fort Caroline from Lake George (Laudonnière 1975:115). Patica was north of Chilili and south of Coya. The latter was where the French tied up their small boats in a small branch of the river and then went inland to visit Utina. We have suggested that the branch of the river was the mouth of Etoniah Creek just north of Palatka. Laudonnière says that Patica was eight or nine leagues from Utina's village, which suggests that it was several leagues south of Coya.

The Le Moyne map has "Patchica" and "Choya" placed in the proper relative positions on the west bank of the river, but Choya (Coya) is on the outside of the large bend near Jacksonville, too far north. The map also shows a "Patica" as the village closest to the mouth of the St. Johns River, on the south bank.[13] This latter Patica may be the same as "Palica," the location of a blockhouse Menéndez had built on the Matanzas River, five leagues south of St. Augustine (Hann 1990:430–431).

Utina seems to have held sway over much of the lower St. Johns River, at least from Picolata and Clarkes Creek south to Lake George. This stretch of river was home to a large number of natives, and villages were said to be present along both sides of the river (Bennett 1964:90). Today numerous archaeological sites, especially shell middens, offer mute testimony to the native societies living there in the sixteenth century. Goggin has placed many of the St. Johns River archaeological sites on a map (1951). There are two very dense regions of sites north of Lake George. One is from the lake north to Palatka; this probably correlates with the region of the villages mentioned in the French accounts as vassals of Utina. Another dense distribution is from about Jacksonville east to the mouth of the St. Johns River. These sites might well include the river towns that were subject to Saturiwa. Between them, from about Palatka to Jacksonville, there are many fewer sites. That region may be the buffer between the two powerful chiefs. South of Lake George is a third region of dense site distribution, most likely the territory of the Mayaca, Mayaguaca, and other south Florida native groups. The northern rival of Chief Utina, Chief Saturiwa, and his allied native chiefs and peoples are examined in the next section.

SATURIWA AND OTHER NORTHEAST FLORIDA INDIANS

The nearest neighbor of the French was Chief Saturiwa, who controlled the territory from the mouth of the St. Johns River down the coast to St. Augustine (True 1945:35). He also controlled the area inland and upriver for a distance, although, as noted, there may have been a buffer between his territory and that of Utina. One of Laudonnière's men wrote that the "Tymangoua" (or Thimogona), Saturiwa's enemies, were a three-day journey upriver (Bennett 1964:66). Saturiwa himself only took two days by canoe to reach the land of his enemies when he went to raid them (Laudonnière 1975:85).

Saturiwa (also "Sotoriva," "Saturiba," and "Satouriona") had the title of *paracousi* or war chief (Laudonnière 1975:61), the same title as the powerful chief located inland from Tampa Bay whom de Soto's men had visited. As war chief, Saturiwa was said to have had thirty other chiefs as vassals, ten of whom were his brothers (Laudonnière 1975:76). The term "brother" was probably an example of fictive kinship, signifying an alliance between chiefs. For example, Chief Calanay told Menéndez that he "held him [Menéndez] to be his elder brother, which is all the obedience the caciques of Florida can give" (Solís de Merás 1964:207). "Brother" was frequently used to describe relationships among other Florida chiefs.

Saturiwa's village was located on the south bank of the St. Johns River near its mouth. Barrientos provides a description: "One enters the harbor (the river mouth) . . . , and on the left hand there is a pueblo of 25 large houses, where in each one live eight or nine Indians with their wives and children, because (those of) one lineage live together. The pueblo is called Saturiba: by this name do the Lutherans [French] call the cacique who is the lord of this place" (Solís de Merás 1964:159).

This suggests that each house contained about 35 persons, meaning the village population could have been as large as 875. Possibly married females of the same lineage or clan lived with their husbands and children in reasonably large multifamily houses. Such a matrilineal pattern of residence was present elsewhere among native groups in the southeast United States.

Saturiwa's most important vassal was perhaps Atore, his son, who also was called *paracousi*, probably reflecting his eventual

Figure 46

A 1591 engraving by de Bry (based on Le Moyne) depicting Chief Saturiwa preparing for war.

inheritance of that title (Laudonnière 1975:61, 132, 140). It is not certain that Atore had his own village. The Le Moyne map shows Atore's and Saturiwa's names together at one village, but Laudonnière mentions a separate village called "Athore" (Laudonnière 1975:132). When the French sailed north to the Satilla River to get corn, they found an assembly of principal leaders, meeting "to have a good time," and one of these was Atore (Laudonnière 1975:139–140).

Another of Saturiwa's vassals was Chief Omoloa, named as one of the chiefs who accompanied Saturiwa's war party up the St. Johns River (Laudonnière 1975:85). Omoloa (also "Emola") was said to live in a village near the fort (Laudonnière 1975:156; see the above section on Utina). Omoloa is probably the same as the chief called Molona, who lived three leagues from the fort and five from the mission of San Juan on Fort George Island (Hann 1990:454–455). Le Moyne's map shows "Homoloua," evidently referring to the Omoloa, not far from the mouth of the river and the fort, which is labeled "Carolina" on the map.

This chief's son was one of six natives whom Menéndez took to Spain in 1567. This individual and two others, also from northeast Florida, were referred to as "principal Indians" or highly ranked individuals. The other three were from Tequesta (Solís de Merás 1964:236, 238, 243). At least one of the Tequestas was returned to Florida in 1568 (Hann 1990:7); the others died in Spain. Before their death, while being taken through a town in Córdova on the way to be presented to the king in Seville, one of the de Soto expedition veterans spoke with them (Varner and Varner 1951:641). That account says there were seven Indians taken to Spain and that six died. Omoloa is certainly the same as Molo or Moloa, a village under the jurisdiction of San Juan del Puerto in 1602.

Several other chiefs who lived near the fort and were probably vassals of Saturiwa are mentioned, although none are specifically said to be allies or vassals. Malica, a "brother" of the above Chief Molona, lived near the fort (Laudonnière 1975:80, 156). Le Moyne places him on the river on the opposite side of Homoloua from the fort. Across the river from Malica, according to Le Moyne's map, is Casti, also said to be near the fort (Laudonnière 1975:156). From Casti it is a great distance to the next upriver towns, Molona and Choya, located on opposite sides of the river at the bend near Jacksonville, but rather far apart.

Next to Molona is a town labeled "Timo" with "ga" underneath, probably "Timogona" (Thimogona). Although engraved as a single village, that name probably indicates the northern extent of Saturiwa's enemies, i.e., the point on the river where Utina's power began. This relative location on the river fits well with our knowledge that Molona and probably Coya were vassals of Utina, Saturiwa's enemy. The relative distances among the various towns also suggests that a buffer existed between the territories controlled by Utina and Saturiwa and that the buffer was specifically between Molona and Coya, on the one hand, subjects of Utina, and Casti, on the other hand, subject of Saturiwa.

Two other allies or vassals of Saturiwa, said to live near the French fort, were Allicamany (also "Allicomany") and Saranay (also "Serranay") (Laudonnière 1975:156). Meleneche confirms that "Macani" was near the French settlement, and Le Moyne places the town ("Alimacani") just north of the mouth of the St.

Figure 47

The locations of Saturiwa (below the mouth of the St. Johns River) and Timo-ga (upper left below Choya) on the Le Moyne map.

Johns River (Lorant 1946:34–35). "Alimacani" is also mentioned by Fontaneda, who seems to verify that he was a vassal of Saturiwa (True 1945:35).

Further north on Le Moyne's map is the river "Sarrauahi," which must represent Saranay (the "Carava" of Meleneche). The river could be the inland waterway between Fort George Island and Black Hammock Island, or else between Fort George Island and either Little Talbot or Talbot islands. Laudonnière said that the village of "Sarravahi" was located about one and a half leagues from the fort, "on an arm of the river," and he sent men there to obtain clay for bricks and mortar (1975:96). In 1602 "Calanay" was a village one-quarter league from San Juan; another document refers to the "high gullies" of "Saravay," possibly a reference to the mine where clay was quarried (Hann 1990:456). "Carabay," "Sarabay," and "Saravay" also appear as place-names near the mouth of the St. Johns River.

The village or place of Saranay was most likely located on Fort George Island itself, or nearby on Little Talbot or Talbot islands. One clay source has been found on a small marsh island in between Fort George and Little Talbot islands. If, as Fontaneda said, Saturiwa's political influence extended down to St. Augustine, then the Seloy living there were also subject to him (True 1945:35; Laudonnière 1975:159).

Several other native chiefs and groups are also mentioned in the French accounts and probably lived in northeast Florida or farther north. The "Tacadocorou" or Tacatacuru were encountered at the mouth of the Satilla River (called the Somme by the French), along with the "Apalou." Their leaders were part of the group present at the assembly where Atore also was present. The Tacatacuru lived on Cumberland Island, site of the mission of San Pedro de Mocama founded by Baltasar López (Deagan 1978:100–104; Hann 1990:431). *Taca-curu* is "black or charcoal colored" in Timucuan, and, as we have seen, *apalu* is "fort." Le Moyne's map does show "Appalou," but it is well inland, beyond Potano and east of Yustaga. The town on the map may represent the town of Apalu through which de Soto passed before arriving at Uzachile (Yustaga), but it seems doubtful that anyone from that town would travel to the coast of Georgia to confer with coastal chiefs. There was also an Apalu in Potano, suggesting that there might have been several villages with that name.

Another native group was the Hioacaia, said to be twelve leagues north of the fort, probably just north of Cumberland Island. The chief of this town was dead, but his widow gave the French baskets of corn, acorns, and cassina leaves (Laudonnière 1975:114). These leaves, similar to *mate*, were used to brew a caffeine-containing beverage (see Hudson 1979). The Le Moyne map shows "Hiouacara" north of Saranay near the coast. In 1602 "Hicachirico" was a town one league from San Juan del Puerto (Hann 1990:456), but this probably was not the same village.

The widow of the chief of Hioacaia was carried on the backs of her subjects as a sign of reverence and esteem, and she was said to rule over a land that was the most productive of any along the coasts. She may have lived on the mainland in northeast Florida or on Amelia Island.

It is uncertain if Hioacaia's widow was a chief, although she clearly was awarded high status. The French documents do mention at least one female chief, Niacubacany, "queen of the village and neighbor of our fort" (Laudonnière 1975:132).[14] Female chiefs seem to have been not uncommon among the Timucuan speakers in northeastern Florida and southeastern Georgia (e.g., see Deagan 1978:103; cf. Hudson 1990:93).

Let us now leave the native societies of north and northeast Florida and return to our reconstruction of the route of the de Soto expedition, picking up the story at the Aucilla River, the eastern margin of Apalachee territory. All that the Spaniards had seen or experienced on their way to the Aucilla River would pale once they reached the territory of the Apalachees, who were the first exemplars of the magnificent native societies the army would encounter in the interior of La Florida.

CHAPTER VIII

TO APALACHEE

The Aucilla River marked the boundary between the Timucuan-speaking Uzachile and the Muskhogean-speaking Apalachee. That drainage is also an archaeological division. To the east, the Uzachile, Aguacaleyquen, Uriutina, and other north Florida peoples were associated with the Suwannee Valley archaeological complex; from Agile west into northwest Florida was the Apalachee-related Fort Walton assemblage. Archaeologists can trace this boundary back to about A.D. 800, roughly the time when maize agriculture began to be integrated into the native economies.

When de Soto's army marched into Apalachee, the Spaniards entered a region where the political complexity and military might were much more like the populous native chiefdoms of the interior of the Southeast than they were like the smaller aboriginal societies in peninsular and northern Florida. These differences are clearly reflected in the observations of the de Soto chroniclers and those of later Spaniards.

On October 1, de Soto and his army departed the village of Agile and marched into the territory of the Apalachee. The Spaniards first came to the River or Swamp of Ivitachuco, the Aucilla River (Biedma 1922:7; Ranjel 1922:79).[1] On the other side of the river lay the chiefdom toward which the Spaniards had been heading since departing from Ocale nearly two months earlier.

The Aucilla River, for the space of a stone's throw, was said to be over one's head. Then for the distance of a crossbow shot it was waist deep, and past the river channel there was tall swamp grass and then a dense growth of woods (Elvas 1922:46; Ranjel 1922:79).[2] This description of the River or Swamp of Ivitachuco is similar to the description provided by the Stuart-Purcell map, which says the "Assilly River" was "fordable, but in high freshes . . . (it has) wide swamps and marshes on each side which are chiefly overflowed in great freshes" (Boyd 1938a:19). Judging from the Spaniards' experience in crossing the Aucilla, it was out of its banks when they approached it. Garcilaso says it was one and a half leagues wide, perhaps reflecting the total distance through the woods, flooded river backswamp and river (Hann 1989a), or else this is an exaggeration.

Only a narrow footpath led through the foliage on either side of the river (Varner and Varner 1951:176). From the cover of this foliage, the Indians of Apalachee attacked the Spaniards as they attempted their crossing. De Soto's men were able to fell some trees across the channel, and in this way they reached the other side and secured a place where they could cross (Elvas 1922:46). Then they built a bridge over the river. This crossing was probably near the present U.S. 27 highway bridge, on the Mission Trail.

THE MARCH TO INIAHICA

On October 3 the army crossed over the bridge and began making its way through the swamp and flooded woods. By noon the Spaniards had succeeded in crossing to the other side, and they went on to the town of Ivitachuco, only to find that the inhabitants had set it on fire and then fled. The army may have pitched camp in the fields next to the destroyed village (Varner and Varner 1951:181–182).

It is not clear how far de Soto's army traveled on its first day west of the Aucilla River. But considering that it had to spend a half day making a difficult crossing of the river and swamp, fighting Apalachee warriors every foot of the way, it is doubtful that the army moved as much as five leagues. Garcilaso says that it only traveled two leagues after crossing the river and swamp (Varner and Varner 1951:181).

Ivitachuco, a major Apalachee town throughout the mission period, was probably on or near the Mission Trail, close to the site of the later Apalachee mission of San Lorenzo de Ivitachuco.

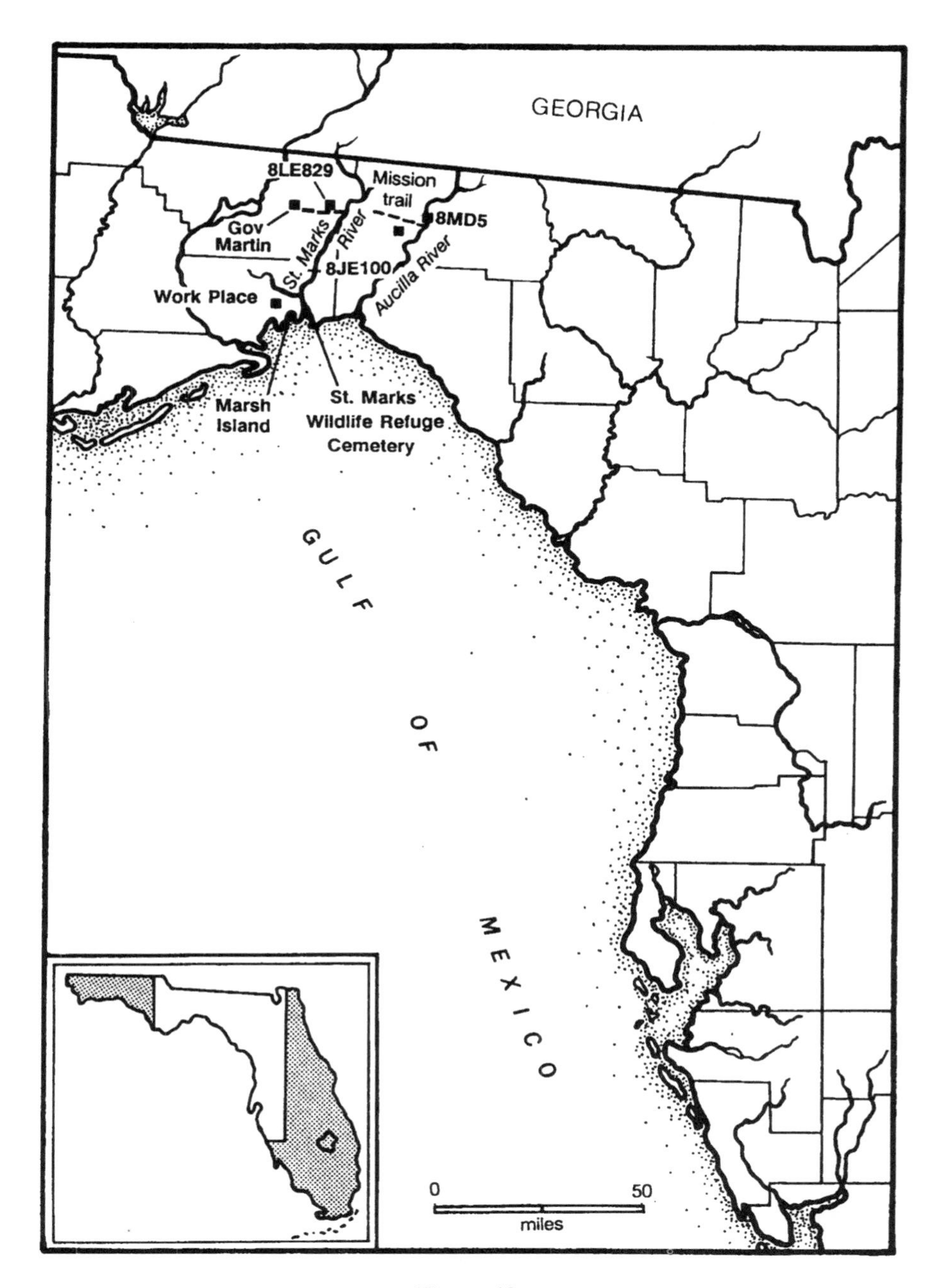

Figure 48

Archaeological sites (in bold) and the Mission Trail in northwest Florida.

That mission (8JE100), located by B. Calvin Jones, is about one-half mile south of Lake Iamonia (the one in Jefferson County, not the one in Leon County) and south of U.S. 27, which runs on or near the main Mission Trail. Except for when it was misled by guides, the army probably followed what later became the Mission Trail into the heart of Apalachee.

In addition to seventeenth-century ceramics, the mission site of Ivitachuco contains aboriginal pottery dating from the early sixteenth century, varieties of types that are the same as those found at the excavated de Soto winter camp in downtown Tallahassee (the village of Iniahica). The Ivitachuco that was burned as de Soto and his army approached could well have been at the later mission site proper, but it was more likely to have been one of the several other sites located close by, roughly around Lake Iamonia (e.g., 8JE242–249, 251). That mission Ivitachuco is different from the Ivitachuco visited by de Soto is hinted at in an early 1650s document found by Hann that speaks of an "Old Ivitachuco" (1990:476).

A third possibility is that the 1539 Ivitachuco was somewhat farther north, where there is another cluster of sites (8JE216–219) that are closer to the Mission Trail and U.S. 27. The route from the Aucilla River would have taken the army north of Anderson Bay to this cluster of sites, all of which contain Fort Walton pottery. Either location (one is a mile and a half north of the other) is about seven miles from the Aucilla River crossing, which fits with Ranjel's statement that the crossing was completed at noon and that by nightfall the army had reached the village.

The Spaniards apparently remained at their camp at Ivitachuco on October 4, resuming travel on October 5. They took a route toward the west, following the Mission Trail that took them near Waukeenah and Lake Catherine and then Wooten Lake and Crow Pond. Along the way they passed by many homesteads and maize fields (Elvas 1922:47; Hann 1989a). That evening they reached a village called Calahuchi, where they captured three Indians and found a large quantity of dried venison (Ranjel 1922:79).[3]

In the course of this day's travel, Garcilaso describes an incident that may help locate the route precisely. As always, there is the question of whether Garcilaso has correctly located this incident with respect to the entire route. In any case, according to Garcilaso, two leagues after departing from an unnamed village (which must have been Ivitachuco), the Spaniards came to a deep arroyo containing a great quantity of water and bordered on either side by dense forest. The Indians had built a barricade in this ravine to impede the Spaniards. When they passed through it, the Indians attacked them in a strong assault (Varner and Varner 1951:182–183; Hann 1989a).

If the Spaniards were following the Mission Trail, which is most likely, this ravine would have been Burnt Mill Creek. The incident, if true, could have taken place just north of the intersection of U.S. 27 and the creek.

Then, if we are to trust Garcilaso, in the remaining two leagues the army traveled that day, the country was devoid of agricultural fields and habitations. Garcilaso makes no mention of a town at the end of this day's march, but Ranjel says the army spent the night at the village of Calahuchi (1922:79). This is a Muskhogean name, and the *-huchi* ending would lead one to believe that it was located on a creek, river, or lake. The accounts of Garcilaso and Ranjel, the most detailed for the route through Apalachee, do not exactly correspond. Because of the discrepancies in Garcilaso's account of the journey elsewhere in Florida, we put more trust in Ranjel's version of the events.

Frank Keel's survey suggests that Calahuchi was one of a number of sites located west of the St. Marks River and south of Lake Lafayette. The sites, spread out over about three miles in a roughly north-to-south direction, include 8LE156, 158–161, 169, 172, 173, 829, 845, and 903, and straddle the Mission Trail (Keel 1989). These are the first recorded sites encountered when traveling west of Burnt Mill Creek that are of the proper time period. Their distance from Ivitachuco is about fifteen miles, one day's travel, and Burnt Mill Creek is almost exactly halfway to our proposed location for Ivitachuco.

Keel (1989) suggests that a likely candidate for Calahuchi is the Sharpe's site (8LE829) located by Stephen Bryne and Rochelle Marrinan in 1986. It is an eleven-acre village on the south side of Lake Lafayette just north of the Mission Trail. The site contains aboriginal pottery dating from the early sixteenth century. Garcilaso's description of fields of corn, beans, and squash on both sides of the road in this area, with small settlements scattered about, fits with the presence of the other sites in this locale (Varner and Varner 1951:182).

WINTER CAMP

On October 6 the army continued traveling, but was at first impeded by the loss of its guide, who had run away at Calahuchi. An old man replaced him, but he was said to have led the Spaniards astray. When they discovered that he was leading them at random, they got an Indian woman to guide them to Iniahica, the main town of Apalachee "where the lord of all that country and Province resided" (Elvas 1922:47; Ranjel 1922:79). Elvas calls the town "Anhayca Apalachee" and Biedma (1922:7) says "Iniahico." We will refer to the town as "Iniahica," following Ranjel, but supposing that the "v" in Ranjel's rendering of the name—"Iviahica"—has been mistranscribed.

Because the Indian man misled it, it is unlikely that the army traveled five leagues that day. If we are to trust Garcilaso, the main town of Apalachee was only two leagues, about seven miles, from the place where the army spent the previous night (Varner and Varner 1951:183), but again we are not certain his account is correct.

After setting up a base of operations in Apalachee, de Soto sent a party of men back to the Tampa Bay camp to order the men there to move forward. On this journey, Garcilaso says that the main town of Apalachee was eleven leagues, about thirty-eight miles, from the swamp of Ivitachuco (Varner and Varner 1951:197). We would also expect that Iniahica was on the main trail, the Mission Trail (approximated by U.S. 27), which de Soto and his army had been following, but from which they were misled for a time. If Garcilaso's coordinates are correct, we would expect that Iniahica was somewhere in the vicinity of Tallahassee, near U.S. 27, seven miles (two leagues) from the Sharpe's site, and thirty-eight miles (eleven leagues) from the Aucilla River. And indeed it was.

In 1987 B. Calvin Jones of the Florida Bureau of Archaeological Research made what is the most spectacular archaeological discovery to date related to the route of the Hernando de Soto expedition in Florida. Jones found the site of the Apalachee town of Iniahica where de Soto and his army spent the winter of 1539-1540. His discovery, verified by archaeological excavations at the site (called the Governor Martin site, 8LE853; Ewen 1988, 1989), has pinpointed the only aboriginal town on the route in Florida whose identification and location are virtually certain. The Governor

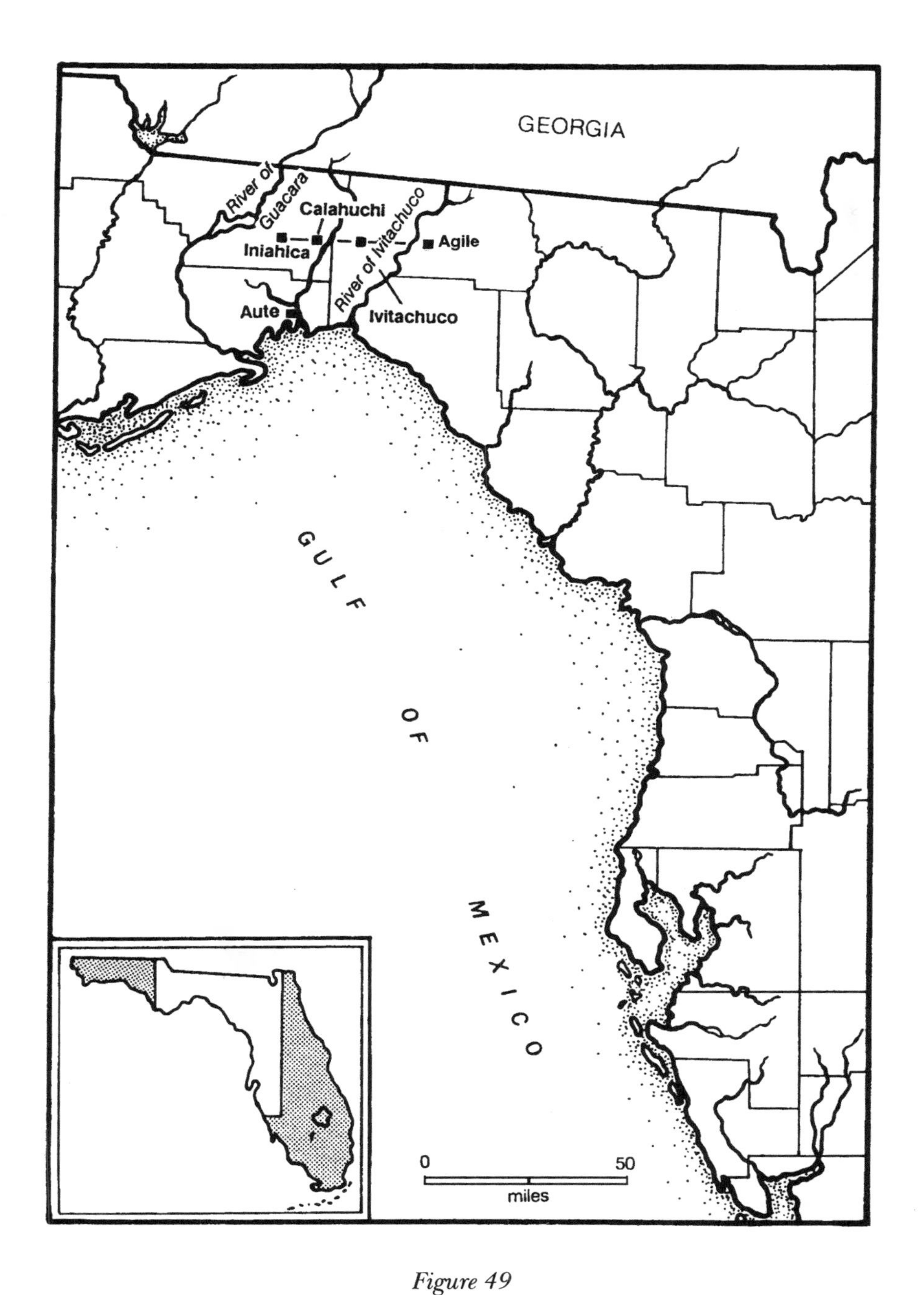

Figure 49

Route of the de Soto expedition from Agile into present Georgia. De Soto names are in bold.

Martin site is located in downtown Tallahassee, one block south of U.S. 27 and seven miles from the Sharpe's site. It is also roughly thirty-five miles along the Mission Trail from the Aucilla River.

That the location of the site matches information in Garcilaso's account may be fortuitous. However, the archaeological site's location is consistent with our contention that it would be near the Mission Trail and within three days' travel time from the Aucilla River.

The Spaniards spent five months in the town, which the native Apalachees had deserted. Garcilaso describes the town: "The Adelantado returned to the village, which consisted of two hundred and fifty large and good houses. In these he found all his army lodged, and he took quarters in those of the Cacique, that were to one side of the village, and as houses of the lord, surpassed all the rest" (Hann 1989a).

Although this description does not specify that there were mounds in the main town, it does imply that it contained a plaza. The army was assigned lodging "round about this settlement" of Iniahica (Hann 1989a).[4] In addition to the principal town, Garcilaso notes there were many more villages scattered throughout the vicinity at one-half, one, one and one-half, two, and three leagues away (Hann 1989a). This pattern of dense settlement is reflected in the similarly dense distribution of archaeological sites in the Tallahassee area (Keel 1989).[5] According to Garcilaso, some of these villages were said to be composed of 50 or 60 dwellings to more than 100, and some had less. There were also a great number of houses (homesteads), which were scattered over the landscape and not arranged as a town (Hann 1989a).

The entire province was said to be pleasant and the land fertile, with an abundance of food, and fish were caught throughout the year (Varner and Varner 1951:184; Hann 1989a). The Spaniards sent foraging parties out to the outlying villages to gather food to store at Iniahica for the winter. Elvas (1922:47) says maize, pumpkins, beans, and dried plums (persimmons) were collected.

Shortly after de Soto arrived in Apalachee, he sent out explorers to the north and to the south. Captains Arias Tinoco and Andres de Vasconselos went in two different directions toward the north. One was gone eight days and the other nine days, and both traveled fifteen or twenty leagues before returning. These men almost certainly reached what is now the state of

Georgia, entering the counties of Decatur, Grady, or Thomas, and they may have reached as far north as Mitchell or Colquitt counties. They reported that they found many towns, with abundant food, and that the land was clear of swamps and extensive forests (Varner and Varner 1951:185).

Their reports were very different, however, from that of Captain Juan de Añasco, whom de Soto had sent south. In that direction the country was very hard to cross because of the swamps and the dense undergrowth. The farther south Añasco went, the worse the terrain became. This implies that the center of Apalachee was located in the hilly region north of the coastal lowland, which Iniahica, the Governor Martin site, indeed is.

The chroniclers describe in some detail Añasco's exploration to the coast, said to be ten leagues away (Hann 1989a).[6] Añasco and the infantry and cavalry who accompanied him crossed a couple of small streams when they set out. When they approached the coast, they came to the Indian village of Ochete, six leagues from Iniahica (Hann 1989a).[7] Garcilaso (Varner and Varner 1951:188) calls the town Aute, the name we will use.

Near the coast the Spaniards located the remains of Pánfilo de Narváez's camp where in 1528 he and his men had built vessels in which they attempted to sail to Mexico. Ranjel (1922:79) says the camp was eight leagues from Iniahica. De Soto's men found the skulls of Narváez's horses, the slips in which the vessels had been built, the site of a forge, and mortars in which Narváez's men had ground corn (Elvas 1922:48; Ranjel 1922:79–80; Hann 1989a). Narváez's camp was located on a broad and spacious bay, but it was some distance from the coast itself. Garcilaso says the camp was three leagues from the coast and twelve from Iniahica, but both distances may be overestimations of the actual distance (Varner and Varner 1951:192).

Mitchem (1989a) suggests that Aute was on the Wakulla River, which meets the St. Marks River just before the latter flows into Apalachee Bay, south of Tallahassee. The town is most likely the Work Place site (8WA11) on the west bank of the river. A large amount of early sixteenth-century artifacts have been found in the nearby Marsh Island Mound (8WA1), including iron tools, glass beads, brass bells, and other items. Downriver is the St. Marks Wildlife Refuge Cemetery site (8WA15), which also contained European items. Clarksdale hawks bells, faceted chevron beads, and other glass bead types tie the site to the early sixteenth

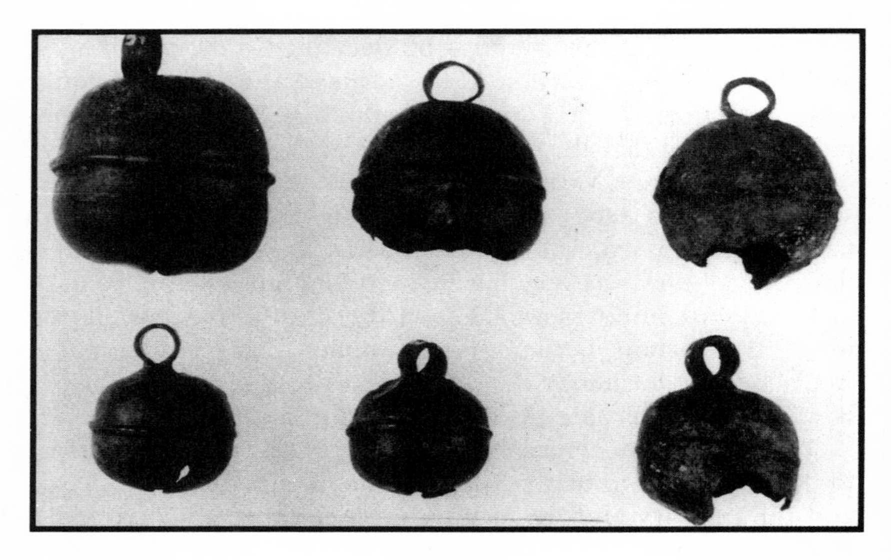

Figure 50

Clarksdale bells, a type of small bell found on early Spanish contact sites in the southeastern United States (see, e.g., Brain 1975; Mitchem and McEwan 1988). All but the lower right specimen are from the St. Marks Wildlife Refuge Cemetery site (courtesy Jeffrey Mitchem). The sixth bell, slightly less than an inch in diameter, is from a site in Glades County, Florida.

century (see also Marrinan, Scarry, and Majors 1990). That site is probably near Narváez's camp, which was on the wide mouth of the St. Marks River, a distance inland from Apalachee Bay.

The Work Place site is about twenty miles—six leagues—south of Tallahassee. State roads 319 and then 363 probably follow the old trail south. The short trip to Aute was uneventful. However, once the Spaniards reached that village, the rest of their journey to Narváez's camp and then to the Gulf of Mexico was a nightmare (Varner and Varner 1951:186–193). A guide tricked them and continually got them lost, leading them on a wild goose chase through the estuarine and coastal marshes. Eleven years before, in June 1528, the Narváez expedition had faced similar difficulties in reaching Aute and the same inlet, the mouth of the

St. Marks River, where it had camped and built its vessels. It had taken that expedition eight or nine days from Apalachee to reach Aute (Bandelier 1905; Hann 1989a). Quite likely, Narváez had not come from Iniahica but from another Apalachee town, and had traveled southward to the coast and then through the coastal marshes, finally coming to the St. Marks River and Aute. The Narváez expedition might well have also been misled by an Apalachee guide.

On October 20 de Soto sent Juan de Añasco with thirty cavalry back to Tampa Bay to tell Captain Calderón to move forward and join them at Apalachee (Biedma 1922:7–8; Elvas 1922:48; Ranjel 1922:81; Varner and Varner 1951:196). Añasco made this journey in just ten days (Elvas 1922:48). If our reconstruction is accurate, the straight-line distance he covered in this time was about 320 miles, or 93 leagues. Biedma (1922:7) notes it was 110 leagues from the port to Iniahica, a slightly longer distance that may more accurately reflect the more sinuous route of the expedition.

After returning to the camp on Tampa Bay, Añasco ordered the two caravels back to Havana, taking on board twenty native women he had captured on his return trip (Elvas 1922:48). Calderón burned the village in which they had been staying, along with surplus supplies. Only Garcilaso says Calderón gave much of the supplies to Chief Mocoso, whose men carried away not only food and clothing, but also curiasses, bucklers, pikes, lances, and steel helmets (Varner and Varner 1951:227–228). Calderón then led the cavalry and some crossbow men northward on the route to Apalachee, and Añasco sailed with other of the foot soldiers on the brigantines and boats for Apalachee Bay (Ranjel 1922:81).

In the meanwhile, de Soto had sent men to the coast with planks and spikes with orders to build a small vessel that would hold about thirty armed men (Elvas 1922:49). Each day they would go out two leagues into the bay, looking for Añasco's sails. Añasco did, in fact, have difficulty in sighting the markers he had previously placed on trees on the coast, but eventually he made contact with the men in the boat (Biedma 1922:8). Añasco reached Iniahica on December 28, and Calderón arrived six days later (Varner and Varner 1951:246). De Soto had sent men to the coast to help guard the Spaniards when they arrived.

De Soto immediately sent the brigantines under the command of Maldonado in search of a port to the west. Maldonado was absent on this mission for about two months, during which time he coasted the shore, entering the rivers, creeks, and coves, until he came to a good protected port with deep water where a ship could come very close to shore (Varner and Varner 1951:248). An Indian town that lay beside this coastal port (Biedma 1922:8–9) was called Achuse (Ranjel 1922:81).[8] The Bay of Achuse was said to be sixty leagues from Apalachee Bay. Both this description and the distance fits Pensacola Bay very well. From Apalachee Bay, taking a straight route after rounding Cape St. George, it is 200 miles to Pensacola Bay—61 nautical leagues. In 1559 the Spaniards led by Tristán de Luna y Arellano would attempt to place a colony in the Bay of "Ochuse" (see chapter 9).

By this time de Soto was ready to continue his expedition to the north. On February 26 he sent Captain Maldonado in the two brigantines to Havana with instructions to meet him at Achuse the following summer. Moreover, if de Soto did not appear at Achuse during the coming summer, Maldonado was to return to the same place the summer after that, and de Soto would definitely be there (Elvas 1922:50). Biedma, on the other hand, says that de Soto told Maldonado that if he had not heard from him in six months, he should run the shore looking for him as far as the river Espiritu Santo—the Mississippi River (Biedma 1922:9). Before tracing de Soto's route into the interior of La Florida, we will first look at the archaeological evidence from the Governor Martin site and then see what other information about the Apalachee Indians is contained in the narratives.

THE GOVERNOR MARTIN ARCHAEOLOGICAL SITE

Spanish artifacts from seventeenth-century mission-related archaeological sites are reasonably common in Leon County. Over the years many such sites have been found by B. Calvin Jones, archaeologist for the Florida Division of Historical Resources. In March 1987, Jones sought permission from a developer in Tallahassee to put several exploratory excavations in a potential mission site in the downtown section of the town, less than one mile from the capitol building itself. He indeed found artifacts from the mission that he thought was in the vicinity, but

Figure 51

Fort Walton archaeological culture pottery from the Governor Martin archaeological site (courtesy Roy Lett and the Florida Bureau of Archaeological Research).

he also found Spanish and Fort Walton culture aboriginal artifacts that dated to a century before the first Apalachee missions were established. It was soon apparent that Jones had found the village of Iniahica, where de Soto and his army had wintered for those five months in 1539–1540.

The Governor Martin site, named for Florida Governor John Martin who had a home built on the site in the 1930s (quite unaware it was an archaeological site), was the subject of intensive excavation in 1987, with analysis and other investigations continuing into 1988. Research was funded by private donations, the Florida Bureau of Archaeological Research, the Florida Division of Recreation and Parks, and a grant from the National Endowment for the Humanities administered by the University of Florida's Center for Early Contact Period Studies and the Florida Museum of Natural History. The research was directed by Charles R. Ewen (see Ewen 1988, 1989).

The de Soto encampment was just that: a military camp set up by the Spaniards where they could wait out the winter that was approaching. We would expect to find aboriginal artifacts discarded or left behind by the Apalachee, who had abandoned their town at the approach of the Spaniards. We would also expect to find trade goods—beads and the like—that the Spaniards carried with them as gifts for native peoples. These trinkets should be the same types found at the Ruth Smith, Tatham Mound, and other de Soto contact sites (see chapter 4).

Because the army lived in the village for five months, setting up housekeeping, the site of Iniahica should also contain refuse left as a result of everyday activities—such things as hardware and broken Spanish ceramics. At least some buildings were constructed by the Spaniards, and it is known that the army had horses and a drove of pigs, providing the opportunity for still more archaeological evidence to be recovered from the site. As it turned out, examples of all of these artifacts, and more, were excavated from the Governor Martin site. Most of the Apalachee pottery is of types dating from ca. A.D. 1450–1660, and it constituted about 90 percent of the artifacts found. Ewen's research identified new varieties of aboriginal pottery that are excellent time markers for the de Soto era, and those types can now be sought at other Apalachee sites, providing chronological markers.

Small amounts of Spanish majolica pottery of types common in the sixteenth century (one type from the early sixteenth century), were recovered, as were pieces of Spanish olive jars known to date from ca. 1490–1570. The latter were used to transport olives and olive oil and other liquids. Several varieties of sixteenth-century glass beads recovered were of the types found at other de Soto–contact sites in Florida, including the site thought to be near Aute on the Gulf coast south of Tallahassee.

Iron nails, some possible horseshoe nails, and an iron point from a crossbow dart lend evidence of the army's presence. Ewen and Jones and their field crew members also found thousands of small U-shaped and S-shaped pieces of iron about one-third to three-quarters of an inch in size, which have been proven to be fragments of chain mail. An X-ray of a clump of the rusty fragments revealed fourteen of them still linked together, confirming that the links were indeed from armor.

Of the five copper coins recovered, two could be dated between 1505 and 1517. The other three are thought to be Por-

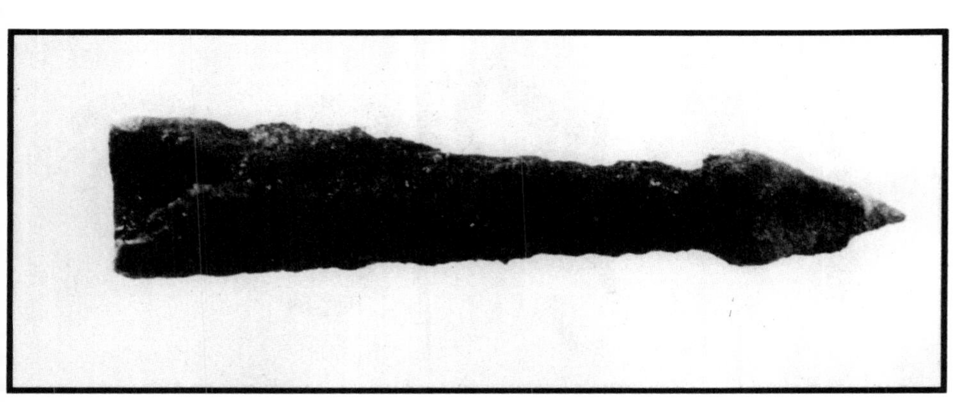

Figure 52

This iron crossbow dart tip is from the Governor Martin site (courtesy Roy Lett and the Florida Bureau of Archaeological Research). It is about two inches long.

tuguese *ceitils* from the sixteenth century or earlier. One of the most dramatic recoveries was a pig mandible, probably from one of the pigs brought to Florida by the expedition as meat-on-the-hoof.

The excavation at the Martin site not only provided a firm location for Iniahica, it gave us a detailed list of the kinds of artifacts that should be found at other de Soto campsites. Recently, Emlin Myers, a scientist with the Smithsonian Institution's Conservation Analytical Laboratory, has analyzed some of the sixteenth-century Spanish ceramics from the Governor Martin site to determine their manufacturing source. This is done by detailed analysis of the pastes of the ceramics and comparison with clays used to make the same kinds of ceramics at manufacturing sites both in Spain and in Spanish colonies in the New World (Myers and Olin 1990).

The analysis demonstrated that the Governor Martin/Iniahica ceramics were from no known manufacturing center. The ceramics, whose paste types are similar to one another, were made at a center that has thus far escaped identification. One

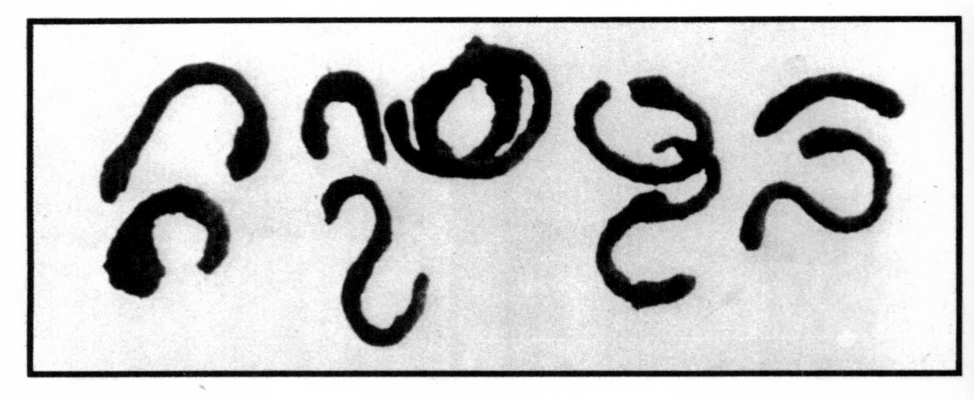

Figure 53

Pieces of chain mail also excavated from the Governor Martin site (courtesy Roy Lett and the Florida Bureau of Archaeological Research). The larger pieces are about three-quarters of an inch long.

hypothesis to be tested is that the de Soto–expedition ceramics came from Cuba, purchased there by participants during the months the army resupplied and outfitted itself in preparation for the Florida entrada.

Portions of the Governor Martin site have been purchased by the state of Florida and preserved, thanks to the efforts of the Trust for Public Lands. This historically and scientifically important Apalachee town will thus be available for research and interpretation to future generations of archaeologists, as well as to the public.

THE APALACHEE

Although the de Soto expedition spent five months among the Apalachee, the three chroniclers—Biedma, the Gentleman of Elvas, and Ranjel—provide little information on this native province that had gained such fame and notoriety among the other Florida Indians. Even Fontaneda, shipwrecked in southern Florida, had heard stories of "Abalachi," located in the direction of Panuco (i.e., along the Gulf coast toward the route to Mexico) and "where resounds the fame of its abundance of pearls." According to the shipwrecked Spaniard, the Apalachee were "the best Indians in Florida; superior to those of Tocobaga, Carlos, Ais, Tegesta, and the other [natives] I have spoken of" (True 1945:29, 38).

The narratives do tell of the fertility of the region, the large population, and numerous settlements—including hamlets or homesteads—and the ability of the Apalachee to wage warfare. Ranjel (1922:79, 82) describes the large quantity of dried venison at one town and notes the abundance of maize, kidney beans, and pumpkins. Elvas (1922:47) and Biedma (1922:7) tell us that the province was well inhabited with much corn and many towns and hamlets. Fish were plentiful along the coast and were apparently brought inland to the towns there (Ranjel 1922:82).

However, this view contrasts sharply with that provided by Cabeza de Vaca, the chronicler and one of the survivors of the Narváez expedition. That army had spent twenty-five or twenty-six days in Apalachee in a small village that had forty houses. Cabeza de Vaca's account mentions a great quantity of maize and deerskins, but in general paints a pretty dismal picture of the province. Narváez sent three scouting parties into the interior of La Florida, but they found few people and the land was poor (Bandelier 1905; Hann 1989a). There are several references to downed trees that made travel difficult. Perhaps storms or a hurricane had swept through the province.

It seems clear that Narváez and his army did not reach the heartland of Apalachee. This also is indicated by the length of time it took them to reach Aute and the coast (eight days). In fact, on their journey northward through peninsular Florida the members of the expedition saw few natives. Either Cabeza de Vaca's account is faulty, or, more likely, the army hugged the coast as it marched north, only going farther inland when it needed to cross a large river, such as the Suwannee. The army probably never reached Apalachee proper, but only a small town subject to Apalachee, one perhaps in western Taylor County. The northward excursions could well have been into and north of the buffer between Apalachee (whose major settlements were in the western portion of the province) and Uzachile, whose towns were toward the Suwannee River, not the Aucilla. Garcilaso (Varner and Varner 1951:186) says the same thing: Narváez probably never reached Apalachee, but was in a province "nearer the sea," one "under the jurisdiction of the province of Apalachee."

In contrast to the rather sparse accounts of Apalachee by Biedma, Ranjel, and the Gentleman of Elvas is the lavish account written by Garcilaso, based on his interviews with survivors of the de Soto expedition (Varner and Varner 1951:175–260; Hann 1989a). The picture presented by Garcilaso is of a proud people who lived in a land of agricultural plenty. The Apalachee continually harassed de Soto's army for five months, employing guerillalike tactics at every opportunity. The Spaniards lived almost in a state of siege, venturing out only to gather food and at times fighting off attacks, sometimes with great cruelty.

Much of Garcilaso's account dwells on the battles that took place. There was a fierce encounter when the army first crossed the Aucilla River; a second battle at the same place when Calderón and the foot soldiers returned from the Tampa Bay camp; a battle when de Soto personally led a group of soldiers to capture Capafi, the Apalachee chief, who had withdrawn to a heavily fortified settlement within eight leagues (three days' travel) of Iniahica; and many other skirmishes. Garcilaso also recounts in some detail Juan de Añasco's journey back to Tampa Bay and the return by Calderón and the men with him.

The Spaniards in Garcilaso's account, many of them professional soldiers, were fascinated with the bravery and archery skill of the Apalachee, as well as with their agility and speed in attacking and retreating. Apalachee military tactics were to ambush or attack small groups of Spaniards, especially in wooded locales, where the advantages afforded by the war horses and mounted lancers were lessened. Apalachee warriors avoided warfare in open settings, where the Spanish soldiers had all the advantages.

Spaniards on foot were often bested by the Apalachee, and whenever possible the natives used their bows and arrows to kill or disable the horses of cavalrymen. On several occasions, the Apalachee scalped their Spanish victims and displayed the scalps on their bows. When the Spaniards traveled south to find Aute, the natives put long thorns into the ground in the trails, causing pain to the Spaniards' horses and to the foot soldiers (Varner and Varner 1951:187–188, 257, 258; Hann 1989a).

The bows and arrows of the Apalachee were particularly fearsome. Some arrows were tipped with flint points. The archers' skill allowed them to shoot an arrow into a horse past the knee of the rider, avoiding armor that the animal might have. On two occasions, native archers shot arrows into two horses' chests, killing the animals. The Spaniards dissected the horses and found the arrows had penetrated the animals nearly their entire length (Varner and Varner 1951:234, 258).

To demonstrate the effectiveness of the bow, a captive Apalachee was made to shoot an arrow into a cane basket over which was placed a coat of chain mail (Varner and Varner 1951:235–236). From fifty paces the arrow passed through the target with such force that a person standing behind it would have been injured also. A second coat of mail was placed over the first, another arrow was shot, and the arrow again penetrated both layers of chain mail and the basket. The Spaniards were quick to learn from this, and soon began to wear quilted fabric coats three or four fingers thick under the chain mail. Apparently, these deflected the arrows better than mail alone. The padded coats of mail were worn by the soldiers and similar padded armor was used to protect the horses. It is perhaps no coincidence that Ewen found so many links of chain mail at the Governor Martin site.

The chief of the Apalachee was called Capafi. He had fled Iniahica and, well guarded, moved to a camp some distance away. De Soto thought that if he could capture Capafi, he could use him as a hostage to force the Apalachee to halt their harassing raids against the Spanish camp. Capafi was captured, but the raids did not halt. Garcilaso says that because of his great corpulence and some type of infirmity, the chief was unable to walk normally and was carried in a litter (Varner and Varner 1951:205; Hann 1989a). We might expect, though, that his being carried in a litter—as true among other southeastern United States native societies—was a sign of reverence and a reflection of his status. However, when Capafi was not being carried, as in his own house, he was forced to crawl on all fours because of his infirmity.

Capafi told his captors that his people would not believe any of his orders given them through the Spaniards. He convinced them to take him to a meeting with some of his vassals, where he could tell them directly to halt the guerilla raids. This was done, but that night Capafi and the Apalachee with him literally crawled out of the field camp under the noses of their Spanish guards. On their return to Iniahica, the chagrined soldiers could only claim that the Apalachee had used magic. Capafi was never seen again by the Spaniards (Varner and Varner 1951: 207–210).

Garcilaso's informants described to him the agricultural fertility and natural bounty of Apalachee. He makes the point that during the five months the army camped at Iniahica—with 1000 or more Spaniards and native captives and more than 200 horses—there was never any problem in getting food. Indian corn, maize (apparently differentiating two types), many other seeds, beans, and squash were grown; and cherries and three kinds of nuts could be collected (one with oil, and acorns from the live oak and another oak) (Varner and Varner 1951:260; Hann 1989a).

Apalachee was one of the many native provinces in La Florida that stood out in the minds of the survivors of the de Soto expedition who reached Mexico in 1543. In recounting the stories of their odyssey, they could not help but remember the "fierceness and unconquerable passion" of the Indians of that province (Varner and Varner 1951:627).

Following their five-month encounter with the de Soto expedition, the Apalachee remained relatively free of European intervention for nearly a century. Neither the French under Ribaut or Laudonnière nor the Spanish under Pedro Menéndez interacted with the Apalachee, although the Spanish colonists certainly knew of the province. As Hann (1988:9) has pointed out, this isolation was probably due to a shortage of personnel and the relative remoteness of Apalachee from St. Augustine. As we shall see in the next chapter, all this would change after 1633 when the Franciscans expanded their mission system into Apalachee Province. Let us now return to the de Soto expedition on its trek out of Apalachee.

NORTH FROM APALACHEE

On March 3, 1540, de Soto and his army marched northward out of Apalachee. Their immediate goal was to find a land called Yupaha. A young man captured in Napituca had told the Spaniards about Yupaha, a land toward the rising sun. Yupaha, the young man's home "from which he had been a long time absent visiting other lands," was governed by a woman who had many vassals and whose village was of remarkable grandeur (Elvas 1922:50–51; Hann 1989a). Garcilaso tells us that the young man was the servant for native traders (Varner and Varner 1951:253), apparently explaining this absence from home. What convinced the Spaniards to seek this land was the young man's seemingly accurate description of how the people of Yupaha mined gold, which the chief was said to possess in quantity. Yupaha turned out to be Cofitachequi, a native province in South Carolina that the expedition reached nearly two months later. Apparently, the young man had come south with the traders and had been in north Florida when captured by the Spanish.

When de Soto and his army, led by native guides, broke camp and marched northward out of Apalachee, they took with them food to last for sixty leagues of travel because they expected to pass through a wilderness, or region with few settlements, for a considerable distance (Elvas 1922:51; Ranjel 1922:82). Because so many of the Indians they had enslaved as bearers had died over the winter, the Spaniards carried the food and their other supplies on the backs of horses and in packs carried by the infantry.

At the end of the first day they came to the river Guacuca, which they apparently forded, and the next day arrived at a broad river, the River of Capachequi, over which they had trouble building a bridge (Elvas 1922:51–52).[9] The River of Guacuca is probably the Ochlockonee River, and the River of Capachequi is the Flint River. Hann (1989a) suggests that "Guacuca" is a garbled version of "Bacuqua," a town in the seventeenth century that was located on the trail north out of Apalachee that led to a crossing point on the Flint River. Two missions were established in or near Bacuqua, one of which had a satellite town called Guaca (Hann 1988:354, 1990:482–483). It had required only one day of travel for the expedition to leave the territory of the powerful Apalachee and reach a wilderness or buffer that separated the Apalachee from the first native group to the north in southeast Georgia, the Capachequi.

While in Spain, de Soto had probably heard tales of Chicora, the rich native province believed by the Spanish to be located in interior South Carolina. The rumors had begun as a result of the voyages to the Carolinean coast in the early 1520s, just before the failure of the ill-fated Ayllón colony (see Hoffman 1984 and chapter 1). The possibility of finding Chicora, along with the other area described by the young native guide captured in north Florida, must have enticed de Soto to lead his army north-northeast across Georgia.

The route of the de Soto expedition north of Apalachee has been reconstructed by Hudson and his associates, whose results are quite different from the earlier work of Swanton (DePratter, Hudson, and Smith 1985; Hudson 1989; Hudson, DePratter, and Smith 1984, 1989; Swanton 1939). After leaving Florida and the Apalachee, the army continued across Georgia, crossing the Savannah River into South Carolina and reaching the native province or chiefdom of Cofitachequi, where it found freshwater pearls, but not the gold or silver it sought. The army also found Spanish artifacts, which it interpreted as evidence that the people of Cofitachequi had been in contact with the Ayllón expedition.

Leaving Cofitachequi, in the interior of South Carolina, the Spaniards marched to the northwest, traveling into western North Carolina and across the Appalachian Mountains into the Tennessee River Valley in eastern Tennessee. There they entered one end of the vast native province of Coosa. De Soto and his army next turned southwesterly, marching the length of Coosa, passing through one town after another for more than 200 miles. They traveled through the heartland of a very large native province. De Soto and the other Spaniards saw firsthand native societies that no European had ever seen before and that would never be seen again. By the time members of the Tristán de Luna expedition reached Coosa twenty years later, disease and the aftermath of de Soto's entrada had already begun taking its toll.

In south-central Alabama, south of Coosa Province, the Spaniards were assaulted by warriors of Chief Tuscaluza at his town of Mabila. The bloody battle resulted in the death of as many as 3000 natives and the destruction of much of the Spaniards' supplies, a potentially disastrous loss. At that point in the journey, de Soto could have chosen to march his battered army southward to the Gulf coast, where he previously had arranged to rendezvous with Francisco Maldonado. Indeed, de Soto's route up to the time of the battle at Mabila had led him to a location roughly north of Pensacola. De Soto's options were few. His army was dispirited, and perhaps mutinous. It was already October, and Maldonado may have already left the port. However, instead of abandoning his quest, going to the coast, locating the port, and trying to locate Maldonado, de Soto chose to turn toward the north and explore more of the interior of the Southeast, seeking the wealth that was proving so elusive.

From Mabila the army marched north-northwest into Mississippi, where it spent its second winter. The Spaniards fought another great battle at Chicaza, remaining there from late December 1540 until late April 1541. In May 1541, two years after having left Cuba, the army reached the Mississippi River.

The Spaniards spent the next year in Arkansas traveling from town to town, some of which were quite large. They saw remarkable things, and their firsthand accounts provide us with extraordinary information and descriptions of the native peoples. But Arkansas, like the lands east of the Mississippi River, did not contain large deposits of mineral wealth. De Soto was unable to find the mines that would furnish him a location to establish settlements.

In late spring 1542, the army returned to the Mississippi River, where de Soto died "of fevers" on May 21, 1542 (Elvas 1922:155, 161). Luis de Moscoso took over as leader of the army. Tattered, torn, and unsuccessful in their quest to find wealth and establish a colony, the Spaniards turned from conquest to survival. The backswamps along the Mississippi thwarted their attempts to follow its banks southward to its mouth, from which point the army could reach New Spain (Mexico) by marching along the Gulf of Mexico. Instead, the Spaniards decided to march overland across southern Arkansas and eastern Texas to Mexico. But that attempt proved unsuccessful. The native societies of eastern Texas did not possess the stored food supplies that had sustained the Spaniards elsewhere in La Florida. Faced with possible starvation if they continued, Moscoso and his army turned around and traced their footsteps back to the Mississippi River. Six months, the last half of 1542, had been spent on the failed journey.

During the first six months of 1543, the Spaniards camped adjacent to the river and built boats. In late June they set out, rowing down the Mississippi and reaching the Gulf of Mexico twenty days later. On September 10, 1543, the 311 survivors reached safe haven, a Spanish settlement on the River of Panuco, near present Tampico, Mexico. Their incredible odyssey of more than four years had ended.

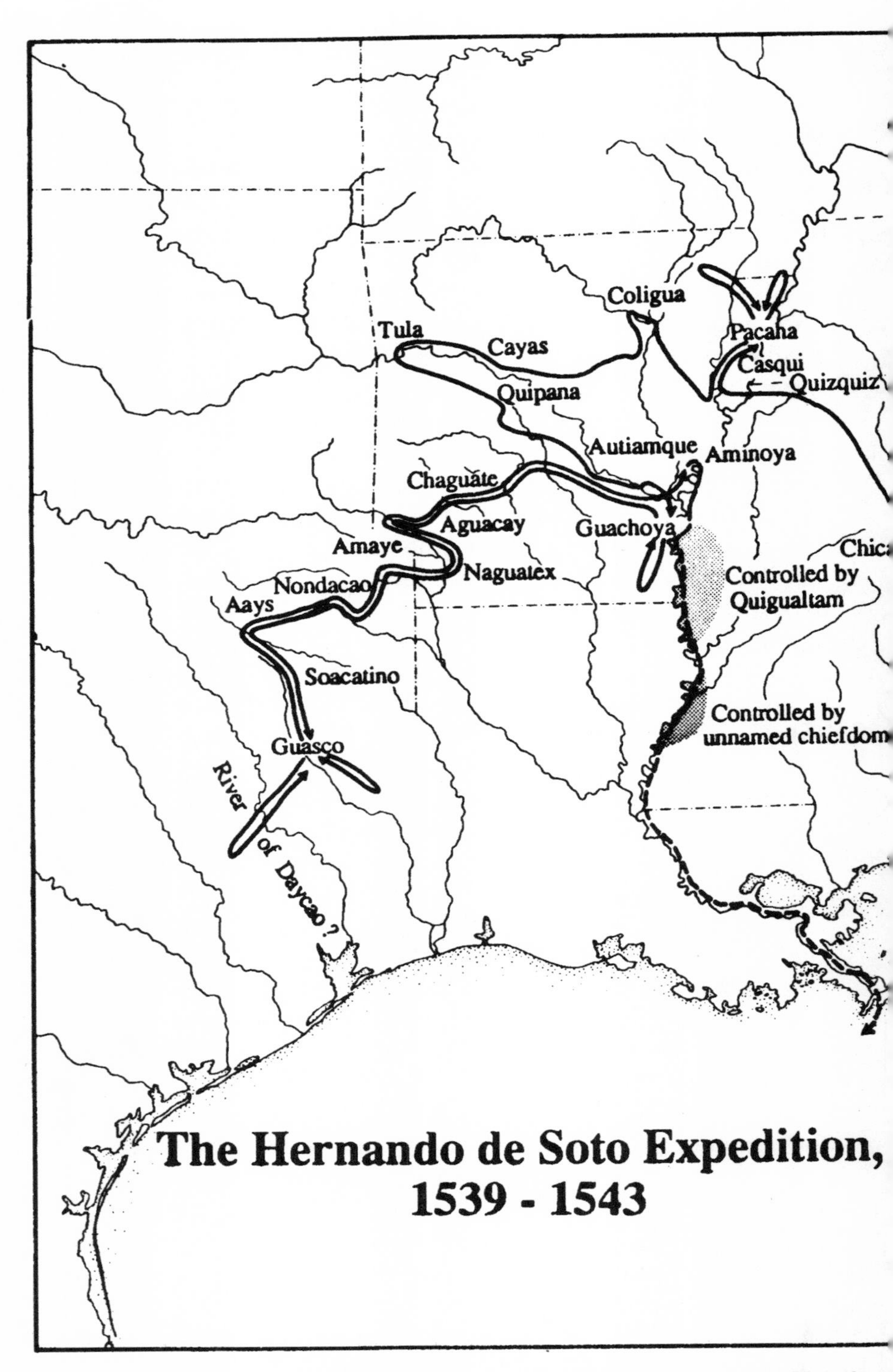

Figure 54. The route of the de Soto expedition through the southern United

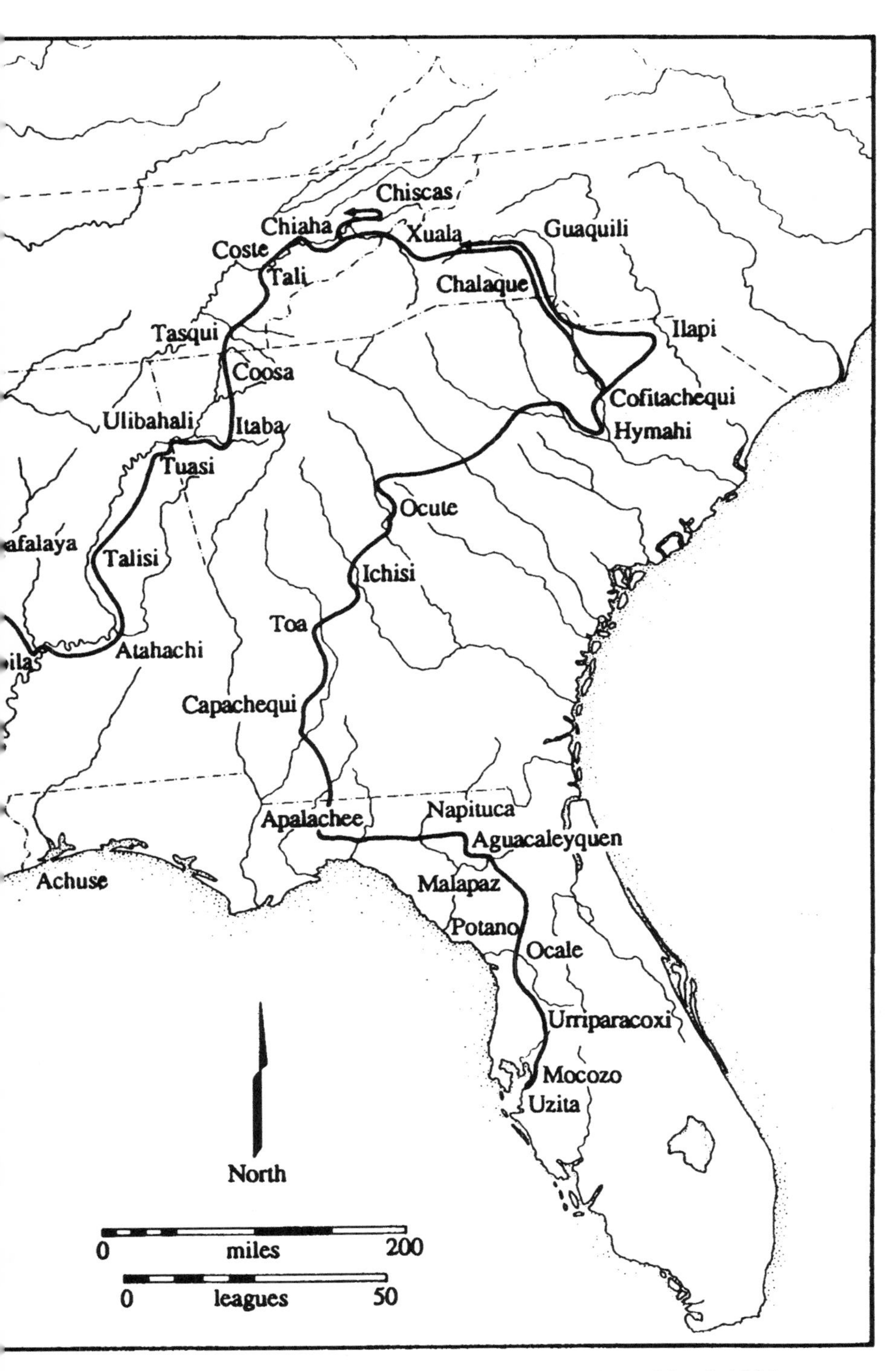

States, as reconstructed by Charles Hudson and his associates, March 1991.

The Hernando de Soto expedition was a failure. Its leader and half the participants had died, and not a single one of its chartered goals was accomplished. On the other hand, the expedition did provide Spain with a great deal of information on the interior of La Florida and its people. Had gold or silver been found, no doubt Spanish colonists would have been brought in to establish interior settlements and create overland links to Mexico.

CHAPTER IX

AFTER DE SOTO

SPAIN IN SIXTEENTH- AND SEVENTEENTH-CENTURY LA FLORIDA

Despite de Soto's failure, the Spanish crown continued to seek a permanent colony in La Florida. Coastal settlements were needed to help protect the shipping lanes that ran near the Gulf and Atlantic coasts of the Southeast United States before turning east across the Atlantic to Spain. And the crown still sought an overland route from Mexico east to the Atlantic coast, passing near the northwest Florida coast. Such a route would eliminate the necessity of shipping cargoes along the dangerous and storm-prone coasts of Florida. A Spanish settlement was needed to anchor the Atlantic coast end of the route, and it was to be placed at Santa Elena, the name given to modern Parris Island, South Carolina. Such a settlement would also help to deflect growing French interest in establishing a colony on the Atlantic coast, perhaps near the presumed location of Chicora, in the region where Ayllón's colony had failed previously.

MORE FAILED SETTLEMENTS: LUNA AND VILLAFAÑE

To accomplish these tasks, still another Spanish colonization effort was organized, funded by the viceroy of New Spain, and led by Tristán de Luna y Arellano. Luna was to establish a colony at Ochuse on Pensacola Bay, from which the overland route to Santa Elena would pass, then put an inland settlement in the

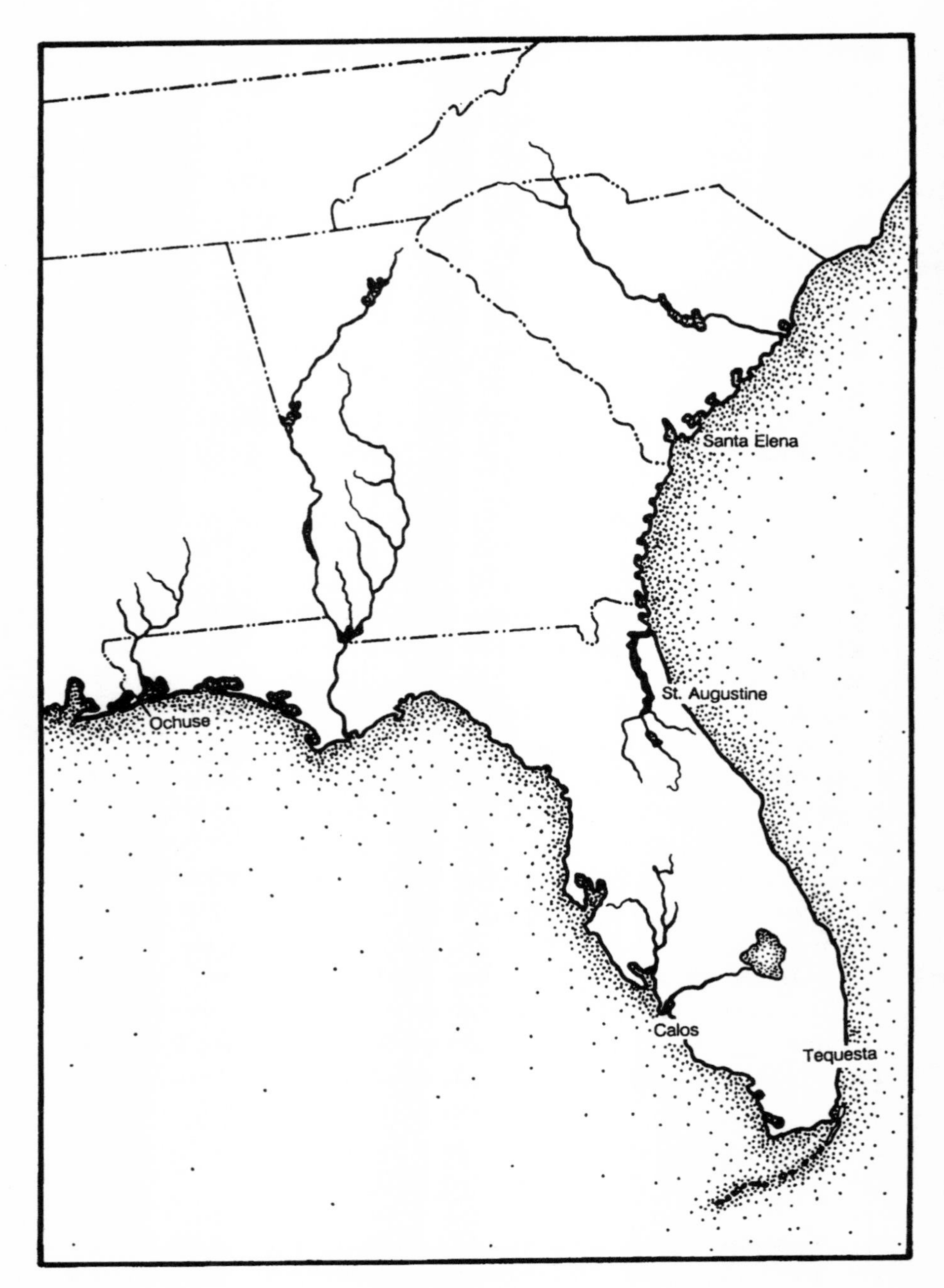

Figure 55

Sixteenth-century Spanish settlement and garrison locations.

native province of Coosa, visited by Hernando de Soto and his army two decades before. He was also to establish coastal missions (Hoffman 1984:429; Weddle 1985:253–255) because Christianized native peoples might help to protect shipwrecked Spanish sailors. "Ochuse" was the port of "Achuse" found by Maldonado on his voyage west while de Soto and the army were wintering at Iniahica.

Luna's expedition of 1500 people, including Mexican Indians, left New Spain in thirteen ships in the summer of 1559. Some of the soldiers and settlers had apparently marched with de Soto in La Florida. Luna himself had been with Coronado in the southwest United States twenty years earlier. At first his fleet landed at Mobile Bay, but later the ships moved on to their goal, the port of Ochuse at Pensacola.

Once a camp was established, Luna sent a party inland to explore. The men marched into the interior country north of the bay, but found the region almost depopulated. There was little food that could be taken from native stores to feed the colony. To add to Luna's problems, a hurricane struck and sank seven of his ships, destroying needed supplies and drowning some of the colonists.

In order to feed his colonists, Luna sent an even larger party inland to find villages in which they could settle. A large town, Nanipacana, forty leagues from the bay was found, and a portion of the colony moved to it. A party was then sent farther into the interior to revisit Coosa and determine if it was suitable for a colony. The Spaniards succeeded in finding Coosa, but it had changed greatly since de Soto's army had marched through it, the result of disease and depopulation.

Faced with failure, some of Luna's men sought to have the colony withdrawn. The viceroy in Mexico failed to grasp the seriousness of the situation, and Luna himself became ill and began acting irrationally. Finally, in March 1561, Angel de Villafañe arrived at Ochuse with orders to assume command and move the colony to Santa Elena. Taking a number of colonists with him, he sailed to Cuba and then north toward South Carolina, arriving in May with four ships and sixty people. But he failed to find a suitable landing site and continued sailing northward. A hurricane struck and sank two of his ships, ending his attempt to place a settlement at Santa Elena. Once again, Spain's efforts to settle La Florida had failed.

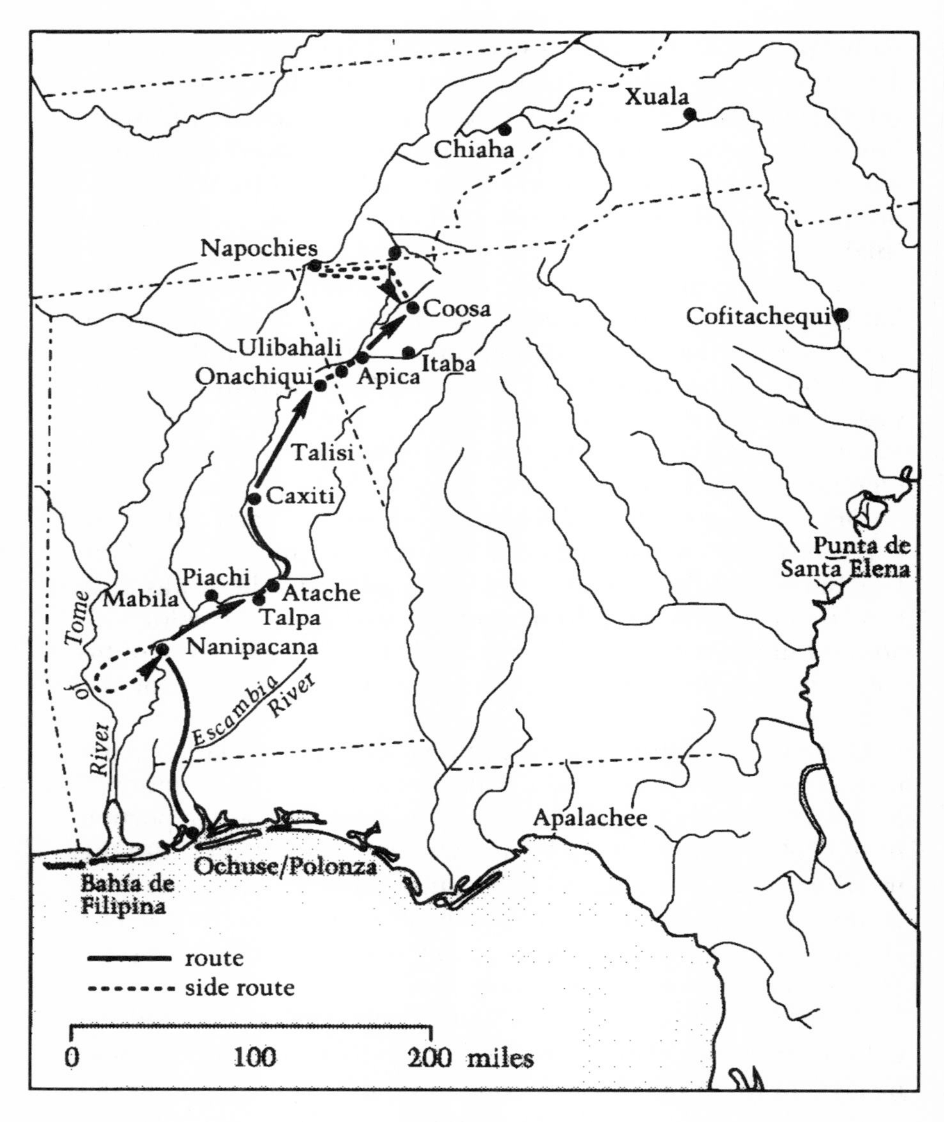

Figure 56

Route of the Tristán de Luna expedition into the interior of the Southeast from Ochuse (from Hudson et al. 1989a).

Recently, Hudson and his associates have reconstructed the location of the Ochuse colony and the inland treks of the various parties sent into the interior of La Florida from Pensacola Bay (Hudson et al. 1989a,b; see also Priestley 1928 and Hoffman 1990:144–181). Studies of Coosa have also been undertaken and are important to understanding the impact of the de Soto and Luna expeditions (Hudson et al. 1985; Smith 1989).

MENÉNDEZ, ST. AUGUSTINE, AND SANTA ELENA

In 1563 the need for a colony in La Florida and reports that the French were seeking to establish a settlement on the Atlantic coast prompted Philip II to summon Pedro Menéndez de Avilés, leader of Spain's Caribbean fleet, to Spain to plan a course of action. The need for military retaliation became a reality when rumors of a French settlement reached the Spanish court. But it was not until early 1565 that Spain was able to devise a plan for ousting the French and establishing its own colony (see Lyon 1976 and Hoffman 1990:205–230).

Pedro Menéndez would lead the effort. He was to remove the French from Spanish-claimed lands and, partially funded by the crown, establish a colony. He was successful on both counts, destroying France's Fort Caroline near the mouth of the St. Johns River in northeast Florida and placing small towns at Santa Elena on the South Carolina coast and at St. Augustine on the coast of northeast Florida.[1] As we have seen, the accounts of the French and Spaniards in sixteenth-century La Florida provide important information about the Timucuan-speaking groups in northern Florida, some of whom previously had witnessed the march of de Soto's expedition through their territory. The accounts, as we have seen, also provide descriptions of the native peoples in northeast Florida and along the upper St. Johns River north of Lake George.

Menéndez's plan for the settlement of La Florida included both Spanish missions and coastal and inland garrisons (Lyon 1988, 1989). Almost immediately after his successful ouster of the French he put small garrisons, some with Jesuit missionary priests, on both the Atlantic and Gulf coasts of Florida. One was placed among the Tocobaga at Tampa Bay, one among the Calusa on the southwest Gulf coast, and one at Tequesta (see chapter 5). Others were located on the lower Atlantic coast. One goal of these coastal outposts was to provide havens for shipwrecked Spaniards. Another was to make allies of the native population.

Accompanying Menéndez was Hernando d'Escalante Fontaneda, the Spaniard who had been shipwrecked in south Florida in 1545 and probably rescued by the French seventeen years later. Menéndez undoubtedly received intelligence about Florida and its native peoples from Fontaneda as well as from French captives. Lyon's discovery of the Cañete fragment, a portion of a previously unknown fourth firsthand narrative from the de Soto expedition, among Menéndez-related papers in the Spanish archives, suggests that Menéndez was gathering information about La Florida, including information from the de Soto expedition a quarter century earlier (Lyon 1982).

Menéndez's La Florida capital was originally established at Santa Elena on the South Carolina coast, not at St. Augustine, a reflection of Spain's long desire to establish an overland route to Mexico. To find the best route to Mexico, as well as to reexplore the interior Southeast native provinces seen by Hernando de Soto in 1540, Menéndez sent an expedition under Juan Pardo inland from Santa Elena. Between 1566 and 1568, Pardo twice traveled well into the interior with an army, including priests. He was not only to explore, but he was to establish a string of forts and placate native peoples.

On the first journey Pardo and 125 soldiers marched into western North Carolina. On the second he followed the same route into North Carolina and then continued farther, crossing the Appalachian Mountains and reaching Tennessee, in the general vicinity of Newport (see DePratter and Smith 1980; DePratter, Hudson, and Smith 1983; Hudson 1987, 1990). On these journeys he revisited some of the same native towns that de Soto and his army had seen in 1540.

Pardo never found the route to Mexico because the Spaniards greatly underestimated the distance from the Atlantic coast to New Spain. Their idea that the Appalachian Mountains reached all of the way to northeast Mexico was greatly in error. Pardo did establish several forts, but most of them lasted only a few months, just as did the coastal garrisons among the Florida natives, such as the Tequesta and Calusa. In 1587 Santa Elena itself was abandoned, and St. Augustine remained the only Spanish town in the vastness of La Florida.

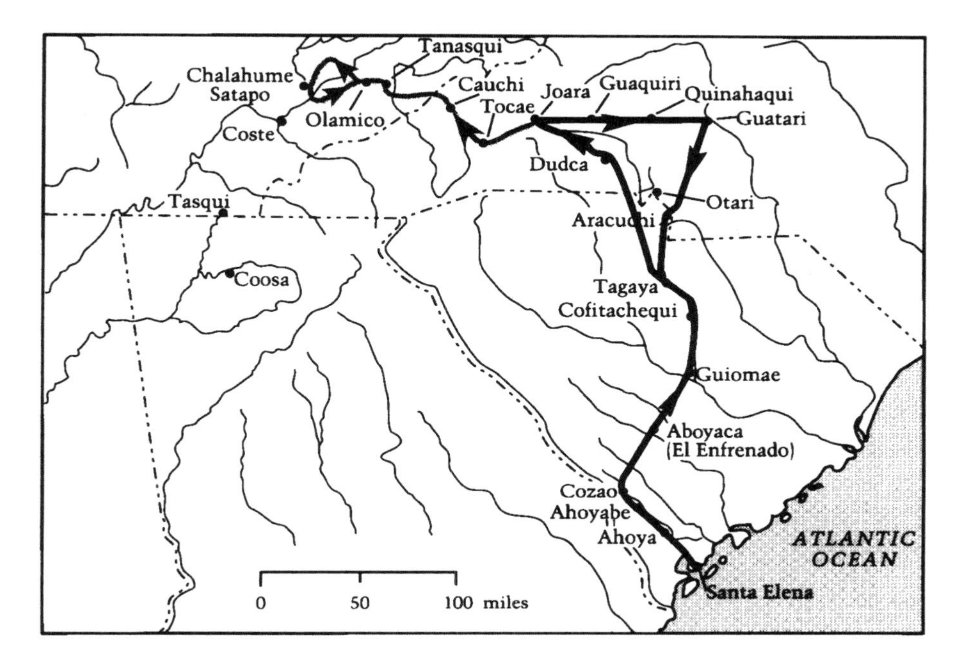

Figure 57

Route of the expeditions of Juan Pardo into the interior of the Southeast from Santa Elena. The second expedition traced the route of the first expedition and then traveled further westward. That portion of the second expedition is shown in a lighter shade.

THE MISSION SYSTEM

A part of Menéndez's plan to colonize La Florida had been to establish missions among the native peoples. Making Christians and allies out of the various native peoples was much easier than trying to control them by military force. The natives also were a potential labor force to be exploited by the colony. Efforts by the Jesuit missionary priests at the coastal outposts were to begin this process.

But, as noted above, these initial attempts, which took place between 1567 and 1572, were not successful. By and large the native groups among whom these first missions were established were not sedentary agriculturists like the Potano, Aguacaleyquen, Uzachile, or Apalachee, and it was extremely difficult to direct the changes that would make them loyal Christian subjects of the Spanish crown. This was especially true in the Tampa Bay region and in south Florida, where the Spaniards never were successful in missionizing native peoples.

In these first missionary efforts several Jesuits were soon killed by the Indians. And at some outposts there were frequent disagreements between soldiers and priests over the approach to be used in the pacification of the natives. As a result of these incidents, the Jesuit priests, never more than a handful, withdrew from Florida.

To fill the void, Menéndez quickly made arrangements for the Franciscan order to provide missionaries to his colony. In 1573 the first Franciscans reached Santa Elena, and by 1578 a friar had been assigned to St. Augustine, where, like his counterparts at Santa Elena, he served as chaplain to the garrisoned soldiers (Geiger 1940:8, 41–42). The extent of these priests' early missionary activities among the native peoples near Santa Elena and St. Augustine is unknown.

The next step was the establishment of *doctrinas*, missions with churches and resident friars who could instruct the native peoples. The coastal peoples between and around Santa Elena and St. Augustine were to be missionized first, helping to assure safe passage and communication by the Spaniards between the two coastal settlements. Missions and priests were also needed in the interior of northern Florida, where native allies were sought and where Spanish farms could be established.

To begin to accomplish these tasks, a group of eight Franciscans sailed from Spain in May 1584, led by Father Alonso de Reinoso. Reinoso perhaps had been with the small group of Franciscans who arrived at Santa Elena in 1573 and had returned to Spain to accompany the new group to Florida. Some of this group of eight Franciscans never actually arrived in Florida, and one left soon after coming (Geiger 1936:46–47).

In 1587 Reinoso brought twelve additional Franciscans to Florida, but a half decade later only five remained. One of the friars who came with Reinoso was Baltasar López, who was to play a major role as one of the first, if not *the* first, Franciscan priest to regularly visit the Timucuan-speaking peoples in interior northern Florida. When still another group of twelve friars arrived in Florida in 1595, missionary efforts began in earnest. By the next year nine missions were established: Nombre de Dios,[2] San Juan del Puerto,[3] San Pedro,[4] Ibi,[5] Asao,[6] Tolomato,[7] Tupique,[8] Ospo,[9] and St. Catherine[10] (Oré 1936:66–86; Geiger

1936:5364, 1940:120). By 1595 Father López also had visited the town of Timucua, fifty leagues inland from Cumberland Island. Timucua, as we have seen, may have been the Aguacaleyquen of the de Soto narratives and the location of the later San Martin de Timucua mission founded by Martín Prieto.

In September 1597 a revolt by the Guale peoples of the Georgia coast took place largely in reaction to Franciscan missionary activities, including attempts to alter native marriage and inheritance patterns. Five Franciscans were killed in the rebellion, and all of the Guale missions were destroyed. In October and early November a Spanish military force sailed northward from St. Augustine to retaliate, destroying abandoned villages and stored crops (Geiger 1936:86–115), the same tactic Pedro Menéndez had used as a threat against St. Johns River native groups.

TIMUCUAN MISSIONS

For the next two decades after the rebellion, the Guale missions were rebuilt, and the chain from St. Catherines Island south to St. Augustine was reestablished. During that same period, beginning with Prieto's founding of the San Francisco mission in 1606, several *doctrinas* were founded among the Potano, Aguacaleyquen and other northern Utina peoples, and the Uzachile, all Timucuans. Apparently mission stations were also placed in nearby villages. By 1612 the westernmost mission probably was San Juan de Guacara, located near the Mission Trail and the Suwannee River in southern Suwannee County (*Guacara* is the Timucuan name for that river). As we have seen, other missions established about that same time or shortly after included Santa Cruz de Tarihica in southern Suwannee County (on the Mission Trail), San Martin de Timucua, and Santa Fe de Teleco (Geiger 1940:123–124). Missions soon were established among the Uzachile (Yustaga).

A list of missions made in 1655 and two lists compiled in 1675 give the names of 38, 37, and 38 missions, respectively, for Guale on the Georgia coast, including the coastal Timucuan missions from St. Augustine northward to Cumberland Island; the inland Timucuan missions among the Potano, Aguacaleyquen and related northern Utinan groups, and Yustaga; and the Apalachee. The latter two lists, both dating from 1675, also provide data on distances between and among the missions, giving modern researchers important clues as to the locations of the missions, especially those in interior Florida (Geiger 1940: 125–131).

By the midseventeenth century the mission system among the Timucuans and other northern Florida and coastal Georgia peoples was well established. To administer this large geographical region, the Spaniards utilized the concept of provinces. The provinces roughly correlated with geographical areas and native linguistic groups. Apalachee was the westernmost province and corresponded to the traditional territory of the Apalachee peoples. Timucua included the territories of the north Florida Timucuan speakers (largely the Yustaga, northern Utina, and Potano). Other provinces were Guale (the Georgia coast from St. Catherines Island to Cumberland Island); the Freshwater or Agua Dulce district (the region of the various peoples living along the upper St. Johns River down to Lake George, including the Oklawaha); and Mocama (the coastal peoples below Guale down to about St. Augustine).[11] These provinces were the major regions of Spanish-Indian interaction in the last two-thirds of the seventeenth century.

Although the mission system was well established by 1655, it was not static. Missions were moved, new ones founded, and old ones abandoned. New missions were attempted in the interior of central Florida (as among the Acuera), as well as in coastal regions. We still have much to learn about these missions. For example, Hann (1991b) has shown that there is a rich, previously little used, documentary record regarding Franciscan efforts to establish a Hispanic presence among the Calusa on the southwest Florida coast in the 1690s. That record contains much information about the Calusa in the late seventeenth century. Documents pertinent to the Franciscan mission activities in Timucua and elsewhere in Florida also remain to be discovered and used.

What about the Timucuan populations who lived at the missions or who resided in nearby satellite villages and were administered to by the mission priests? Unfortunately, the population decline begun with the introduction of European diseases by Spanish sailors and explorers in the early sixteenth century continued at the seventeenth-century missions of Timucua. Numerous epidemics, such as those documented for the Apalachee (see below), were recorded by the Spaniards. As mission village populations fell, other nonmissionized people were moved to the decimated missions. At times whole villages were moved. Rebellions, which led to Spanish retribution, contributed to the turmoil in the missions.

The year 1656 seems to have been pivotal in the history of the missions and the native peoples. A rebellion broke out among the mission natives in the province of Timucua, and many of the missions were abandoned. That rebellion occurred during a decade of epidemics that killed thousands of natives (between 1649 and 1659). To put down the eight-month-long rebellion and punish its leaders, Spanish soldiers executed eleven native chiefs. Disease and military punishment must have devastated the already dwindling mission populations. In 1657 the Spanish governor of Florida, Diego de Rebolledo, wrote that the Indians of Guale and Timucua were few in number "because they have been wiped out with the sickness of the plague (*peste*) and smallpox which have overtaken them in the past years." In 1659 Governor Francisco de Córcoles y Martínez reported that 10,000 Indians had died of a measles epidemic (Hann 1986:111, 133–134, 1988:22–23).

The midseventeenth century thus seems to have marked the demise of most of the Potano and northern Utina. Many of the missions that existed previously in Timucua Province and that were abandoned or destroyed in the 1656 rebellion were apparently not rebuilt. A few were rebuilt and new ones were established, but in order to assure adequate native support, Indians had to be enticed or forced to move to the missions from elsewhere. For instance, the mission of Santa Fe in Alachua County was repopulated in 1657 with "Arapaja" (from northern Madison County?) and by Yustaga in 1659 (Hann 1990:460; *arapaha* means "many houses" in Timucua).

The repopulation of the late seventeenth-century missions in the Potano region is reflected in the archaeological record. For example, at the Zetrouer site (8AL67), a late seventeenth-century Spanish-Indian site on the Alachua Trail, 68 percent of the aboriginal pottery collected is from Georgia Indians—most likely Guale and/or Yamassee—rather than from the indigenous Potano. It seems likely that the ethnicity of the mission Indians in Timucua in the late seventeenth century was quite different from that prior to 1656.

APALACHEE MISSIONS

In 1608, Martín Prieto, the same Franciscan who had established missions among the Potano and Aguacaleyquen, traveled to Ivitachuco in Apalachee with a delegation of Timucuan chiefs and warriors. He sought to put a halt to warfare between the various Timucua groups and the Apalachee. Prieto said the entire province came out to receive him, including 70 chiefs and 36,000 villagers (Hann 1988:11). Hann's excellent account of the Apalachee peoples, *Apalachee: The Land between the Rivers*, tells how the province and its people were represented by the chief of Ivitachuco. Peace was agreed to, and the chief of Iniahica, said to be a brother of the chief of Ivitachuco, was directed to pay a visit to the Spanish governor in St. Augustine. Quite likely the term "brother" conveyed the same fictive, political relationship of equality that it did among the Timucuan chiefs in north and northeast Florida (see chapter 7).

Hann (1988) has carefully documented the growth and history of the Apalachee mission system, which began in 1633 and continued until it was essentially destroyed in 1703–1704. He recounts in detail the interaction between the Spanish and the Apalachee in the mission period. As he notes, the names of Iniahica and Ivitachuco, names of towns at the time of de Soto's expedition, remain prominent throughout the mission period.

At various times in the seventeenth century eleven missions were established to serve the Apalachee, and most had satellite villages. Together, mission and satellite villages at any one time totaled about forty (Hann 1988:30). This is a very large number compared to the Timucuan-speaking peoples to the east and reflects the larger and denser population of Apalachee.

Hann's study of the Apalachee makes them the best documented of any of the Florida Indian groups during the colonial period. That study includes a thorough interpretation of Apalachee demographic data (Hann 1988:chap. 7). Unfortunately, as is true for all of the Florida aborigines, there are no hard data on the Apalachee population at the time of European contact. Henry Dobyns (1983) has estimated Apalachee population at contact as 100,000, but Hann (1988:161) believes this is too high. A contact population of 50,000 for the Apalachee is more likely, although not at all certain. The population could certainly be higher. The 50,000 figure correlates with a population density of about 30 people/square mile.

In 1608, nearly fifty years after de Soto's expedition, the Apalachee were still unified under a system of village chiefs who recognized a paramount chief. Prieto's estimate of 36,000 Apalachee is not out of line with estimates of 30,000 given by other Franciscans before the establishment of the missions, including one from 1617 (Hann 1988:164). A parish census done by a resident priest in 1638 just after the founding of the missions listed 16,000 Apalachee living under Spanish aegis. Other Apalachee may not have been included in the census because they were not residing at mission villages. A friar writing in ca. 1648 put Apalachee's population at 20,000. The Apalachee population continued to decline, however, reaching about 10,000 by 1675 and stabilizing at that level or slightly less until the English raids of 1704 that destroyed the Apalachee missions (Hann 1988:164–169).[12]

There is reasonably good information on the presence of epidemics among the Apalachee and other north Florida aborigines. Hann (1988:175–180) has reviewed this evidence to determine the effects on Apalachee population levels. According to the priests, between 1613 and 1617 there were a number of "great plagues and contagious diseases" that affected half of the missionized Florida Indians, as well as Spanish soldiers (quoted in Hann 1988:175). During that period missions had only recently been established in Timucua, although the missions in Guale and along the coast north of St. Augustine had been in existence since the late 1580s. The impact of those epidemics on the Apalachee is uncertain, but from the demographic figures cited above the Apalachee were apparently little affected.

A second epidemic is documented for St. Augustine in 1649–1650. One friar stated that several of his colleagues died at that time, suggesting that the epidemic also reached the missions. In 1655 a severe smallpox epidemic ravaged Guale and Timucua as well as St. Augustine, but the Spanish governor noted that the effects in Apalachee had been less severe. A measles epidemic hit the missions in 1659; that episode along with the Timucuan rebellion of 1656 caused the temporary abandonment of several of the Timucuan missions. These later epidemics, all taking place during the mission period, apparently were what reduced the Apalachee from 30,000 to 10,000, the approximate level at which they remained throughout the last quarter of the seventeenth century.

DEMISE OF THE MISSIONS

Although the number of Spanish missions in 1675 was the same as that in 1656 before the rebellion, the numbers are deceiving. Many of the missions present in 1655 were not rebuilt following the rebellion and new ones were established. In reality indigenous population levels were severely reduced, and natives from elsewhere were brought in to reside at the missions established after the rebellion.

But even so the mission system soon came to an end. The reason was not continued depopulation, because there was a large native population north of Florida that could sustain the missions. Rather, the missions were destroyed by raids by other European colonials and their native allies.

The main antagonists were the English who were intent on colonizing the eastern seaboard. Through their Carolina colonies they were developing a lucrative trade in deerskins and Indian slaves, posing a threat to Spain's La Florida colony. In 1670 the English founded Charles Town (Charleston) and began to lay the groundwork for usurping Spanish land and influence among native peoples. That same year, 1670, saw the signing of the Treaty of Madrid between Britain and Spain, which affirmed each country's rights to lands they controlled in the West Indies and America. But control of the region from the Carolinas to St. Augustine, largely the provinces of Guale and Mocama, was not resolved and it remained an area of contention. This set the stage for military hostilities between the two European colonies, encounters that would lead to the destruction and abandonment of both the coastal and interior missions (Bolton and Ross 1925). For the next three decades, from the early 1670s into the early 1700s, an "undeclared war was waged" (Arnade 1959:1).

In 1680 the English attacked the Spanish mission and garrison on St. Catherines Island and the mission on Jekyll Island on the Georgia coast. The St. Catherines settlement was withdrawn and first moved farther south in Guale to Sapelo Island. But the harassing raids, some by English-inspired pirates and some by the English in league with Indian allies, continued.

By the early 1680s all of the missions in Guale and northern Mocama, the entire Georgia coast, had been withdrawn. The St. Catherines mission was moved to Amelia Island in northeast Florida by 1686. The natives who had lived at the Guale missions, many of them Yamassee from the interior of Georgia who had repopulated the Guale missions, either fled from the coast or were moved to the new St. Catherines mission or to missions on Amelia Island. Still other natives sought refuge among the English (Gannon 1965:71–72; Thomas 1987:56–57).

In early 1685 Yamassee allies of the English raided into Timucua Province and destroyed the mission of Santa Catalina located near the Mission Trail in southeast Suwannee County. On August 31, 1691, the mission of San Juan de Guacara on the Suwannee River in western Suwannee County was also destroyed, raided by the English and their Indian allies from Apalachicola.[13] Santa Cruz de Tarihica was destroyed about this same time or shortly after. These raids not only demolished the buildings and villages of the missions but decimated the Indian inhabitants, some of whom were killed and others of whom were taken back to South Carolina to be sold as slaves (Boyd, Smith, and Griffin 1951:8, 11; Gannon 1965:72).

In retaliation for these raids, the Spaniards in 1686 organized a military advance intended to drive the English from Charles Town. The raiders did not attack all the way to Charles Town, but they did destroy Port Royal. In St. Augustine work was continued on the stone castillo that was begun in the 1670s to replace the previous wooden fort.

After a decade-long respite following the attack on Port Royal the raids into Timucua resumed. San Pedro y San Pablo de Potohiriba (in Madison County near Lake Sampala) and Santa Fe (in northwest Alachua County) were attacked in 1702. The Apalachicola Indians who raided Santa Fe had been armed by the English. They were repulsed by the Spanish garrison stationed at the mission, but in an ill-advised retaliatory skirmish against the attackers, ten Christian natives were killed (Boyd, Smith, and Griffin 1951:11–12, 36–37).

The Spanish governor of Florida, Don Joseph de Zuñiga y Zerda, wrote the Spanish king, relating what had occurred in the initial raid:

> *On Saturday, the 20th of May of this year 1702, they entered in the dawn watch and burned and devastated the village of Santa Fé . . . , attacking the convent with many firearms and arrows and burning the church. . . . Finally, the fight having lasted for more than three hours, our force repulsed them, after the hasty strengthening of an indefensible stockade which served as a fence to the gate of the convent. (Boyd, Smith, and Griffin 1951:37)*

In November 1702, English soldiers led by Carolinean governor James Moore sailed from Port Royal and landed on the northern end of Amelia Island. The army marched down the island, destroying Spanish outposts and missions. The mission that by 1686 had been moved to Amelia Island from St. Catherines Island, Georgia was one of the first to be destroyed. The belief that closer proximity to St. Augustine would bring safety proved false. Apparently the Spanish soldiers who manned a blockhouse on the north end of the island could put up little resistance. Using accounts from the Spanish captain on the scene and the governor of Florida, Arnade (1959:14–15) has described the raid:

> *At one o'clock in the morning of November 4 the fleeing Indians from the northern part of the island arrived at the stockade, reporting the unexpected English invasion. . . . The captain and the two Franciscan friars, Manuel de Urissa and Domingo Santos, immediately rang the church bells, alerting the people . . . panic broke out. . . . the captain ordered complete evacuation of the fort, mission, and island. He and the friars collected the church ornaments and statues. Just at this moment the English arrived and showered the fort and mission with burning spears which fell on the palmetto roofs. At once flames engulfed the structures. . . . Apparently everyone got out. . . . They fled to the next important Spanish outpost [the mission of San Juan del Puerto on the island to the south].*

The English raiders continued southward, routing the Spanish soldiers at San Juan del Puerto on Fort George Island, and taking the missions that lay between them and their goal, St. Augustine, which they besieged (Arnade 1959). They destroyed most of the town, but failed to capture the castillo.

Apalachee would be next. An initial raid in 1703 destroyed at least one mission. Then, in early and mid-1704, two more military campaigns were waged, effectively wiping out the Apalachee missions and killing, enslaving, or scattering the mission villagers. The Apalachee and the other native peoples living among them at the missions were devastated (Boyd, Smith, and Griffin 1951; Jones 1972). As a result of the raids perhaps half the Apalachee population was killed or enslaved and the remainder forced to leave their traditional lands. Remnants of the Apalachee were scattered over the Southeast, and by the 1720s most had ceased to exist as ethnic Apalachee. One colony, however, moved westward to French Louisiana before moving into Texas where they still lived in 1834 (Hann 1988:chap. 13). Had the English not destroyed the Apalachee missions, it is very likely that some of the Apalachee would have continued to adjust to the European colonial presence and might have survived to the present day.

In 1705 and 1706 additional raids into Timucua completed the destruction of those missions. By 1706 the Florida missions were destroyed, and as many as 10,000 to 12,000 Christian Indians had been displaced or taken as slaves. The few hundred remaining villagers were moved to the vicinity of St. Augustine and placed in mission villages. There village populations slowly declined from the hundreds to tens. For example, after the 1702 raid the Santa Fe population was initially moved to San Francisco, and then to the outskirts of St. Augustine. Placed in a village named Esperanza (Hope), the population was only 51 persons in 1717. After 1736 the village's name is no longer found in documents (Milanich 1978:80).

During the period shortly before and after 1720, Franciscan missionaries returned to the field in Florida, serving eleven towns, all composed of remnants of Guale, Timucuan, and Apalachee Indians, as well as a few other native groups originally from south-central Florida and Georgia. Apparently these missionary efforts continued into the mideighteenth century, although little research has been done on them (but see Hann 1988:316,

326–327, 356, 363–364, 1989b). Effectively, however, the mission system in Florida ended with the English raids of 1702–1704.

The descendants of the indigenous Florida native groups—the Uzita, Ocale, Potano, Aguacaleyquen, and others who are described in the narratives of the Hernando de Soto expedition—did not survive. It is ironic that those very colonial powers—England, France, and Spain—that provided the modern world with our only firsthand descriptions of those native peoples, also led to their demise.

AFTERWORD

At various times Hernando de Soto has been judged a heroic explorer and a bloody conquistador. How he is portrayed reflects prevailing attitudes in American society. For example, at the time of the World Columbiana Exposition held in Chicago in 1893 to celebrate the quatrocentenary of Christopher Columbus's "discovery" of the New World, Columbus, de Soto, and other European explorers of the Western Hemisphere were seen as culture heroes who spread European domination to another world and its peoples. One hundred years later, on the occasion of the Columbian Quincentenary, these same individuals are being judged in a harsher light. The celebration of 1892 has been replaced in 1992 by a commemoration that is referred to as an "encounter." At the insistence of native peoples, one theme in this commemoration is "the people who discovered Columbus."

Whatever one's moral judgments about Hernando de Soto and the impact of his army's trek through Florida and the southern United States, one fact must be acknowledged: the de Soto expedition was a historical event. It occurred. The native peoples encountered by the army and the battles and other events recorded in the de Soto narratives are real. Individuals like Urriparacoxi and Capafi were historical actors, and their roles are as important as those of de Soto and the members of his army.

Our task in this volume has been to take the accounts of these people and the events in which they participated and interpret them in the light of other sources of information. This allowed us to draw a preliminary line on a map, a line representing a tentative reconstruction of the expedition's route through Florida. We then tested this reconstruction a segment at a time against new archaeological data, altering and refining the reconstruction as appropriate to arrive at a "best fit"—or, in some instances, best "fits"—reconciling the documentary, archaeological, cartographic, and other sources of evidence. The fruit of this exercise is the reconstruction of the de Soto route through Florida presented here. We have also sought to place the expedition in its historical context, that of the expansion of Spain's New World empire northward from the Caribbean.

Another of our goals was to apply the information about native peoples contained in the de Soto narratives to our reconstruction of the route to begin developing a picture of the social geography of the Florida Indians. We know from the narratives, for example, that the Uzita were a distinct native group in 1539 who occupied territory at the de Soto army's landing site. Likewise, the Aguacaleyquen were a group living north of the River of Discords somewhere in northern peninsular Florida. When these bits of information are combined with our reconstruction of the route, we can place both the Uzita and the Aguacaleyquen in their respective specific locations at a specific time, the summer of 1539.

This is true for the native groups all along the route from Tampa Bay into northwest Florida. And we have used other sixteenth-century documentary sources to provide additional interpreted information that has allowed us to venture beyond the route proper to create a social geography of other Florida Indians, such as the various Timucuan speakers living along the St. Johns River and the Calusa and Tequesta in southern Florida. Although the names of all of these sixteenth-century groups have been known by scholars for many years (e.g., Swanton 1922: 320–345), the social geography we present here is far more consistent with available information. And, using archaeological data not available in the past, we can in many instances correlate particular native groups with specific archaeological sites and material cultural assemblages.

What were once only names found in documents are now cultural entities that exist in time and space and are tied to concrete material remains. The Uzita, Aguacaleyquen, and their contemporaries take on enhanced historical and anthropological significance, allowing us to view them in a new light. In this way we can clarify difficult questions about taxonomy and geography. For example, we now are confident that the Utina encountered by René de Laudonnière and by Pedro Menéndez in the 1560s were a quite different group from the Aguacaleyquen and other north Florida peoples mistakenly called "Utina" by scholars.

We also can clarify relationships between ethnic groups and archaeological assemblages. One example is the Ocale, previously thought to be associated with the north-central Florida Alachua tradition archaeological assemblage, but now thought to correlate with ceramic types that in the late pre-Columbian period are found with the Safety Harbor archaeological culture found in west-central peninsular Florida.

Using such new data, we can begin to trace specific groups through time and we can study, for example, the impact of the European presence on them. We can see that peoples like the Acuera and the Tocobaga, who existed in the midsixteenth century, maintained their ethnic identities and continued to interact with Europeans for at least a century, while others, like the Uzita, quickly disappeared from the documentary record. We also can trace the history of groups like the Potano from their first encounters with Europeans in the summer of 1539, through their battles with the French and Spanish in the 1560s, into the seventeenth-century mission period, and to the time of their demise.

And with increased understanding comes increased ability to investigate more complex anthropological issues. For example, at the time of the de Soto expedition, were the Potano organized into a chiefdom—a form of complex social integration—or did a confederation of previously semiautonomous villages united under the leadership of a single warchief occur in response to the European presence?

Our study of Hernando de Soto and the Florida Indians has prompted us to conceive of the native peoples of Florida in a new fashion. We can now both better delineate and study specific groups and their material remains in time and space, *and* we can more clearly see the larger picture—the geographical and political relationships within and among the Florida native groups. Our research on the de Soto expedition has allowed us to begin fleshing out a more comprehensive interpretation of Florida's native peoples.

De Soto's trek through Florida more than 450 years ago has helped to lead us today to an enhanced understanding of the native peoples he met. This is indeed his most important legacy.

NOTES

CHAPTER 1

1. Hernández de Biedma is the author's actual name, but it has been Americanized to Biedma.

2. See Swanton (1939:4–11) for a discussion of the various translations and editions of the three de Soto expedition narratives to that date; also see Hann 1989a.

3. See Robertson (1933:397–428) for a discussion of these and other sources and documents.

CHAPTER 2

1. For biographical information on de Soto, see Albornoz (1986), Buckingham Smith's "Life of de Soto," in Smith (1866), and Swanton (1939:65–74).

2. See Lyon (1976:220–223) for a comparison of de Soto's contract with those of Ayllón and Narváez.

3. This translation was originally published as an appendix to the 1866 edition of the Elvas and Biedma narratives translated by Buckingham Smith (Smith 1866).

CHAPTER 4

1. Elvas (1922:34) places the numbers at fifty cavalry and thirty or forty footmen.

2. Elvas says thirty cavalry and seventy infantry along with provisions for two years were left at the camp (1922:36).

3. Garcilaso says 120 men were left at the camp, and gives the figures as forty cavalry and eighty infantry.

4. Elvas (1922:36) called it Acela.

5. Ranjel's account (1922:68) suggests some of the maize was taken from Acuera, a nearby province or town. The region of Ocale itself may not have been a good agricultural region.

6. Information on Bullen's survey comes from the Florida Museum of Natural History's archaeology files.

CHAPTER 5

1. See Mitchem (1989b) for a discussion of these sites and the collections from them.

CHAPTER 6

1. Ranjel (1922:69) says 100 on foot.

2. Elvas (1922:38–39) calls Itaraholata "Ytara," and refers to Utinamocharra as "Utinama."

3. Elvas (1922:40–41) calls the village "Caliquen."

4. Hann (1989a) notes that in the Biedma account (1922:5) this is mistakenly translated as four to five days.

5. Hann (1989a) notes the word used, *ferragem*, could refer to "horseshoes."

6. Ranjel (1922:72) mistakenly says this was a Friday.

7. Elvas (1922:45) calls these towns "Hapaluya" and "Uzachil." Biedma (1922:6) calls the latter "Veachile."

8. Biedma (1922:6) calls the town "Aguile" and notes that it was in the confines of Apalachee. Ranjel (1922:46) says the town's name is "Axille."

CHAPTER 7

1. This mission was sometimes called "Tari"; *tari-hica* is "strong village" (Granberry 1989:167, 184).

2. Santa Maria was probably in Hamilton County. "Arapaha" is the source of the name for the Alapaha River. *Ara-paha* means "many houses."

3. *Chua* is "sinkhole" or "spring."

4. *Ajohica* also appears as "Afuica." *Hica* means "village."

5. *Cha-mili* could be "where the light shines" (Granberry 1989:161, 174).

6. *Cachu-pile* is "pretty cabin" (Granberry 1989:160, 180).

7. Throughout this chapter we refer to the de Bry–engraved map as the Le Moyne map.

8. *Hiereba*, in Timucuan, is "metal, gold, iron, silver" (Granberry 1989:167), perhaps a reference to metal controlled by the Yustaga?

9. *Machaba* is "marsh, swamp" (Granberry 1989:173), suggesting it was close to San Pedro Bay.

10. *Sile* may be akin to "chile," a chiefly reference.

11. *Tola-patafi* is "at the foot or under the laurel" (Milanich 1978:65; Granberry 1989:179, 185).

12. This general location was first proposed by Charles Hudson, who was attempting to reconcile French accounts and the Le Moyne map with his reconstruction of de Soto's route in Florida. Hudson surmised that "Etoniah" was a corruption of "Utina." Kenneth Johnson first realized that the crescent-shaped shaded feature on Le Moyne's map probably referred to an ancestral Lake Grandin, and that this was probably Utina's main territory.

13. In Timucuan, *pacha-hica* is "old town" (Granberry 1989:167, 179).

14. *Nia* is "female" in Timucuan (Granberry 1989:177).

CHAPTER 8

1. Elvas (1922:47) spells it "Uitachuco." The *V* may have been mistranscribed as a *U.*

2. Garcilaso says the actual channel was about forty paces wide (Hann 1989a).

3. Elvas (1922:47) calls the town "Uzela."

4. Hann has corrected the Buckingham Smith translation of Elvas that stated the men were lodged "half a league to a league apart" (Elvas 1922:27).

5. Keel (1989) quotes B. Calvin Jones as saying the distribution of sites in Apalachee is like a triangle, with the wide base around Iniahica extending east to the apex at Ivitachuco.

6. Hann (1989a) notes that the Elvas account (1922:47), which says the coast was eight leagues, is mistranslated.

7. Hann (1989a) notes that the distance to Ochete in Elvas (1922:47) is again mistranslated by Buckingham Smith, who gives the distance as eight leagues.

8. Elvas (1922:50) calls it "Ochus," and Garcilaso (Varner and Varner 1951:248) says "Achusi."

9. Elvas says the River of "Capachiqui" was a four-day journey from Iniahica.

CHAPTER 9

1. For the story of the French settlements and Menéndez's successful overthrow of them, see Bennett (1964), Laudonnière (1975), Lorant (1946), Lyon (1976, 1988, 1989), and Ribaut (1964).

2. Nombre de Dios was at St. Augustine and probably served the Seloy.

3. San Juan del Puerto was located toward the northern end of Fort George Island north of the mouth of the St. Johns River.

4. San Pedro, on the southern portion of Cumberland Island, Georgia, served Timucuan speakers.

5. Ibi, which means "water, lagoon, lake, canal, or sea" in Timucuan (Granberry 1989:169), was in southeast Georgia near the coast.

6. Asao was in the province of Guale, the name of which was derived from the Guale Indians who lived on the Georgia coast and who spoke a Muskhogean language quite different from Timucuan. Asao was on the Altamaha River, probably near its mouth. Later, Asao became the name of St. Simons Island.

7. Tolomato, another Guale mission, was on the mainland north of the Altamaha River.

8. Tupique was north of Tolomato.

9. Ospo was in northern Guale.

10. St. Catherine, probably the northernmost Spanish outpost after Santa Elena was abandoned in 1587, was on St. Catherines Island.

11. *Moca-ma* is "ocean" in Timucuan (Granberry 1989:174). Most references to Mocama as a province, however, link it to Guale, rather than Timucua, although it is known that Timucuan speakers resided in coastal southeasternmost Georgia.

12. We are grateful to John Hann for providing demographic data used here that are not in his 1988 publication.

13. Hann provided the information on the destruction of San Juan de Guacara. He found the information in a letter to the king by Governor Diego de Quiroga y Lossada, April 10, 1692 (AGI, SD 228, document number 32 in John Tate Lanning's Colección "Missiones Guale," Vol. IV, Thomas Jefferson Library, University of Missouri–St. Louis).

BIBLIOGRAPHY

Albornoz, Miguel

1986 *Hernando de Soto: Knight of the Americas.* New York: F. Watts.

Allerton, David, George M. Luer, and Robert S. Carr

1984 Ceremonial Tablets and Related Objects from Florida. *Florida Anthropologist* 37:5–54.

Anonymous

1829 [Map of north Florida]. Filed as map PKY 240, P.K. Yonge Library of Florida History, University of Florida. Gainesville.

Arnade, Charles

1959 *The Siege of St. Augustine in 1702.* Gainesville: University of Florida Press.

Avellaneda, Ignacio

1990 *Los Sobrevivientos de la Florida: The Survivors of the de Soto Expedition.* Edited by Bruce Chappell. Research Publications of the P.K. Yonge Library of Florida History, No. 2, University of Florida Libraries. Gainesville.

Bandelier, Ad. F., ed.

1905 *The Journey of Alvar Núñez Cabeza de Vaca and his Companions from Florida to the Pacific, 1528–1536.* Translated by Fanny Bandelier. New York: A. S. Barnes and Co.

Barnett, E. (Capt.)

1861 *The West Indian Pilot,* Vol. I. London: J. D. Potter.

Bennett, Charles

1964 *Laudonnière & Fort Caroline.* Gainesville: University of Florida Press.

Benyaurd, William H. H.

1897 (Map of Tampa Bay.) From a survey made under the direction of Lieut. Col. Wm. H.H. Benyaurd, Corps of Engineers,

U.S. Army, December 1896 to March 1897, and from Charts of the U.S. Coast and Geodetic Survey. Map PKY 1659, P.K. Yonge Library of Florida History, University of Florida. Gainesville.

Biedma, Luys Hernández de

1922 Relation of the Conquest of Florida. In *Narratives of the Career of Hernando de Soto in the Conquest of Florida, . . .* Vol. II, pp. 1–40. Translated by Buckingham Smith, edited by Edward G. Bourne. New York: Allerton Book Co.

Bien, Julius, and Co. (Lithographers)

n.d. *Atlas to Accompany the Official Records of the Union and Confederate Armies, 1861–1865.* New York: Bien and Co.

Black, William H. (Capt.)

1889 Improvement of Caloosahatchee River, Florida. In *Report of the Chief of Engineers, U.S. Army,* pp. 1337–1339. Report of the Secretary of War, Messages and Documents Communicated to the Two Houses of Congress, 1st Session, 51st Congress, vol. 2, part 2. Washington, D.C.

Bloodworth, Bertha E., and Alton C. Morris

1978 *Places in the Sun, The History and Romance of Florida Place-Names.* Gainesville: University of Florida Press.

Blunt, Edmund M.

1822 *The American Coast Pilot . . .* (Tenth Edition). New York: William Hooker.

Bolton, Herbert E., and Mary Ross

1925 *The Debatable Land.* Berkeley: University of California Press.

Bourne, Edward G., ed. and trans.

1904 *Narratives of the Career of Hernando de Soto in the Conquest of Florida, as Told by a Knight of Elvas and in a Relation by Luys Hernández de Biedma, Factor of the Expedition, Translated by Buckingham Smith Together with an Account of de Soto's Expedition Based on the Diary of Rodrigo Ranjel, his Private Secretary, Translated from Oviedo's Historia General y Natural de las Indias,* 2 vols. New York: A. S. Barnes and Co.

Boyd, Mark F.

1938a Map of the Road from Pensacola to St. Augustine, 1778. *Florida Historical Quarterly* 17:1–23.

1938b The Arrival of de Soto's Expedition in Florida. *Florida Historical Quarterly* 16:188–220.

Boyd, Mark F., Hale G. Smith, and John W. Griffin

1951 *Here They Once Stood, the Tragic End of the Apalachee Missions.* Gainesville: University of Florida Press.

Brain, Jeffrey P.

1975 Artifacts of the Adelantado. *Conference on Historic Site Archaeology Papers* 8:129–138.

Brown, James A.

1985 The Mississippian Period. In *Ancient Art of the American Woodland Indians,* pp. 93–145. New York: Harry N. Abrams, Inc.

Bullen, Ripley P.

1951 *The Terra Ceia Site, Manatee County, Florida.* Florida Anthropological Society Publications 3.

1952a De Soto's Uçita and the Terra Ceia Site. *Florida Historical Quarterly* 30:317–323.

1952b *Eleven Archaeological Sites in Hillsborough County, Florida.* Florida Geological Survey, Report of Investigations 8.

1955 Archaeology of the Tampa Bay Area. *Florida Historical Quarterly* 34:51–63.

1975 *A Guide to the Identification of Florida Projectile Points.* Gainesville: Kendall Books.

1978 Tocobaga Indians and the Safety Harbor Culture. In *Tacachale, Essays on the Indians of Florida and Southeastern Georgia during the Historic Period,* pp. 50–58. Edited by Jerald T. Milanich and Samuel Proctor. Gainesville: University of Florida Press/Florida Museum of Natural History.

Burger, William B.

1982 Cultural Resource Management in Manatee County, Florida: The Prehistoric Resources Base. Master's thesis, Department of Anthropology, University of South Florida. Tampa.

Castañeda, Paulino, Mariano Cuesta, and Pilar Hernández

1983 *Transcripción, Estudio y Notas del "Espejo de Navegantes" de Alonso Chaves.* Madrid: Instituto de Historia y Cultura Naval.

Chamberlain, Robert S.

1948 *The Conquest and Colonization of Yucatan, 1517–1550.* Carnegie Institution of Washington Publication 582. Washington, D.C.

Chardon, Roland

1980 The Linear League in North America. *Annals of the Association of American Geographers* 70:129–153.

Cordell, Linda

1989 Durango to Durango: An Overview of the Southwest Heartland. In *Columbian Consequences.* Vol. I: *Archaeological and Historical Perspectives on the Spanish Borderlands West,* pp. 17–40. Edited by David Hurst Thomas. Washington, D.C.: Smithsonian Institution Press.

Crane, Verner W.

1956 *The Southern Frontier, 1670–1732.* Ann Arbor: University of Michigan Press.

Cumming, W. P., R. A. Skelton, and D. B. Quinn

1972 *The Discovery of North America.* New York: American Heritage Press.

Davis, T. Frederick

1935 Juan Ponce de León's Voyages to Florida. *Florida Historical Quarterly* 14:5–70.

Deagan, Kathleen A.

1978 Cultures in Transition: Fusion and Assimilation among the Eastern Timucua. In *Tacachale, Essays on the Indians of Florida and Southeastern Georgia during the Historic Period,* pp. 89–119. Edited by Jerald T. Milanich and Samuel Proctor. Gainesville: University of Florida Press.

1987 *Artifacts of the Spanish Colonies of Florida and the Caribbean, 1500–1800.* Vol. I: Ceramics, Glassware, and Beads. Washington, D.C.: Smithsonian Institution Press.

DePratter, Chester B., Charles Hudson, and Marvin T. Smith

1983 The Route of Juan Pardo's Explorations in the Interior Southeast. *Florida Historical Quarterly* 62:125–158.

1985 The Hernando de Soto Expedition: From Chiaha to Mabila. In *Alabama and its Borderlands from Prehistory to Statehood,* pp. 108–126. Edited by Reid Badger and Lawrence A. Clayton. Tuscaloosa: University of Alabama Press.

DePratter, Chester B., and Marvin T. Smith

1980 Sixteenth-Century European Trade in the Southeastern United States: Evidence from the Juan Pardo Expeditions (1566–1568). In *Spanish Colonial Frontier Research,* pp. 57–77. Edited by Henry F. Dobyns. Albuquerque: Center for Anthropological Research.

de Salazar, Pablo Hita (governor of Florida)

1675 (Letter to the Spanish Crown. St. Augustine, August 24, 1675.) Photostat, P.K. Yonge Library of Florida History, University of Florida. Gainesville.

de Soto, Hernando

1866 Letter of Hernando de Soto at Tampa Bay to the Justice and Board of Magistrates in Santiago de Cuba. In *Narratives of the Career of Hernando de Soto in the Conquest of Florida. . . .* Translated by Buckingham Smith. New York: Bradford Club.

Dobyns, Henry F.

1983 *Their Number Become Thinned, Native American Population Dynamics in Eastern North America.* Knoxville: University of Tennessee Press.

Elvas (Gentleman of Elvas)

1922 True Relation. . . . In *Narratives of the Career of Hernando de Soto in the Conquest of Florida, . . . ,* Vol. I, pp. 1–222. Edited by Edward G. Bourne. New York: Allerton Book Co.

Ewen, Charles R.

1988 *The Discovery of de Soto's First Winter Encampment in Florida.* De Soto Working Paper 7. Alabama De Soto Commission, University of Alabama, State Museum of Natural History. Tuscaloosa.

1989 Anhaica: Discovery of Hernando de Soto's 1539–1540 Winter Camp. In *First Encounters, Spanish Explorations in the Caribbean and the United States, 1492–1570,* pp. 110–118. Edited by Jerald T. Milanich and Susan Milbrath. Gainesville: University of Florida Press.

Fairbanks, Charles H.

1968 Early Spanish Colonial Beads. *Conference on Historic Site Archaeology* 2:3–21.

Featherstonhaugh, Thomas

1897 [Untitled.] *American Anthropologist* 10:200.

1899 The Mound-Builders of Central Florida. *Publications of the Southern History Association* 3(1):1–14.

Fernández de Oviedo y Valdés, Gonzalo

1851 *Historia General y Natural de las Indias,* Vol. I. Madrid: Impresa de la Real Academia de la Historia.

Fewkes, Jesse W.

1924 Preliminary Archeological Investigations at Weeden Island, Florida. *Smithsonian Miscellaneous Collections* 76(1):1–26.

Gannon, Michael V.

1965 *The Cross in the Sand: The Early Catholic Church in Florida, 1513–1870.* Gainesville: University of Florida Press.

Gatschet, Albert S.

1880 The Timucuan Language. *Proceedings of the American Philosophical Society* 18:465–502.

Gaytan, Juan, Johan de Añasco, and Luis Hernández de Biedma

1866 *Letter to the King of Spain from Officers at Havana in the Army of Soto [May 18, 1539]. Narratives of the Career of Hernando de Soto in the Conquest of Florida. . . .* Translated by Buckingham Smith. New York: Bradford Club.

Geiger, Maynard

1936 *The Franciscan Conquest of Florida, 1573–1618.* Washington, D.C.: Catholic University of America Press.

1940 *Biographical Dictionary of the Franciscans in Spanish Florida and Cuba (1528–1841).* Franciscan Studies 21. Paterson, NJ: St. Anthony's Guild Press.

Goggin, John M.

1940 The Tekesta Indians of Southern Florida. *Florida Historical Quarterly* 18:274–284.

1951 *Space and Time Perspective in Northern St. Johns Archaeology, Florida.* Yale University Publications in Anthropology 47. New Haven.

1953 An Introductory Outline of Timucuan Archaeology. *Southeastern Archaeological Conference Newsletter* 3(3):4–17.

1960 *The Spanish Olive Jar, an Introductory Study.* Yale University Publications in Anthropology 62. New Haven.

1968 *Spanish Majolica in the New World.* Yale University Publications in Anthropology 72. New Haven.

Goggin, John M., and William C. Sturtevant

1964 The Calusa: A Stratified Nonagricultural Society (with Notes on Sibling Marriage). In *Explorations in Cultural Anthropology: Essays in Honor of George Peter Murdock*, pp. 179–219. Edited by Ward H. Goodenough. New York: McGraw-Hill.

Granberry, Julian

1989 *A Grammar and Dictionary of the Timucuan Language.* (Second Edition.) Anthropological Notes 1. Horseshoe Beach, FL: Island Archaeological Museum.

Griffin, John W.

1975 Conclusions. In *Excavations at the Granada Site. Archaeology and History of the Granada Site*, Vol. I, pp. 365–394. Prepared under contract for the City of Miami by Florida Division of Archives, History and Records Management. Tallahassee.

Griffin, John W., and Ripley P. Bullen

1950 *The Safety Harbor Site, Pinellas County, Florida.* Florida Anthropological Society Publications 2.

Hann, John H.

1986 Translation of Governor Rebolledo's 1657 Visitation of Three Florida Provinces and Related Documents. *Florida Archaeology* 2:81–145.

1988 *Apalachee: The Land between the Rivers.* Gainesville: University of Florida Press/Florida Museum of Natural History.

1989a Pánfilo de Narváez and Hernando de Soto in Apalachee. (Including: "Luys Hernández de Biedma, Report of the Outcome of the Journey that Hernando de Soto Made and of the Characteristics of the Land through which He Traveled [Transcription of the Spanish Text Dealing with Apalachee and a Translation of the Same]"; "Translation of the Apalachee Section of the Narrative about the de Soto Expedition Written by Gonzalo Fernández de Oviedo and Based on the Diary of Rodrigo Ranjel, de Soto's Private Secretary"; "Transcription and Translation of the Apalachee Section of the Fidalgo de Elvas's True Relations of the Labors that the Governor Don Fernando de Soto and Certain Portuguese Gentlemen Experienced in the Exploration of Florida. Now Newly Made by a Gentleman of Elvas"; "Translation of the Apalachee Section of The Florida of the Inca . . ."; and, "Translations of the Florida Sections of the Alvar Núñez Cabeza de Vaca Accounts of the 1528 Trek from South Florida to Apalachee Led by Pánfilo de Narváez.") Typescript manuscript on file, Florida Bureau of Archaeological Research. Tallahassee.

1989b St. Augustine's Fallout from the Yamassee War. *Florida Historical Quarterly* 68:180–200.

1990 Summary Guide to Spanish Florida Missions and Visitas with Churches in the Sixteenth and Seventeenth Centuries. *The Americas* 46:417–513.

1991a The Mayaca and Jororo and Missions to Them. Typescript manuscript on file, Florida Bureau of Archaeological Research. Tallahassee.

1991b *Missions to the Calusa.* Gainesville: University of Florida Press/Florida Museum of Natural History.

Harrisse, Henry

1961 *The Discovery of North America: A Critical, Documentary, and Historical Investigation.* Amsterdam: N. Israel (Publishing Department). (Originally published in 1892, London.)

1968 *John Cabot, Discoverer of North America, and his Son.* New York: Argosy-Antiquarian Ltd. (Originally published in English 1896, London.)

Hemming, John

1978 *Red Gold: The Conquest of the Brazilian Indians.* Cambridge: Harvard University Press.

Henige, David

1986 The Context, Content, and Credibility of La Florida del Ynca. *The Americas* 43:1–24.

Hoffman, Paul E.

1984 The Chicora Legend and Franco-Spanish Rivalry. *Florida Historical Quarterly* 62:419–438.

1990 A *New Andalucía and a Way to the Orient, The American Southeast during the Sixteenth Century.* Baton Rouge: Louisiana State University Press.

Hudson, Charles

1984 The Hernando de Soto Expedition: The Landing. Paper presented at the annual meeting of the American Society for Ethnohistory, November 8, New Orleans.

1987 Juan Pardo's Excursion beyond Chiaha. *Tennessee Anthropologist* 12:74–87.

1989 *De Soto in Alabama.* De Soto Working Paper 10. Alabama De Soto Commission, University of Alabama, State Museum of Natural History, Tuscaloosa.

1990 *The Juan Pardo Expeditions: Spanish Explorers and the Indians of the Carolinas and Tennessee, 1566–1568.* Washington, D.C.: Smithsonian Institution Press.

Hudson, Charles, ed.

1979 *The Black Drink—A Native American Tea.* Athens: University of Georgia Press.

Hudson, Charles, Chester DePratter, and Marvin T. Smith

1984 The Hernando de Soto Expedition: From Apalachee to Chiaha. *Southeastern Archaeology* 3:65–77.

1989 Hernando de Soto's Expedition through the Southern United States. In *First Encounters, Spanish Explorations in the Caribbean and the United States, 1492–1570,* pp. 77–98. Edited by Jerald T. Milanich and Susan Milbrath. Gainesville: University of Florida Press.

Hudson, Charles, Marvin Smith, David Hally, Richard Polhemus, and Chester DePratter

1985 Coosa: A Chiefdom in the Sixteenth-Century Southeastern United States. *American Antiquity* 50:723–737.

Hudson, Charles, Marvin T. Smith, Chester B. DePratter, and Emilia Kelley

1989a The Tristán de Luna Expedition, 1559–1561. In *First Encounters, Spanish Explorations in the Caribbean and the United States, 1492–1570*, pp. 119–134. Edited by Jerald T. Milanich and Susan Milbrath. Gainesville: University of Florida Press.

1989b The Tristán de Luna Expedition, 1559–1561. *Southeastern Archaeology* 8:31–45.

Hutchinson, Dale L.

1991 Post-contact Native American Health and Adaptation: Assessing the Impact of Introduced Disease in Sixteenth-Century Gulf Coast Florida. Ph.D. dissertation, Department of Anthropology, University of Illinois. Urbana.

Ives, J. C.

1856 Military Map of the Peninsula of Florida South of Tampa Bay. Washington, D.C. Copy on file, P.K. Yonge Library of Florida History, map PKY 581, University of Florida. Gainesville.

Johnson, Kenneth W.

1986 *Archaeological Survey of Contact and Mission Period Sites in Northern Peninsular Florida.* Miscellaneous Project Report 37. Department of Anthropology, Florida Museum of Natural History. Gainesville.

1987 *The Search for Aguacaleyquen and Cali. Miscellaneous Project Report 33.* Department of Anthropology, Florida Museum of Natural History. Gainesville.

1991 The Utina and the Potano Peoples of Northern Florida: Changing Settlement Systems in the Spanish Colonial Period. Ph.D. dissertation, Department of Anthropology, University of Florida. Gainesville.

Johnson, Kenneth W., Bruce C. Nelson, and Keith A. Terry

1988 *The Search for Aguacaleyquen and Cali, Season 2.* Miscellaneous Project Report 38. Department of Anthropology, Florida Museum of Natural History. Gainesville.

Jones, B. Calvin

1972 Colonel James Moore and the Destruction of the Apalachee Missions in 1704. *Florida Bureau of Historic Sites and Properties Bulletin* 2:25–33.

Keel, Frank J.

1989 Research on the de Soto Expedition in Northwest Florida. (With accompanying notes and maps.) Manuscript on file, Department of Anthropology, Florida Museum of Natural History. Gainesville.

Kunz, George F.

1887 On Gold and Silver Ornaments from Mounds of Florida. *American Antiquarian and Oriental Journal* 9:219–227.

Laudonnière, René de

1975 *Three Voyages.* Translated by Charles Bennett. Gainesville: University of Florida Press.

Lewis, Clifford M.

1978 The Calusa. In *Tacachale, Essays on the Indians of Florida and Southeastern Georgia during the Historic Period,* pp. 19–49. Edited by Jerald T. Milanich and Samuel Proctor. Gainesville: University of Florida Press/Florida Museum of Natural History.

López, Atanasio

1933 *Relación Histórica de la Florida Escrita en el Siglo XVII,* Vol. II. Madrid: Librería General de Victoriano Suárez.

Lorant, Stefan

1946 *The New World, the First Pictures of America.* New York: Duell, Sloan & Pearce.

Luer, George M., and Marion M. Almy

1981 Temple Mounds in the Tampa Bay Area. *Florida Anthropologist* 34:127–155.

Lyon, Eugene

1976 *The Enterprise of Florida.* Gainesville: University of Florida Press.

1982 The Cañete Fragment: Another Narrative of Hernando de Soto. Manuscript on file, St. Augustine Foundation. St. Augustine.

1988 Pedro Menéndez's Strategic Plan for the Florida Peninsula. *Florida Historical Quarterly* 67:1–14.

1989 Pedro Menéndez's Plan for Settling La Florida. In *First Encounters, Spanish Explorations in the Caribbean and the United States, 1492–1570,* pp. 150–165. Edited by Jerald T. Milanich and Susan Milbrath. Gainesville: University of Florida Press.

McMurray, Judith A.

1973 The Definition of the Ceramic Complex at San Juan del Puerto. Master's thesis, Department of Anthropology, University of Florida. Gainesville.

McNicoll, Robert E.

1941 The Caloosa Village Tequesta, a Miami of the Sixteenth Century. *Tequesta* 1:11–20.

Marquardt, William H.

1987 The Calusa Social Formation in Protohistoric South Florida. In *Power Relations and State Formations*, pp. 98–116. Edited by Thomas C. Patterson and Christine W. Gailey. Washington, D.C.: Archaeology Section, American Anthropological Association.

1988 Politics and Production among the Calusa of South Florida. In *Hunters and Gatherers*. Vol. I: *History, Environment, and Social Change among Hunting and Gathering Societies*, pp. 161–188. Edited by David Richies, Tim Ingold, and James Woodburn. London: Berg Publishers.

Marrinan, Rochelle A., John F. Scarry, and Rhonda L. Majors

1990 Prelude to de Soto: The Expedition of Pánfilo de Narváez. In *Columbian Consequences*. Vol. II: *Archaeological and Historical Perspectives on the Spanish Borderlands East*, pp. 71–82. Edited by David Hurst Thomas. Washington, D.C.: Smithsonian Institution Press.

Meigs, J. L.

1880a Report of Mr. J. L. Meigs, Assistant Engineer, Mobile, Alabama, August 1, 1879. In Examination of Caloosahatchee River, Florida; Report of the Chief of Engineers, pp. 864–870. *Executive Documents of the House of Representatives, 2nd Session, 46th Congress, 1879–1880*, vol. 3; Engineers no. 1, part 2, vol. 2, part 1. Washington, D.C.: Government Printing Office.

1880b Report of Mr. J. L. Meigs, Assistant Engineer. In Examination of Tampa Bay and the Mouth of Hillsborough River, Florida; Report of the Chief of Engineers, pp. 871–873. *Executive Documents of the House of Representatives, 2nd Session, 46th Congress, 1879–1880*, vol. 3; Engineers no. 1, part 2, vol. 2, part 1. Washington, D.C.: Government Printing Office.

Meyer, F. W.

1962 *Reconnaissance of the Geology and Ground Water Resources of Columbia County, Florida*. Florida Geological Survey, Report of Investigations 30.

Milanich, Jerald T.

1971 *The Alachua Tradition of North-central Florida.* Contributions of the Florida State Museum, Anthropology and History 17. Gainesville.

1972 Excavations at the Richardson Site, Alachua County, Florida: An Early 17th-Century Potano Indian Village (with Notes on Potano Culture Change). *Bureau of Historic Sites and Properties, Florida Department of State, Bulletin* 2:35–61.

1978 The Western Timucua: Patterns of Acculturation and Change. In *Tacachale, Essays on the Indians of Florida and Southeastern Georgia during the Historic Period,* pp. 59–88. Edited by Jerald Milanich and Samuel Proctor. Gainesville: University of Florida Press/Florida Museum of Natural History.

1989 Where Did de Soto Land? Identifying Bahía Honda. *Florida Anthropologist* 42:295–302.

In press Franciscan Missions and Native Peoples in Spanish Florida. In *The Forgotten Centuries: Europeans and Indians in the American South, 1513–1704.* Edited by Charles Hudson and Carmen McClendon. Athens: University of Georgia Press.

Milanich, Jerald T., and Charles H. Fairbanks

1980 *Florida Archaeology.* New York: Academic Press.

Milanich, Jerald T., and Kenneth W. Johnson

1989 *Santa Fe: A Name Out of Time.* Miscellaneous Project Report 41. Department of Anthropology, Florida Museum of Natural History. Gainesville.

Mitchem, Jeffrey M.

1989a Artifacts of Exploration: Archaeological Evidence from Florida. In *First Encounters, Spanish Explorations in the Caribbean and the United States, 1492–1570,* pp. 99–109. Edited by Jerald T. Milanich and Susan Milbrath. Gainesville: University of Florida Press.

1989b Redefining Safety Harbor: Late Prehistoric/Protohistoric Archaeology in West Peninsular Florida. Ph.D. dissertation, Department of Anthropology, University of Florida, Gainesville.

Mitchem, Jeffrey M., and Dale L. Hutchinson

1986 *Interim Report on Excavations at the Tatham Mound, Citrus County, Florida: Season II.* Miscellaneous Project Report 28. Department of Anthropology, Florida Museum of Natural History. Gainesville.

1987 *Interim Report on Archaeological Research at the Tatham Mound, Citrus County, Florida: Season III.* Miscellaneous Project Report 30. Department of Anthropology, Florida Museum of Natural History. Gainesville.

Mitchem, Jeffrey M., and Jonathan M. Leader

1988 Early Sixteenth-Century Beads from the Tatham Mound, Citrus County, Florida: Data and Interpretations. *Florida Anthropologist* 41:42–60.

Mitchem, Jeffrey M., and Bonnie G. McEwan

1988 New Data on Early Bells from Florida. *Southeastern Archaeology* 7:39–49.

Mitchem, Jeffrey M., and Brent R. Weisman

1984 Excavations at the Ruth Smith Mound (8CI200). *Florida Anthropologist* 37:100–112.

1987 Changing Settlement Patterns and Pottery Types in the Withlacoochee Cove. *Florida Anthropologist* 40:154–166.

Mitchem, Jeffrey M., Marvin T. Smith, Albert C. Goodyear, and Robert R. Allen

1985 Early Spanish Contact on the Florida Gulf Coast: The Weeki Wachee and Ruth Smith Mounds. In *Indians, Colonists, and Slaves: Essays in Memory of Charles H. Fairbanks*, pp. 179–219. Edited by Kenneth W. Johnson, Jonathan M. Leader, and Robert C. Wilson. Florida Journal of Anthropology Special Publication 4. Gainesville.

Mitchem, Jeffrey M., Brent R. Weisman, Donna L. Ruhl, Jenette Savell, Laura Sellers, and Lisa Sharik

1985 *Preliminary Report on Excavations at the Tatham Mound (8CI203), Citrus County, Florida: Season I.* Miscellaneous Project Report 23. Department of Anthropology, Florida Museum of Natural History. Gainesville.

Moore, Clarence B.

1900 Certain Antiquities of the Florida West-Coast. *Journal of the Academy of Natural Sciences of Philadelphia* 11(3):350–394.

1903 Certain Aboriginal Mounds of the Florida Central West Coast. *Journal of the Academy of Natural Sciences of Philadelphia* 12:361–439.

Morison, Samuel Eliot

1971 *The European Discovery of America, the Northern Voyages.* New York: Oxford University Press.

Myers, J. Emlin, and Jacquelin S. Olin

1990 Where Did the De Soto Expedition's Ceramics Come From? Paper presented at the Southeastern Archaeological Conference, November 7–10, 1990. Mobile, AL.

Neill, Wilfred

1978 *Archeology and a Science of Man.* New York: Columbia University Press.

Oré, Luis Gerónimo de

1936 *The Martyrs of Florida (1513–1616).* Translated by Maynard Geiger. Franciscan Studies 18. New York: Joseph F. Wagner.

Oribe, Gonzalo de (Scribe)

1866 Memorial of Alonso Vázquez. In *Narratives of the Career of Hernando de Soto in the Conquest of Florida. . . .* Translated by Buckingham Smith. New York: Bradford Club.

Pareja, Francisco

1627 *Cathecismo, y Exámen para los que Comulgan.* Mexico City: Impresa de Juan Ruyz. (Microfilm, National Anthropological Archives, Smithsonian Institution, Washington, D.C.)

Parks, Arva Moore

1985 *Where the River Found the Bay, Historical Study of the Granada Site, Miami, Florida. Archaeology and History of the Granada Site,* Vol. II. Prepared under contract for the City of Miami by Florida Division of Archives, History and Records Management. Tallahassee.

Portinaro, Pierluigi, and Franco Knirsch

1987 *The Cartography of North America, 1500–1800.* New York: Facts on File, Inc. (Bison Books Corp.).

Priestley, Herbert I., ed.

1928 *The Luna Papers, Documents Relating to the Expedition of Don Tristán de Luna y Arellano for the Conquest of La Florida in 1559–1561,* 2 vols. Florida State Historical Society, Publication 8. Deland.

Purdy, Barbara A.

1991 *The Art and Archaeology of Florida's Wetlands.* Boca Raton: CRC Press Inc.

Quinn, David B., ed.

1976 *The Extension of Settlement in Florida, Virginia, and the American Southwest. New American World: A Documentary History of North America to 1612,* Vol. V. New York: Harper and Row.

Ranjel, Rodrigo

1922 A Narrative of de Soto's Expedition. . . . In *Narratives of the Career of Hernando de Soto in the Conquest of Florida, . . .*, Vol. II, pp. 41–158. Edited by Edward G. Bourne. New York: Allerton Book Co.

Ribaut, Jean

1964 *The Whole & True Discoverye of Terra Florida.* Gainesville: University of Florida Press. (Facsimile of the London edition of 1563.)

Robertson, James Alexander, ed. and trans.

1933 *True Relation of the Hardships Suffered by Governor Hernando de Soto and Certain Portuguese Gentlemen during the Discovery of the Province of Florida. Now Newly Set Forth by a Gentleman of Elvas,* 2 vols. Florida State Historical Society, Publication 11. Deland.

Romans, Bernard

1962 *A Concise Natural History of East and West Florida.* Gainesville: University of Florida Press. (Facsimile of the 1775 edition published in New York for the author.)

Schell, Rolfe F.

1966 *De Soto Didn't Land at Tampa.* Ft. Myers Beach: Island Press.

Simpson, J. Clarence

1937 Report on Activities in Hillsborough County. In *Second Biennial Report to State Board of Conservation, Archaeological Survey, Biennium Ending June 30, 1936,* pp. 109–116. Florida State Board of Conservation. Tallahassee.

1939 Notes on Two Interesting Mounds Excavated in Hillsborough County. In *Third Biennial Report to State Board of Conservation, Archaeological Survey, Biennium Ending June 30, 1938,* pp. 56–62. Florida State Board of Conservation. Tallahassee.

Smith, Buckingham, trans.

1866 *Narratives of the Career of Hernando de Soto in the Conquest of Florida as Told by a Knight of Elvas and in a Relation by Luys Hernández de Biedma, Factor of the Expedition.* New York: The Bradford Club.

Smith, Hale G.

1956 *The European and the Indian.* Florida Anthropological Society Publication 4.

Smith, Marvin T.

1987 *Archaeology of Aboriginal Culture Change in the Interior Southeast: Depopulation during the Early Historic Period.* Gainesville: University of Florida Press/Florida Museum of Natural History.

1989 Indian Responses to European Contact: The Coosa Example. In *First Encounters, Spanish Explorations in the Caribbean and the United States, 1492–1570*, pp. 135–149. Edited by Jerald T. Milanich and Susan Milbrath. Gainesville: University of Florida Press.

Smith, Marvin T., and Mary Elizabeth Good

1982 *Early Sixteenth-Century Glass Beads in the Spanish Colonial Trade.* Greenwood, MS: Cottonlandia Museum.

Solís de Merás, Gonzalo

1964 *Pedro Menéndez de Avilés. Adelantado, Governor and Captain-General of Florida.* Translated by Jeannette Thurber Connor. Gainesville: University of Florida Press. (Originally published 1923, Florida State Historical Society, Publication 3. Deland.)

Stearns, R. E. C.

1870 Rambles in Florida. *American Naturalist* 3:349–360, 397–405, 455–470.

1872 Research on the Mounds and Shell Heaps of Tampa Bay. *Proceedings of the California Academy of Sciences* 4:214–215.

Stirling, Mathew W.

1930 Prehistoric Mounds in the Vicinity of Tampa Bay, Florida. *Explorations and Field-Work, Smithsonian Institution in 1929*, pp. 183–186. Washington, D.C.: Smithsonian Institution.

1931 Mounds of the Vanished Calusa Indians of Florida. *Explorations and Field-Work, Smithsonian Institution in 1930*, pp. 167–172. Washington, D.C.: Smithsonian Institution.

Sturtevant, William C.

1978 The Last of the South Florida Aborigines. In *Tacachale, Essays on the Indians of Florida and Southeastern Georgia during the Historic Period*, pp. 141–162. Edited by Jerald T. Milanich and Samuel Proctor. Gainesville: University of Florida Press/Florida Museum of Natural History.

Swanton, John R.

1922 *Early History of the Creek Indians and Their Neighbors.* Smithsonian Institution, Bureau of American Ethnology, Bulletin 73. Washington, D.C.

1932 Ethnological Value of the De Soto Narratives. *American Anthropologist* 34:570–590.

1934 The Landing Place of De Soto. *Science* 80(2076):336–337.

1938 The Landing Place of De Soto. *Florida Historical Quarterly* 16:149–173.

1952 De Soto's First Headquarters in Florida. *Florida Historical Quarterly* 30:311–316.

Swanton, John R., ed.

1939 *Final Report of the United States de Soto Expedition Commission.* United States House of Representatives Document 71, 76th Congress, 1st Session. Washington, D.C.

Terry, Keith

1990 Suwannee County Survey, October–November 1990. Manuscript on file, Department of Anthropology, Florida Museum of Natural History. Gainesville.

Thomas, David Hurst

1987 *The Archaeology of Mission Santa Catalina de Guale: 1. Search and Discovery.* Anthropological Papers of the American Museum of Natural History, vol. 63, pt. 2. New York.

True, David O., ed.

1945 *Memoir of D. d'Escalante Fontaneda respecting Florida, Written in Spain, about the Year 1575.* Coral Gables, FL: Glade House.

Vanderhill, Burke G.

1977 The Alachua Trail: A Reconstruction. *Florida Historical Quarterly* 55:423–438.

Van Doren, Mark, ed.

1928 *Travels of William Bartram.* New York: Dover Publications.

Varner, John G., and Jeanette J., trans. and eds.

1951 *The Florida of the Inca.* Austin: University of Texas Press.

Walker, S. T.

1880 Report of the Shell Heaps of Tampa Bay, Florida. *Annual Report for 1879, Smithsonian Institution,* pp. 413–422. Washington, D.C.: Smithsonian Institution.

Weddle, Robert S.

1985 *Spanish Sea, the Gulf of Mexico in North American Discovery, 1500–1685.* College Station: Texas A&M University Press.

Weisman, Brent R.

1986 The Cove of the Withlacoochee: A First Look at the Archaeology of an Interior Florida Wetland. *Florida Anthropologist* 39:4–23.

1988 *1988 Excavations at Fig Springs (8CO1), Season 2, July–December 1988.* Florida Archaeological Reports 4, Florida Bureau of Archaeological Research. Tallahassee.

Wenhold, Lucy L.

1936 *A Seventeenth-Century Letter of Gabriel Díaz Vara Calderón, Bishop of Cuba.* Smithsonian Miscellaneous Collections 95(16). Washington, D.C.

Widmer, Randolph

1988 *The Evolution of the Calusa, a Nonagricultural Chiefdom on the Southwest Florida Coast.* Tuscaloosa: University of Alabama Press.

Wilkinson, Warren H.

1954 *Opening the Case against the U.S. de Soto Commission's Report and other de Soto Papers.* Jacksonville Beach: Alliance for the Preservation of Florida Antiquities.

Willey, Gordon R.

1949 *Archeology of the Florida Gulf Coast.* Smithsonian Miscellaneous Collections 113. Washington, D.C.

Williams, John Lee

1837 *The Territory of Florida.* New York: A. T. Goodrich.

Williams, Lindsey W.

1986 *Boldly Onward.* Charlotte Harbor, FL: Precision Publishing Co.

1989 A Charlotte Harbor Perspective on de Soto's Landing Site. *Florida Anthropologist* 42:280–294.

Winsor, Justin, ed.

1884–1889 *Narrative and Critical History of America,* 8 vols. Boston: Houghton, Mifflin and Co.

Zubillaga, Félix, ed.

1946 *Monumenta Antiquae Floridae (1566–1572).* Monumenta Historica Societatis Iesu 69; Monumenta Missionum Societatis Iesu 3. Rome.

INDEX

Page numbers given in italics indicate that the reference is to a figure on that page.

Aboriginal peoples. *See* Indians
Achuse, Bay of. *See* Pensacola Bay
Acuera (territory), *95,* 169; Franciscan missionaries at, 98; location of, 96, 98; scouting expeditions to, 18
Acuera (town), 72; location of, 73, 74, 93
Acuera Indians, material culture of, 131
Agile (town), 11, 166–67, 211
Aguacaleyquen (chief), 177–78, 184
Aguacaleyquen (town), 154–58; de Soto expedition at, 157, 158; de Soto's route to, 150; location of, 156, 160; political organization of, 177
Aguacaleyquen Indians, xii, 143, 144, 256; confrontation with de Soto, 157; missions to, 245; population of, 158; relationship with Utina, 150
Ais Indians, 118, 195
Ajohica (mission), 182
Alachua County, 5, 93, 134
Alachua Lake, 140
Alachua tradition archaeological culture, 99, 129, 131, 138–40, 146; at Florahome Trough, 193; in Potano region, 170; pottery of, *139;* at Robinson Sinks locale, 147
Alachua Trail, *137,* 145–46
Alafia River, 60, 61, 76–81; archaeological evidence at, 62; fording of, 76–77
Alaminos, Anton de, 43, 45
Allen, Robert, 108
Allicamany (vassal of Saturiwa), 207
Alligator Lake, 153, 160, 177
Alvarez de Pineda, Alonzo, 22; voyage of, *23,* 41
Amelia Island, 209; destruction of missions at, 251, 252
American Coast Pilot, The (Blunt), 47
Añasco, Juan de, 48–49; attack on Uzita, 124; exploration of coast, 219; letters of, 9; at Tampa Bay, 49, 57, 221, 228; at Uzita's village, 68
Ancón Bay, 45
Andrade, Captain, 174, 176
Anna Maria Key (Tampa Bay), 43, 49
Apalachee (chief), 166; power of, 167
Apalachee Bay, Chaves's account of, 43, 45
Apalachee Indians, xii, 143; agricultural activities of, 227; attacks on de Soto expedition, 228; and Pánfilo de Narváez expedition, 23–24; population of, 248–49; weapons of, 228–29
Apalachee "mountains," 180–81
Apalachee region, 180–82, 226–30; archaeology of, 15; boundary with Uzachile, 211; de Soto at, 103, 163, 216; English attack on, 253; fertility of, 230; Franciscan missions in, 248–49
Apalu (village), 164, 176, 209
Appalachian Mountains, 184; de Soto expedition in, 232
Aquera (vassal of Utina), 198. *See also* Acuera
Aquouena. *See* Acuera
Arapaha Indians, 247

Archaeological evidence, destruction of, 62, 94–95, 100, 142
Archery: among Apalachee Indians, 229; among Tampa Bay Indians, 123
Archivo General de Indias (Seville), 9
Arias, Gómez, 53
Armor, Spanish, 17, 106, *107,* 226, 229; at Governor Martin site, 224
Arnade (governor of Florida), 252
Arrow points, 80; of eastern Utina, 173; at Tampa Bay, 123
Artifacts, Spanish, 15–17, 76; at Alafia River, 78; in Cofitachequi region, 232; at de Soto winter camp, 224–26; at Lake Butler, 74; at Mill Point archaeological site, 80; north of Santa Fe River, 148; at Ocale region, 101, 104–10; at Tampa Bay, 63–64, 66–67
Asao (mussion), 244, 261n6
Astina (vassal of Utina), 193, 199
Atahualpa (Inca), 27
Atore (son of Saturiwa), 205–6
Aucilla River, 11, 13, 210, 211; fording of, 212; Mission Trail at, 165, 166
Aucilla Trail, 165
Aute (village), 219, 221
Avellaneda, Ignacio, 10
Axile. *See* Agile

Bahía de Juan Ponce. *See* Charlotte Harbor
Bahía de Miruelo. *See* Apalachee Bay
Bahía Honda. *See* Tampa Bay
Barbu (European captive), 118–19
Bartram, William, 203
Beads, 66, 84; at Governor Martin site, 224; at Marsh Island Mound, 219; at Mill Point archaeological site, 80; Nueva Cadiz Plain, 69, 74, 81, 100, 104, *109;* from Tatham Mound, *105, 106;* at Thomas Mound 68; in Weeki Wachee Mound, 108
Bellamy Road. *See* Mission Trail
Belleview, 92
Bells, brass, 219, *220*
Bell Shoals (Alafia River), 76, 78
Beverages, ceremonial, 104
Biedma, Luys Hernández de, 7, 11, 259nl; on the Apalachee, 226–27; on arrival at Aguacaleyquen, 156; on de Soto's landing site, 46; letters of, 9; on Ocale region, 73, 92, on return to Tampa Bay, 221; on route to Urriparacoxi, 57, 58, 59; and size of de Soto expedition, 38
Big Sand Lake, 74
Bimini (island), 21
Bishop's Harbor, 62
Bobadilla, Isabella de (wife of de Soto), 9, 27
Boca Ratones (Indians), 115–16
Bourne, Edward G., 8
Boyd, Mark F., 48, 58, 59
Buck Island Mound, 81
Bullen, Ripley P., 67, 69, 80, 94
Burger, William B., 15, 69
Byrne, Stephen, 215

Cabbage Key (Tampa Bay), 43
Cabeza de Vaca, Alvar Núñez, 8, 41; on Apalachee region, 227; captivity of, 23, 24; at Spanish court, 26; at Tampa Bay, 57
Cacique (Arawak word), defined, 122
Cadecha (vassal of Utina), 196
Cades Pond culture, 193
Calahuchi (village), 214, 215
Calanay (vassal of Utina), 197–98, 205
Calderón, Captain (de Soto expedition), 76, 221; and battle with the Apalachee, 228
Calderón, Gabriel Díaz Vara (bishop), 186
Caloosahatchee River, as landing site, 4, 7, 41–42
Calos (Calusa chief), 21; power of, 117–19; wealth of, 118–19
Calusa Indians, 21, 22, 112, 117–21, 256; archaeological culture of, 129; decline of population of, 121–22; effect of epidemics on, 120, 121; Franciscan missions to, 120, 246; at Jesuit mission, 115; wealth of, 72
Canary Islands, de Soto's stop at, 37
Cañete, Father Sabastián de, 9
Cañete fragment (de Soto expedition document), 242
Canoes, use of by Indians, 192
Capachequi, River of (Flint River), 231
Capafi (Apalachee chief), 228–29
Capaloey Indians, 122; identification with Pohoy Indians, 125
Cape Canaveral, 119

Cape Kennedy, 118
Caribbean Islands, 19, *20*
Carlos (chief). *See* Calos (Calusa chief)
Carlos V (king of Spain), charter to de Soto, 27, 28–38
Casti (town), 207
Cavally, of de Soto expedition, 56, 82, 87
Center for Early Contact Period Studies (University of Florida), 223
Ceramics, Spanish, 17, 64; at de Soto winter camp, 224–26; at Florahome Trough, 193; at Ivitachuco mission site, 214; at Peacock/White Lake locale, 162; at Richardson site, 146. *See also* Artifacts, Spanish
Chain mail, of de Soto expedition, 17, 226, 229. *See also* Armor, Spanish; Artifacts, Spanish
Charles Spring, 152, 153
Charles Town (Charleston), 250
Charlotte Harbor: Chaves's account of, 42–43, 45, 48; as landing site, 4, 7, 39, 42; modern surveys of, 47–48; Ponce de León at, 21, 22, 41
Charnel houses, 123; of Ocale region, 102, 103–4; at Tampa Bay, 63, 64
Charters, royal, form of, 35. *See* also de Soto, Hernando: *asiento of*
Chaves, Alonso de, 9–10, 39, 42–43, 45
Chequescha Indians. *See* Tequesta Indians
Chicora (South Carolina province), 231–32
Chicora (town), 22, 237
Chilili (vassal of Utina), 196
Cholupaha (town), 170, 172, 177; de Soto expedition at, 134, 143, 144, 154; de Soto's route from, 150; location of, 145, 147, 148
Christianity, conversion of natives to, 35, 243–45
Citrus County, artifacts in, 16
Clarkes Creek, 189, 190
Cockroach Key, 62
Coffeepot Bayou, 58
Cofitachequi (Indian territory, South Carolina), 9, 230, 231, 232
Coins, of de Soto expedition, 17, 224. *See also* Artifacts, Spanish
Columbia County, 154
Columbus, Christopher, 19
Coosa (province), 232; Spanish settlement at, 239
Copper, 185
Córcoles y Martínez, Governor Francisco de, 247
Coronado, Francisco Vásquez de, 9, 26
Cortes map (1524), 41
Cortéz, Hernán, 9, 26
Cosa, Juan de la, map of, 19
Cove of the Withlacoochee. *See* Withlacoochee, Cove of the
Coya (town), 204
Creek Indians, 120
Crossbow tips, at Governor Martin site, *225*. *See also* Artifacts, Spanish
Cuba: de Soto's arrival at, 37; in de Soto's charter, 30
Cuellar, Father Antonio de, 183

Dade City, 59, 83, 169
Dávila, Pedrárias, 26
De Bry, Theodore, 140, 174, 184
DePratter, Chester, 4
Derroteros (navigation rutters), 21
De Soto, Hernando: arrival at Acuera, 73; *asiento* of, 9, 27, 28–38; barter with Indians, 68; and battle at Napituca, 178; and Cabeza de Vaca, 26; correspondence with Cuba, 93, 96; death of, 38, 233; early life of, 26; embassy to Urriparacoxi, 71–73, 84, 86; governorship of Cuba, 37; heirs of, 9; marriage of, 27; military exploits of, 27; mistreatment of Indians by, 148; moral judgments on, 255; obligations under royal charter, 28, 32; pages of, 87; at Tampa Bay, 38, 49–50; titles conferred on, 29; at Uzita's village, 55, 59; visit to Mocoso, 56
De Soto expedition, 3, 234, *235;* at Aguacaleyquen, 157; artifacts of, 13, 15–17; attack by Chief Tuscaluza, 232; battles with Indians, 86, 101–3, 162–63, 178, 179, 228; camp at Luca, 84; composition of, 38, 53, 76; confrontation with Aguacaleyquen, 157; departure from Florida, 232; departure from Ocale, 134; departure from Tampa Bay, 76; departure from Uzachile, 166; documents relating to, 9–11;

De Soto expedition—*continued*
early accounts of, 7–11; end of, 38, 233; entry into Apalachee territory, 163, 211; entry into Mississippi, 233; epidemics caused by, 103, 239; failure of, 236; fording of Aucilla River 212; fording of Withlacoochee River, 87–90, 92; gifts to Indians, 104, 105; historical importance of, xi; and Indian political culture, 179; landing site of, 39–48; march to Apalachee region, 134; march to Iniahica, 212–15; on Mission Trail, 160, 214–15, 216; at Napituca, 162; at Ocale region, 91–96, 99; organization of, 17–18; at Pánfilo de Narváez's camp, 220–21; provisions for, 82, 83, 91–92, 96, 101, 128, 133, 157, 230; reconstruction of route, 5–6, 7–18; route from Aguacaleyquen to Asile, 158, *159,* 160–66; route from Apalachee, 230–33; route from Asile, *217;* route from Ocale, 134–48, *135;* route to Ocale, *77,* 81–87; at Tampa Bay, 15, 48–50, *51,* 52–53, 56–61, 63, 69–70; and Tampa Bay Indians, 55–57, 122–25; voyage from Cuba, 49; winter camp of, 216–21, 223–24
De Soto Trail Committee, 5; establishment of, 3–4
Disease, European: effect on Indians, xii, 239, 246. *See also* Epidemics
Dobyns, Henry, 248
Doctrinas (mission system), 244
D'Ottigni (French lieutenant), 173, 202
Dowling Park, 163, 164
Duval Island archaeological site, 86

Ecita. *See* Uzita (chief)
Eclavou (vassal of Utina), 196
Edelano (village), 202–3
Egmont Key (Tampa Bay), 43, 46
Eloquale. *See* Ocale region
Elvas, Gentleman of, 11, 78; account of landing, 53; on Aguacaleyquen, 154, 156, 178; on the Apalachee, 226–27; on gifts to Indians, 104, 105; on mound sites, 67; on Ocale region, 87–88, 93; on Tampa Bay camp, 63
English, attacks on Franciscan missions, 250–51
Epidemics, 112; among the Apalachee, 249; among mission Indians, 246–47; effect on Calusa, 120, 121; at Ocale, 103, 110; severity of, 116. *See also* Disease, European; Fontaneda, Hernando d'Escalante
Espejo de Navigantes (Chaves), 39, 42–43, 45–46
Espíritu Santo. *See* Tampa Bay
Etoniah Creek, 189–90
Eucappe (vassal of Utina), 197
Ewen, Charles R., 16, 223, 224
Explorers, Spanish, 21–26
Extremadura, Spain, 26

Face painting, 180
Featherstonhaugh, Thomas, 74
Fernández de Olivera, Juan, 46
Fernández de Oviedo y Valdés, Gonzalo, 8
Ferrière, La Roche, 184
Final Report of thc United States de Soto Commission (Swanton), 4, 5
Flint River, 231
Florahome Trough, 189, 193
Floral City, 86
Florida: archaeological research in, 13–17; central, *97;* coastal geography of, 39, *40,* 41–42; early maps of, 11–13, 19, 41, 83, 84, *85,* 95, 98; east, *188;* northern archaeological sites, *149;* northern native sites, *171;* northern trails of, 148–54; northwest, *213*
Florida, La (Garcilaso de la Vega), 6–7
Florida Archaeological Site Files, 74
Florida Bureau of Archaeological Research, 13, 223
Florida Division of Historical Resources, 222
Florida Division of Recreation and Parks, 3, 5, 223
Florida Santa Fe Trail, 136, 138, 145, 147; intersection with Mission Trail, 142, 144
Florida State Board of Conservation, excavations by, 66, 68, 78
Fontaneda, Hernando d'Escalante, 95, 202, 226–27, 242; on Calusa Indians, 117–18; on Chief Tocobaga, 117–18; on Chief Utina,

193; on Mocoso, 124; stories of gold, 185; and Tequesta Indians, 114; on Tocobaga Indians, 126–27
Fort Caroline (French fort), 118, 140, 172, 190, 204; Spanish capture of, 187, 200, 241
Fort George Island, 208, 209, 261n3
Fortification, plans for, 29–30
Fort Myers, 42
Fort Walton archaeological culture, 166–67, 170; association with Apalachee, 211; at Ivitachuco mission site, 214; pottery of, *223*
Fountain of Youth archaeological site, 104
Fox Pond archaeological site, 176
French: contact with eastern Utina Indians, 187, 189–90, 192; exploration and settlement of Florida, 11, 95, 172–74, 189–91, 193, 261nl; at Fort Caroline, 118

Gallegos, Baltasar de, 50; mission to Urriparacoxi, 57–58, 71–73, 81, 84, 93; at Uzita's village, 55
Gambaye, Pierre, 203
Gambel Creek, mound at, 64
Garcilaso de la Vega: accuracy of account, 6–7; on Aguacaleyquen, 158; on Apalachee region, 228–29; on Aucilla River, 212; on Indian chiefs, 178, 221; on march to Iniahica, 212, 214–15; on Ocale region, 88, 93; on the Suwannee River, 163; translations of, 8; on Uriutina, 160–61; on Urriparacoxi, 72, 73, 76
Gaytan, Juan, 9
Gentleman of Elvas. *See* Elvas, Gentleman of
Gift-giving, to Indians, 104, 105–6, 190
Gilchrist County, 134
Glass, at Thomas Mound, 68
Goggin, John, 74, 141, 176, 204
Gold: in de Soto's charter, 33; rumors of, 72, 118–19, 184–85, 231; sources of, 180–81
Governor Martin archaeological site, 105, 216, 218, 219, 222–26; chain mail at, 229. *See also* de Soto expedition, winter camp of; Iniahica (Apalachee village)
Granberry, Julian, 76
Grantham Mound, 81
Great Abaco Island, 21
Green Bacín Ware (pottery), 100
Groutauld (French explorer), 184, 185
Guacara River. *See* Suwannee River
Guacozo, savannah of, 83
Guacuca, River of (Ochlockonee River), 231
Guale (mission province), 251, 261n6
Guatutima (Indian guide), 158
Gum Slough (Dead River), 92

Hann, John H., 7, 98, 246, 262nl2; study of the Mayaca, 201; translation of early accounts, 8, 9
Harbor Key, 123
Harisse, Henry, 10
Hatchett Creek, 146
Hernández de Córdova, Francisco, 22
Hernando County, artifacts in, 16
Herrera, Antonio de, 21
High Road Trail, 153, 160, 161, 180; in Apalachee territory, 185
Hillsborough River, 59
Hioacaia Indians, 209–10
Hirrihigua (chief), 56, 122
Hispañiola, 19
Historia General y Natural de las Indias (Fernández de Ovjedo y Valdés), 8
Houstaqua (chief), identification with Uzachile, 179
Hudson, Charles, 4, 260nl2
Hudson, Joyce, 158
Hurrah Creek (Alafia River), 78
Hutchinson, Dale, 101

Ibi (mission), 244
Ichetucknee–Rose Creek–Alligator Trail, 154, 160
Ichetucknee–Rose Creek River, 13, 154, *155*, 160
Indian Mounds Spring archaeological site, 94
Indians: account of de Soto's landing, 46; agricultural activities of, 128, 169, 172, 190, 227, 230, 259n5; alliance with the English, 120; attacks on de Soto expedition, 86, 101–3, 162–63, 178, 179, 228; captives of de Soto, 87, 158, 162–63, 172, 183; during colonial period, 112; in de Soto's charter, 31;

Indians—*continued*
effect of European contact on, xi–xii, 111–12; enslavement of, 19, 22; as guides to de Soto expedition, 53, 87, 158, 216; introduction of diseases to, xii; names used by, 114–15; of northwest Florida, 205–10; political structure of, 169–70, 177; presentation to the king, 207; reaction to de Soto expedition, 53, 72; reaction to *requerimiento,* 35; rebellion (1656), 152, 247, 249; settlement pattems of, 17; social geography of, 5, 256–57; Spanish policy concerning, 35; at Tampa Bay, 55–57
Iniahica (Apalachee village), 216, 218, 219; artifacts of, 16–17; Garcilaso's description of, 218; during mission period, 248. *See also* Governor Martin archaeological site
Iniahica region, de Soto's march to, 212–15
Inverness, 87
Isabella, La (Columbian settlement), 19
Itaraholata (chief), 172
Itaraholata (town), 134, 136, 170; de Soto expedition at, 140; location of, 138, 146
Ivitachuco, River of. *See* Aucilla River
Ivitachuco (Apalachee town), 11, 212, 214; location of, 215; during mission period, 248

Jeaga Indians, 118
Johnson, Kenneth, 13, 15, 146, 260nl2; on eastem Utina, 187, 193; excavation at Peacock–White Lake locale, 161; excavations at Ichetucknee–Rose Creek River, 154; excavations of Hammock Belt, 148; excavations of Ocale region, 93, 136; on Utina peoples, 177, 189
Jones, B. Calvin, 16; and Apalachee sites, 261n5; and discovery of Governor Martin site, 216, 218, 222–24; excavations at Lake Sampala, 165; location of San Lorenzo mission, 214; location of San Pedro mission, 165
Jones Mound, 81, 124
Justicias (legal documents), 9

Keel, Frank, 215
Key Indians, 115
Kissimmee River, 119

Lacoochee, 74, 84
Lake Butler, 74, 84
Lake George, 201, 202
Lake Gibson, 83
Lake Grandin, 189, 190, 193, 260nl2
Lake Lafayette, 215
Lakeland, 81, 83
Lake Louisa, 74
Lake of the Rabbit, 81–82
Lake Okeechobee, 119
Lake Parker, 83, *85*
Lake Sampala, 165
Lake Thonotosassa, 81, 124
Lake Tibet, 74
Lake Tsala-Apopka, 13, 86, 87, 101
Lake Weir, 84, 98
Laudonnière, René de, 118–19, 180, 185, 257; and eastern Utina, 187; and murder of Pierre Gambaye, 203; St. Johns River expedition of, 172–74, 189–90, 195, 199, 202, 204; on Uzachile, 184
League (unit of measure), 42
Le Moyne, Jacques, *95,* 174, 180
Le Moyne map, *95,* 118, 124, 260n7; "Apalatci" mountains on, 181; Calanay on, 198; Coya on, 204; Lake Grandin on, 189; Mayacans on, 201; Onotheaqua on, 180; and Potano Indians, 140–41; St. Johns River on, 194, *195;* Saturiwa on, 206; Utina's vassals on, 193–94; Uzachile on, 184
Leon County, archaeological sites in, 222
Le Vasseur (French captain), 172–73, 199; at Molona's village, 202
Levy Lake, 136
Little Manatee River, 15, *52,* 60, 61, *65;* archaeological evidence at, 62, 66, 69; sterility of soil at, 71
Lochloosa Lake, 193
Longboat Key (Tampa Bay), 43, 49
López, Father Baltasar, 175–76, 182, 244; visit to Timucua, 245
López Cacho, Juan, 87
López de Velasco, Juan: description of San Carlos Bay, 41; and Tequesta Indians, 114

Lower Mission Trail, 165, 166
Luca (village), 73, 74, 129; arrival of de Soto expedition at, 84
Luna y Arellano, Tristán de, 222, 232; colonizing expedition of, 237, 239, *240*
Lykes Mound, 81
Lyon, Eugene, 9

Mabila (town), 232
Macoya (chief), 200–202
Madeline Key (Tampa Bay), 43
Maize, cultivation of, 169, 190, 227, 230; at Acuera, 259n5
Majolica, Spanish, 78, 84; at de Soto winter camp, 224. *See also* Artifacts, Spanish
Malapaz (town), 134, 147, 170, 172; de Soto's arrival at, 143
Maldonado, Francisco, 222, 232, 233
Malica (vassal of Saturiwa), 207
Manatee County, mounds in, 64
Manatee River, 60, *65;* archaeological evidence at, 62
Marion County, 5, 92, 93, 99, 136; archaeological sites in, 94
Marion Oaks archaeological site, 94
Marracou (chief), 118
Marrinan, Rochelle, 215
Marsh Island Mound, 219
Martín, Alonso (de Soto's pilot), 39, 49
Martin, John, Governor of Florida, 223
Martin site. *See* Covernor Martin archaeological site
Martínez, Hernán de, 115
Mathiaca (chief), 118
Mathiaqua (village), 202–3
Meinecke, Adolph, 74
Meleneche, Roberto, 198, 200, 202; on St. Johns River Indians, 207–9
Méndez, Ana, 9; in the Ocale region, 90
Menéndez de Avilés, Pedro, 59, 111, 115, 257; alliance with Saturiwa, 197; and colonization of Florida, 241–42; defeat of French, 119–20, 261nl; deployment of Franciscans, 244–45; and eastern Utina, 187; gifts to Indians, 190; St. Johns River expedition by, 124, 127, 187, 189, 192, 194–96; and Tequesta Indians, 114; voyage from Fort San Mateo, 200–201
Micanopy, 145, 146
Middens, 62; shell, 66, 78, 99, 192, 204; at Tampa Bay, 63
Middle Florida Hammock Belt, 138–39, 162, 170; archaeological excavations of, 148
Milanich, Jerald T., 4
Mill Point mound archaeological site, 78, *80,* 124
Miruelo, Diego de, 22, 43
Missionaries, 16; Franciscan, 98, 111; Jesuit, 111, 241, 243, 244
Missions: documents kept by, 11; Menéndez's plans for, 241
Missions, Franciscan, 120, 129, 150, 151–52, 176, 182–83, 201, 261nn2–10; after English attacks, 253–54; in Apalachee region, 230, 245, 248–49; artifacts of, 148; demise of, 250–54; destruction by the English, 249; Menéndez's establishment of, 244–45; at Potano, 140; to Timucuans, 176, 245–48; to the Uzachile, 185–86
Missions, Jesuit, 120; at Tequesta, 115
Mission system, 243–45; provinces of, 246
Mission Trail, 136, *143, 155,* 180, *191;* in Apalachee territory, 185; de Soto expedition on, 160, 214–15, 216; intersection with High Road Trail, 153; intersection with Santa Fe Trail, 142, 144; in northwest Florida, *213;* route from St. Augustine, 150–53; on Stuart–Purcell map, 138, 165
Mississippi, de Soto's entry into, 233
Mississippi River, 42, 222
Mitchem, Jeffrey, 74; on Aute village, 219; excavation of Ocale region, 93, 102, 105
Mobile Bay, 42
Mocama (mission province), 251, 261n11
Mocoso, River of. *See* Alafia River
Mocoso (chief), 56, 57, 58, 78; alliance with de Soto, 80, 81, 157, 221; kinship with Urriparacoxi, 122
Mocoso (town), 123

Mocoso Indians, 121; association with Safety Harbor culture, 129; demise of, 125; territory of, 63, 123, 124
Molona (vassal of Utina), 172–73, 179, 193, 199–200
Montejo, Francisco de, 34
Moon Lake archaeological site, 136, 141–42, 147, 176
Moore, Clarence B., 66, 67, 78
Moore, Governor James, 252
Moquoso (vassal of Utina), 198–99
Moscoso, Luis de: as de Soto's successor, 86; en route to Ocale, 86; at Uzita's village, 55
Mound Key, 120
Mounds, 15; excavation of, 66–70, 74, 76, 78, 80–81, 100–110; shell, 69; at Tampa Bay, 59, 63–64, 66, 123; at Uzita's village, 55, 56
Mounds, burial, 62, 78, 145; at St. Johns River, 192
Mounds, temple, 62; at Tampa Bay, 63, 122
Mt. Royal archaeological site, 203
Mullet Key (Tampa Bay), 43
Murphy Island, 203
Muskhogean language, 261n6
Myers, Emlin, 225

Naime, Thomas, 183
Nanipacana (town), 239
Napituca (village): battle at, 162–63, 178, 179, 183; location of, 163; political organization of, 177
Narváez expedition. *See* Pánfilo de Narváez expedition
Native peoples. *See* Indians
Navidad, La (Columbian settlement), 19
Neguarete Indians, 122, 125
Neill, Wilfred, 84
Niza, Fray Marcos de, 26
Nombre de Dios (mission), 244, 261n1
North Carolina: de Soto expedition in, 232; Pardo expedition in, 242

Oathchaqua (chief), 118, 119
Ocala, 99, 145
Ocale, River of. *See* Withlacoochee River
Ocale (town), 15; de Soto expedition at, 88; location of, 92–93, 95–96
Ocale Indians: association with Safety Harbor culture, 129; cultivation of maize, 169
Ocale region, 58, *77, 95;* agriculture in, 259n5; archaeology of, 93–95, 98–110; de Soto expedition at, 91–96; food supply of, 133; location of, 86; material culture of, 99; wealth of, 72–73, 92. *See also* Withlacoochee River
Ochete. *See* Aute (village)
Ochlockonee River, 231
Ochuse. *See* Pensacola Bay
Official Records of the Union and Confederate Armies, 1861–1865, 83
Oklawaha River, 93, 96
Oleno State Park, 144
Omittaqua (vassal of Utina), 198
Omoloa (vassal of Saturiwa), 206–7
Onachaquara (vassal of Utina), 198
Onotheaqua (chief), identification with Aguacaleyquen, 179–80
Orange Lake, 92, 176
Orange Lake archaeological site, 147
Oré, Luis Géronimo de, 46, 98, 176, 198
Orriygua. *See* Hirrihigua
Ortiz, Juan: captivity of, 56, 58, 123; flight from Uzita, 78, 124; as translator, 178, 194; on Urriparacoxi, 71, 73
Ospo (mission), 244, 261n9
Oustaca. *See* Uzachile; Yustaga

Palestine Lake, 157, 160
Pánfilo de Narváez expedition, 41, 111; at Apalachee region, 157, 227–28; at Aute, 219, 220–21; contact with Indians, 121; in de Soto's charter, 28; route of, *25;* survivors of, 56; at Tampa Bay, 43; and Tocobaga Indians, 126
Paracousi (war chief), 205
Pardo expedition (Juan Pardo), 100, 136, 194; forts established by, 242; route of, *243*
Pareja, Father Francisco, 98
Parrish Mounds, 64
Parris Island, South Carolina, 237; Spanish colony at, 239, 242
Passage Key (Tampa Bay), 43
Patica (town), 204
Payne, Claudine, 165
Paynes Prairie, 136, 140, 146, 147

Peacock–White Lake archaeological site, 161–62
Pensacola Bay, 222, 237, 239; Spanish colony at, 241
Philippi Point (Tampa Bay), 48, 59
Picnic Mound, 78
Pinellas Peninsula (Tampa Bay), 48
Pinellas Points (arrowheads), 123
Piney Point (Tampa Bay), 60, 61
Pizarro, Francisco, 26, 27
Place–names, Spanish, 115
Plant City, 81
Poarch Farm archaeological site, 104
Pohoy Indians, 125, 127
Pojoy (Indian province), identification with Tampa Bay, 46
Polygyny, among Indians, 122
Ponce de León, Hernán, 9; frienship with de Soto, 26
Ponce de León, Juan: and Calusa Indians, 117; encounter with Tequesta Indians, 114; Florida expedition of, 21–22, 111; landing at Charlotte Harbor, xii, 41
Porcallo de Figueroa, Vasco, 50, 53; attack on Uzita, 123; return to Cuba, 71; at Uzita's village, 55, 57
Port Royal, destruction of, 251
Potano (chief), 140, 172, 173–75; battle with Utina, *175*
Potano (town), 134, 140, 170, 174; location of, *141,* 146
Potano Indians, 99; agricultural activities of, 172; association with Alachua tradition, 140; decline of, 177, 247; missions to, 143, 148, 245
Potano region, 170–77
Pottery, 13; of Alachua tradition, *139;* Apalachee, 224; Fort Walton, 214, *223;* at Lake Lafayette, 215; near Moon Lake, 142; of Ocale region, 100; Pasco, 99; Seminole, 74; Suwannee Valley, *151,* 162; Weeden Island, 74
Pottery, Spanish. *See* Ceramics, Spanish
Pottery Hill archaeological site, 84
Prieto, Father Martín: founding of San Martin mission, 156; founding of Santa Fe mission, 145; and Potano missions, 148, 176, 182
Purdy, Barbara, 192

Quexo, Pedro de, 22
Quiroga y Lossada, Governor Diego de, 262nl3

Ranjel, Rodrigo, 11; account of landing, 53, 60; on Aguacaleyquen, 156, 178; on the Apalachee, 226–27; on gifts to Indians, 105–6; en route to Ocale, 87–88; on Santa Fe crossing, 154; and size of de Soto expedition, 38; skirmish with Indians, 101; on Tampa Bay site, 7–8, 49; at Tocaste, 86; on Uzachile, 164
Rebolledo, Diego de, 247
Reinoso, Father Alonso, 244
Requerimiento (declaration read to Indians), 35–37
Residencia (posthumous investigation of de Soto), 9
Ribera, Diego, world map of, *24*
Richardson archaeological site, 176
Río de Canoas (Caloosahatchee River), 4, 7, 41–42
Río de Flores (Mobile Bay), 42
Río del Espíritu Santo (Mississippi River), 42, 222
River of Discords. *See* Ichetucknee–Rose Creek River
River of the Deer. *See* Suwannee River
Rivers, in establishing de Soto route, 11, 13
Robertson, James Alexander, 8
Robinson Sinks archaeological sites, 144–45, 147, 148, 151
Rodríguez de Cortaya, Juan, 46
Rogel, Juan, 126
Romans, Bernard, 83, 153
Ross Prairie, 94, 95, 99
Rotz, Jean, 41
Ruiz Lobillo, Juan, 55–57, 124
Ruskin, 66; shell mound at, 70
Ruth Smith Mound, 100, 104, 106, 107, 158
Rye Bridge Mound, 66

Safety Harbor archaeological culture, 257; at Alafia River, 78; at Lake Tsala–Apopka, 86; of Ocale region, 101, 138; at Pottery Hill archaeological site, 84; pottery of, *130;* at Sarasota Bay, 50; at Tampa Bay, 62–63; at Tatham Mound, 108
St. Augustine, 241, 242; English attack on, 253; epidemics at, 249

St. Catherine (mission), 244, 251, 261n10
St. Catherines Island, 245
St. Johns archaeological culture, 129, 131, 193
St. John's Lake, 81–82
St. Johns River, 96; on Le Moyne map, 194, *195;* Menéndez expedition on, 124, 127, 187, 189, 192, 194–96
St. Johns River area, 186–205; archaeology of, 192
St. Marks River, 13; Pánfilo de Narváez expedition at, 24
St. Marks Wildlife Refuge Cemetery archaeological site, 104–5; European artifacts at, 219
San Antonio de Enecape (mission), 176, 197
San Augustin de Urica (mission), 161
San Carlos Bay, as landing site, 4, 41, 42
Sand Key (Tampa Bay), 43
San Francisco de Potano (mission), 176, 182
San Juan de Guacara (mission), 182; destruction of, 183, 262nl3; establishment of, 245
San Juan del Puerto (mission), 200, 207, 209, 244, 252, 253
San Lorenzo de Ivitachuco (mission), 11, 212, 214
San Luis de Acuera (mission), 98
San Martin de Timucua (mission), 151, 152, 156, 182; epidemics at, 249; establishment of, 245
San Mateo. *See* Fort Caroline (French fort)
San Matheo de Tolapatafi (mission), 186
San Miguel de Asile (mission), 11, 152, 186; location of, 166
San Miguel de Gualdape (colony), 22
San Pedro de Mocama (mission), 175, 209
San Pedro y San Pablo de Potohiriba (mission), 152, 165, 186; English attack on, 251
San Salvador de Mayaca (mission), 201
Santa Catalina (mission), 183, 251
Santa Cruz, Alonso de, 10
Santa Cruz de Tarihica (mission), 152, 182; destruction of, 183, 251; establishment of, 245
Santa Elena. *See* Parris Island, South Carolina
Santa Fe de Teleco (mission), 145, 245; English attack on, 251–52
Santa Fe River, 13, 93, 134, 136; archaeological sites near, *137;* fording of, 147, 154
Santa Fe Trail. *See* Florida Santa Fe Trail
Santa Helena de Machaba (mission), 186
Sanu Isabel de Utinahica (mission), 182
Santa Lucia de Acuera (mission), 98
Saranay (vassal of Saturiwa), 207; identification with Calabay, 208–9
Sarasota Bay, 50
Saturiwa (chief), 180, 198, 204–5, *206,* 207–9; alliance with Menéndez de Avilés, 197; territory of, *208*
Saturiwa (village), 205
Scalping, 228
Scouts, in de Soto expedition, 17, 18, 82, 218
Second Seminole War (1837–42),12, *14,* 84, *191*
Serrano, Alonzo, 176
Serrope Indians, 119
Shaw's Point (Manatee River), 60
Shell dippers, 104, 108
Shell Point (Tampa Bay), 69
Silvestre, Gonzalo, 87
Sinkholes, limestone, 162, 163, 178
Slavery, Spanish, 19, 22, 24; in de Soto's charter, 31
Smith, Buckingham, 8; translations by, 9, 34, 166
Smith, Hale, 74
Smith, Marvin T., 4
Snavely Mounds, 81
Snead Island, 123
Sobrevivientos de la Florida, Los (Avellaneda), 10
Sotoriva. *See* Saturiwa (chief)
Spain: colonies in Florida, *238;* colonization activities of, xii, 19, 22–23, 237, 239, 241–42; exploration of New World, 19–26, 35–37

Spender Mound, 81
Spider effigy tablets, 68
Stokes Ferry (Withlacoochee River), 87
Stuart–Purcell map, *142, 143,* 146, 165, 186, 189; Aucilla River on, 212
Sumter County, 92; archaeological sites in, 94
Suwannee River, 13, 46; fording of, 163–64, 165; intersection with Mission Trail, 152
Suwannee Valley archaeological complex, 156, 166, 172, 211
Swanton, John R., 4; on landing site, 60; reconstuction of de Soto route, 17, 232

Tacadocorou Indians, identification with Indians of Apalu, 209
Tampa Bay, 10, *44, 65;* archaeology of, 15, 48, 61–70, *79;* Chaves's description of, 10, 43, 45–46; de Soto's camp at, 15, 53, *54,* 55–61, 63; harbor of, 39–48; Indians of, *113,* 121–26, 243; landing site at, 4, 5, 7; modern surveys of, 46–48; Santa Cruz map of, *10*
Tatham Mound, 100–107, 158
Tennessee River Valley, de Soto expedition in, 232
Tequesta (village), 207
Tequesu Indians, 112, 114–17, 118, 256; decline of population, 116; Juan Ponce's visit to, 21
Terra Ceia Mound archaeological site, 60
Terry, Keith, 162
Thimogona Indians, 181–82, 199, 205, 207
Thomas Mound (Tampa Bay), 15, 66, *67,* 68–69, 123
Timucuan language, 118, 150, 161, 164, 169, 173, 202; place-names in, 115
Timucuan missions, 98, 245–48; English attacks on, 253; rebellion at (1656), 152, 247, 249
Tinoco, Arias, 218–19
Tocaste (village), 13, 86–87; de Soto expedition at, 101
Tocobaga (chief), 179
Tocobaga Indians, 59, 125–27; association with Safety Harbor culture, 129
Tolomato (mission), 244, 261n7
Tools, 66, 74–75; from Tatham Mound, *108. See also* Artifacts, Spanish
Tovar, Nuño de, 87
Trails, Indian, *12, 14*
Treasure, in de Soto's charter, 33
Treaty of Madrid (1670), 250
Tupique (mission), 244, 261n8
Tuscaluza (chief), 232
Tymangoua Indians. *See* Thimogona Indians

Union County, 154
United States Corps of Engineers, survey of Tampa Bay, 46, 47
Uqueten (town), 15; de Soto expedition at, 92, 191
Uriutina (chief), 178, 184
Uriutina (village), 179; de Soto's arrival at, 160–61; location of, 164; political organization of, 177
Urriparacoxi, meaning of word, 76
Urriparacoxi (chief), 57–58; de Soto's embassy to, 71–73, 84, 86; kinship with Mocoso, 122; power of, 128
Urriparacoxi (territory), *75;* artifacts in, 16; location of, 73–76, 93; scouting expeditions to, 18
Urriparacoxi (village), 84, 87, 169; location of, 73–74
Urriparacoxi Indians, 127–29; archaeological culture of, 129; crops cultivated by, 128, 169; fate of, 129
Utina (chief), 128, 172–75; battle with Potano, 174, *175;* capture by French, 192; French embassy to, 184; and Menéndez expedition, 201; power of, 193; territory of, 204; vassals of, 96, 196–200; village of, 187
Utina Indians, 144; branches of, 177, 257; missions among, 151–52; relationship with Aguacaleyquen, 150
Utina Indians, eastern, 172–74; contact with French, 187, 189–90, 192; crops cultivated by, 190; military tactics of, 192; territory of, 186–205
Utina Indians, northern: decline of, 247; missions to, 245; surrender to de Soto, 162

Utinamocharra (chief), 172
Utinamocharra (town), 134, 170; de Soto's arrival at, 141, 144; location of, 146–47, 176
Uzachile (chief), 161, 163; alliance with de Soto, 167; power of, 177, 179, 184
Uzachile (town): Garcilaso's description of, 164; location of, 165–66
Uzachile Indians, missions to, 142, 245
Uzachile region, 183–86, 227; boundary with Apalachee, 211
Uzita (chief), 59
Uzita (village), *52, 54,* 55, 58; location of, 123–24; Spanish fortification of, 68
Uzita Indians, xii, 256; association with Safety Harbor culture, 129; demise of, 125; diet of, 62; and Pánfilo de Narváez expedition, 121; territory of, 63

Varner, John, 6, 8
Vasconselos, Andres de, 218
Vásquez de Ayllón, Lucas, 28, 29; colonizing expedition of, 22, 232, 237
Vázquez, Alonso, 9, 88–89
Veachile. *See* Uzachile
Vicela (village), 86
Villafañe, Angel de, 239
Village of Many Waters, 161, 177; location of, 164
Villareal, Francisco, 115
Vizcayano Indians, 116

Wealth, rumors of, 92, 117, 231–32
Weeden Island archaeological site, 161
Weeki Wachee Mound, 104, 108–9
West Indian Pilot, The (Barnett), 47
Weisman, Brent, 101
Williams, John Lee, 98; map of Florida, *12*
Withlocoochee, Cove of the (wetlands area), 15, 86, *89, 91;* agriculture at, 128; archaeology of, 98–110; fording of, 87–90, 103
Withlacoochee River, 8, 13, 58, 84, 164; fording of, 92
Women, aboriginal, 122; as chiefs, 209–10
Work Place archaeological site, 219, 220
Works Progress Administration (WPA), excavations by, 66, 68, 78, 80
World Columbiana Exposition (Chicago, 1893), 255

Yupaha. *See* Cofitachequi (Indian territory, South Carolina)
Yustaga, identification with Uzachile, 179, 245
Yustaga region, 183–86

Zephyrhills, 82, 83
Zetrouer archaeological site, 247
Zuñiga y Zerda, Don Joseph, 252

Library of Congress Cataloging-in-Publication Data
Milanich, Jerald T.
Hernando de Soto and the Indians of Florida / Jerald Milanich and Charles Hudson.
p. cm. — (The Ripley P. Bullen series) (Columbus quincentenary series)
Includes bibliographical references and index.
ISBN 0-8130-1170-1 (alk. paper)
1. Indians of North America—Florida—First contact with Europeans. 2. Soto, Hernando de, ca. 1500–1542. 3. Indians of North America—Florida. 3. Florida—Discovery and exploration—Spanish. I. Title. II. Series. III. Series: Columbus quincentenary series.
E78.F6M557 1992 92-22868
975.9'01—dc20 CIP

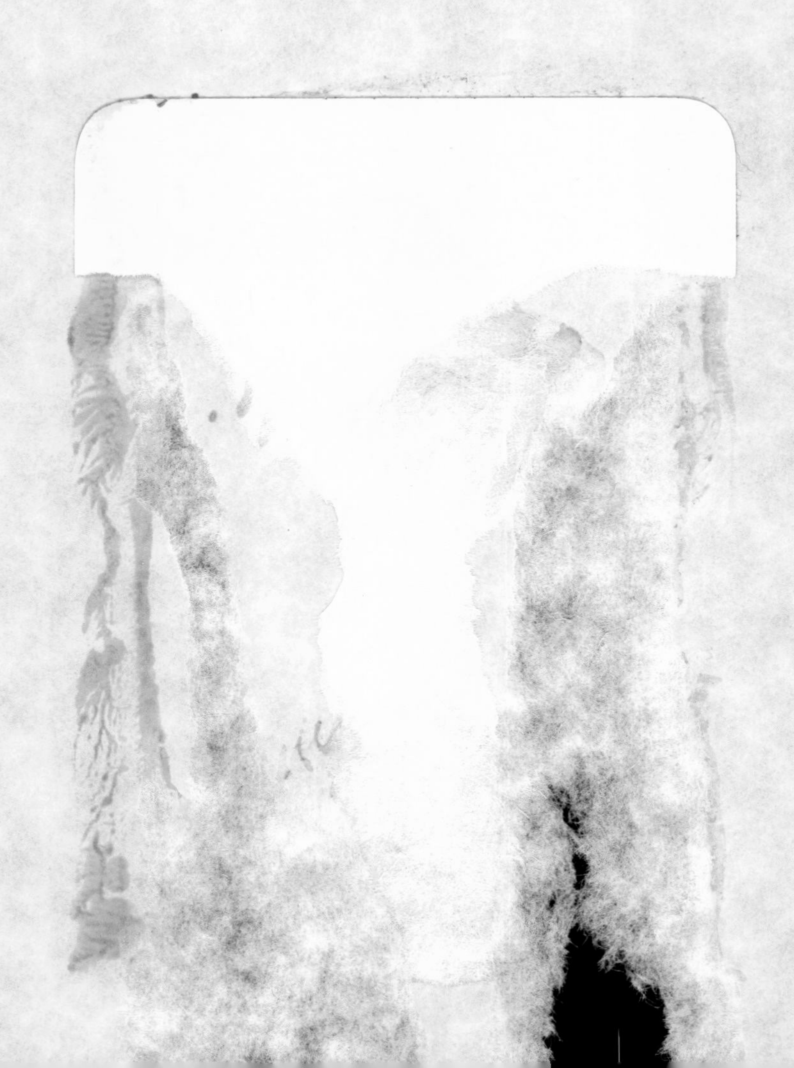